TRAVELLERS IN FAITH

SOCIAL, ECONOMIC AND POLITICAL STUDIES OF THE MIDDLE EAST AND ASIA

(S.E.P.S.M.E.A.)

(Founding editor: C.A.O. van Nieuwenhuijze)

VOLUME 69

TRAVELLERS IN FAITH

Studies of the Tablīghī Jamā'at as a Transnational Islamic Movement for Faith Renewal

EDITED BY

MUHAMMAD KHALID MASUD

BRILL
LEIDEN · BOSTON · KÖLN
2000

This book is printed on acid-free paper.

Library of Congress Cataloging-in-Publication Data

Travellers in faith : studies of the Tablīghī Jamā'at as a transnational Islamic movement for faith renewal / edited by Muhammad Khalid Masud.
p. cm. — (Social, economic, and political studies of the Middle East and Asia, ISSN 1385-3376 ; v. 69)
Includes bibliographical references and index.
ISBN 9004116222 (alk. paper)
1.Da'wa (Islam) 2. Islam—Missions. 3.Tablīghī Jamā'at (Pakistan) I. Masud, Muhammad Khalid, 1939- II. Series.

BP170.85.T73 2000
297.7'4—dc21 00-041351
CIP

Die Deutsche Bibliothek - CIP-Einheitsaufnahme

Travellers in faith : studies of the Tablīghī Jamā'at as a transnational Islamic movement for faith renewal / ed. by Muhammad Khalid Masud. – Leiden ; Boston ; Köln : Brill, 2000
(Social, economic, and political studies of the Middle East & Asia ; Vol 69)
ISBN 90-04-11622-2

ISSN 1385-3376
ISBN 90 04 11622 2

PRINTED IN THE NETHERLANDS

CONTENTS

PREFACE

This volume has grown out of papers read at a workshop on Tablīghī Jamāʿat, a twentieth century transnational movement for the renewal of Islamic faith. The workshop was held in London on 7–8 June 1990, as part of the "Muslim Transnationalism" project under the leadership of James Piscatori. It was organized by the Committee on Comparative Study of Muslim Societies, jointly sponsored by the Social Science Research Council, U.S.A., and the American Council of Learned Bodies, with Barbara Metcalf as Chair. "Muslim transnationalism" refers to the varieties of linkages through which Muslims express themselves on the transnational level. *Daʿwa* (call to Islam) is one such linkage.

The center of the Tablīghī Jamāʿat is in Delhi, India, and the movement currently operates in more than eighty countries. Among the several Muslim *Daʿwa* groups, organizations and associations working around the world, Tablīghī Jamāʿat is perhaps the most successful transnationally. The movement's annual gatherings in India, Pakistan and Bangladesh, and meetings in London, Chicago and elsewhere, have been so spectacularly well-attended that they have attracted the attention of the media worldwide. Mumtaz Ahmad remarked that "The Raiwind International Conference of the Tablīghī Jamāʿat has become the second-largest congregation of the Muslim world after the Ḥajj" (Aḥmad 1991a, 510).

The global spread of the Jamāʿat and the massive number of its participants would by themselves justify academic attention, and the religious and sociological problematics of the Jamāʿat as a phenomenon of *Daʿwa* further warrant focused study.

Recent writings on the Jamāʿat have offered varied explanations for its rise and spread. Authors have emphasized different aspects of the movement, ranging from the family background of its founder (Nadwī 1985), to the local religious history of Mēwāt (Qādirī 1971), to Sufism (Haq 1972), and to the social and economic conditions in Mēwāt during the 1920–1930s (Ali 1970; and Sikand n.d.).

Writings about Tablīghī Jamāʿat at first appeared in the Indian journals in 1940s, such as Mawlānā Mawdūdī's report in the *Tarjumānul Qurʾān* (1939). Academic studies probably began in the 1970s. The first analytical study, to our knowledge, was published by Muḥammad Ayyūb Qādirī (1971). Previous studies had been either partisan, such as that of Mawlānā Abul Ḥasan ʿAlī Nadwī (1985, originally 1944/1948), or hostile, for example that by Rāshid al-Qādirī (1960).

The first academic dissertation on Tablīghī Jamāʿat was probably that of Anwārul Ḥaq (1972). Other dissertations about the movement have included Muḥammad Aslam (1976), Jacobus Lodewicus Cilliers (1983), Mohammad Zain b. Husin (1984–1985), Mohamed Tozy (1984), ʿAbdul Khāliq Pīrzāda (1990), Yoginder Singh Sikand (1994), Elke Faust (1996), M. Amer (1999), and Khurram Mahmood (1999).

Other studies of the Jamāʿat that have appeared in academic journals are listed in the bibliography. A serious difficulty in studying the Tablīghī Jamāʿat lies in the sources of information available. The movement has no official writings and discourages interviews with the elders. Accounts written by the Tablīghīs are often far from objective. This volume offers studies of the Jamāʿat by scholars who have watched its activities very closely for a considerable length of time, and most of them have personally participated in those activities.

The volume consists of an Introduction, followed by papers grouped into two parts. The Introduction analyzes the historical and social context in which the Jamāʿat was founded, and serves as a background chapter to the studies in the volume. The first group of papers—"Tablīghī Jamāʿat: A *Daʿwa* Organization"—are four general studies dealing respectively with the growth of the Jamāʿat in India, the issues of gender within the movement, the movement's worldview, and its ideology. The second part, "The Tablīghī Jamāʿat: A Transnational Movement," is made up of seven studies of the Jamāʿat as a transnational movement in nine countries in Asia, Africa and Europe. These studies are not simply country reports; they are written by scholars well-acquainted with the Tablīgh work in each country who have studied and written about the movement there. The essays address the Tablīgh's history, linkages, activities, structure, literature, and translations. They explore how the movement has adopted to local environments, how it has been accepted, its ethnic linkages, and its method of communicating its message.

Many features of *Daʿwa*, such as its organization and structure, the centrality of the mosque, and international travel, are common to the Jamāʿat in all these countries. Nevertheless, the practice of *Daʿwa* varies in several significant aspects. The chapters on Belgium and France by Dassetto and Kepel illustrate the role of the Jamāʿat's *Daʿwa* in the development of socio-religious consciousness among minorities, particularly regarding their relationships with majority communities. The Jamāʿat in both countries has linkages and commonalties with Morocco (Tozy). In all these three countries it is a registered society, unlike in India and other countries where it is not. Azmi's study of Canada illustrates a typical case of an English-speaking environment which in some respects resembles Great Britain and the United States. *Daʿwa* in Canada is evidently connected very closely in its organization and spread with South Asian Muslim communities. In Britain, Jamāʿat is also associated with institutions of learning that are similar to the Madrasas in the Muslim World. In Germany, the Turkish linkage, though very small, also plays an important role in the spread of the Jamāʿat.

Morocco (Tozy) illustrates the adaptation of this India-based *Daʿwa* movement to an Arab environment. This occurs not only linguistically, namely in choice of literature and emphasis, but also in the legal framework of its operation. The case of South Africa (Moosa) illustrates how issues of ethnicity intervene with the spread of *Daʿwa*. There we find a divided reaction to the movement among local and immigrant Muslim communities, and according to their affiliation to traditional institutions of learning and reformist trends.

The volume thus explores the ideology and background of the Jamāʿat, and how it became a successful transnational movement. We hope that it will help students and scholars understand the international nature of Islamic *Daʿwa* and the elements of transnationalism within Muslim social and political perceptions of their religion.

I have translated the essays by Gilles Kepel and Mohamed Tozy from the French, with their permission. Other translations in the text and the appendices are also mine, unless otherwise indicated. I must thank Editions du Seuil, Paris, for permission to translate part of chapter 4 Gilles Kepel's *Les banlieues de l'Islam* (1987). I must also express my gratitude to the Social Science Research Council for their initial funding. Finally, I want to thank all the contributors to this volume whose cooperation and patience made it possible. I am particularly indebted to Barbara D. Metcalf and William Roff who read the entire manuscript and suggested valuable improvements.

Muhammad Khalid Masud

TRANSLITERATION TABLE

ء ', ا a, ب b, پ p, ت t, ٹ ṯ, ث th, ج j, چ ch, ح ḥ, خ kh, د d, ڈ d̲, ذ dh, ر r, ز z, س s, ش sh, ص ṣ, ض ḍ, ط ṭ, ظ ẓ, ع ', غ gh, ف f, ق q, ک k, گ g, ل l, م m, ن n, و w, ه h, ة (*tā' marbūṭa* at the end) a, ی y.

VOWELS

Short: َ a, اے e, ِ i, او o, ُ u.
Long: اَ ā, اے- ē, ِی ī, و- ō, اُو ū.
Diphthongs: َو aw, َے ay, ُوّ uww, ِیّ iyy.

Notes:

1. Article ال is transliterated as *al-*, but in the construct form it is abbreviated and vocalized, e.g. Abul, *fil*, 'Abdush Shakūr, etc., according to the sound of the moon and sun letters.
2. Persian/Urdu construct short vowels, both possessive and adjectival, are omitted to avoid confusion.
3. The Persian/Urdu conjunction vowel is transliterated as *wa* in Arabic.
4. Proper names, when cited from European sources, are not transliterated. When cited from non-European sources, they are transliterated as Arabic alphabets. For instance, Ziyaul Hasan (if so cited in the source), and *Ḍiyā* (if cited from non-western source), or Moosa and *Mūsā* respectively.

CONTRIBUTORS TO THIS VOLUME

Shaheen H. Azmi received his Ph.D. from the University of Toronto, Canada in 1996. He is working in Canada as an independent researcher and consultant on issues of Muslim community affairs. His most recent publications are *Professionalism and Social Care, Concepts of Care: Developments in Health and Social Care* (1997) and "Traditional Islamic Social Welfare: Its Meaning, History and Contemporary Relevance" in *Islamic Quarterly* (1991:3,4; 1992:1).

Felice Dassetto is a professor of sociology at the Université Catholique de Louvain, Belgium, with a special interest in the sociology of knowledge and the socio-anthropology of European Islam. He is the team leader of the programme of the European Science Foundation on "Individual and Society in the Mediterranean Muslim World," section on contemporary Islam. His publications include: *Europa nuova frontiera dell'Islam* (1994), *La construction de l'Islam european* (1996), and with A. Bastenier, *L'Islam transplanté, vie et organisation des minorités musulmanes en Belgique* (1984). He is the editor of the book *The New Islamic Discourses in Europe* (1999).

Elke Faust received her M.A. (1996) in Islamic Studies and Sociology and is currently doing her Ph.D. at the Institute for Development Research and Development Policy, Ruhr-University Bochum. Her recent publications include "Islam on Tour: Die indo-pakistanische Bewegung Tablīghī Jamā'at," *Orient* (1998) 39:2.

Marc Gaborieau, a specialist in the historical anthropology of South Asian Muslims in their Hindu environment, is a senior research fellow at CNRS (National Centre for Scientific Research), a professor at EHESS (School of Higher Studies in Social Sciences), and Director, Centre d'Etudes de l'Inde et de l'Asie de Sud, Paris. His recent publications include *Nī brahmanes, ni ancêtres: colporteurs musulmans du Népal* (1993) and *Madrasa: La transmission du savoir dans le monde musulman*" (1997), co-edited with Nicole Grandin.

Gilles Kepel is a Professor at the Institut d'Études Politiques, Paris. Among his latest books are *Muslim Extremism in Egypt/The Prophet and Pharaoh* (1993), *Les banlieues de L'Islam* (1987), *The Revenge of God* (1994) and *Allah in the West* (1997).

Muhammad Khalid Masud formerly a professor at the Islamic Research Institute, Islamabad, Pakistan, is currently the Academic Director of the International Institute of Islam in the Modern World, Leiden, The Netherlands. His recent books include *Shāṭibī's Philosophy of Islamic Law* (1995) and *Iqbal's Reconstruction of Ijtihad* (1995). He co-edited, with D. Powers and B. Messick, *Islamic Legal Interpretations: The Muftis and their Fatwas* (1996).

Barbara Metcalf is Professor of History at the University of California, Davis. She has published a history of the early period of the Deoband movement (*Islamic Revival in India*, Princeton 1982) and a partial translation of the *Bihishti Zewar* (*Perfecting Women*, 1991). Her ongoing work on Tablīghī Jamā'at has produced articles in the *Journal of Asian Studies* (52, 1993, 3) and in the volume *Accounting for Fundamentalism*, edited by Martin Marty and Scott Appleby (1993).

Ebrahim Moosa is Visiting Associate Professor, Department of Religious Studies, Stanford University, California, USA. His interests are Islamic thought and culture, with a special focus on law, ethics and political thought.

Mohammad Talib is Professor of Sociology at Jamia Milia Islamia, New Delhi, India. His research interests focus on migrant labor, sociology of education, and sociology of Islam. He is currently associated with an experiment in teaching and learning of sociology called Participatory Sociology.

Mohamed Tozy is Professor of Political Science and Sociology at Université Hassan II and the Head of the Department of Political Science. He is also supervisor of research works on Muslims in Morocco and Maghreb. His recent publications include *Monarchie et l'Islam politique au Maroc* (1999).

INTRODUCTION

Tablīghī Jamāʿat, from its rise in a rural setting in Mēwāt in India to its global spread in less than a decade, illustrates a significant variety of Muslim transnationalism. The present volume is an attempt to understand this phenomenon. Studies of the Tablīghī Jamāʿat generally refer to "Muslim transnationalism," "*Daʿwa*" and "faith renewal" as essential aspects of the movement. To provide background to the chapters, the first section of this Introduction analyzes these three concepts from theoretical and historical perspectives. The second section explores Islam in Mēwāt, and the third the challenge of modernity and the Muslim response.

I. *Terms and Concepts*

Tablīghī Jamāʿat as a transnational movement has sometimes been regarded as a potential threat to nation-state polities. Some see it as another pan-Islamic movement, others as a fundamentalist Islamic movement opposing the nationalistic basis of the state. These fears reflect general debates about transnationalism and nation-states in theoretical studies in political science and international relations. Let us begin by briefly outlining these debates.

"Transnationalism" implies the preexistence of nationalism and nation-states. Historically, the phenomena of transnationalism (e.g. imperialism) existed long before nationalism. Recent ideologies like industrialism, capitalism, communism and socialism have also idealized a supranational order. Transnationalism has raised several political, cultural, religious and economic questions. For instance, does the rise of transnationalism imply necessarily the irrelevance of the concept of nation-state? Is the advancement of transnational interests like trade, peace, world politics, international laws, knowledge and education possible within nation-state systems? Culturally, transnationalism tends to define the relationship between transnational and other cultures in terms of great/little or centre/periphery civilizations. We must ask how and why certain cultures assume the status of transnational cultures?

James Piscatori (1992) has analyzed recent theoretical studies of the phenomenon of transnationalism in the disciplines of political science and international relations. He observes that scholarly interest in transnationalism's impact on the working of nation-states began only in 1970s. "The obvious common supposition was that nation-states were the decisive components of international affairs" (Piscatori 1992, 4).

Joseph S. Nye (1972) and Robert Keohane (1977) observed that state based international politics had failed. Roland Robertson (1978) and others found that international interaction in social, political, economic and cultural spheres had expanded to the extent that the nation-state was becoming irrelevant. Further, global concerns like the environment, human rights, and international capital made national boundaries less significant.

Piscatori remarks that the functionalist theory had predicted that cooperation between states and non-state sectors in such matters as health and environment would promote interstate cooperation for peace. The world culture would lead to 'an erosion of not only specific forms of authority such as nation-states but authority in general' (Piscatori 1992, 4). Some scholars, on the other hand, argued that such developments would not weaken nation-states but instead would strengthen weaker states by connecting them with greater networks of power (Huntigton cited in Piscatori 1992, 4). In any case, until now, transnationalism has not made the states irrelevant, although it has subjected their absolute sovereignty to higher world interests.

Regarding the cultural aspects of transnationalism, political economists find transnationalism hegemonic, spreading the cultures of the developed states. Some scholars have noticed a powerful trend toward homogenization in favour of European-American culture (Ernest Gellner cited in Piscatori 1992, 7).

Piscatori observes that the theoretical literature on transnationalism has paid "minimal attention to religious phenomena." According to him, two assumptions in the social sciences might explain this indifference. First, "The future of the integrated nation-state lies in secular and participatory politics." Since religion encourages dogmatism and 'intolerance', it has no future. Second, because religion favors society over the individual, it is regarded as irrational. Piscatori questions these assumptions and argues that the role of religion in shaping the language of politics, creating new communities and generating self-awareness of one's tradition has been too crucial in transnational politics to be ignored. He particularly refers to Muslim societies in this regard.

Muslim Transnationalism

Muslim transnationalism differs significantly from its Western conception. Politically, religion does not seem to threaten the state. This is first because the state is not necessarily correlated with nationalism. The most prominent movement of nationalism among Muslims, namely Arab nationalism, was not confined to the geographical boundaries of a particular nation-state. Second, the Muslim nation-states have mostly come into existence after independence from colonial regimes. The element that has most united Muslim communities during their struggle for independence has been, not the usual components of nationalism, namely language, race, culture and territory, but rather religion. Third, the present Muslim-dominated territories are mostly based on arbitrary boundaries introduced by the European colonial regimes. Thus, even though Muslim states are defined territorially, the political sense of nation-state is not historically rooted in most cases.

Indeed, Arabic language, travel to Arab centres of religious learning and the annual pilgrimage to Mecca have long provided transnational linkages among Muslim communities of the world. Nevertheless, although movement from peripheries to the centre has been quite constant, during the premodern period, the Muslim world always had multiple cultural centres. Muslims living in the peripheries now outnumber those living in the Arab world, and an increasing number now reside in the West. Which Muslim culture is central and which is peripheral has become, therefore, contestable.

The peripheral Muslim communities appear to have been more sensitive of their transnational linkages. For instance, South Asian Muslim communities have played a more active role than their Arab counterparts in keeping Muslim transnationalism alive. *Daʿwa* has served as an important transnational linkage in this regard. The South Asian Muslim communities have also carried their religious sensitivity and concern for faith renewal to other Muslim communities abroad.

Although the term nation-state may be an imperfect description of Muslim states or states in the contemporary Muslim world, Muslim transnationalism has not weakened these states. It has rather helped in the routinization of the idea of nation-state by defining 'transnationalism' as a network of linkages between various Muslim states.

Transnational movements have been mostly operating within a nation-state framework. That is, even with their branches in several countries, they have been concentrating their activities with the framework of their respective nation-states. But then, why have these movements transformed themselves into transnational movements?

With reference to Tablīghī Jamāʿat, we can point to two reasons. First, Tablīghī Jamāʿat has adopted physical movement and travel as the most effective method of personal reform. The Jamāʿat has gradually expanded this from local to national to transnational travel. Second, the Jamāʿat has adopted transnationalism as a means of seeking legitimacy for its ideology. The more the Jamāʿat expands transnationally the more universally its ideology is recognized.

The Tablīghī Jamāʿat has adopted transnational travel and physical movement as a means of *Daʿwa*, and travel appears to have become a characteristic feature of the movement. Reports about the gatherings of the Jamāʿat in the news media typically carry pictures of Tablīghīs walking along roadsides with bedding on their shoulders or riding the trains in spectacularly large numbers. Groups of Tablīghīs knocking at neighborhood doors inviting people to come out to the mosque is a common sight in South Asia and in many other places. The most important and frequent activity of an adept of the Jamāʿat is going out for God's sake.

When combined with time and space, 'travel' has a special meaning in the Tablīghī discourse. It is a physical movement from one's present space (house, city, or country) to another. It is comparable with the concept of Hijra, both in the sense of migration and withdrawal. In these senses it is travel within one's self. One temporarily migrates from *dunyā* (wordly pursuits) to *dīn* (religious concerns), a favorite dichotomy among the Tablīghīs. It is a migration from corruption to purity, withdrawing from wordly attachments to the Path of God.

Reform of self becomes feasible when one travels out of one's present setting. Staying in one's usual environment one cannot discriminate between the vital and the trivial in one's life. Temporal withdrawal enables one to give up the trivial (*tark lā yaʿnī*), one of the fundamental principle of the Jamāʿat (see chapter one). It is thus a journey within one's self. While going out and meeting others and speaking to them, one is urged to keep addressing one's self. Knocking at others' doors, one is expected to arrive at one's own doorsteps.

During this travel a Tablīghī creates a different space and time, sacred in several respects. One repeatedly listens to the stories of the Prophet and his companions and is expected to imitate their model in one's daily routines, like eating and sleeping (see Tozy, this volume). A Tablīghī is constantly reminded of the presence of the angels around him who inhabit the sacred space that the Tablīghī has created. With these travels a Tablīghī begins to live in a world that has different measures of success and failure (see Talib, this volume).

A Tablīghī crosses several types of frontiers in this travel. It is a travel across the boundaries of gender since a Tablīghī assumes certain roles and modes of behaviour that, in his original setting, belong to the opposite gender (Metcalf, this volume). He also travels across the frontiers of ethnicity. The Jamāʿat appeals to different Muslim communities across continents. A Tablīghī is not the only one made aware of the fact that he can transcend national, geographical, and language boundaries across Muslim communities in the world; other Muslims, too, are sensitized to the bond that creates an 'imagined' boundary that encloses them all. Finally, the transnational linkages also convince a Tablīghī of the legitimacy of his *Daʿwa*.

Let us now turn to *Daʿwa*, which has provided an important linkage to Muslim transnationalism.

Daʿwa, or call for the renewal of faith, appears to be a common phenomenon in almost all religions in the twentieth century. Some of these movements share an emphasis on a return to scriptures, and an aversion to modernization. These movements have been called revivalist, reformist, fundamentalist, puritan, evangelical and so on, depending upon the perspective of the scholar. Notwithstanding their utility as convenient terms for a comparative study of religious movements in other communities, one must not forget that these terms were developed in specific contexts in Europe and America during the last two centuries. The semantic implications might be distorting in other religious contexts.

For instance, revivalism and renewal might have different specific semantic structures in different religious traditions. Similarly, the phenomena of reformism, fundamentalism and evangelicalism may share commonalities in, say, Christianity and Islam, but their historical and local contexts may shape them very differently.

Revivalism in the Western context refers to the restoration of religious values which secularism and scientism claim to have replaced. It does not necessarily mean restoration of the authority of church and clergy, but rather the authority of scriptures that are believed to contain pure religion and its fundamentals. The fundamentalists defend scriptures against modern historical criticisms of Bible and the challenge of the scientific tradition. The evangelical movements take a missionary and transnational stance to reach out to the adherents of other religions.

The concept of "revivalism" has quite different connotations for the Muslim movements who define their agenda, religious or political, in terms of *daʿwa*. The four terms, namely, *iḥyā, tajdīd, tablīgh* and *daʿwa*, to which Muslim movements refer are analyzed below to explain the Muslim sense of 'revivalism.'

Iḥyā (Revival)

In the *ḥadīth* literature the term *iḥyā* is used to denote the revival of *Sunna*, often meaning the practice of the Prophet. An example of this *ḥadīth* usage is the following saying of the Prophet: "Whoever revives my *Sunna* (practice) revives me. And whoever revives me he will be with me in Paradise" (Tirmidhī n.d., 4:151). The other *aḥādīth* explain the meaning of revival as eliminating *bidʿa*, or deviation from Islamic tradition. *Bidʿa* could be a survival of pre-Islamic customs in a society, or it could be ideas and practices introduced under foreign influence.

The use of the term *iḥyā* was often prompted when there was a threat of deviation from the tradition due to either foreign or local influences. For instance, Ghazālī (d. 1111) called his book *Iḥyā ʿUlūm al-Dīn*, revival of religious sciences, to counter the impact of Greek sciences in his day (Al-Ghazālī n.d.). Again, Ibn Taymiyyah (d. 1328) used it against Sufism and philosophy, which he believed were foreign to Islam. He also opposed *taqlīd* (adherence to one particular school of Islamic law), an internal development in the Islamic legal tradition, which he regarded as a religious innovation (Harās 1952). One must follow the ancients (*salaf*, usually meaning the first generation of Islam), and deviation from their ways is called *bidʿa*, and must be avoided. The term *salafiyya*, which means those who follow ancients as opposed to moderns, is closely associated with the revivalism of *Sunna*.

The revivalism of the *iḥyā* movements is not, however, a return to or restoration of an agreed 'tradition.' Instead, we find in it a "reconstructed tradition," one that is contested by others. To seek legitimacy, the *iḥyā* movements invoke the authority of scriptures. The scriptures under debate are not simply the Qur'ān; more often they are *aḥādīth* texts. Compared to other Fundamentalisms that call for a return to their primary scriptures, the *iḥyā* movements place little stress on a return to the Qur'ān, the premier scripture in Islam. Instead they emphasize *Sunna*, the practice of the Prophet and his companions. The focus is on scriptures, but of a different type. *Iḥyā* movements also employ transnational linkages to seek legitimacy and to surpass local authorities, and in this sense *iḥyā* is very close to *tajdīd*. Indeed, both terms are sometimes used together.

Tajdīd (Renewal)

Tajdīd has the same root as *jadīd* (new, modern), but it is understood as 'renewal or renovation.' It is distinguished from modernization, which is pejoratively called in Urdu *tajaddud* (Aḥmad 1991a, 471). *Mujaddid* is the person who renews the religion. In Islamic tradition, as the following *ḥadīth* describes, this renewal is believed to take place centennially:

> The Prophet (peace be upon him) said, "Allah will raise for this community at the end of every hundred years the one who will renovate its religion for it" (Abū Dā'ūd 1989, 3:80).

Muslim scholars have not unanimously recognized this *ḥadīth* as essential. It is not included in five other reputed collections of *aḥādīth*. Later collections have also classified it under nonessential topics such as eschatological matters (e.g. Ṣaʿīdī n.d., 8). *Tajdīd*, in this *ḥadīth*, refers to a view of the history of religion according to which the original teachings become corrupted with the passage of time. New matters are added to the religion's core. The function of *tajdīd* is to purify the religion by eliminating these later additions, and to renew faith by returning to the pure and original religion. Gaborieau (1997) regards *tajdīd* as a Muslim concept of the renewal of time, according to which there is a continuous deterioration after the period of Prophet Muhammad. A *mujaddid* averts this process of deterioration by renewing the religion. This conception of *tajdīd* is not found in the literature of the renewal movement. They believe that the early centuries were the best period of Islam and that they constitute the ideal to be imitated. They do not state that the period can be repeated or recreated; no *mujaddid* can bring it back. *Tajdīd* is nevertheless a conservative concept.

Several persons in Islamic history have been claimed as *mujaddids* or renovators. Jamālud Dīn Afghānī (d. 1897), Muftī Muḥammad ʿAbduh (d. 1905) and Mawlānā Ashraf ʿAlī Thānawī (d. 1941) have recently been claimed as the *mujaddids* of the modern period (see Ṣaʿīdī n.d., 12; ʿAbdul Bārī Nadwī 1962, 35). Mirzā Ghulām Aḥmad, the founder of the Aḥmadiyya Mission, is also claimed to be a *mujaddid* by a section of his followers. Some Tablīghī writers also explain Mawlānā Ilyās's mission within the framework of the *mujaddid* concept (Ferōzpurī n.d., 5; also see Chapter four, this volume).

In India, *tajdīd* responded to the challenges of modernity in the twentieth century by developing a special meaning of resistance to changes and reform in religion. Mawlānā Sulaymān Nadwī defined *tajdīd* as 'overhauling' (Nadwī 1962, 35) to emphasize restoration to the original position. The Tablīghī Jamāʿat uses the terms *iḥyā* and *tajdīd* interchangeably, but the term *tablīgh* is more central to this movement.

Tablīgh

Balagha (*b-l-gh*), the root verbal form of *tablīgh*, connotes the following meanings: to reach one's destination, to arrive, to achieve one's objective, to come to hear, and to come of age. The verbal form *ballagha*, from which the noun *tablīgh* is derived, means to cause something to reach, to communicate, and to report. This verb appears frequently in the Qur'ān (e.g., 5:67; 33:39; 7:62, 68, 79, 93), in association with *risāla* (mission of a prophet), meaning the communication of the revelation or message. The Qur'ān does not use the term *tablīgh*. The word *balāgh*, which is used, is considered synonymous with *tablīgh* by Qur'ānic lexicographers (Iṣfahānī 1961, 60). The Qur'ānic usage signifies that communication of the message alone is the objective. Conversion is not the duty or the mission of a prophet or a preacher; this is left to the free choice of the addressees.

> And say to the People of the Book and to those who are unlearned: Do you submit yourselves? If they do, they are in right guidance. But if they turn back, your duty is only to convey the message (Balāgh) (3:20).

> Had God willed, they had not been idolaters. We have not sent you as a Keeper over them, nor are you responsible for them (6:107).

These and other verses (e.g., 5:99, 105; 13:40; 16:35, 82; 42:48) emphasize a very significant aspect of the Islamic concept of *tablīgh*, that the duty of a preacher ends with the communication of the message.

Another literal meaning of *tablīgh* is communication. The meaning of preaching or a mission is produced when *tablīgh* is combined with *risāla* or *Daʿwa*. The Qurʾān uses the term *risāla* in conjunction with the word *balagha* or *ballagha*. *Daʿwa* often replaces the word *risāla* in common usage to produce the phrase *tablīgh al-Daʿwa* (communication of call). In modern usage, *tablīgh* and *Daʿwa* are often used interchangeably. In modern Urdu usage *tablīgh* by itself has acquired the meaning of mission or proselytization. Qāḍī Sulaymān Manṣūrpurī defined *tablīgh* as follows: "*Tablīgh* means calling others toward one's religion" (1928, 4). This particular sense of *tablīgh* is a product of developments in the twentieth century, especially within the context of Hindu and Christian missionary activities during this period, discussed in the next section. The Tablīghī Jamāʿat defined *tablīgh* without reference to conversion, probably to avoid this particular sense of *tablīgh* and *Daʿwa*.

Daʿwa

Daʿwa (root *d-ʿ-w*), literally meaning 'to call,' connotes the following: invitation to a meal, prayer, invocation, vow, appeal, claim and lawsuit. Usually, the verb *daʿā* means to 'call on,' and 'pray' if it is addressed to God. If it is suffixed with the preposition *ilā*, it means 'to invite to something.' The word *Daʿwa* has been used in the Qurʾān to mean 'invocation,' 'prayer' (2:186; 13:14), 'claim' (40:43), and 'call' (14:44; 30:25). *Daʿwa* and its related words mean mission when used with reference to the Prophets and other people who were assigned such missions (12:108; 14:22, 44; 33:46; 71:5–8). The following Qurʾānic verses illustrate this point:

> Who could be a better person than the one who called (*daʿā*) toward God and acted righteously (41:33).
>
> There should be a group of people among you who call (*yadʿūna*) to good, enjoining [what is known to be] good and forbidding [what is known to be] evil (3:104).

The Tablīghī Jamāʿat defines its mission within the framework of these verses. According to them, *Daʿwa* means enjoining good and forbidding evil (*Amr bil-maʿrūf wa nahī ʿanil munkar*). The acceptance of the message is left to the free choice of a person. "There is no compulsion in religion. Truth is henceforth distinct from falsehood" (2:256). The Qurʾān, therefore, considers the mission accomplished when the Truth has been made known to a person.

> When it is said to them, "come to what God has revealed, come to the Apostle," they say, "Enough for us are the ways we found our fathers following." What! Even though their fathers were void of knowledge and guidance? Oh you who believe! You have charge of your own souls. He who errs does not harm you if you follow guidance. All of you will return to God, He will then inform you of what you used to do (5:104–105).

Mawlānā Ilyās, the founder of the Tablīghī Jamāʿat, elaborates this point as follows:

> One cannot call others to religion by compulsion, but it is possible only in the manner that truth may be sifted from the untruth and the genuine must be distinguished from the counterfeit. To use human force to make people accept the divine message does not mean obedience to God, but it is rather compliance of human orders (Kāndhalwī 1962, 15).

It appears from the Qurʾān that *Daʿwa* combines two acts simultaneously: invitation and claim. When someone invites another to God he also claims the truth of his mission. His duty is complete with the call, because truth and falsehood are clear to the human mind, which is free to choose between them. The person who denies this invitation denies also the claim to the truth. It is then for God to take action; the preacher has no further charge. This sense also reflects the pre-Islamic usage of *Daʿwa* meaning 'a call to help,' mostly in tribal wars (Ibn Manẓūr 1988, 4, 361). In the Qurʾān '*Daʿwa*' means also calling upon God to help and establish the proof of that truth. The Qurʾān narrates stories of prophets who were denied and whose people were consequently punished as a proof (16:113; 26:189; 29:37; 39:25; 54:18).

The Qur'ān prescribes *Daʿwa* as both an individual and a collective duty of Muslims. Prophet Muḥammad explained the scope of the performance of the duty, saying that a believer must correct evil by hand or by tongue, respectively, depending on his or her abilities. Failing that, one should at least condemn the evil in one's heart (Muslim 1954, 1:69). The three levels in this *ḥadīth*, hand, tongue and heart, provided a basis for the doctrine of *Tartībud Daʿwa* (priority in *Daʿwa*), as three levels or phases of Islamic mission in the following descending order: *Jihād* (physical struggle), *Daʿwa* (communication) and *hijra* (abandoning, migration), respectively.

Theology

Among the early Muslim sects, the Muʿtazilīs and the Ashʿarīs differed regarding the basis of religious obligations. The Ashʿarīs argued that obligations come into effect with Revelation or its *Daʿwa*. The Muʿtazilis believed that reason was the true source of obligation, religious or otherwise (Aḥmad 1965, 69; Zuḥaylī 1986, 146; Ibn Humām 1898, 165–166; Baghdādī 1928, 262–264; Bayhaqī n.d., 76). Consequently, the Ashʿarīs believed that *Daʿwa* was necessary to communicate Revelation to the people. The people who do not receive Revelation or *Daʿwa* have no obligation. The Muʿtazilīs held that such people were still obliged to do good and avoid evil according to their rational perception and that they would be judged by God accordingly. It is clear from these discussions that the subject of *Daʿwa* in this period was enjoining good and forbidding evil (*amr bil maʿrūf wa nahī ʿanil munkar*). Its audience included both Muslims and non-Muslims. After the conquest period in Islam, Muslim theologians generally came to consider it impossible to imagine a community in any part of the world that was ignorant of Islam. Consequently, *Daʿwa* was no longer a perennial obligation. Only in times of war was *daʿwa* required as a form of legitimation.

In Fiqh books, *Daʿwa* was treated as a problem of communication. *Bulūghud Daʿwa*, or the question whether the call to Islam has reached its destination, was a question on which the jurists differed among themselves. The followers of Mālik b. Anas (d. 795), Zayd b. ʿAlī (d. 740) and a Shāfiʿī jurist al-Māwardī (d. 1031), regarded *Daʿwa* as obligatory before every battle with non-Muslims, regardless of whether the enemy had knowledge of Islam or not. The Imāmī Shīʿa, the Ibāḍī, and a majority of Sunnī scholars maintained that

Daʿwa was obligatory only if the enemy had not heard of Islam at all. The Ḥanbalī School did not consider it an obligation because Islam was universally known (Zuḥaylī n.d., 136ff.; Zuḥaylī 1989, 419).

The Ḥanafīs in India held similar views in the twentieth century. The *ʿulamā* of Deoband maintained that every non-Muslim was obliged to accept Islam because the message of Islam had reached the whole of mankind (Shērkōtī 1985, 134). Mawlānā ʿUbaydullāh Sindhī (1872–1945), a convert from the Sikh religion to Islam, disagreed with this view, saying that *Daʿwa* was the duty of Muslims and that non-Muslims could not be held responsible for not accepting Islam. During the debate, the Qur'ānic verses (2:62; 5:69) that promise reward in the hereafter for believing and practicing Christians and Jews as well was cited. The verse implied that conversion to Islam was not necessary. Mawlānā Manāẓir Aḥsan Gīlānī rebutted this claim by arguing that the beliefs mentioned in these verses included belief in the prophethood of Muḥammad (Gīlānī 1962, 223).

Institutionalization

In the light of the above discussion it is easy to understand why Muslims had no regular missionary organization. Among modern scholars, Wahba Zuḥaylī (n.d., 55), Muḥammad al-Ghazālī (1988, 80) and Thomas Arnold (1968, 443; 1958, 746) have explicitly noted the absence of such an organization in Islam. Ṣāliḥ (1968), in his history of the institutions in early Islam, does not mention the existence of any proselytizing organization. Muslim writers frequently criticize past Muslim rulers for not establishing such institutions (Ghazālī 1988, 80).

The absence of such a referent for *Daʿwa* in nineteenth century encyclopedias also supports our point. *The Shorter Encyclopedia of Islam* (Juynboll 1961) defines *Daʿwa* only as an accusation or arraignment of a legal claim. *A Dictionary of Islam* (Hughes 1885/1964, 472) mentions several terms under *Daʿwa*, but not preaching. On the other hand, under "preaching" it refers to *khaṭīb, mudhakkir, wāʿiẓ* and *nāṣiḥ*, but not to *Daʿwa* or *tablīgh*. This means that during the nineteenth and early twentieth centuries when these works appeared, no institution for *Daʿwa* existed, nor did Western writers yet associate the term *Daʿwa* with preaching.

In fact, Westerners generally believed that Islam was not a missionary religion. T.W. Arnold had to argue at length that the concept of *Daʿwa* existed among Muslims and that Islam was indeed a missionary religion, although it had no organized missionary institutions as did Christianity (Arnold 1968, 413). He noted that when the British Government of the Sudan marked out zones of influence for various Christian missionary societies, Muslims in Egypt demanded a zone for Islamic *Daʿwa*. The demand was turned down because Muslims had no missionary organization (Arnold 1968, 443; Goldziher 1952, 343).

Certain historical factors discouraged the organization of *Daʿwa* as a state institution. First, *Daʿwa* was regarded as a function of prophets. Since prophecy came to an end with Prophet Muḥammad, the concept of *Daʿwa* had to be redefined. Although *Daʿwa* is still characterized as "a prophetic work" (Mawdūdī 1940, 76), it came to be seen as a responsibility of the Muslim Umma. Second, *Daʿwa* was considered a function of *Jihād*. Like *Jihād*, after the period of conquests it came to be classified as a collective duty (*farḍ kifāya*) rather than a personal duty.

During the Umawī period (660–750), *Daʿwa* began to be politicized. The state obliged a new convert to change his name and to adopt Arabic as his language (Fāṭimī 1963, 124, 129). This emphasis on Arabic led to protests by the non-Arabs. The Khawārij, Shīʿa, Fāṭimī and ʿAbbāsī movements politicized *Daʿwa* against the Umawīs and called for alternative political orders. The Khawārij condemned their political opponents as disbelievers and declared *Jihād* against them to be a personal religious duty. The Fāṭimīs organized *Daʿwa* more efficiently, with a distinct hierarchical structure and secrecy at various levels (Hamdānī 1976, 86).

The politicization of *Daʿwa* had serious implications for its further growth. First, the state tried to control *Daʿwa* movements. Since in *Jihād* permission of the *imām* (ruler) was needed, and *Daʿwa* was closely linked with *Jihād*, the state made permission of the ruler necessary also for *Daʿwa*. The state, however, did not develop an official organization for this purpose. Second, theologians and jurists redefined the concept of *Daʿwa* within the framework of *amr bi'l-maʿrūf wa nahiy ʿanil munkar* (enjoining good and forbidding evil) in order to assign *Daʿwa* to *ʿulamā*, although it was still subject to the ruler's permission (ʿAwda 1959, 1:495–500). Consequently, *Daʿwa* came to be limited to the forms with which the *ʿulamā* were familiar. Al-Ilūrī (1979) mentions the following as forms of *Daʿwa: waʿẓ* (speech), *tadrīs* or *taʿlīm* (teaching), *taṣnīf wa tālīf* (writing books), *irshād* (guidance) and *tadhkīr* (reminding). They all typified individual efforts, not missionary organizations.

Political *Daʿwa* movements often worked secretly. Some of them, like the Fāṭimīs in India, operated in such a fashion that it was hard to distinguish them from Hindus.

The Ṣūfī *Daʿwa* also developed its own system independent of the state. The Ṣūfīs defined conversion as *tawba*, meaning to return. In other words, it placed stress on making Muslims true Muslims. The Ṣūfī orders were closely connected with education, guilds and soldiers. Ṣūfī *Daʿwa* included welfare and health programmes in the form of charms, amulets and prayers for the sick and needy, and also the fear of divine wrath for those who denied the Ṣūfīs. The Ṣūfī *Daʿwa* was nonpolitical and nonmissionary. The focus of *Daʿwa* on conversion of non-Muslims to Islam reemerged in reaction to European Christian missions.

Modern Daʿwa Movements

There are numerous *Daʿwa* organizations working at present, and it is not possible to list them all in this essay. A selected list is given in appendix 1. Instead of a detailed analysis of them, a comparative analysis is provided in the form of a chart, which requires some brief explanation.

This chart analyzes sixteen aspects of these movements. The first three categories are year of foundation, country of origin and sectarian affiliation. In this list only one movement belongs to the Shīʿī sect; others are Sunnī, one of which was declared non-Muslim. The next three categories analyze their relationship with the state and aspects of their organization. Four of them are state sponsored *Daʿwa* movements and the others are privately established. Besides the state organizations, only one, the Aḥmadiyya Mission, is registered. The Tablīghī Jamāʿat is not registered in its country of origin. It does, however, operate as a registered society in some countries in Europe and Africa. All organizations have a system of registered regular membership, with the exception of the Tablīghī Jamāʿat, which does not maintain regular membership. Anyone can join in or leave the Jamāʿat activities at any time, and there is no membership fee.

The next ten categories analyze the agenda of *Daʿwa.* Most of these movements are non-political; only five have an explicit political agenda. Three of them are state sponsored and two (Muslim

Brotherhood and Jamāʿat Islāmī) are private. Most of these movements work among Muslims; only four work among non-Muslims for their conversion to Islam. Five movements have Ṣūfī affiliations. All of them operate transnationally in at least one or two countries outside their country of origin. Most have mosques as the centre of their activities, and some have their own mosques.

With the single exception of Tablīghī Jamāʿat, all of them have their own publication programs and periodicals. Only three support militancy and have participated in militant operations. Except for Tablīghī Jamāʿat, all have educational and welfare programs as part of their *Daʿwa*. The Tablīghī Jamāʿat has educational institutions attached to some of its centres but these are not part of its *Daʿwa* activities.

Lastly, the movements are usually ambiguous regarding the question of female participation in *Daʿwa* activities. Most of them have programmes for women, and some even have women members, but their activities are generally limited. No clear information on this is available for four of the organizations. The Tablīghī Jamāʿat allows limited female participation under due care (see Metcalf and Faust, this volume).

Daʿwa organizations in the modern period have generally worked in four areas. First is the defence of Islam against Christian and other non-Muslim missionaries, and to make counter or parallel missionary efforts to gain new converts to Islam. Organizations such as the Aḥmadiyya Mission in India, founded by Mirza Ghulām Aḥmad (d. 1908), and PERKIM (Pertubuhan Kebajikan Islam Se Malaysia) are examples of this type. The missionary form of *Daʿwa* often follows the model of modern Christian missionaries. Organizations like the World Council of Mosques, the Organization for the Distribution of the Qurʾān, and Jamʿiyyatul Shubbānil Muslimīn resemble the World Council of Churches, the Bible Society, and the YMCA, respectively.

The second area in which *Daʿwa* organizations have worked is for the education and welfare of the Muslim community. Abd al-Raḥmān al-Kawākibī's Jamʿiyyat Taʿlīmil Muwaḥḥidīn in Egypt, and several other educational movements in India like the Aligarh Movement, laid the foundation for this type of *Daʿwa*. The early educational movements favoured modernization of education, with emphasis on Western sciences. The educational movements led by the *ʿulamā*, such as the Deoband School, stress purely traditional religious education. Tablīghī Jamāʿat found *Daʿwa* work in this area to be quite ineffective.

SOME *DAʿWA* MOVEMENTS*

Serial Number	Name / Categories	AM (1)	ICS (2)	MB (3)	PM (4)	HDI (5)	DAM (6)	MWL (7)	JI (8)	MA (9)	TJ (10)
1	YEAR	1889	1972	1928	1960	1957	1968	1962	1941	1960	1934
2	COUNTRY	India	Libya	Egypt	Malaysia	Iraq	Malaysia	Arabia	India	Egypt	India
3	SECT	Aḥmadi	Sunni	Sunni	Sunni	Shiʿa	Sunni	Sunni	Sunni	Sunni	Sunni
4	SPONSOR	Priv	State	Priv	State	Priv	Priv	State	Priv	State	Priv
5	REGISTERED	Yes	Yes	No	Yes	No	No	?	No	?	In some countries
6	OPEN	No	No	No	No	No	No	No	No	No	Yes
7	POLITICAL	No	Yes	Yes	Yes	No	No	Yes	Yes	No	No
8	NON-MUSLIM	Yes	No	No	Yes	No	No	Yes	No	Yes	No
9	ṢŪFĪ	Yes	No	Yes	No	No	Yes	No	No	No	Yes
10	MOSQUE	Yes	Yes	Yes	Yes	Yes	Yes	Yes	Yes	Yes	Yes
11	TRANSNATION	Yes	Yes	Yes	Yes	Yes	Yes	Yes	Yes	Yes	Yes
12	PUBLICITY	Yes	Yes	Yes	Yes	Yes	Yes	Yes	Yes	Yes	No
13	MILITANT	No	No	Yes	No	Yes	No	No	Yes	No	No
14	EDUCATION	Yes	Yes	Yes	Yes	Yes	Yes	Yes	Yes	Yes	In some countries
15	WELFARE	Yes	Yes	Yes	Yes	Yes	Yes	Yes	Yes	Yes	No
16	WOMEN	Yes	?	Yes	Yes	?	Yes	?	Yes	Yes	Yes

* Organization names are given in abbreviated forms corresponding with those listed alphabetically in appendix 1.

The third area of *Da^cwa* relates to politics, either state sponsored or independent. State sponsored *Daʿwa* goes back in recent history to the Ottoman Sulṭān ʿAbdul Ḥamīd I (1725–1789), who claimed authority over Muslims everywhere as a defender of religion. Sulṭān ʿAbdul Ḥamīd II (1876–1909) sent emissaries to Muslims outside Turkish borders to obtain recognition as a caliph of Islam. This *Daʿwa* sat well with Europeans, who were used to comparing Muslim *khalīfa* with the Pope (Arnold 1968, 167–173, 190–194). Modern examples of the state sponsored *Daʿwa* are al-Majlisul Aʿlā lish Shuʾūn al-Islāmiyya in Egypt, Rābiṭatul ʿĀlamil Islāmī founded in Saudi Arabia and Jamʿiyyatul Daʿwatil Islāmiyya in Libya.

Muslim Brotherhood and Jamāʿat Islāmī illustrate political *Daʿwa* movements that are not state sponsored. This type of *Daʿwa* is transnational as well as national in that they seek the unity and solidarity of the Muslim Umma and have established branches and offices in other countries. They are national insofar as they work for the formation of Islamic states in particular countries.

The fourth area of *Daʿwa* is the reform of religion and religious practices. In this area we find three general approaches: modernization, revivalism and faith renewal. Modernists aim at reforming traditional Islam to meet the challenges of modernity. They interpret Islam from a liberal, dynamic and forward looking perspective. They do not reject the value of *fiqh* (texts) but they reject adherence to them. Revivalists reject modernity as well as tradition as expressed in *fiqh* schools and Ṣūfī orders. They call for the revival of the original Islam, and oppose modernity as secularism and materialism. Several revivalist trends with various interpretations are contested by other Muslim groups.

The faith renewal approach, such as Tablīghī Jamāʿat's *Daʿwa*, addresses similar issues. It also speaks of revival and reform, but these are comparatively more objectified. Revivalism here refers to the restoration of the religious tradition, which is established in Ṣūfī orders and schools of Islamic law. It rejects modernity as manifested in materialism and secularism. The focus on faith renewal is explained by saying that the faith has been corrupted and needs to be renewed. The faith renewal movements are often rooted deeply in their local environments. Their *Daʿwa* can be properly understood only with reference to their local contexts, to which we now turn.

II. *Mēwāt*

Having analyzed the concepts of transnationalism and *Daʿwa*, we now examine the concept of faith renewal, with particular reference to South Asia. The *ʿulamā* and the Ṣūfīs both emphasize faith renewal in their *Daʿwa*. They differ, however, in their emphasis on *sharīʿa* (Divine Law). The *ʿulamā* stress the supremacy of *sharīʿa* as expressed in *fiqh*. The Ṣūfīs find *fiqh* concerned only with the external aspects of *sharīʿa*, disregarding the inner meanings which the Ṣūfī *Daʿwa* highlights. Tablīghī Jamāʿat's approach is closer to that of the *ʿulamā*. South Asian Muslims, especially the *ʿulamā* and the elite, regarded both Hinduism and modernity as threats to their faith and identity, and these threats intensified in twentieth century Mēwāt where Tablīghī Jamāʿat originated.

Mēwāt, the land of the Meo Rajput tribes, is a vast area in Central India to the south of Delhi and north of Hadūtī. The river Jamna lies to its east and to the west is Kōt Qāsim. During the British period, Mēwāt included the princely states of Alwar and Bhartpur and the district of Gurganwa, and some parts of the district Mithrā. Present day Mēwāt consists of the area from Sohna to Fērōzpūr Jhirka and Alwar, and some parts of Bhartpur (Shams 1983, 17).

The geographical conditions in the area shaped the habits and lives of the Mēwātīs. They lived a hard life and were constantly occupied in robberies, raids and rebellions. They trace their genealogy to Meeds from Central Asia (Cunningham cited in Shams 1983, 18; Mewātī 1979, 35). Shams (1983, 30) says that the Meos claim to be a warrior class, the Kashatriya, and adds that they belong to the same stock as the Minas of Rajputana, who later mixed with the Rajputs. In Indian history they are mentioned frequently as attacking and plundering Delhi (Nadwī 1985, 74). Qādirī (1971) explains that the Mēwātīs found it hard to integrate with the Delhi Sultanate because the rulers treated them as inferior to the privileged nobles, who were mostly from Arab, Persian or Turkish families.

The Meos continually rebelled against Delhi and suffered the consequences. Sulṭān Balban massacred many to subdue the tribe in 1267 (Mēwātī 1979, 38). Mēwātīs, under Bahādur Nāhar and Lakhan Pal, fought against the Tughlaqs (1320–1413). Sulṭān Fērōz Shāh Tughlaq (1351–1388) integrated Mēwāt into Delhi Sultanate. Lakhan Pal accepted Islam, and the Sulṭān founded a cantonment in Fērōzpūr

Jhirka, also known as Ḥiṣār Fērōz (Nadwī 1985 [1944], 74; Mēwātī 1979, 38). Opposition to Delhi continued during the Mughal period. Shahjahān's armies raided Mēwāt to crush a rebellion. After the British conquest of Delhi in 1807 Lord Lake also massacred Meos to subdue them completely (Mēwātī 1979, 38), and after 1857 William Frazer did so again (Ali 1970, 24ff.). We see then that historically Mēwāt has been unable to integrate politically into Muslim India.

It is generally claimed that Maḥmūd Ghaznawī and Sālār Masʿūd Ghāzī converted Meos to Islam in the twelfth century (Mīr Maḥbūb ʿAlī Mēwātī d. 1853 cited in Mēwātī 1979, 52; Kaye Watson and W. Hunter cited in Shams 1983, 34). Ḥabībur Raḥmān Khān Mēwātī, however, argues that Meos, as Meeds, had accepted Islam already during Muḥammad b. Qāsim's rule in Sind (Mēwātī 1979, 52).

In fact, Islam came to India gradually and in several phases through soldiers and the Ṣūfīs. Of several Ṣūfī orders working in India the following five came to Mēwāt: Chishtiya,[1] Qādiriya,[2] Suhrawardiya,[3]

---

[1] Shaykh Khweshgī (d. 1155) introduced the Chishtiya order among the Afghans (Ikrām 1992, 190). The second important inroad was made by Khwāja Muʿīnud Dīn (d. 1235) in Ajmer, who arrived during the reign of Sulṭān Muḥammad Ghawrī (d. 1206). The Chishtīs worked mainly among the Rājputs. Bābā Farid's disciple Makhdūm Ṣābir (d. 1291) is buried in Kalyar, Sahāranpūr. The Chishtīs were popular among the local population because they never accepted financial support or estates from the kings (Ikrām 1992, 192). Delhi became the centre of the Chishtiya from Khāwja Niẓāmud Dīn Awliyā (d. 1325); one branch of their order was called Niẓāmiyya after him. The area around the hospice later became known as Bastī Niẓāmud Dīn. Mawlānā Ilyās belonged to the Ṣābiriyya branch of the Chishtiya, yet he began his work in this Bastī where the headquarters of the Jamāʿat are now located.

The Ṣābiriyya, attributed to Makhdūm ʿAlā'ud Dīn ʿAlī Aḥmad Ṣābir of Kalyar Sharīf (d. 1291), a relative and disciple of Bābā Farīd Ganj Shakar (d. 1265), became popular in Northern India during the fifteenth century. This branch was known for its active interest in the propagation of religion. Ṣābiriyya rose to prominence through the efforts of Shaykh ʿAbdul Quddūs of Gangōh (d. 1537), who supported the Lodīs in their battle against the Mughals. The Ṣābiriyya was frequently in conflict with Mughal Delhi, and only Dārā Shikōh had cordial relations with them.

[2] The Qādiriya Ṣūfī order, attributed to Shaykh ʿAbdul Qādir Jilānī (d. 1165), was introduced into India by Makhdūm Muḥammad Gilānī (d. 1517), who came from Iran and settled in Uchch, near Multān (Panjab), during the period of Sulṭān Sikandar Lōdī (d. 1516).

[3] The Suhrawardiya order, attributed to ʿAbdul Qāhir Abū Najīb al-Suhrawardī (d. 1168), was introduced into India by Bahā'ud Dīn Zakariyyā (d. 1262), and spread to Kashmir, Bengal, Gujarat, Sind and Baluchistan. This order remained close to the Muslim kings and accepted grants from them. They generally worked among the Muslim elite and in political centres.

Naqshbandiya[4] and Madāriya.[5] Mewātī (1979, 182–440) mentions the names of more than forty Chishtī Ṣūfīs in Mēwāt, including Muʿīnud Dīn Ajmērī (d. 1235), Shaykh Muḥammad Turk Nārnawlī (d. 1244), Shaykh Chāpan (d. 1589), Shāh Chōkhā (d. 1591) and Miyān Mastān Shāh (d. eighteenth century). Among the Qādiriyya, more than twenty Ṣūfīs came to Mēwāt (Mēwātī 1979, 473–610). One Qādirī Ṣūfī Miyān Lāl Khān, alias Lāl Dās (d. 1754), is claimed to have instructed Dārā Shikōh on spiritual matters (Mēwātī 1979, 600–601). Nine Suhrawardī Ṣūfīs of the Rasūl Shāhī Majdhūb order (Mēwātī 1979, 639–664) and seven Naqshbandī Ṣūfīs came to Mēwāt (Mēwātī 1979, 611–638).

The Madāriya order became more popular among the Rajput tribes of Mēwāt. Their soldierly appearance and organizational structure probably appealed to the warrior Meo tribes. According to Ḥabībur Raḥmān Khān Mēwātī, Shāh Madār came to Mēwāt in the later days of his life. Miyān Chānd Shāh (d. 1395), whose tomb is in Ghansōlī, became Shāh Madār's disciple in Alwar (Mēwātī 1979, 412). Another Ṣūfī of the Madāriya order was Khwāja ʿAbdur Raḥmān, popularly known as Chuhrsiddh (d. 1599). His tomb in Chandoli is a popular shrine. The tomb of another Madārī Ṣūfī known as Ghāzī Gaddan, probably Ghazanfar ʿAlī (d. 1599), was built in the days of Shāh Jahān (Mēwātī 1979, 416).

Two notable Madārī Ṣūfīs—Bābā Kapūr and Bābā Gopāl—are revered by the Mēwātīs. Shāh ʿAbdul Ghafūr (d. 1571), popularly

[4] The Naqshbandiya order, attributed to Shaykh Bahā'ud Dīn Naqshband (d. 1390), came to India with Bābur who was devoted to Khāwjā ʿUbaydullāh Aḥrār. Khāwja Bāqī Billāh, a disciple of Khāwja Aḥrār formally introduced the order. His disciple Shaykh Aḥmad Sirhindī, known as the Mujaddid Alf Thānī, transformed the Naqshbandiya order into a reformist and politically active Ṣūfī order. His branch later came to be known as Naqshbandiya Mujaddidiya.

[5] The Madāriya, more popular among the illiterate masses than among the *ʿulamā*, is attributed to Shāh Badīʿud Dīn Madār (d. 1434). Shāh Madār came to Kalpi (India) from Hurmuz (Iran) and quickly gained popularity among the people for his ascetic practices. The Madāriya were accused of living naked and using ashes to cover their bodies. Probably their emphasis on asceticism and minimal clothing led to such exaggerations. There are nine orders of his successors, all called *ʿāshiqān* (devotees): Imām Nawrōzī, Sōkhta Shāhī, Kamar Basta, Laʿl Shahbāzī, Bābā Gōpāl, Lakhā Shāhī, Kalāmī, Kamāl Qādirī and Karīm Shāhī. These orders take their names from the disciples of Shaykh Kapūr. Imām Nawrōz was a soldier who joined Shaykh Kapūr. Sōkhta Shāh refers to Sayyid ʿĀbid who used to play with fire in his states of *jadhb* (spiritual states of possession) without being burned. Laʿl Shahbāz refers to Shāh Amānullāh.

called Bābā Kapūr, came to Mēwāt from Kālpi. A water carrier by profession, he had served in the Muslim army. Shaykh ʿAbdul Ḥaq describes him as a majdhūb (possessed person) who ate and wore very little. He is known as Shaykh Madār's successor (Mewātī 1979, 424ff.), and his tomb is in Gawalior. His disciple Bābā Gōpāl, a convert from Hinduism, is described as a prince who abdicated his throne for asceticism. In a competition of ascetic (*yōga*) feats, he lost to Bābā Kapūr and became his disciple (Mēwātī 1979, 422). It is significant to note that most converts to Islam adopt Arabic names, but he retained his Hindi name. Both these Ṣūfīs were reponsible for the spread and organization of the Madāriya order in this area. An annual festival was held in Makanpur at the tomb of Shāh Badīʿud Dīn Madār, which Mēwātī disciples celebrated in a ceremonious manner. First they gathered for two or three days in the places where branches of the Madāriya order were already established. From there they traveled in groups, carrying flags, to Makanpur. The flags were offered at the grave and fixed there.

Madāriya attracted more people among the masses of the lowest strata than other Ṣūfī orders. The Madārī Ṣūfīs belonged to lower service classes like water-carriers, private soldiers and jugglers. One may suppose several reasons for their popularity; their miraculous feats such as playing with fire, and their soldier-Ṣūfī image, known popularly as *ghāzī*, must have attracted the Meo warriors.

Comparing the various Ṣūfī orders, Shaykh Ikrām concludes that all of them stressed the significance of *dhikr* (chanting God's names). Yet while the Chishtiya performed *dhikr* loudly while moving their bodies, the Naqshbandiya insisted on silent *dhikr*. The Suhrawardiya and the Qādiriya allowed both loud and silent *dhikr*. On the question of *samāʿ* (listening to music), again, the Chishtiya practiced it, while the Qādiriya and the Naqshbandiya forbade it. The Suhrawardiya gave it no importance, with the exception of a few prominent individuals among them. The Qādiriya distinguished themselves by including *darūd* (salutations to the Prophet) in the *dhikr*. Of the four orders, the Naqshbandiya were most strict in observing *sharīʿa*. Others believed that Ṭarīqat (Ṭarīqa, Ṣūfī Order) was concerned with the inner meaning of religiosity while *sharīʿa* cared more for the external form (Ikrām 1992, 254). The Ṣūfī order of Madāriya obviously focused the least on external forms of religiosity and scholars like Massignon classify it as a Hindu sect (1961, 676).

Nominal Islam

It is quite common to describe Mēwātīs as Muslims in name only. Allow me to reproduce some typical descriptions, which will then be analyzed.

Mawlawī Murād ʿAlī, who accompanied his father on a *tablīgh* tour in Mēwāt recalled that Rājū Khān, a head of one town, had long whiskers, no beard, and wore a small cloth around his loins, barely covering his private parts (Ali 1886, 11–12). His father's advice to give up Hindu practices and to dress like Muslims earned no positive response.

Mawlawī ʿAbdul Bāqī Sahsawānī, a contractor in Taḥṣīl Rāi Sēn, wrote that Mēwātīs worshiped Hindu deities. Their only Islamic trait was that they ate cow meat and revered Shāh Masʿūd Ghāzī and Shāh Madār, sometimes prostrating at their graves. The people of Mēwāt were said to be very cunning and deceitful. Theft and dacoity were their profession (Sahsawānī 1924, 33).

Major Powlett, a settlement officer in the Alwar State, described Mēwātīs in the Alwar Gazetteer as follows:

> The Meos are now all Musalmans in name, but their village deities are the same as those of Hindus, they keep several Hindu festivals. Thus, the Hōlī is with Meos a season of rough play, and is considered as important as Muḥarram, ʿĪd and Shabi Barāt; and they likewise observe the Janam Ashtamī, Dasahara and Dīvalī. They often keep Brahmin priests to write the note (Pīlī Chiththī) fixing the date of marriage.
>
> They call themselves by Hindu names, with the exception of Ram; and Singh is a frequent affix, though not so common as Khan is. On the Amass [Amaawas], or monthly conjunction of the sun and moon, the Meos, in common with Hindu Ahirs, Gujars etc., cease from labor; and when they make a well, the first proceeding is to erect a platform to Bhaironji or Hanuman. However, when plunder was to be obtained, they have shown little respect for Hindu shrines and temples.
>
> As regards their own religion, the Meos are very ignorant. Few know the Kalima, and fewer still the regular prayers, the seasons of which they entirely neglect.... Indeed, in Alwar, at certain places where there are mosques, religious observances are better maintained and some know the Kalima, say their prayers... As already stated, Brahmins take part in the formalities preceding a marriage, but the ceremony itself is performed by the Qazi.... The men wear loin and waistcloth (dhoti, kamari) and not drawers (pajamas). Their dress is in fact Hindu. The men often wear gold ornaments....

> Meos in their customs are half Hindu. In their villages there are hardly any mosques. In the Tajara Tehsil, in fifty-two Meo villages there are only eight mosques. . . . The Meo places of worship are similar to those of their Hindu neighbors (as) for example, Panch Pir, Bhaiyya and Chahand. Chahand or Khera Deo is dedicated to Mahadevi to whom sacrifices are made. . . . During Shab-i Barat the flagstaff of Sayyid Salar Masud Ghazi is also worshipped in every Meo village (Powlett quoted in Nadwī 1985, 66–67).

> Recently religious teachers have become numerous among them and some Meos now keep the Ramadan fast, build village mosques, say their prayers and their wives wear trousers instead of the Hindu petticoat—all signs of revival (Gazetteer Gurgaon District 1911, 4 A, 70, quoted in Haq 1972, 106).

Shamsuddin Shams, during his field studies of Mēwāt in the 1980s, also remarked that the Meos were only nominal Muslims until 1947. Their Islam did not go beyond male circumcision and burial of the dead (1983, 35). According to him, the conversion of the Malkānās of Rājpūtāna and Meos of Panjab was incomplete; they adopted only what was suited to their rural setting. He observed that "A large number of Meos do revere Hindu gods and goddesses while believing in Allah as true Muslims" (1983, 187). Shams mentions Ghānsōlī and Choorsid among the Hindu temples that the Meos revered (1983, 187).

Let us now analyze the non-Muslim (Hindu) elements in these descriptions. As far as Hindu names and dresses are concerned, this phenomenon was common among most North Indian Muslim communities in Awadh, Balgaram, Kashmir, Sind and Bengal. In Northern India it was customary to request a Hindu Brahman to suggest a Hindu name for a Muslim child at its birth. After due study of horoscopes the name was given. In Balgaram, the Sayyid families invited the Brahmans to name their children. In Soni Pat, for instance, Muslims used to have two names: one Muslim, the other local and given by the local Hindu ruler. This was often a "Hindu name" and used as an alias or *ʿurf*[6] (Qādirī 1971, 52). Local names were used as aliases in addition to Arabic names in Lucknow and other areas. It is significant that the above mentioned areas belonged to a high Muslim culture that produced renowned *ʿulamā* in the pre-modern period.

[6] *ʿUrf* literally means 'known as' or alias. The term also refers to the distinction between *ʿurf* and *sharīʿa*, the former referring to the local customs.

It is questionable if Muslims were obliged Islamically to have only Arabic names. A number of *ʿulamā* in the medieval period are known by their non-Arabic local names, for instance Qāḍī Jaggan, Shaykh Budhdhan or Mullā Jīwan. Sometimes they were local pronunciations of Arabic names, for instance Kapūr for Ghafūr.

Muḥammad Ḥabībur Raḥmān Khān Mēwātī explains that Mēwātīs did maintain a distinction between local and typically Hindu religious names. He says that the Mēwātīs used names like Singh and Mall because they indicated their Chattari (Kashatriya) identity, but they never used names like Ram or Krishan, since they were typically Hindu names. The Meo never had Brahmans prescribe Hindu names for their children.

Similarly, Muslim Meos participated in local seasonal festivals; they were never involved in *mūrtī pūja* (idol worship). Even the Mēwātī dialect spoken by Muslims differs from that spoken by the Hindus (Mēwātī 1979, 6). The question of worshiping Hindu deities also needs further investigation. Madārī saints are often mistaken as Hindus. We have already mentioned Massignon regarding Madāriya as Hindus. Ghānsōlī and Choorsid, which Shams regards as Hindu temples (1983, 187) are Madārī Ṣūfī shrines. Ghansōlī (Alwar) belongs to Miyān Chānd Khān, alias Chānd Shāh Madārī, known as a disciple of Badīʿud Dīn Shāh Madār (Mēwātī 1979, 413). Similarly, Choorsid or Chuhr Sidh Shrine (Chāndōlī, Alwar) belongs to Khāwja ʿAbdur Raḥmān, another Madārī Ṣūfī (Mēwātī 1979, 416). Ḥabībur Raḥmān Mēwātī categorically refutes that the Meo worshiped any Hindu deities.

Some recent studies have remarked that the term 'nominal Islam' was a product of British ethnic and religious classification. It was British administrative policy to distinguish between the backward rural and the progressive urban societies. One may note with interest that in the above descriptions Hindu customs imply backwardness while revival of Muslim customs is a sign of progress which is credited to British schools and religious teachers.

Studying a similar phenomenon in Bengal, Asim Roy (1983) argues that the British dismissed the Muslim majority in that area as nominal. They argued that either the Muslim conversion was incomplete or that their beliefs had corrupted or degenerated under local influences (Roy 1983, 5).

It is significant to note that the theme of Mēwātīs being nominal Muslims appears prominently from the nineteenth century onward. It is usually the British or Indian officials working for them who underscore this aspect of Mēwātī Islam. Sahsawānī frequently characterizes the Mēwātī peasants as lethargic, ignorant, cunning and dishonest, while the landowners are always described in laudable terms (Sahsawānī 1924, 33). The reformist Muslims and the Tablīghīs generally rely on these sources. Obviously, both the British and the reformists exaggerated this state of affairs to justify their respective reform agendas.

Some scholars regard 'nominal Islam' as 'syncretic' because they assume conversion to Islam was a result of Muslim raids, in between which the Muslim converts reverted back to Hindu practices (e.g. Atulananda Chakrawarti 1934, cited in Ali 1970, 22). We find it difficult to call this phenomenon "syncretism" or assimilation in the proper sense. Muslim Mēwātīs continue to distinguish themselves from Hindus. Other scholars have called it a phenomenon of 'regional Islam.' According to them, due to geographical distance from the centre, the process of Islamization accommodated a wide variety of local religio-cultural elements and there developed a regional type of Islam (e.g., Tarafdar 1986, 93). Apparently, this view assumes that the local Muslims were completely isolated from the Muslim culture, that they had no access to Islamic tradition, and therefore retained their local Hindu traditions. Mēwātī (1979) has rejected this view. He notes that thirteen religious educational institutions existed in Mēwāt when Tablīghī Jamāʿat arrived there. He argues that Mēwāt was known for its intellectual centers in Bayāna, Nārnawl, Alwar and Palōl in the Islamic period. We have already mentioned several Ṣūfīs and scholars who lived in Mēwāt and whose tombs are there.

Islam came to Mēwāt by Ṣūfī *Daʿwa*, which, as we have indicated, differs from the reformist *Daʿwa*. Before we analyze the characteristics of the Ṣūfī *Daʿwa*, let us briefly examine a popular cult in Mēwāt that is quite close to Ṣūfī *Daʿwa*.

The Cult of Sālār Masʿūd Ghāzī

As noted above, according to popular belief the Meos were converted to Islam by Sālār Masʿūd Ghāzī. His cult offers an interesting example of the Ṣūfī *Daʿwa*. Sālār Masʿūd Ghāzī, a nephew of Sulṭān Maḥmūd Ghaznawī died in Bharāʾich in 1030 in a battle against the local Hindu Raja. There is an annual festival in the form of a wedding (*ʿurs*) held at his tomb because it is believed the he died young before marrying. The people come to his shrine with flags of cloth and fix them on and around the grave.

Ghāzī is a relatively small figure historically but he looms large in the folk literature. The folk stories transcend historical and religious boundaries to make him a living personality in people's minds. Ghāzī's cult is not confined to Mēwāt. The Chhatī fair is celebrated every year in May in Ambala in the name of Ghāzī, known as Bālā Miyān (bridegroom). All the inhabitants of the military cantonments in northern India consider him their patron saint (Temple 1962, 102).

Shaykh ʿAbdur Raḥmān Ambethawī wrote the story of the Ghāzī in a peculiar style of a *jangnāma* (war epic) told by an eyewitness. ʿAbdul Ḥayy Ḥasanī affirms the historicity of Sālār Masʿūd Ghāzī and the battle in which he died, but he rejects stories narrated by Ambethawī as fictitious[7] (Ḥasanī 1947, 112–114). Hindu poets in Punjab composed the stories of Gajjan, apparently a local pronunciation of Ghāzī, and Gōgā Pīr (Temple 1962, 267), reflecting the spread of the cult in these areas. We find in the cult folk songs Hindu, Sikh, Sunnī, Shīʿa and Madārī Ṣūfī elements. It is, however, significant that there has been no attempt to integrate them into a syncretic cult.

The stories stress the separate religious identities of the characters. Gōgā Pīr's song, composed in the Krishna devotional tradition with a background of pastoral life, describes Bālā Ghāzī (Sālār Masʿūd) as a supporter of Gōgā who fought against Muslim Kings. He is nevertheless a Muslim and a Sayyid (Temple 1962, 102). The song also includes the names of Gōrakh Nāth, a Hindu saint, as the Pīr of Gōgā, and Gurū Gōbind Singh, a Sikh hero. References to the Qurʾān (*Pāk Kalām*, the Pure Words), Houris, and Imām Ghāʾib, the last Shīʿa Imām, are invoked during the preparation for the battle. Most interesting is the part about the death of Gōgā Pīr. Gōgā requests the earth to accept him in her bosom. The earth refuses saying that, "I have made a pact with the Prophet (Pāk Rasūl) that I will not accept any Hindu in my bosom. You are a Hindu by birth and caste. First recite the *Kalima* (the Muslim profession of faith), then you will be accepted." He repeats the *Kalima* and the earth takes him in (Temple 1962, 267). Written versions, composed by Muslims, abound with the names of Shīʿa Imāms. Sālār Masʿūd is a descendent of Imām Muḥammad b. al-Ḥanafiyya and his companion Sayyid

[7] Ibn Baṭṭūṭa (1934, 2,111) and Muḥammad b. Qāsim Farishta (1962, 483) mention this festival. Shaykh ʿAbdur Raḥmān Ambēthawī in the sixteenth century wrote *Mirʾāt Masʿūdī*, on Sālār Masʿūd's life. It is available to us in Urdu translation (Ḥusayn, 1870).

Ibrāhīm of Imām Mūsā Raḍā. The martyrs of the army of Imām Ḥusayn also appear in the story. Despite these Shīʿa elements, the author warns against vilifying the first two caliphs Abū Bakr and ʿUmar, who are highly regarded by the Sunnīs.

The Ghāzī cult story employs established places of reverence and symbols. For instance, the Sūraj Kund where Ghāzī's tomb was erected was already revered by the local Hindu population. This confirms Rahim's view that conversion might be seen as a phenomenon of socio-religious continuity. "Most of the Ṣūfī hospices were located on the ruins of shrines or temples" (1959, 164).

The Ṣūfīs used spiritual phenomenon for the purpose of healing without discriminating between Hindus and Muslims, and the Ghāzī cult does also. One of the stories refers to a miracle in which Zuhra, the blind daughter of a Muslim noble, Sayyid Jamālud Dīn, regains her sight and erects a mausoleum for the Ghāzī at the Suraj Kund. She died young before marriage. Since she had fallen in love with the Ghāzī, her parents would return each year in the month of Jeth (harvesting season) to Bhara'ich in a procession and celebrate the *ʿurs*, the wedding ceremony at the tomb (Husayn 1870, 70). Atulananda Chakrawarti (cited in Ali 1970) mentions that Hindus also worship the Ghāzī as the one who gives eyesight to the blind.

The Ghāzī cult stories reflect a religious world where people of different religious identities interact without fear of assimilation or absorption by others. This self-confidence was provided by the Ṣūfī *Daʿwa*.

Ṣūfī Daʿwa

According to Shaykh Muḥammad Ikrām, the Chishtī Ṣūfīs in India did not focus on conversion. Their objective was to provide spiritual guidance to the people. That they did not discriminate between Hindus and Muslims in this regard as becomes clear from the study of Ṣūfī texts like *Fawā'idul Fuwād, Safīnatul Awliyā* and *Khazīnatul Asfiyā* (Ikrām 1992, 190). Gradually, this became a specific strategy of the *Daʿwa* of this Ṣūfī order.

The Ṣūfīs certainly differed from the *ʿulamā* in their conception of an ideal Muslim. They focused on devotional aspects of religion, stressing the unity of God and man's devotion to Him. They trained their devotees to be faithful to their spiritual guide (the *Ṣūfī*, the *Pīr*) by taking an oath of allegiance (*bayʿa*) to him. The *Ṣūfī* as *Pīr* was responsible for the guidance and spiritual well being of his disciples (*murīd*) and was believed to intercede before God for them. This *Daʿwa* approach was quite different from that of the *ʿulamā*, who stressed the accuracy of belief and practices in accordance with the scripture as interpreted and agreed upon by the *ʿulamā*. The ideal Muslim, according to the *ʿulamā*, was a person who acquired knowledge of *sharīʿa* and translated it into practice. In the Indian context a Muslim must consciously distinguish his beliefs and practices from any that would resemble those of the infidel Hindus.

While the Chishtiya and the Madāriya worked among the masses, the Suhrawardiya, like the *ʿulamā*, preferred to target the elite and the rulers in their *Daʿwa*. The rulers gave land grants to support the educational institutions and the Ṣūfī hospices. Ṣūfīs and the *ʿulamā* became fief-holders like the Hindu and Buddhist priestly classes. They served as revenue farmers to the state in an agrarian based economy where the land system was linked with the collection of taxes. Socially, the system worked quite well with the Hindu hierarchical caste system, which the Muslim elite replicated so as to keep benefiting from it. Occupational and service groups continued to have a lower status even after conversion to Islam. They were not integrated into the main community, but they found hospitality at the Ṣūfī hospices.

Anwārul Ḥaq (1972) considers the Tablīghī Jamāʿat to be a Ṣūfī reform movement, for two primary reasons. First, because of its founder's connection with Ṣūfism, and second because it borrowed extensively from Indian Ṣūfī practices. He traces the origin of several terms and practices of Tablīghī Jamāʿat (e.g. *chilla* and *dhikr*) to Ṣūfism. In fact Haq concludes his discussion by saying:

> Ilyās adopted Ṣūfī terms and practices such as *zikr, murāqaba* and *chilla*, with certain changes, to popularize Sūfism and create a better understanding of it among the masses. At the same time, he sought to eliminate the abuses which had crept into Ṣūfī orders, contributing to their popularity among certain sections of the community (Haq 1972, 173).

We find it hard to accept Anwarul Haq's conclusion. Tablīghī Jamāʿat does not seem to be a Ṣūfī movement, nor does it focus on the reform of Ṣūfism. It is more in line with the ʿulamā's reformist activities, to which we now turn.

Tablīgh Activities in Mēwāt

Ayyūb Qādirī (1971) finds Tablīghī Jamāʿat in the Mēwāt a continuation of *tablīgh* efforts that began in the nineteenth century among the Meo tribes. Mostly, these were the *ʿulamā* of the reformist school of Shāh Waliullāh of Delhi who came to Mēwāt for Tablīgh. They also belonged to the Qādirī and Chishtī Ṣūfī orders. Among them Shāh Muḥammad Ramaḍān Muhimī (d. 1825), Muḥammad Ismāʿīl Muhimī (d. 1857), Maḥbūb ʿAlī Dihlawī (d. 1864), and Karīmud Dīn (d. 1857) were disciples of Shāh ʿAbdul ʿAzīz (d. 1824), the son of Shāh Waliullāh (Qādirī 1971:54–60). Some Mēwātī scholars, like Miyān Rāj Shāh (d. 1888) and ʿAbdullāh Khān (d. 1879), also carried out Tablīghī activities in Mēwāt. These *ʿulamā* wanted to eliminate non-Islamic practices among the Meos such as infanticide and worship of Sītlā Dēvī, Shaykh Siddū, and Māmūn Allāh Bakhsh, and to establish the wearing of Muslim dress (Qadiri 1971, 55) and the observance of Islamic obligations. *Waʿẓ* (sermons) were employed as a method of *Daʿwa*. They wrote in local languages and dialects, sometimes in the form of poems that could be recited, and held debates with the scholars of other religions.

Shāh Muḥammad Ramaḍān Shahīd (d. 1825) was a prominent reformer of Mēwāt who typified this *Daʿwa*. He was dissatisfied with the Ṣūfī religious system under his father Shāh ʿAbdul ʿAẓīm, whose Rājput devotees presented him with a tithe from everything taken in their raids. Shāh Ramaḍān therefore left his family to study with Shāh ʿAbdul ʿAzīz in Delhi. Shāh Ramaḍān made the Rājput Muslims conscious of their separate identity from Hindus. He countered Hindu practices by introducing new rites to replace them. For instance, where people had offered sweet food (*gulgulē* and *pūrē*) to Sītlā Dēvī, Shāh Ramaḍān instead introduced the practice of fasting on that day. To lessen the reverence for cows among Muslims he introduced the practice of *Bībī Maryam kā Rōza* (Mary's Fast) that was broken with *Rōt Bōt* (Beef Bread), a special kind of fried bread containing a large chunk of beef (Mēwātī 1979, 487).

Shāh Ramaḍān observed two types of idolatry worship being practiced; one due to fear of harm, the other to revere beauty and majesty in nature. People feared that if they did not make offerings to Shaykh Siddū, Sarwar Sultān or Gōgā, these three beings would punish them by respectively turning them into lunatics, making them lepers, or visiting a poisonous snake upon them. (Mēwātī 1979, 488).

Hindus also revered Shāh Ramaḍān, and in several Hindu villages there were *Shāh Ramjān kē Chabūtrē* (raised platforms for Shāh Ramaḍān).

Like the other British officials discussed above, Shāh Ramaḍān's biographer, a British district officer in Ḥiṣār, describes Meos as being almost Hindus. He compares Mēwāt with pre-Islamic Arabia and the Rajputs in Ḥiṣār with the Arabs of that period. Each tribe had its own idol, worshiped trees, fire, and Sītlā Dēvī, practiced infanticide, celebrated festivals of Hōlī and Dīvālī, and made offerings to Zayn Khan, Gōgā, Lūnā Chamārī and Shaykh Siddu (Mēwātī 1979, 474). We have already analyzed the exaggerations contained in these 'nominal Islam' descriptions.

III. *The Challenge of Modernity and South Asian Responses*

We have seen that the South Asian Muslim community has remained conscious of its minority status throughout its history. Situated on the periphery of the Muslim world, the fear of absorption into the local Hindu majority kept the community sensitive about its separate religious identity. This sensitivity was heigthened with the advent of modernity and the Christian missions under British rule. A number of Muslims converted to Hinduism and Christianity under the British, and it was feared that modernity was corrupting the faith.

In India, the nineteenth century introduced far-reaching political and social changes. A number of ideas and movements current in Britain at that time circulated in India such ideologies as reformation of religion, liberalism, and scientism. More significantly, a number of Christian missionary, reformist and evangelical organizations established missions in the country. British officials believed in promoting religious reforms in India and provided official patronage to Christian missionaries who debated with Muslims and Hindus. These efforts, however, presented modernity as being a religious, or to be more exact, a Christian missionary programme, which challenged the Indian religious traditions (See Peter van den Veer 1994, 1999).

Traditional economic, educational, social and religious institutions, in India were changing. The religious literature in this period reflects the resulting anxiety of Muslims. Religious leaders were being asked about the religious doctrines challenged by the nineteenth century scientism and about Christian missionary activities. People inquired about the permissibility of wearing English dress, using the banking system, and learning English language and foreign sciences (Masʿūd 1969). Self-rule and other political reforms were generating a new consciousness that large numbers meant political power.

Indian society responded to these changes in a number of ways. Generally speaking, both Hindus and Muslims developed two approaches. Modernists viewed the issue as one of modernization and reform, and tried to interpret the teachings of their respective religions to accommodate scientism, modernity and liberalism. Conservatives, on the other hand, perceived those changes as a threat to their traditions and religions. They developed defense mechanisms against the challenges of modernity, especially against materialism and scientism.

To better understand this development let us look briefly at the six prominent movements: the Brahmo Samaj, Arya Samaj and Shuddhī movements among Hindus, and the Aligarh, Deoband and Khilāfat movements among Muslims. They are significant not only as reformist movements but also because they are referred to frequently in connection with the Tablīghī Jamāʿat.

Brahmo Samaj

The Brahmo Samaj was founded in 1843 by Raja Rammohun Roy, who some writers have called "the father of modern India" (Kopf 1988). The Samaj supported modernity and science, stressing that the Hindu religion was itself scientific and promoted scientific methods and education. The movement at the same time criticized religious taboos. It stood for social reforms, advocated remarriage of widows and the abolition of child marriages, encouraged intercaste marriages, and supported equality for women. In politics it called for democracy and Indian nationalism. The Brahmo Samaj introduced religious reformation by stressing the authority of scriptures, and the Vedas as the only source of Hinduism. It systematized Hindu religious thought as a rational theology. The Samaj explained Hindu rituals in symbolic terms and developed a this-worldy Hindu ethic, stressing the social role of the Dharma (Kopf 1988, 314).

Despite its significant contribution toward the modernization of Hindu society, the Brahmo Samaj movement was confined to the educated middle classes, and never became popular among the masses.

The movement was more influential in Bengal where it had leaders like Rabindranath Tegore and Chandra Keshab Sen, but gained little ground in places like Panjab and North India. One reason, perhaps, was its close association with the British administration and Christian Unitarian missionaries. The Christians continuously tried to convert Rammohunroy and others. Its critics, especially the Arya Samaj, which we shall discuss shortly, saw Brahmo Samaj as an extension of Christian missionary efforts in India (Rai 1977, 130).

Aligarh

More than the Hindus, Muslims found it harder to adjust to the new changes. First, the Muslim aristocracy lacked the skills and education to find employment and influence within the British system, nor were they trusted by the British. Sir Syed (Sayyid Aḥmad Khān, d.1898), who founded the Aligarh movement in 1858, believed that only by gaining British trust could they restore the aristocracy to its former position. Toward this goal he took four steps. First, he refuted William Hunter and other British officials who claimed that the Muslims were religiously duty-bound to rebel against the British. In his *Asbāb Baghāwat Hind* (Khan 1858), Sir Syed analyzed the causes of the 1857 Indian revolt and suggested that British attitudes and Christian missionaries were mainly responsible for the mutual misunderstanding, and that the Muslims were loyal to the British government. Second, to encourage scientific attitudes among Indians and particularly among Muslims, he founded a scientific society in 1863, "to foster and encourage the growth of an enlightened public spirit in the population" (Jain 1979, 18). Among its other objectives were the "appraisal of the British crown, improving Urdu literature, and improving the method of agriculture in India" (Jain 1979, 19). The bylaws of the society also advocated translating works on art and sciences from European into native languages, and the publication of rare and valuable oriental works. The document specifically excluded religious works (Muḥammad 1986, 1:4).

Sir Syed's third step was to encourage Muslims to seek modern education. He was convinced that all-embracing reforms were needed in education and religious thought for the revival of Indian Muslims. He believed that education must proceed along Western lines, with an emphasis on the English language. After his return from England he established for Muslims Mohammedan Anglo Oriental College.

The college's policy was to teach major subjects in English. The spirit of fraternity, love for the Urdu language and a sense of Muslim identity were the values that Aligarh inculcated among the students. Various other Muslim groups also began working for modern education among Muslims. These included the Anjuman Ḥimāyat Islām (1865) in Lahore, Panjab (Mathur 1983, 33), Nawwāb ʿAbdul Laṭīf's (d. 1893) Mohammedan Literary and Scientific Society (1863) in Calcutta, and Syed Amir Ali's Central National Mohammedan Association (1876) in Bengal.

The Aligarh movement had several aspects in common with Brahmo Samaj, including its scientific spirit, its modern interpretation of religion, and its loyalty to the British. It was, however, more politically oriented than the Brahmo Samaj, and it emphasized a separate Muslim identity. Dr Tara Chand summarized the achievements of the movement: "The Aligarh Movement exercised a tremendous influence on the Muslims. It created among them the ambition to obtain for their community its proper place among the communities of India, and turned their thought from the fruitless contemplation of their past glories and defeats to the actual pursuits of the idea of progress and advancement in the modern world" (quoted in Muḥammad 1986, v).

Sir Syed's fourth step, for which he may be rightly called the father of Muslim modernism in India, was his active pursuit of religious reformism. He wrote extensively to argue that there was no conflict between science and Islam, and that indeed the Qur'ānic teachings were in accord with the laws of nature. The *ʿulama* disagreed with his views on scientism and called him a *nēcharī* (naturist), one who preached for the supremacy of nature. He supported scientism, rationalism and reformism, and also rationalism in Islam on the basis of *ijtihād* as a principle of research and investigation. He opposed *taqlīd* (the doctrine of adherence to schools of law), *qiyās* (analogical reasoning) and *ijmāʿ* (consensus) as doctrines of stagnation (Masud 1995, 64). In addition to several books, Sir Syed also published magazines, such a *Tahdhībul Akhlāq* in 1870. He was joined by a like-minded group of writers and thinkers like Chirāgh ʿAlī (d. 1895), Alṭāf Ḥusayn Ḥālī (d. 1914), Deputy Nadhīr Aḥmad (d. 1912) and Shiblī Nuʿmānī (d. 1914). These were the vanguard of modernism among Indian Muslims, and they introduced new approaches to the study of Islamic laws, literary criticism, Urdu poetry, Islamic history and historiography. Their efforts, aimed at "a complete regeneration of Muslims in all phases of life and enabling them to acquire strength and qualities, which they need to secure and stabilize their position" are what is known as the Aligarh movement (Moin, 1976, 8). Moin distinguishes two phases of the movement. The first, that ended with the death of Sir Syed, was primarily concerned with the education of Muslims. The second, from 1898 to 1947, was more political and culminated in the emergence of Pakistan.

As we shall see, several relatives of Tablīghī Jamā'at's founder were associated with Aligarh, although it was never a source of inspiration for the movement itself. Aligarh was also associated in some respects with the Nadwatul 'Ulamā, at Lucknow, an institution of religious learning founded in 1894. The Nadwa originally aimed at finding a middle way between the traditionalism of Deoband and the modernism of Aligarh, but it eventually came to resemble Deoband (Metcalf 1982, 316–347). Shiblī Nu'mānī, a close associate of Sir Syed, brought to Nadwa the concerns of Aligarh, such as its interests in Islamic history, research and publication, modern Islam, and the modern Arab world. Shiblī was nevertheless extremely critical of Aligarh's principle of loyalty to the British and to Westernization. Nadwa's stress on learning modern Arabic led its scholars to have close contacts with their contemporaries in the Arab world. Many graduates from Nadwatul 'Ulamā, such as Mawlana Abul Ḥasan 'Alī Nadwī and their disciples, joined Tablīghī Jamā'at. The Jamā'at benefited from their Arab contacts in building its network in the Arab world (Nadwī 1983, 278ff., Khān 1984).

The Deoband School

While the Aligarh movement, in the words of Barbara Metcalf, was "committed to collaboration of the more privileged classes of Indian Muslim society with the imperial regime" (1982, 11), the *'ulamā* in Deoband and elsewhere avoided British institutions. They set out to preserve and disseminate instruction in authentic religious practice and belief and to create personalities that embodied Islam. They felt that the British system of administration and justice had deprived the class of *'ulamā* of the prestigious positions they had enjoyed under the Mughals. In 1857 they were suspected of instigating the Indian revolt and persecuted. Consequently, they "feared for the fate of their class and culture" (Metcalf 1982, 91), and therefore withdrew into their old institutions like Farangī Maḥal in Lucknow.

Dārul ʿUlūm Deoband was founded in 1867 in Deoband, a small town in northern India for the revival of Islam and renewal of faith among Muslims. Although the Deoband school rejected the teaching of English and Western sciences, it modernized the system of education. It did so with the help of teachers from Delhi College, which had been founded by the British for the training of officials. Traditionally, an individual teacher had imparted the religious education using a specific set of books. Upon their completion, the teacher would award a certificate testifying that the student had studied them. Deoband, however, offered a new system of religious education including classrooms, a fixed curriculum, and a system of examinations and certificates along the lines of Delhi College. It differed from other institutions of learning in other ways; it had its own magazines and other publications, and a Dārul Iftā (a department to answer queries on matters of Islamic law and other religious issues).

Deoband also grew as a school of thought (*maslak*) that differed from the modernism of Aligarh. While we cannot go into details, the main differences between Deoband's *maslak* and other religious groups are important to us here because, due to Tablīghī Jamāʿat's affinity with Deoband, its opponents often call it a "Deobandī sect" and characterize it as a Deobandī *Daʿwa*.

Apart from the Shīʿa, there are two major Sunnī religious schools of thought with which the Deobandīs differ: Ahli Ḥadīth and Brēlwīs. Ahli Ḥadith follow ḥadīth instead of Fiqh schools and Sufi orders, and trace their origins to the ḥadīth movement in early Islam. Adherence to ḥadīth was revived in the pre-modern period by Muḥammad b. ʿAbdul Wahhāb (d. 1787) in Ḥijāz, in the footsteps of Ibn Taymiyya. In India, Shāh Ismāʿīl Shahīd (d. 1831) called for return to the Qurʾān and ḥadīth in place of their diverse schools of thought. He died fighting along with Sayyid Aḥmad in the *Jihād* movement against the Sikhs. In his *Taqwiyatul Īmān* he expounded unity of God, and refuted the doctrines leading to association of others with God, innovations and heresies. Ahli Ḥadīth are generally close to the Salafī movement of Muḥammad b. ʿAbdul Wahhāb, although they are not a product of that movement.

The Brēlwīs (Ahlus Sunnat wa'l Jamāʿat), named after Aḥmad Riḍā Khān of Breilley (d. 1922), stress the centrality of the Prophet Muḥammad and love for him. In their definition of his role and place they attribute to him such qualities as knowledge of the unseen, omnipresence and omniscience.

The main points of difference among these three religious groups center around the doctrines of *taqlid, taṣawwuf* and *bidʿa.* The Deobandīs and Brēlwīs follow the Ḥanafī School and the Ṣufī orders, while the Ahli Ḥadīth follow none. They differ also on the definition of *bidʿa*; Deobandīs and Ahli Ḥadīth regard certain religious practices, like visiting graves of the ancestors to seek their help, as *bidʿa*, while the Brēlwīs consider them Islamically justified.

Despite its reformist appearance, the Deoband school is conservative and traditional in its stance toward modernity. Modernity has caused the rise of "unbelief" in the form of materialism, fascination with worldly matters, and indifference to one's religious duties. This view is not limited to Muslims; other religious communities have also reacted strongly against the perceived threat of modernity, and the religious literature has decried the prevailing trend of neglecting religion for wordly concerns.

The Deobandīs identified Islam with religious observances and avoidance of *bidʿa* practices. It is significant that most of the *bidʿa* practices, largely related to life crises situations such as rites related to birth, marriage and funerals, were believed to be survivals of Hinduism, or due to its influence. Muslim identity in India was thus inversely related with Hinduism. Consequently, *iṣlāḥ* (reform) activities were intended to eliminate such practices.

The Deoband School bitterly opposed Aligarh for its loyalty to the British. Deoband gradually became politically conscious and active. The Jamʿiyyat ʿUlamāi Hind, a political association mainly consisting of the *ʿulamā* of Deoband persuasion, supported the Indian National Congress. The influence of Deoband on Indian Muslim religious and political views increased with the establishment of sister religious institutions that followed the same system of education and shared their religious ideology. Nevertheless, a few institutions stayed away from politics. The Maẓāhirul ʿUlūm was established in Sahāranpūr a few months after the Deoband as its sister institution, but was not active in politics. It developed close relations with the Tablīghī Jamāʿat and influenced its ideology more than Deoband because Mawlānā Zakariyyā, the Shaykh of Maẓāhirul ʿUlūm, became its ideologue. All four of these institutions, Deoband, Aligarh, Nadwa and Maẓāhirul ʿUlūm provided the Tablīghī Jamāʿat with needed manpower.

Arya Samaj

Pandit Dayanand Sarswati (d. 1883 in Ajmer) founded the Arya Samaj in Bombay in 1875. Born into an orthodox Brahman family, Dayanand revolted against traditional Hinduism quite early in life. He debated with Muslims, Christians and orthodox Brahmans. One debate was held at the well known Mēlā Khudā Shanāsī (Festival for the study of God) held in Chandpur (District Shahjahanpur, UP) in 1875–1877. At this huge gathering representatives of all the religions were asked to present their religious views. Dayanand represented the Hindus and Mawlānā Muḥammad Qāsim, the founder of the Deoband School, and Sayyid Abul Manṣūr Dihlawī represented the Muslims. Samuel Knowels, the Head of the American Methodist Mission School participated as a Christian representative, and Munshī Piyārē Lāl, a local government official, and Mōtī Miyān, a local Muslim Magistrate, took part as government officials. The festival soon turned into a polemical debate, each participant fighting for the superiority of his religion (Metcalf 1982, 221, 234).

Dayanand believed that the British threat was greater than that experienced during the Muslim rule. The British technology and literature was generating a sense of inferiority and the aggressive Christian missionary work was making Hindus indifferent to religion, even if it did not succeed in converting them. Dayanand taught that Hindu religion was scientific and that ancient Hindus had contributed a great deal to science and technology (Rai 1977, 142). He considered Brahmanism, Christianity, Muslim *tablīgh* activities, rationalism and the pragmatic methods of science all to be a serious threat to the survival of Hindu Society (Rai 1977, 135).

D. Vable (1983, 124), reviewing the role of the Arya Samaj, describes it as primarily a nonpolitical religious and social reform movement. Yet, since Dayanand had very strong views on self government, Hindu unity and pure Arya society, the movement soon became politically active against both the British and the Muslims. It supported agitation for Hindu causes, like the protection of cows, and gained increasing popularity among the Hindu masses. On the national level, it supported the Indian National Congress. However, because the Congress supported Muslim causes, the Arya Samaj decided to part with them, and consequently began to lose its popularity as a political movement. A large number of Arya Samaj members left to join more extremist Hindu movements like Hindu Mahāsabhā, founded in 1924, and Rashtrya Sēvak Sangh. The Arya

Samaj, according to its critics, gradually drifted toward sectarianism (Vable 1983, 90).

Brahmo Samaj and the Arya Samaj shared several traits. Both believed in the authority of Vedas and in returning to them. Both supported monotheism and opposed idol worship. Both wanted to reform some Hindu customs and practices like the caste system, child marriages and extravagant celebrations of events like marriages. They also favoured marriage of widows and the education of women. Like Brahmo Samaj, the Arya Samaj also spread among government servants and modern educated Hindus, but it became more popular among the masses.

Dayanand realized that both Christianity and Islam were missionary religions and therefore could be countered only by Hindu missionary activities. He decided in 1860 to target first those Hindus who had joined Islam or Christianity, and he launched a movement to call them back to Hinduism. This doctrine came to be known later as "Shuddhī" (purification). The transformation of Arya Samaj into a missionary movement reflects the peculiar milieu of India at that time. The question of religious identity among religious communities eventually led the movement into communalism. Dayanand Sarsawati's book *Satyārath Parkāsh*, supposedly a critique of contemporary religions, contained contemptuous and derogatory remarks about Islam and the Prophet. This and other events, to which we now turn, sparked a turning point in Hindu-Muslim relations.

The Khilāfat Movement

After World War I South Asian politicians realized that European colonialism, whose military power and superior technology had so impressed them in the nineteenth century, was subsiding. Better means of communication, the printing press and news media had brought an end to Indian isolation. It also increased Muslim awareness of Muslim communities elsewhere. These developments contributed to a rebuilding of solidarity.

The Khilāfat Movement (1919–1924) was a protest movement against the British policy of partitioning the Ottoman Empire. It emerged as the first mass political movement in India in which Hindus joined hands with Muslims. An Arya Samaj leader, Swami Shardhanand, even addressed Muslims in the Delhi mosque, an act that was applauded by most Muslims though debated by others.

Hindu-Muslim cooperation, however, proved to be shortlived—as soon as the movement failed they went their separate ways, and both were soon involved in missionary activities against each other. Swami Shardhanand became active in Arya Samaj missionary activities, and Dr. Sayfud Din Kitchlew of the Khilāfat Committee founded the Tablīghī mission Tanẓīm, in Amritsar.

Of these movements, Khilāfat had the most far-reaching effects on Muslim society, as Khilāfat symbolized the transnational unity of the Umma. These events made Muslims critically aware of Muslim transnationalism. This sharpened their focus on mass politics. The political involvement of Muslim masses required an emphasis on religious identity. The Khilāfat movement utilized the techniques of missionaries and shaped the methodology of *Daʿwa* in India along modern lines. Muslim leaders learned skills of modern organization, publicity techniques, mass contact and the use of the printing press from Khilāfat. According to Mumtāz Aḥmad (1991a, 511), Mawlānā Muḥammad Ilyās, the founder of the Tablīghī Jamāʿat, benefited from this movement greatly.

The Khilāfat movement had exposed the thin line dividing political and religious views of politics in India, and shifted the focus of politics toward religious identity. This focus was defined in both ideological and communal terms. On the political level, however, religious identity was perceived in terms of Hindu-Muslim separation.

Recent studies (e.g., Mathur 1983) show that the identity crises in India deepened when the British imposed, for political or scientific reasons, a new system of classification of the population based on ethnic and religious identities. The censuses of 1901 and 1911, separate electorates, and the idea of self-government successively made numbers the critical variable in political power, and generated conflicts and missionary efforts for conversion; rioting increased from 1925–1928.

The Shuddhī Movement

The Arya Samaj began to assert the doctrine of Shuddhī forcefully in 1908. Rajput Shuddhī Sabha, a special group of the Arya Samaj, was working to reconvert Muslims and Christians, especially Muslim Rajputs. The Arya Samaj claimed that these tribes had originally been Hindus. According to 1911 census reports, between 1907 and 1910, 1052 Muslim Rajputs were converted to Hinduism (Rai 1977,

153). Among them there were a large number of Malkāna Rajput tribes living in Mēwāt and in areas around Delhi and Agra. Swami Shardhanand transformed Shuddhī into an aggressive movement in 1922, and that same year Dr. Monje started another movement called Sanghatan (unity) to support the Shuddhī. Both movements targeted Muslim Rajputs.

These missionary activities alarmed Muslims across India. In 1924, riots broke out in Agra and Bhartpur, where the Arya Samaj had converted a number of Muslims. Several Muslim *tablīgh* organizations were founded during these years and sent missions to Mēwāt. These included Anjuman Riḍā-i Muṣṭafā (1923) in Bareilley; Ghulām Bhīk Nairang's Tablīgh-i Islām in Ambala; Jamʿiyyat ʿUlamai Hind's All India Anjuman Tablīgh Islam; Dr. Sayfud Dīn Kitchlew's Tanẓīm in Amritsar; Markazī Jamʿiyyat Tabligh Islām (1926) in Poona; and Khwaja Ḥasan Niẓāmī's Tablīghī Mission in Niẓāmud Dīn in Delhi (Mathur 1968). The Aḥmadiyya Mission also denounced Christianity and Arya Samaj.

Missionary activities and riots made the situation extremely tense. Leaders of both communities, including Pandit Madan Mohan Malwiyah and Muftī Kifāyatullāh, came together to discuss Hindu-Muslim unity. The influence of Arya Samaj was, however, too strong for Hindu leaders to find any fault in its methods. The Hindu leaders demanded that Muslims abandon *tablīgh* and suspend their condemnation of the apostates from Islam to death. The Muslim leaders accepted the proposal with some amendments and signed a resolution to that effect (Kifāyatullāh n.d., 9:331–344). There was a general resentment among the Indian Muslims at this reconciliation, particularly since the Hindu and Christian missions were actively working among Muslims.

The first political outburst in Mēwāt took place in 1932 in Alwar. Various factors had already built tension between Muslims and Hindus. So long as the Muslim Meos kept to the status quo and the caste system, the Brahmans treated them as Kashatriya, a caste lower than Brahmans but higher than others (Shams 1983, 17). Sikand (n.d.) argues that the status quo suited the economic conditions in Mēwāt and guaranteed Meo domination in the system. The situation, however, began to change in the twentieth century when a series of social and economic disruptions eroded Meo domination and prosperity. The 1916 Government of Panjab Report describes the Meos as follows:

> The condition of the Meos is rapidly becoming hopeless. They live so literally from hand to mouth, carelessly contracting debt for marriages, funerals and petty luxuries even in average years that when a year of drought comes they are thrown on the moneylender who can make them with what terms he likes (quoted in Sikand n.d., 7).

Sikand adds that by 1910 nearly forty percent of Meo lands were under mortgage to the Banias, the Hindu moneylenders (n.d., 8). Sikand suggests that this situation probably led to Meo disenchantment with Hindus. The Hindu revivalism further escalated the tension between Brahmans and Meos. In this new social situation, the British and the Hindus replaced the Mughals as the threatening 'other.' From this perspective, Meo identity had therefore to be re-defined.

The frustration among the Meos increased due to changes introduced by the British and the general economic depression in the third decade of the twentieth century. The agriculture situation worsened, and heavy taxes and maladministration in Mēwāt caused Meo uprisings in 1932 in Alwar. In 1933 the Raja of Alwar raised the tax four times, and the whole of Mēwāt rose up. The Meo historians call this rebellion Alwar Taḥrīk ('Abdul Ḥayy 1966, 298). The Muslim organizations supported the Meos. Other Hindu states, like Kapūrthala, had similar conditions, and the Alwar movement spread to them. The Majlis Aḥrārul Islām, a religious political organization, sent a delegation to support the Alwar refugees. The Raja of Alwar, a Hindu nationalist, and a supporter of the Indian National Congress, and Mawlana Shaukat Ali of the Khilāfat movement, also an ally of the Congress, persuaded Ghulām Bhīk Nairang to withdraw his support to Aḥrār.

The Mēwātī Muslims were at a loss because neither the Muslim political parties nor the Muslim officials in the state would help them. The Jamʿiyyat ʿUlama-i Hind, because of its alliance with the Congress, preferred to support the Raja. According to Janbaz Mirza, the Aḥrār leader of the Muslim movement against the Raja, the Majlis Aḥrār reacted by deciding to help the Muslims in Alwar state. Janbaz Mirza (Mirza n.d., 1:280) describes how the Maharaja banned all types of religious activities in the state on 30 June 1932. The religious organizations were obliged to maintain registers. He made a special point of forbidding the Jamʿiyyat Markaziyya Tablīghul Islām, Ambala to hire residents in the state to be preachers. On 2 July 1932, a Hindu was murdered and the state sentenced a number of Muslims to death for the crime.

The Majlis Aḥrār declared 22 July as Alwar Day to launch a public protest against the repression of Muslims in the state. They announced that Muslims would leave the state en mass if their demands were not met. In the end the Maharaja agreed (Mirza n.d., 283), but the British quikly took the opportunity to dethrone the Raja and appoint a political agent of their own (Alī 1970, 29).

This was the context within which Mawlānā Ilyās decided to launch Tablīghī Jamāʿat in Mēwāt. We shall discuss the emergence of the movement in chapter one, but here it is important to note that the Tablīghī Jamāʿat was not the only or the first *Daʿwa* movement in Mēwāt—Tablīgh activities were already in progress. The Jamāʿat, however, succeeded where others failed because it improved upon the method and strategy of *Daʿwa*.

Mawlānā Ashraf ʿAlī Thānawī

Mawlānā Ashraf ʿAlī Thānawī (d. 1941) was a renowned scholar from Deoband who came to Mēwāt in 1922 and preached in Rēwārī, Nārnawl and Ismāʿīlpur in Alwar. He planned to go to Nūḥ and Fērōzpūr Jhirka but was unable to (Ḥasan 1985, 3:238, 239). Mawlānā Thānawī also wrote several short treatises on the subject of *tablīgh*, including *Al-insidād li-fitnatil irtidād* (Eradication of the evil of apostasy), *Ḥusn Islām kī ēk Jhalak* (A view of the beauty of Islam), *Namāz kī ʿaqlī khūbiyān* (Rational explanation of the merits of prayer) and a treatise justifying the sacrifice of cows, from the Vedas. He also wrote three other sermons entitled *al-Daʿwat ila Allāh, Maḥāsinul Islām* and *Ādābut tablīgh* (Ḥasan 1985, 3:239) on the merits of missionary activities.

When Mawlānā Thānawī came to know of the Arya Samaj missionary work in Gajnēr in the district of Kānpūr, UP, he paid a visit. This story is quite instructive about the state of Islam in this area and *ʿulamā*'s method of *Daʿwa*. Mawlānā gathered the nobles of the Gajner village, among them two men named Nathhū Singh and Adhār Singh. He found that in government records their names were Nathhū Khān and Adhār Khān, indicating their Muslim origin. Mawlānā offered them drinks but they refused saying that they did not accept any food from Muslims. They said that they were neither Muslims nor Hindus, but "Naw-Muslim" (neo-Muslims, converts). Mawlānā also came to know that these people practiced some Hindu customs like "*phērē*" (ritually making seven rounds around a fire) at wedding ceremonies and they wore *chōṭī* (a lock of hair left on top of the head while the rest is shaven) like Hindus. Only those who could afford it practiced circumcision. Adhār Singh further explained that they were not Hindus since they built *taʿziya* (models of the tombs of Imām Ḥasan and Ḥusayn carried in the *muḥarram* procession). The Mawlānā instructed them to continue the practice of *taʿziya*. When his companions objected to this Shīʿa practice, Mawlānā remarked that it saved them from committing *Kufr* and apostasy. The Mawlānā announced that a Muslim *kithā* (story-telling) would be held in the village, and a *Mīlād* (Prophet's birthday) ceremony was arranged. The *Mīlād* consisted of the recital of stories from the life of Prophet Muḥammad and songs in his praise, and sweets were distributed at the end. The *Mīlād*, a Brēlwī practice, was condemned by the Deobandīs as *bidʿa*. The people in the village promised that they would not commit apostasy, but they said they would continue to be Naw-Muslim, not Muslims (Ḥasan 1985, 3:233).

There are several points to be noted from this story. First, the use of Singh in the names and the peoples' adherence to some apparently Hindu social practices resemble practices from Mēwāt that we have discussed. It demonstrates further that the phenomenon of nominal Islam was not confined to Mēwāt. Second, Muslims and Hindus treated converts to Islam as a separate caste which retained certain Hindu customs and practices. Third, it appears from the mention of *taʿziya* that Shīʿa *Daʿwa* was active in the area, and, probably due to this fact, the locals were distinguished from other Muslims. Fourth, Mawlānā Thānawī used Shīʿa (*taʿziya*), Brēlwī (*mīlād*) and even Hindu (*kithā*) practices as entrance points for his *Daʿwa*. We have seen that the Ṣūfī *Daʿwa* also used this strategy, but Mawlānā Thānawī employed these measures only temporarily.

In 1924, Mawlānā Thānawī prepared a program (*Dastūrul ʿAmal*) of *Daʿwa* called "Tafhīm al-Muslimīn", consisting of twelve points, including *kalima, namāz, zakāt, Ramaḍān, ḥajj, taʿlīm, ittifāq Muslimīn* (Muslim unity), *tanẓīm* (organization) and *tablīgh* against moral evils. The program also recommended reading material, mostly Mawlānā Thānawī's books. In 1931, he developed a special method of *tablīgh* which he presented in his booklet *Āthār Raḥmat*. He established an organization of *tablīgh* in Sahāranpūr (Ḥasan, 1985, 3:244) called Majlis Ṣiyānatul Muslimīn (Association for the protection of Muslims), aimed at the reform of Muslims in general. He wrote *Iṣlāḥī Niṣāb* (Course for reform) for this particular purpose. In its latest edition it includes the following books: *Ḥayātul Muslimīn, Aghlātul ʿawāmm,*

Ḥuqūqul Islām, Jazā'ul Aʿmāl, Ḥuqūqul wālidayn, Furūʿul īmān, Ādābul muʿāsharat, Taʿlīmud Dīn, and *Tashīl qaṣdis sabīl.* Apparently, this course was prepared for the *ʿulamā*, because the introduction to the book was written in Arabic and the Urdu language was heavily Arabized. The style of writing and focus on legal and theological topics also indicate that the book was not addressed to common Muslim men, who were mostly illiterate. Mawlānā Ilyās admired Mawlānā Thānawī's efforts, and the Tablīghī Jamāʿat even adopted certain of his ideas like devising a course for the Tablīghīs and developing the rules of Tablīgh in the form of a set number of points. The Tablīghī Jamāʿat, however, differs with Mawlānā Thānawī's method of *Daʿwa* in two significant respects. First, it dismisses the idea that Tablīgh is the function of the *ʿulamā* alone—it addresses the common man and assigns to him also the duty of *Daʿwa.* Second, Jamāʿat stresses collective physical movement in groups.

Conclusion

South Asia's intellectual encounter with the West began earlier than in the Arab world. It sensitized South Asian Muslims, more than others, to the threats to faith, not only from Hinduism but also from modernity. *Daʿwa,* therefore, came to be defined not only as a missionary activity of calling non-Muslims to Islam, but more significantly, as a call to Muslims to become *good* Muslims. Faced with the challenges of modernity, materialism and secularism, the definition of a good Muslim became contestable among modernists, revivalists and reformists. Dissatisfied with the prevailing conception, several new definitions of a good Muslim were claimed. The Tablīghī Jamāʿat's stress on faith renewal and Muslim transnationalism reflects specifically South Asian Muslim concerns. The studies in this volume explore various dimensions of these topics as they are developing within different political and cultural settings.

Appendix

Some Modern Daʿwa Movements[8]

1. *Aḥmadiyya Mission* (AM), India
Mirzā Ghulām Aḥmad (1830–1908) launched the Aḥmadiyya movement in 1889 in Qādiyān, India. Initially, his mission was to defend Islam against Christian and Hindu missionaries, including the Arya Samaj. Subsequently he also called for reforms within Islam itself. He claimed to be the Mahdī who, it was believed, would end war in the world. He therefore declared that *Jihad* had come to an end and that henceforth the faith should be spread by preaching and persuasion. He established Aḥmadiyya Mission, which began to operate transnationally, especially in the African continent. The Mirzā offered a liberal interpretation of Islam in certain areas but overall he remained conservative. The point where he came into conflict with the *ʿulamā*, and on account of which his mision was later declared non-Muslim in Pakistan in 1974, was his claim to prophesy. He believed that prophecy was continuous and that he was a prophet within Islam. He claimed to be inspired by the Ṣūfī tradition, especially by the twelfth century Spanish Ṣūfī Ibn ʿArabī. The Aḥmadiyya mission was probably the first transnational movement working in multiple countries outside of India to establish mosques and convert non-Muslims to Islam. It is essentially a missionary organization, similar to Christian missionary societies. It has an extensive publication programme that includes periodicals in several languages.

2. *Dārul Arqam* (DAM), Malaysia
This movement was founded in 1968 by Sheikh Imam Ashaari Muhammad al-Tamimi in Kuala Lumpur in Malaysia. Its objective is defined as the revival of religious belief and values in practice, and it teaches the Qurʾān and basic Islamic duties and doctrines. The overall goal is self-correction. It is a *Daʿwa* organization that is very media conscious, and it organizes cultural shows and concerts to stress multi-ethnicity in Islam. The movement has branches in several other countries. It establishes self-reliant village communities with agricultural complexes, business firms and factories to produce foodstuffs, cosmetics and other items of daily use. The organizational structure is patterned after a state government, with ministers and departments dealing with education, information, economy and propagation. There is a deep association with Sufism. It is not a registered organization, and it was accused of political designs and outlawed in 1994.

3. *Ḥizbud Daʿwatil Islāmiyya* (HDI), Iraq
Founded by Muḥammad Bāqirus Ṣadr in Najaf, Iraq, in 1957, this is a political party with a Shīʿa religious orientation. The Ḥizb called upon the

[8] Main sources of information for this appendix are the relevant articles in the *Oxford Encyclopedia of the Modern Islamic World* (Esposito 1995).

people of Iraq to revive Islam. It worked among both literate and poor urban communities, teaching about the Qur'ān and Islamic tenets. It also spread to other countries. Soon it came into conflict with the ruling Ba'th party in Iraq. After the government executed its leader, the Ḥizb went underground and became militant. It organized mass anti-Ba'th demonstrations, and it fought on the side of Iran during the Iraq-Iran War. Its organizational structure is pyramidal with a General Leadership Committee assisted by a council. The top leadership positions have been given different names from time to time, but at the lower levels the basic units have been "the family" and "the ring." It has a publication programme that takes an ecumenical approach to religious issues.

4. *Jamāʿat Islāmī* (JA), India, Pakistan
Mawlānā Mawdūdī founded Jamāʿat Islāmī in August 1941. Its five-point program included the following: reconstruction of human thought in the light of Divine guidance; purification of individuals; training of these individuals for *Daʿwa*; reconstruction of society and its institutions according to the teachings of Islam; and revolution in the political leadership of the Muslim society to establish an Islamic state.

Jamāʿat Islāmī was originally an intellectual movement, but shifted its focus to power politics. It has been critical of all the other Muslim political parties and associations. As a political party it takes part in electoral politics at every level, and in 1958 the Jamāʿat won the local municipal elections in Karachi. Generally, however, its electoral success has been negligible.

Disillusioned with electoral politics, the Jamāʿat Islāmī reorganized its student wing Islāmī Jamʿiyyatut Ṭalaba as a militia, training them to resist police and security forces. It also decided to penetrate various organizations, associations, labor and trade unions, bureaucracies, the army and educational institutions. In 1977 it joined the Niẓām Muṣṭafā movement to overthrow the government. General Ziaul Haq launched a programme of Islamization fully supported by the Jamāʿat Islāmī.

The organizational structure of the Jamāʿat is complex. The *amīr*, or head of the Jamāʿat is elected by a council called Shūra. There are three cadres of movement members, Rukn, Kārkun and Muttafiq. Rukn are regular members but are selected only after scrutiny. Members in the other two are not regular members and have no voting privileges. The *amīr* is selected for five years. The structure is repeated at the provincial, division, district, and city or town levels. The organizational structure is highly bureaucratic, and the office holders receive salaries and other privileges. Study circles and reading rooms are organized where Jamāʿat literature is placed, and the Jamāʿat has an extensive network of publishing institutions both in Pakistan and abroad.

5. *Jamʿiyyatul Ikhwānil Muslimūn* [Muslim Brotherhood (MB)], Egypt
This movement was founded in 1928 in Egypt by Ḥasan al-Bannā (1906–1949), and soon established its branches in other Arab countries. It began as a purely religious educational and charity association concerned

with Islamic morals, education and social work. Rising against the impending threats of Western culture, secularism and loss of political power, especially after the abolition of caliphate, the Brotherhood became involved in political activities in 1938. Its organizational structure was pyramidal, stressing obedience to the leader, Amīr, who had a council to guide him. The most basic unit was the *usra* (family). Various committees and technical sections supported the organization. National political conditions in the 1940s brought the Brotherhood into active politics, and it began militant activities against the British and Zionist threats to the country.

In 1940 the movement developed a secret military apparatus, with ranger scouts called Jawwāla. The Ikhwān also became financially self-sufficient, establishing its own businesses, factories, schools and hospitals. It also infiltrated the trade unions and the armed forces. The brotherhood came into direct conflict with the Egyptian Government that executed Ḥasan al-Bannā in 1949. In 1952 all political parties were dissolved, but since the Brotherhood was a *jamʿiyyat* (society), not a *jamāʿat* (party), it survived. A shift in the movement's thought came under the leadership of Sayyid Quṭb, who maintained a radical political orientation. He strongly opposed the prevalent ideologies in the Arab world, including modernism and Westernization. The continuous conflict with the government cost the lives of many of the movement's members, including Sayyid Quṭb.

Intellectually, the Brotherhood was an urban, literate group, initially inspired by Sufism and its ideals. It was strongly influenced by Salafi thought, especially that of Ibn Taymiyya. It was not, therefore, in agreement with the orthodox Islam. Its *Daʿwa*, however, remained more concerned with political matters. It was not a missionary movement in the sense of working for the conversion of non-Muslims. Rather, its *Daʿwa* targeted Muslims in order to change their thinking.

6. *Jamʿiyyatud Daʿwatil Islāmiyya* [Islamic Call Society (ICA)], Libya
Qaddhāfi established this movement in Libya in 1972 to propagate his ideology of Islam. The Society defines its five objectives as the spread of Arabic language; purification of Islamic laws; organization of studies for preparing devout Muslims; preparation of preachers; and reforms in Muslim countries. It has three broader goals: Islamic revolution, the reorganization of religious institutions including education, and Islamic missionization. To establish an Islamic mission it initiated an educational programme to train *dāʿīs* (preachers). The Society is a good example of state *Daʿwa*. It is organized on a bureaucratic model that is highly structured and centralized. Largely funded by the state, it is a missionary as well as a political *Daʿwa* organization. It calls for *Jihād*, but means by that *Daʿwa* and relief work. It is transnational, but on a very limited scale. It also operates among non-Muslims and has an extensive publication programme.

7. *Al-Majlisul Aʿlā Lish Shuʾūnil Islāmiyya* [Higher Council of Islamic Affairs (MA)], Egypt
This department, established by Jamāl ʿAbdun Nāṣir in 1960 in Cairo, is

another example of state controlled *Daʿwa*. The Council is a part of the government machinery and works as an organization for publication and propagation. It has also worked for the promotion of Arabic language and culture.

8. *Pertubuhan Kebajikan Islam Semalaysia* [Perkim (PM)], Malaysia
Tunku ʿAbdur Raḥmān founded Perkim in 1960 as a religious and social welfare organization. It was supported mainly by the World Muslim League. Its principal objective was to promote Islam as a national religion. This was a particularly complex problem in multiethnic Malaysian society, where Malays were in the majority. Perkim supported the conversion of non-Muslims but the Malays did not recognize the new converts as equals. During ethnic conflicts in the 1970s Perkim's policy of supporting Muslims irrespective of their ethnicity became problematic. Its conversion programme could not succeed because the converts faced so many ethnic problems. Perkim today operates as a missionary movement that provides services for converts such as religious instruction, hostels, and help and training toward getting government jobs.

9. *Rābiṭatul ʿĀlamil Islāmī* [Muslim World League (MWL)], Saudi Arabia
The League was founded in Saudi Arabia in 1962 during a political crisis in Egyptian-Saudi politics. During this period, communism had made inroads in the Muslim world and Jamāl ʿAbdun Nāṣir in Egypt was supporting socialism and suppressing the Islamists. The League was therefore a purely political organization, but it operated as a transnational missionary organization. It defined itself as a cultural organization that spoke for the whole of Muslim Umma. It is the clearest example of state *Daʿwa*, completely state-funded, organized on a bureaucratic model, and strictly centralized. The objectives of the League are defined as promoting the message of Islam, fighting conspiracies against Islam, and discussing problems relevant to Islam. The character of the League changed in 1968 after the establishment of the Organization of Islamic Countries (OIC). In that same year it established branches in other parts of the world. It has two *Daʿwa* councils: Continental Councils (established in 1974), and the World Council of Mosques (1975). In 1979 it formed the Islamic Fiqh Academy and the International Islamic Relief Fund, and established a centre for training *dāʿīs* (preachers).

PART ONE

TABLĪGHĪ JAMĀ'AT
A *DA'WA* ORGANIZATION

CHAPTER ONE

THE GROWTH AND DEVELOPMENT OF THE TABLĪGHĪ JAMĀʿAT IN INDIA

Muhammad Khalid Masud

Delhi has been the political as well as the intellectual centre of Muslim India. Although important as intellectuals, the *ʿulamā* began to play a leading role in the society only after Muslim political power declined in the eighteenth century. Shāh Waliullāh (d. 1762) tried in vain to check this decline. He asked Muslim rulers in Afghanistan and powerful Muslim nobles in India to stop the rising Marhatas, Jats and Sikhs, but this only weakened further the Muslim state in Delhi. Shāh Waliullāh's son, Shāh ʿAbdul ʿAzīz (d. 1823), therefore, paid more attention to Muslim intellectual growth, and other *ʿulamā*, too, focused more on education than on politics. Consequently, small towns in UP, India, such as Kāndhala, Jhanjhāna, Sahāranpur and Deoband, where *ʿulamā* families had established themselves, rose to prominence in the nineteenth century as *ʿulamā* towns. These families remained connected with Delhi through Shāh Waliullāh and his family.

Shāh Waliullāh's *madrasa* in Delhi established itself as a leading school of thought that advocated the revival of Islam and the study of *ḥadīth*. The school refuted *taqlīd* and the Shīʿa and Ṣūfī doctrines that divided the Muslim Umma. Shāh ʿAbdul ʿAzīz remained on good terms with the British in Delhi, and some of his relatives even took jobs under them. Other *ʿulamā* in Delhi and in smaller towns generally opposed learning the English language and employment with the British. Sayyid Aḥmad Brēlwī (d. 1831), who was associated with Shāh Waliullāh's sons, launched a *Jihād* movement for the revival of Islam. Although this *Jihād* was not against them, the British linked the movement with the 1857 revolt and persecuted the *ʿulamā*. These repressive measures pushed the *ʿulamā* toward an attitude of resistance to the British and to modernity. The *ʿulamā* associated with Shāh Waliullāh's family carried on the spirit of revivalism.

Mawlānā Muḥammad Ilyās, the founder of the Tablīghī Jamāʿat, and his two successors grew up in this milieu. Mawlānā Ilyās was related to two distinguished families of the *ʿulamā* in Jhanjhāna and Kāndhala, two towns in district Muẓaffar Nagar, UP. His father belonged to Jhanjhāna, and his mother to Kāndhala. The Jhanjhāna family traced its ancestry to Mawlānā Muḥammad Ashraf in the period of the Mughal emperor Shāhjahān (d. 1627), while the Kāndhala family was descended from Shaykh Muḥammad, a Qāḍī during Muḥammad Tughlaq's (d. 1351) time. The well-known scholar Muftī Ilāhī Bakhsh (d. 1829) belonged to Kāndhala.

The two families had been linked by marriage since the thirteenth century. Mawlānā Ilyās's father Mawlānā Muḥammad Ismāʿīl (d. 1898) had married into Muftī Ilāhī Bakhsh's family and had settled in Kāndhala. He had three sons: Muḥammad, Muḥammad Yaḥyā and Muḥammad Ilyās. Muḥammad Yaḥyā married in Jhanjhāna and Mawlānā Ilyās in Kāndhala. The elders of the Jamāʿat were also closely related. Mawlānā Zakariyyā was a nephew of Mawlānā Ilyās and father-in-law of Mawlānā Yūsuf and Mawlānā Inʿāmul Ḥasan. Mawlānā Iḥtishāmul Ḥasan was Mawlānā Ilyās's cousin as well as his brother-in-law.

The *ʿulamā* families in Jhanjhāna and Kāndhala were closely associated with Shāh Waliullāh's (d. 1762) school in Delhi. Muftī Ilāhī Bakhsh (d. 1829) had studied with Shāh ʿAbdul ʿAzīz. His two sons Abul Ḥasan and Abul Qāsim were followers of Sayyid Aḥmad Shahīd, and his nephew Muẓaffar Ḥasan Kāndhalawī (d. 1865) and his nephew Nūrul Ḥasan (1868) had studied with Shāh Isḥāq of the Shāh Waliullāh family. Muḥammad Ṣābir and Ḥāfiẓ Muḥammad Muṣṭafā of Jhanjhāna also studied in Delhi and participated in the *Jihād* movement. The latter was killed with the Sayyid in 1831. It is therefore not surprising that *Jihād*, revival of Islam and Sunna would all be familiar topics in the family. Mawlānā Nadwī mentions that stories of Sayyid Aḥmad Shahīd's *Jihād* were frequently told to the children (Nadwī 1985).

Both families were associated with Deoband as well as with Aligarh. Some of their *ʿulamā* took employment with the British government, and a number of *ʿulamā* of the Kāndhala family also studied or worked at the Aligarh College.

The women in these families, too, were devoted to piety and religious education. They were taught the Qurʾān, commentary, Aḥādīth works and Awrād (e.g., *Ḥiṣn Ḥaṣīn*). Some of the women, like Mawlānā

Ilyās's mother, memorized the entire Qur'ān. It was customary in the family to memorize the Qur'ān and perform supererogatory prayers, *Dhikr* and rosary, and both men and women occupied themselves with these forms of worship (Ḥasanī 1988 [1967], 158). Their devotion produced a milieu within which even the family's children developed a deep commitment to religion.

Mawlānā Muḥammad Ismā'īl (d. 1898)

Mawlānā Muḥammad Ismā'īl, Mawlānā Ilyās's father, earned his fame as a Qur'ān teacher. Mirzā Ilāhī Bakhsh, a close relative of Bahādur Shāh Ẓafar, the last Mughal emperor, invited Mawlānā Ismā'īl to Delhi to teach Qur'ān to his children. The Mirzā was on good terms with the British because he had not taken part in the 1857 Revolt. He built a mosque near his bungalow (Bangla) in the Bastī Niẓāmuddin, which came to be known as Banglē Wālī Masjid. When Mawlānā Ismā'īl came to Delhi he took up residence in this mosque. Mawlānā Ismā'īl, while teaching Mirzā's children, developed the mosque into Madrasa Kāshiful 'Ulūm. Mirzā Ilāhī Bakhsh supported the Madrasa, and later, as mentioned in Mawlānā Ilyās's letters, the Madrasa received funds from Nawwāb Chhatārī's trust. Mawlānā Ilyās continued to receive five rupees each year from that trust for some time (Ilyās 1952, 116–117).

According to Mawlānā Nadwī, Mawlānā Ismā'īl while in Delhi came into contact with the Mēwātīs by accident. He used to go out inviting people to come to mosque, and on one such round he found some Mēwātīs who had come to Delhi seeking work. Mawlānā invited them to mosque and promised to pay them their daily wages. Soon they became accustomed to prayers and did not want their wages (Nadwī 1985, 46). Mēwātī scholars have questioned this story (Mēwātī 1979, 329n). It is difficult to believe that Mawlānā Ismā'īl had enough money to pay the wages of even a small number of persons. The story probably refers to the ten to twelve Mēwātī students who came to study in the Madrasa. They were probably given some money to meet their expenses by Mirzā Ilāhī Bakhsh, who also provided for the daily meals of other students. Mawlānā Ismā'īl died in 1898, leaving behind three sons: Mawlānā Muḥammad, Mawlānā Muḥammad Yaḥyā and Mawlānā Muḥammad Ilyās.

Mawlānā Muḥammad Ilyās (1885–1944)

Mawlānā Muḥammad Ilyās was born in 1885 and spent his childhood in Kāndhala and Bastī Niẓāmuddīn with his father. After completing his early education with his father, he went to Gangōh, Sahāranpur, where his brother had already studied with Mawlānā Rashīd Aḥmad Gangōhī. Mawlānā Ismāʿīl was very close to the *ʿulamā* in Deoband and Gangōh. Mawlānā Gangōhī initiated Ilyās into the Ṣābiriyya Chishtiya Ṣūfī order, while Mawlānā Khalīl Aḥmad Ambēthawī, Ashraf ʿAlī Thānawī and Mawlānā ʿAbdul Qādir Rāʾipurī initiated him into other Ṣūfī orders. Ilyās was twelve years old when his father died in 1898, and he became extremely devoted to Mawlānā Gangōhī. Mawlānā Gangōhī's death in 1905 came as a great shock to him. Mawlānā Ilyās had a very frail body. He had suffered from serious illness since early childhood, and he became so weak that he had to discontinue his formal education. In 1908 he resumed his studies in Dārul ʿUlūm Deoband.

Mawlānā Ilyās graduated from Deoband in 1910 and the next year began teaching at Maẓāhirul ʿUlūm, Sahāranpūr, where his brother Mawlānā Muḥammad Yaḥyā was a member of the faculty. After his brother's death in 1915, he continued teaching for another two years. He went to Delhi in 1917 because his second brother Mawlānā Muḥammad, who had been looking after the Madrasa Kāshiful ʿUlūm in Bastī Niẓāmuddin Delhi, had fallen seriously ill there. These were very hard times for Mawlānā Ilyās—both his brother and his mother died within a few months. Mawlānā Ilyās was already quite weak, and the shock affected his health badly. He had been working hard for several years, and when he fell seriously ill he came to Kāndhala to rest. Nevertheless, he soon went back to Bastī Niẓamuddīn, this time to settle there permanently. Life in the Bastī was much harder, and the *madrasa* had no regular income. The voluntary funds had also stopped coming in after Mawlānā Muḥammad's death, and Mawlānā Ilyās and his students often had to go hungry.

During this period of trial in Delhi, Mawlānā Ilyās was supported by the students and colleagues of his father in Mēwāt (Ḥasanī 1988, 149). Mawlānā Ismāʿīl had worked among the Mēwātīs and had established several mosques and *maktabs*, and Mawlānā Ilyās continued his father's mission of religious education in this area. This was the period when he began to doubt the efficacy of *madrasa* for the revival of religion, and he came to the conclusion that they could no longer fulfill this purpose (Fīrōzpurī n.d.c, 13). He expressed his worries about the future of Madrasa Kāshiful ʿUlūm, Delhi, in a letter to Ḥājī Rashīd Aḥmad, one of the school's sponsors:

> I want to draw your attention to the current problems of Niẓāmud Dīn. For fifteen years now I have been observing the changing dispositions of the people. In my humble opinion, two weaknesses currently affect the progress of the *makātib* and *madāris*. First, the interest and concern of the people that led them to found these institutions, that caused them to continue their sincere efforts for the *maktab* and *madrasa* and to donate to them, is coming to an end. . . . Second, the sciences were taught in the *madāris* in pursuit of certain objectives, goals and benefits. These are no longer achievable through these sciences (Ilyās 1952, 114).

Mawlānā's criticism of the religious education system is quite pertinent. He is obliquely referring to the fact that employment was no longer available to the *madrasa* graduates under the British because the subjects they taught did not prepare them with the necessary skills and knowledge. The above letter is undated, but since Mawlānā refers to his fifteen years experience, and he began teaching at Maẓāhirul ʿUlūm in 1910, the letter was probably written around 1925.

Mawlānā Ilyās once explained how he developed his method of *tablīgh*, that he had first employed a method of education for his *Daʿwa* but was disappointed with the system because it brought no change. He then tried the method of *dhikr*, and was again disappointed. He then realized that the true objective was to call (*bulānā*) people to Allah, especially those who were neglectful of or indifferent toward religion. Only through physical movement away from one's place could one leave behind one's esteem for life and its comforts for the cause of God (Nadwī 1985, 244).

Arya Samaj, Christian missionization and Muslim *tablīgh* activities in the area around Delhi, particularly in Mēwāt, were at their peak in the first quarter of the twentieth century (see Introduction). Several *tablīgh* and *Daʿwa* movements had been established, and Mawlānā had been exploring the various forms of *Daʿwa*. Meanwhile, he came into contact with a *tablīgh* movement in Fērōzpūr Namak, a small town of Mēwāt, that led him to further develop his own ideas and methods of *tablīgh*.

Gasht

A movement for religious revival in Mēwāt in early twentieth century had founded several *makātib* (primary schools for the teaching of the Qur'ān). We cannot fix a date with certainty, but most probably this movement began in the early twentieth century. One Qārī Ḥāfiẓ Muḥammad Ismā'īl of Fērōzpūr-Namak (District Gurganwa), and his son Munshī Nūr Bakhsh, founded a *madrasa* and three mosques in Fērōzpūr-Namak. The Munshī had been in contact with Mawlānā Ilyās's brother Mawlānā Muḥammad (Fērōzpūrī n.d.c, 8) who was in the habit of addressing the Friday prayers and sometimes stayed for the entire week (Fērōzpūrī n.d., 8–10). This movement developed a method of making rounds in the vicinity of a mosque, calling people for the study of the Qur'ān and observance of prayers. They called this method *gasht*, a Persian word that means "making rounds." In Indian usage it also meant army or police patrol, and may therefore have appealed to the military minds of the Mēwātīs.

Similar movements were operating elsewhere in Mēwāt, but their efforts were often marred by conflicts of interest and personal differences. They sought an individual on whom the dissenting parties would all agree. Ḥājī 'Abdur Raḥmān, a Meo convert to Islam, and Mawlānā 'Abdus Subḥān Mēwātī, thought of Mawlānā Ilyās and invited him to Mēwāt (Ḥasanī 1988, 139). Another group of people from Fērōzpūr-Namak also called upon Mawlānā Ilyās in 1925. They told him of Munshī Nūr Bakhsh's efforts and Mawlānā Muḥammad's connections with their town. Mawlānā Ilyās thus knew the situation in Mēwāt well.

The delegation explained the details of their work, including the method of *gasht*. Fērōzpūrī remarks that "At the mention of the word *gasht*, Haḍrat Jī [Mawlānā Ilyās] suddenly sat up and asked what *gasht* was. The deputation explained, 'We go to people in the form of groups, invite them to prayer and bring them to mosque" (Fīrōzpurī n.d.c, 14). Mawlānā was fascinated by this idea and agreed to visit the place to observe.

Mawlānā Ilyās was on his way to performing *ḥajj* in 1925, and he promised to visit Fērōzpūr-Namak afterward. According to Mawlānā Nadwī, Mawlānā Ilyās conceived the idea of *tablīgh* during the pilgrimage. Nadwī quotes Mawlānā Ilyās's words: "During this stay in Medina, I received orders to do this work. I was told, 'We shall make you perform this work"' (Nadwī 1985, 91). Upon his return from *ḥajj*, Mawlānā Ilyās visited Fērōzpūr-Namak from 1926–1927. He observed the working of *gasht*, approved, and advised them to add *kalima* with invitation to prayer" (Fērōzpūrī n.d.c, 15; Nadwī

1985, 91). Fērōzpūrī mentions that it was during this visit that Mawlānā Ilyās also approved the formation of a group (*jamāʿat*) to make rounds in various hamlets (*bastī*) in Fērōzpūr-Namak, inviting Muslims to *kalima* and prayer. This group consisted of six persons: Ḥāfiẓ Muḥammad Ishāq, son of Nūr Bakhsh, the village head Miḥrāb Khān, Chaudhrī Namāz Khān, and three youths, including the narrator of the story. It was they who started the *tablīgh* work in the village of Ghāsīra—"This was the first of series of groups that began the work of *tablīgh*" (Fērōzpūrī n.d.c, 19). Mansoor Agha has endorsed this statement (1995), but Mawlānā Nadwī writes that *gasht* work first began in Kāndhala (1985, 99). Both statements could be true since the *jamāʿat* from Fērōzpūr Namak also visited Kāndhala.

The Launching Date

Recent studies differ as to the exact date when the Jamāʿat began its work. According to Ḥasanī, *Tablīghī* work started in Mēwāt in 1926 (1988 [1967], 141). Metcalf (1993a) places the beginning in the 1920s, Troll (1985) in 1925, and Anwārul Ḥaq (1972) in 1927. They have probably derived these dates from the chronology of events given by Mawlānā Nadwī (1985, 84) who says that Mawlānā Ilyās began making *Tablīgh* rounds after his return from Ḥajj in 1926.

In our view, the Tablīghī Jamāʿat was launched officially much later. It appears that the above mentioned authors treat Mawlānā Ilyās's approval of the method of *gasht*, and its local work that was already in progress, as the beginning of the movement. In fact, the Tablīghī Jamāʿat took some years to develop its formal organization. This took place in several phases. During 1926–1928, Mawlānā Ilyās learned of the idea of *gasht* and adopted it with two additions: correction of *kalima*, and expansion into other areas. Up to that point *gasht* had been practiced only as a local operation (*maqāmī kām*).

Between 1920–1930, a number of Samaj and Sabhas in Mēwāt had started working among the Hindus for social and economic reforms. They had made the Hindus aware of their separate identity, and consequently the Muslim peasants became victims of the new economic reforms. The Arya Samaj turned the social reform program into a missionary program aimed to converting Muslim Meos to Hinduism. This aggravated the Muslims, and they responded by forming their own associations. *Panchayat*, a traditional institution of village elders, was a suitable vehicle for the reform programmes. After the 1930s, Muslim Meos began to hold *chaupals* and *panchayats* for this purpose, but internal disputes did not allow the *panchayat* to succeed. Mawlānā Ilyās took this opportunity to introduce *Daʿwa* and a reform programme through the *panchayat* system. The Mawlānā soon earned respect and popularity among the Mēwātīs, who found in him a selfless person who could settle their disputes wisely, and he played an active role in ongoing social and religious reform activities (Ḥasanī 1988, 140; for such reforms see this volume's introduction).

In 1932, Mawlānā performed his third *ḥajj* and decided to extend his activities throughout Mēwāt (Ḥasanī 1988 141). He began holding gatherings of people interested in his ideas of *Daʿwa* and reform. He also started sending small groups to villages and towns in Mēwāt, and inviting local people to the gatherings. Sikand reports this activity, saying, "It was only from late 1933 onwards that the Muballighīn of the Tablīghī Jamāʿat began roving the Mēwātī countryside" (n.d., 12). We may consider this the second phase in the movement's development. Mawlānā dispatched these *jamāʿats* in 1932 to UP religious centers like Kāndhala, Rāʾipūr, Deoband and Nadwa. Obviously, Mawlānā would not send the *jamāʿats* for *tablīgh* to these places where the *ʿulamā* families were already active. More likely, Mawlānā was seeking *ʿulamā* support for his ideas. Mawlānā Ashraf ʿAlī Thanāwī (see Introduction) had already established a *tablīgh* organization in 1931 to work in Mēwāt. Ilyās wanted the *ʿulamā* to attend the forthcoming meetings that he was planning to hold there.

These meetings culminated in a *panchāyat* held in 1934 for which Ayyūb Qādirī has provided details (1971, 92–93). There, the programme of the Tablīghī Jamāʿat was officially launched. This Panchāyat was attended by approximately 107 notables of the area, including *chaudhrīs* (landlords), village officials and elders. Mawlānā Ilyās presented a programme of action that consisted of fifteen points:

1. Correct memorization of the formulae of faith.
2. Regularity in the performance of prayers.
3. Education and promotion of knowledge.
4. Formal appearance in accordance with Islam.
5. Adherence to Islamic customs and elimination of idolatrous practices.
6. Purdah (veiling) for women.

7. Strict observance of Islamic practices in marriage ceremonies.
8. Promotion of Islamic dress for women.
9. Abiding by the Islamic faith and rejection of other religions.
10. Regard for each other's rights.
11. Necessity of the participation of responsible persons of the community in all meetings.
12. Teaching children about religion prior to formal education.
13. Efforts for the propagation of religion.
14. Observing cleanliness.
15. Protecting each other's honor.

According to Ayyūb Qādirī, "As a matter of fact, the work of Tablīghī Jamāʿat began with the holding of this *panchayat* on 2 August 1934" (Qādirī 1971, 92).

In our view, Ayyūb Qādirī's foundation date can be accepted with certainty. This may be considered the third phase in the Jamāʿat's development. In the next phase Ilyās devoted himself to preparing a precise plan of action for the Jamāʿat.

The *panchāyat* agreed that the preaching of Islam was the duty of all Muslims, not of the *ʿulamā* or religious scholars alone. The meeting defined four objectives of the *Daʿwa*: (1) universal participation of all classes of Muslims; (2) focus on action and physical movement; (3) adoption of learning, teaching, serving and promoting religion as a way of life; and (4) temporary migration from one's native place as a religious obligation.

The meeting also stipulated other details of the programme of *Tablīgh*, such as obedience to *amīr*, service to fellow participants, self-financing, utmost humility, devotion to religious learning, lawful means of earning, and avoidance of polemical and sectarian issues.

The fifteen-point programme was put into writing and signed by all the participants. A method of *tablīgh* and a plan of action were also agreed upon. These details were later reproduced in Mawlānā Ilyās's *Call to Action* in 1944.

Mawlānā worked on the fifteen points of the Panchāyat Nāma to condense them into a six-point plan of action, called Chhe Bātēn. He held another meeting in March of 1940 in Nūḥ. By that time, the number of Tablīghī followers had increased; between 125 and 150 were active in Delhi and surrounding areas, and about fifty in Karnāl (Ilyās 1952, 12, 13). In 1939, the national press, particularly the religious journals, began to notice the activities of the Tablīghī Jamāʿat, and a number of *ʿulamā* had also taken an interest (Ḥasanī 1988, 149). Despite this, Mawlānā was not happy with the work's progress. He was particularly worried about the lukewarm Mēwātī attitude toward Tablīgh (Ilyās 1952, 99, 104, 105).

Mawlānā Ilyās was self-conscious about his thin physique and stuttering tongue. When he spoke with emotion his speech became incoherent and his frequent use of Ṣūfī and technical terms often made his presentation difficult to understand. People were nonetheless impressed by his sincerity and commitment (Ḥasanī 1988, 146). Despite his physical weakness and ill health, Mawlānā Ilyās remained active in the Tablīgh work. Mumtāz Aḥmad quotes one of his contemporaries that, "Mawlānā Ilyās, though a mere skeleton, can work wonders when he takes on anything" (Aḥmad 1991a, 512).

Mawlānā Ilyās fell seriously ill in 1943. He heard that the Jamʿiyyat-i ʿUlamā was holding a public meeting in Delhi that year, and he wanted to present his programme of Tablīgh and its objectives before them. Mawlānā Iḥtishāmul Ḥasan Kāndhalawī prepared a statement for this meeting, which Mawlānā approved with amendments, but it could not be placed in the meeting. Two versions of it were published under the titles *Payām-i ʿAmal* and *Musalmānōn kī mawjūda pastī kā wāḥid ʿilāj*, under the names of Mawlānā Ilyās and Mawlānā Iḥtishāmul Ḥasan, respectively (see chapter 4). Mawlānā Ilyās died in 1944 after a long illness and was buried next to his father in Niẓāmuddīn.

Mawlānā Ilyās's Succession

Mawlānā Manẓūr Nuʿmānī recalls being worried about Mawlānā Ilyās's successor. During his illness he discussed the matter with Mawlānā Abul Ḥasan ʿAlī Nadwī. Both agreed that Mawlānā Zakariyyā was the best choice. They talked to Mawlānā Zakariyyā but he asked them to wait. He did, however, assure them that he would not hesitate to take up the responsibility if he was chosen. Mawlānā ʿAbdul Qādir Rā'ipūrī, on the other hand, wished Mawlānā Ilyās's son Mawlānā Muḥammad Yūsuf to succeed him. He asked Mawlānā Zakariyyā to get Mawlānā Ilyās's approval and permission for this choice. Mawlānā Ilyās nominated the following six persons: Ḥāfiẓ Maqbūl Ḥasan, Qārī Dā'ūd, Mawlawī Iḥtishāmul Ḥasan Kāndhalawī, Mawlawī Muḥammad Yūsuf Kāndhalawī, Mawlawī Muḥammad

Inʿāmul Ḥasan Kāndhalawī and Mawlawī Sayyid Raḍā Ḥasan Bhōpālī. Mawlānā Zakariyyā suggested Ḥāfiẓ Maqbūl Ḥasan, but Mawlānā Rāʾipūrī proposed Mawlānā Yūsuf's name. Mawlānā Ilyās considered the proposals and then decided in favour of Mawlānā Yūsuf, as he was sure that the people in Mēwāt would also approve. (Ḥasanī 1988, 189; Bijnawrī 1980, 119).

Nadwī's account confirms this statement. He adds that Mawlānā Rāʾipūrī and Mawlānā Ẓafar Aḥmad both favoured Mawlānā Yūsuf. A formal deed was written for the succession, drafted by Mawlānā Zakariyyā. This deed included a clause permitting Mawlānā Yūsuf to take an oath of allegiance on Mawlānā Ilyās's behalf. Mawlānā Zakariyyā recorded that the sentence originally read: "I allow him to take allegiance of the people," but that Mawlānā Ilyās modified it to read: "I allow him on behalf of the Messenger of God" (Ḥasanī 1988, 196). Mawlānā Ẓafar Aḥmad notes that since Mawlānā Yūsuf had never taken an active interest in *tablīgh* during his father's life, some elders of the Jamāʿat were unhappy with his selection (*Tabṣiratun nās fī tadhkirat Mawlānā Ilyās* cited in Rāshid 1997, 210–211). As we shall see, however, Mawlānā Yūsuf proved himself to be the best choice.

Mawlānā Muḥammad Yūsuf Kāndhalawī (1917–1965)

The second *amīr* of the Tablīghī Jamāʿat, popularly known as Ḥaḍrat Jī, Mawlānā Yūsuf, was the only son of Mawlānā Ilyās. Born in Kāndhala, he spent his childhood in Niẓāmuddīn, Delhi and Sahāranpūr. In Bastī Niẓamuddīn his life was one of hardship and austerity; sometimes the family had to fast for days (Ḥasanī 1988, 163).

He completed memorization of the Qurʾān in 1928 when he was eleven years old, and began studying traditional sciences, mainly with his father in Basti Niẓāmuddīn. In 1932 he went to Sahāranpūr to complete his education. He was especially interested in *ḥadīth* literature and poetry, and had no interest in the rational sciences (Ḥasanī 1988, 63).

Mawlānā Yūsuf was brought up in a strictly disciplined environment. He was frequently scolded even for looking at sweets and other things that visitors brought as gifts, since they were for the family as well as for the students (Ḥasanī 1988, 164). His childhood friends remember that he was never seen strolling or loitering in the market (Ḥasanī

1988, 165). Even the games he played reflected the religious concerns of the family. One of his classmates recalled that, as a child, Mawlānā Yūsuf would arrive carrying a stick in his hand in order to wage *Jihad* against those who did not pray (Nadwī 1985, 52).

Mawlānā wrote *Amānīl Aḥbār* and *Ḥayātus Ṣaḥāba.* The first is a commentary in Arabic language on Ṭaḥāwī's (d. 933) *Sharḥ Maʿānīl Āthār.* Mawlānā had completed only two volumes in 1943 when his father asked him to write *Ḥayātus Ṣaḥāba* (Yūsuf 1959b). This work, in three volumes, concerns the biographies of the Companions of the Prophet. Both books were written in Arabic. He died in Lahore on 2 April 1965 on a Tablīgh tour, and his body was flown to India and buried in Niẓāmuddin.

Mawlānā Yūsuf began taking interest in *Tablīgh* only in 1938 when he accompanied his father on *Ḥajj.* Soon after his election as Amīr of the Tablīghī Jamāʿat in 1943, he began to devote his full attention to Tablīgh.

Mawlānā Yūsuf took some immediate measures to consolidate the achievements of the movement. He held a meeting of Tablīghi elders in Nūḥ in Ramaḍān in 1943 and toured extensively in Mēwāt. Mawlānā Yūsuf's caravan started in Gurgānwa and traveled from village to village, even in areas where the Tablīgh had not yet been introduced. The Mēwātī elders accompanied Mawlānā Yūsuf wherever he went. In Tajarah, a town in Alwar state, people opposed Mawlānā to a degree that he could not stay there. Besides Tablīgh, Mawlānā Yūsuf also conducted collective weddings and Ṣūfī initiation ceremonies. Twelve to fifteen bridegrooms were married at a time in a simple ceremony. He initiated hundreds of persons into his Ṣūfī order. During the initiation ceremonies individuals could not touch his hands when swearing allegiance to him. Instead, a cloth was spread for this purpose. At least fifty persons could join the ceremony by touching the cloth simultaneously (Ḥasanī 1988, 217).

Next, Mawlānā Yūsuf planned tours of the main urban centres of India and in 1944 he visited Muradabad. He was, however, disappointed with the cold response of the people in that city, and he made a passionate appeal to the audience. This speech indicated that Mawlānā had been considering launching the Jamāʿat internationally. He said, "Now you hesitate to travel to nearby places such as Bijnawr, Chandpur and Rampur for three days. A time will come when you will go to Syria, Egypt, and Iraq, but then the work will have spread so extensively that the reward will not be the same"

(Ḥasanī 1988, 233). He was probably referring to the fact that any movement has more difficulties in the beginning, when its ideas are in a formative stage—participation at this time is quite trying and hence earns more rewards from God.

In October 1945 he held a consultative meeting with the elders of the Jamāʿat. It was conceived of as a training camp and planning workshop to explore the possibility of improving upon the Tablīgh methods and increasing its popularity (Ḥasanī 1988, 240). The next year a transnational Jamāʿat programme was launched, with a token *gasht* in London on 20 January 1946 (Ḥasanī 1988, 246; also see Gaborieau, this volume).

The Jamāʿat was making rapid progress when, in 1947, with the independence of India, Hindu Muslim riots broke out and disrupted the work. The riots forced many Muslims to leave their homes, first in Bengal and then in Eastern Panjab. A large number of Muslims around Delhi had taken refuge in a camp near Bastī Niẓāmuddin. Mawlānā Yūsuf asked his followers to work in the refugee camps, distributing food and clothing and introducing the inhabitants to Tablīgh work (Ḥasanī 1988, 267).

The year 1947 was a crucial one for the Jamāʿat in several ways. Apparently, the movement was identified with Muslims during this crisis. This posed a problem for the Jamāʿat's goal of rising above political and ethnic divisions. Mawlānā Yūsuf steered the Jamāʿat out of this trial successfully, gaining the confidence of Muslims, Hindus and the governments of India and Pakistan.

In the wake of the 1947 riots, the government of India held a public meeting in Ghāsīra, Mēwāt, one of the most affected areas, with speakers that included Gandhi, Patel and Jawahar Lal Nehru. This was the area where Tablīgh work had begun, and was the stronghold of the Jamāʿat. Moreover, most Muslims in the area were Mawlānā Yūsuf's followers. The Indian government invited Mawlānā Yūsuf to participate but he declined, citing the meeting's political nature (Ḥasanī 1988, 275).

Similarly, when he visited Pakistan in 1947 soon after the riots, he was invited to address Muslims of Lahore in Nīlā Gunbad mosque. In those days, Mawlānā ʿAbdul Majīd Qarshī, the founder of the Sīrat Committee Patti, had launched a popular movement with the slogan "*Har Ghāzī Namāzī, Har Namāzī Ghāzī*", every soldier should perform religious prayers regularly and every praying Muslim should get military training. He held large gatherings each Friday in the

Nīlā Gunbad mosque and addressed the audience. Mawlānā Yūsuf was invited to speak to this gathering, and he talked about the normal Tablīgh subjects. But when, after his speech, Mawlānā Qarshī wanted to speak, Mawlānā took the microphone from him and commented:

> God's punishment has descended upon us on account of our sins, disobedience and violations of God's commands. More is still to come. This punishment cannot be averted by military training and parades. Your guns, mortars and bombs cannot stop it. The true solution lies in strengthening your faith and in returning to God. Only this way you can save yourselves and the world of Islam (Ḥasanī 1988, 286–287).

Hearing this story in India, an Indian Muslim leader suggested that Mawlānā meet Nehru and tell it to him, apparently to win his sympathy for the Muslims in India. Mawlānā responded, "I said those words to the people in Pakistan. Nehru and his people in the government in India must also be told that military actions alone will not save them or the country from disaster. They should make efforts to win God's pleasure, eliminate oppression and exploitation and promote justice—only then will they be able to save themselves and the country" (Ḥasanī 1988, 287).

Muslims in India suffered from the riots for several years. Most Madrasas and Ṣūfī hospices were closed. The Muslim population took refuge in safer areas, and some migrated to Pakistan or even abandoned their religion. Mawlānā Yūsuf decided to rectify the situation. He sent some *jamāʿat*s into the affected areas, and one left by train for Pakistan. He personally visited cities like Rāʾipūr and Sahāranpūr that had been centres of Tablīgh activity (Ḥasanī 1988, 288). These were brave actions since they risked the workers' lives. Mawlānā considered them indispensible for restoring Muslim self-confidence.

The *Jamāʿat* groups that went into East Panjab in 1951 actually traveled into the riot areas which most Muslims had departed and where the few remaining were in hiding. Hostility toward Muslims was still strong, and the mosques were all deserted. The *jamāʿat* came across mostly Sikhs who were suspicious of Muslims and who often reacted violently. The *jamāʿat* spoke about peace, reconciliation, human values and justice. Most often the non-Muslim audience were impressed, and they would themselves lead the *jamāʿat* to the Muslims who had apostatized, who the *jamāʿat* preached to and invited back to Islam. These people were then sent to Muslim centres in Delhi, Sahāranpūr and Deoband (Ḥasanī 1988, 288). The *jamāʿat* travelling by train to Pakistan had a horrible experience. They witnessed the massacre of Muslims on trains going to Pakistan, and had to hide in the latrine to save themselves. The following is an extract from a letter reporting this experience:

> We reckon that the miscreants (*fasādī*) entered our compartment thirteen times, but by the special grace of God, we narrowly escaped. However, the screams of innocent children, cries of helpless women and moaning of the wounded men around us during this massacre left an indelible mark on our memory" (Ḥasanī 1988, 292).

The Tablīgh workers felt helpless because they could not retaliate or to help the Muslims for fear of exposing their identity and jeopardizing their neutrality.

Another measure that Mawlānā adopted was to hold mammoth public meetings. These made the Jamāʿat more visible and gave Muslims in India self-confidence and courage. They also helped consolidate the Jamāʿat in India and Pakistan. These gatherings were held in Lahore (1947), Karachi (1948), Rāʾipūr, Kursī and Lucknow (1948), Rawalpindi (1948), and in Nūḥ and Bhopal (1952) (Ḥasanī 1988, 309).

Mawlānā had already started working for the transnationalization of the Jamāʿat. First, it was decided to work among the *ḥājjīs* at places like railway stations, ports, waiting rooms and ships, where they stayed on their way to Mecca. Attention was drawn to the need for this work at a 1946 Murādabad meeting. It began in Karachi and Bombay in 1946 and 1947 (Ḥasanī 1988, 388), and in 1951 it spread to the Arab countries. The *ʿulamā* of Nadwa who could speak Arabic fluently and had linkages in the Arab countries proved to be invaluable (Ḥasanī 1988, 426).

Hundreds of the *ijtimāʿat* (public gatherings) were held and thousands of *jamāʿats* were dispatched within India and abroad (see Gaborieau, this volume). When Mawlānā Yūsuf died in 1965, the Jamāʿat had already spread to more than ninety countries.

Mawlānā Yūsuf's Succession

Mawlānā Yūsuf's death was sudden, and neither he nor the elders had discussed a successor. Mawlānā Zakariyyā took the initiative. He had in mind Mawlānā Inʿāmul Ḥasan, who had been closer to

Mawlānā Yūsuf than anyone else. According to Rāshid, it was Inʿāmul Ḥasan who planned and envisioned the transnational work of the Jamāʿat. Mawlānā Zakariyyā consulted selected elders individually, and then announced him to be the successor of Mawlānā Yūsuf as a third *amīr* of the Jamāʿat (Rāshid 1997, 232, 241).

There is evidence that this decision process was not as smooth as the sources would have us believe. Some of the Tablīgh elders from Mēwāt had preferred Mawlānā Ḥārūn, a son of Mawlānā Yūsuf. Mawlānā Zakariyyā, however, prevailed, and opposition to Mawlānā Inʿāmul Ḥasan was short-lived (Rāshid 1997, 246).

Mawlānā Inʿāmul Ḥasan (1918–1995)

Mawlānā Inʿāmul Ḥasan, the third Amīr of the Tablīghī Jamāʿat, was born in 1918 in Kāndhala. His father Mawlānā Ikrāmul Ḥasan (1891–1950) was a son of Mawlānā Ilyās's sister, who had studied law at Aligarh. After graduation in 1917, he had started a legal practice in Kirana and Muzaffar Nagar. Although a successful legal practitioner, he finally decided to abandon his practice and devote himself to Maẓāhirul ʿUlūm. In the last years of his life he was grieved by the successive deaths of several family members.

His son Inʿāmul Ḥasan received his early education in the Qur'ān and the Persian language in Kāndhala. In 1930 he traveled to Niẓāmuddīn and continued his studies at Madrasa Kāshiful ʿUlūm. In 1932 he went to Maẓāhirul ʿUlūm Sahāranpūr, and graduated at the age of eighteen in 1936, after which he returned to Kāshiful ʿUlūm to teach.

Mawlānā Inʿāmul Ḥasan had been very active in sports in his youth. He played football, volleyball, tennis, and hockey. As mentioned earlier, Mawlānā Inʿāmul Ḥasan and Mawlānā Muḥammad Yūsuf became interested in the Tablīgh only in 1938. Mawlānā Inʿāmul Ḥasan took his first Tablīgh tour in 1943 (Rāshid 1997, 205). Inʿāmul Ḥasan was very close to Mawlānā Yūsuf and accompanied him on many Tablīgh travels.

In May 1946 Mawlānā Inʿāmul Ḥasan became seriously ill, and the cause could not be diagnosed. In June he went to Kāndhala to rest, and he remained sick for more than three years. He suffered from depression and lost interest in everything. Although not fully recovered from this mysterious illness he began working for Tablīgh in 1950.

As Amīr of the Jamāʿat, he traveled extensively to foreign countries to attend Tablīgh gatherings. His son Mawlānā Muḥammad Zubayrul Ḥasan accompanied him during most of his travels in Tablīgh. Mawlānā's health deteriorated rapidly, and he died in Delhi on 10 June 1995.

The Jamāʿat had expanded considerably as a transnational movement by the time Mawlānā Inʿāmul Ḥasan took charge, but during his tenure, Jamāʿat's transnational role increased still further. In the beginning the Jamāʿat faced internal conflicts that tested Mawlānā's leadership. Mawlānā Iḥtishāmul Ḥasan withdrew from the Jamāʿat during these years. No details are known about the conflict, but indirect references indicate that Mawlānā had criticized certain changes in the Jamāʿat's policies. Qārī Ṭayyib in 1967 defended the Jamāʿat, without direct reference to Mawlānā Iḥtishāmul Ḥasan, saying that institutions were not to be assessed on the basis of their small errors, but rather as a whole, based on their overall gains. Although the Qārī did not mention any names, Mawlānā Inʿāmul Ḥasan's biographer, Rāshid, is sure that his comments referred to Mawlānā Ihtishāmul Ḥasan's criticisms (Rāshid 1997, 272).

In 1967 the Jamāʿat also came into conflict with Jamāʿat Islāmī in Sahāranpūr. Again, the sources do not provide us with details. It appears that Jamāʿat Islāmī tried to take advantage of a Tablīgh gathering there. After the Tablīghī leaders's speeches, the Jamāʿat Islāmī workers took over the stage to raise the issue of Palestine. The Tablīghī Jamāʿat stopped them and there followed a bitter disputation (Rāshid 1997, 273).

In 1967, again, in the Bhopal gathering, Mawlānā received complaints about two elders of Tablīgh, Iftikhār Farīdī and Raḥmatullāh Mīrathī. Mawlānā dismissed them both from their Jamāʿat responsibilities (Rāshid 1997, 275). Again, the details of the complaints against them are unknown.

Reading the writings of Mawlānā Iḥtishāmul Ḥasan and Mawlānā Iftikhār Farīdī one finds evidence of political concerns in their perception of *tablīgh* and *Daʿwa*. By contrast Tablīghī Jamāʿat avoided politics. In view of the political events in India and in the Muslim world during 1967, the Jamāʿat Islāmī expected support from the Tablīghī Jamāʿat on certain key political issues. Mawlānā Yūsuf had successfully avoided confrontation with Jamāʿat Islāmī, and Mawlānā Inʿāmul Ḥasan continued to keep the Tablīghī Jamāʿat away from politics. Consequently, the gap between the Tablīghī Jamāʿat and the Jamāʿat Islāmī widened (see chapter 4, and Aḥmad 1991a).

During his period, Mawlānā Inʿāmul Ḥasan paid close attention to systemaic organization on the international level. Under Mawlānā Yūsuf, the transnational system of the Jamāʿat was still emergent. He would invite Tablīgh leaders from other countries to Hijaz for consultation and guidance. Mawlānā Inʿāmul Ḥasan began establishing centres in other countries as well (Rāshid 1997, 294).

Mawlānā's first Tablīghī travel abroad was to Sri Lanka in 1967, and in 1972 he toured the important Tablīgh centres in Asia, Africa and Europe. In addition to ten European countries, he visited Kuwait, Iraq, Lebanon, Syria, Jordan, Libya, Turkey and Morocco. In 1975 he again toured African countries, and he traveled frequently until his death. His last trip abroad was to Britain in 1994.

No *amīr* could be appointed to succeed him—The Jamāʿat elected a council (*shūra*), instead of a single *amīr*. The council was comprised of Mawlānā Iẓhārul Ḥasan (an uncle of Mawlānā Ilyās), Mawlānā Zubayrul Ḥasan (son of Mawlānā Inʿāmul Ḥasan), and Mawlānā Saʿdul Ḥasan (son of Mawlānā Muḥammad Yūsuf). Mawlānā Iẓhārul Ḥasan died in 1996.

The Tablīghī Jamāʿat has now been working for more than four years under this council, and has continued to expand as before. In the sixty-four years since its rise in Mēwāt, several million people in South Asia have been associated with the Jamāʿat.

Tablīghī Jamāʿat in Pakistan has forty-eight centres (*marākiz*) across the country, with its headquarters in Raiwind near Lahore. Each centre has an *amīr* and a *Shūra*. The Raiwind Centre holds each year a gathering (*ijtimāʿ*) from which *jamāʿat* groups are dispatched to various destinations within the country and abroad. Each group consists of at least ten people. The following statistics concerning *jamāʿat* groups dispatched from Raiwind attest to the scope of the Jamāʿat's activities in a single country, Pakistan:

1996: 4,008 *jamāʿat*s
1997: 3,287 *jamāʿat*s
1998: 4,173 *jamāʿat*s (Mahmood 1999, 44).

These figures include only *jamāʿat*s dispatched from the annual gatherings. The Raiwind Centre, however, continues its activities throughout the year, and receives and dispatches groups of Tablīghīs almost every day. For instance, during 1997, apart from the number of *jamāʿats* dispatched at the annual gathering, the Centre dispatched 34,000 groups.

Programme

The fundamental objectives and principles of the Jamāʿat's programme, as presented by Mawlānā Ilyās in 1934 at the Nūḥ meeting, were explained in fifteen points. These points were restated as five principles in *Invitation to Action.* They are more popularly known as *Chhe Bātēn* or *Chhe Nambar* (Six Points):

1. *Kalima Ṭayyiba* (the article of faith)
Tablīghī Jamāʿat regards the credal formula of Islam, *Lā ilāha illaʾllāhu Muḥammadur rasūlullāh* (There is no deity worthy of worship except Allah, Muḥammad is the Messenger of Allah) as each individual's covenant with Allah to be a Muslim, to submit oneself to the will of Allah. This point is explained in a way that prepares a Tablīghī for his or her total commitment to the Jamāʿat programme.

The *kalima* is explained so as to endorse orthodox dogma and beliefs about angels, revelation, the Qurʾān and other revealed books, pre-determination, and eschatological matters such as events in the grave, eternal life after death, the day of judgement, and the existence of Heaven and Hell. The second part of the Kalima also rationalizes *tablīgh* as a duty of every Muslim. Since Muḥammad was the last Prophet of Allah, the task of inviting people toward submission to Allah lies now on the shoulders of the Muslim Umma.

2. *Ṣalāt* (prayer)
Among the five pillars of Islam—faith (*kalima*), prayer (*ṣalāt*), fasting (*ṣawm*), alms (*zakāt*) and pilgrimage (*ḥajj*)—the *kalima* forms the first fundamental. *Ṣalāt*, in the Tablīgh description, subsumes the other four pillars as the religious obligations of a Muslim. These obligations are explained in very general terms. The Jamāʿat also stresses that the daily five prayers should be performed in congregation in a mosque. There are multiple rewards for them. This reinforces the centrality of the mosque in Tablīghī space and its conception of *Daʿwa.* These first two fundamentals are not new, but the next four

are peculiar to the Tablīghīs in the sense that other Muslims do not emphasize them as they do. In what follows they are presented from the Tablīghī perspective.

3. *ʿIlm* (knowledge) and *Dhikr* (remembrance)

This principle has two components: (a) *ʿilm* or knowledge (of the principles of Islam) and (b) *dhikr* or remembrance (of Allah). *ʿIlm* and *dhikr* complement each other; *ʿilm* makes *dhikr* effective and *dhikr* gives life to rituals and light to faith. This conjunction also symbolizes Tablīghī Jamāʿat's efforts to reduce the polarization between the *ʿulamā* and the Ṣūfīs.

Islam obliges every Muslim to obtain the knowledge essential for discharging all religious obligations and doing all worldly things in a manner approved by Allah and His Messenger. This emphasis on minimal knowledge is sometimes taken as being an anti-intellectual stance of the Tablīghī Jamāʿat. The Jamāʿat, however, defines *ʿilm* and *dhikr* differently than do the *ʿulamā* and the Ṣūfīs. It deconstructs the Ṣūfī definition of *dhikr*, which contains formulas and litanies that are not necessarily derived from the Scriptures. The Tablīgh literature speaks about the magical effects and extraordinary rewards of the *dhikr*, but it restricts this within the Scriptures and within the *ʿulamā*'s accepted framework. The Tablīghī Jamāʿat defines knowledge as learning the virtues (*faḍāʾil*), and rewards in the Hereafter, of all obligatory acts and other things a person does. Obviously, such knowledge can be obtained by studying the Qurʾān and *aḥādīth* (traditions of the Prophet).

According to the Tablīgh programme, the best form of *dhikr* is the study of the Qurʾān itself. One must, however, learn the invocations or prayers which the Prophet Muḥammad said on different occasions, such as while eating food, entering a town, going to bed, or riding a vehicle (see Tozy, this volume).

4. *Ikrām-i-Muslim* (respect for a Muslim)

Islam requires Muslims to live together in collective peace and tranquillity and mutual affection and trust. Allah likens them to "a single Brotherhood" (Qurʾān 49, 10). Every Muslim must be respectful, kind, courteous, polite and sympathetic towards others and must give them a helping hand in all spheres of life, particularly in matters of religious guidance. No Muslim should be self-righteous, haughty, insolent, envious, rude or disdainful toward another Muslim, and Muslims must never feel happy seeing another Muslim in trouble.

This principle is intended to cultivate an attitude of forbearance, toleration, indulgence and good will toward other Muslims. The humility and respect for others was essential in a society such as India, where social stratification was ubiquitous. It is common to see Tablīghīs helping each other, carrying another's luggage or serving them in some other way, overlooking different social statuses which would be jealously guarded otherwise.

Although Tablīghī public speeches advise kind treatment of all non-Muslims, they do not explicitly promote love and respect for non-Muslims. This point is probably based on a fear that love for non-Muslims may lead to love for religions other than Islam and a compromising of religious matters. This fear appears to be related to the phenomenon of 'nominal Islam' discussed earlier (see introduction).

5. *Ikhlāṣ-i-Niyyat* (sincerity of purpose) *or Taṣḥīḥ-i-Niyyat* (emendation of intention)

Everything that a Muslim does must be done with the intention of earning the pleasure of Allah and avoiding His displeasure. Such intentions are the mark of sincerity, and only things done with such intentions carry rewards in the Hereafter.

This principle appears to be related to the Ṣūfī emphasis on sincerity. On further analysis, however, one finds the Tablīghī stress *niyya* for different reasons. The *ʿulamā* do not regard human acts as simply good or evil by themselves; it is *sharīʿa* that determines their value. The Jamāʿat teaches that an act must have a motive or intention (*niyya*) in accordance with *sharīʿa*. Any act, however good it might be, will not earn any reward in the eyes of God if the *niyya* is incorrect. Even a mundane act can be an act of worship if performed with a correct *niyya*. For example, if one takes food with the intention of gaining strength to perform *ṣalāt*, one is rewarded as for an act of worship (*ʿibāda*).

This principle is basic to the formation of Tablīghī attitudes and it sanctifies most of the actions necessary for the Tablīgh work, since they are justified on the basis of their good intentions. Similarly, this works as a principle of self-criticism because every Tablīghī must be conscious of his or her intentions in all acts.

6. *Tafrīgh-i-Waqt* (sparing time)

This point is central because it relates the most essential requirement of the Tablīgh work. The Tablīghīs define it as "sparing time" from worldly occupations and domestic engagements and donating that time to *Tablīgh.* This principle explains the philosophy, methodology and practice of the Tablīghī Jamā'at. It is described as the most ingenious and effective way of learning the Islamic principles in a practical manner. By moving away from one's home and staying in a group one becomes free from all distractions in order to learn and spread the message of Islam. One may spare any duration of time between one day and four months, according to his situation, capacity and convenience, as well as the money he can afford to pay his way.

Miyānjī ʿĪsā remarks that the Tablīghīs differed about this sixth point—some called it "*tablīgh*", some "*tafrīgh waqt,*" and still others "*nafar fī sabīl Allāh*" (going out in the path of God). He recalls that once the question was posed to Mawlānā Yūsuf in the presence of Bhā'ī (Brother) ʿAbdul Wahhāb (Raiwind), Qurayshī Ṣāhib (Rawalpindi) and other elders as to which was correct. He explained that there was no dispute on this point—the sixth point was "*tablīgh*" because "*tafrīgh*" also meant *tablīgh.* These are only different words with the same meaning. Miyānjī explained further that *Nafar fi Sabīl Allāh* refers to *Jihād.* In Tablīgh usage "*Allāh kē rastē mēn nikalnā*" (to go out on the path of Allah) means local work and movement abroad" (Firozpuri n.d.c. 119). However, "*nafar fī sabīl Allāh*" implies *Jihād,* and is not a Tablīgh principle; *Jihād* is a substantive institution of Islam. *Nafar,* in its meaning as *Jihād,* becomes obligatory only in times of necessity, whereas *tablīgh* is a perennial duty (Fērōzpūrī n.d.c, 103). We shall encounter other debates concerning this point in chapter four.

7. *Tark-i-Lā yaʿnī* (abstention from futile talk)
This principle constitutes a preventive measure against wasting time and energy in talking, or doing things that are unlikely to bring any reward in the Hereafter. The least that a person loses by indulging in useless talk or activity is the time that could have been used for things more rewarding in the Hereafter.

Method

Tablīghī Jamā'at's method of *Daʿwa* differs from the traditional methods of *waʿẓ* (sermon), *tadrīs* (teaching), *munāẓara* (disputation), *tabshīr* (prophesy) and *Jihād.* It is apparently closer regarding others, such as *tadhkīr* (reminding) and *taʿlīm* (learning), but it does not allow the use of force as in *Jihād*. It emphasizes participation, group work, and change of environment by travel out of one's place of work and residence. These travels are organized according to a strict discipline and programme, which includes *taʿlīm* (learning sessions) and the practice of six basic tenets of *tablīgh*. The method of *tablīgh* and its rules and regulations came to the fore in Tablīghī Jamāʿat. Mawlānā Yūsuf required workers to abide by them fully, saying, "The work yields benefits only if it is done in strict accordance with its rules and principles. The violation of rules reduces its positive effects and benefits" (Ḥasanī 1988, 741).

As argued above, the method of *tablīgh* has passed through several stages. For example, the method of *gasht*, and the idea of *panj kōs* and *chilla* were derived from local practice in Mēwāt. Mawlānā developed these and other practices into a formal and systematic Tablīgh method. This method was described briefly in *Payām-i ʿAmal*, and in Mawlānā Iḥtishāmul Ḥasan's *Musalmānōn kī Mawjūda Pastī*. . . . The method was practiced and perfected through the work of the early *jamāʿats*.

Mawlānā Ilyās was very particular about Tablīgh's method, and he believed that Tablīgh work should not be undertaken without proper training in it. This concern is illustrated by an incident that took place in 1942. Impressed by the work of Tablīgh, some Burmese students in Dārul ʿUlūm Nadwa, in Lucknow, decided to introduce the work in their country. Mawlānā learned of this after their departure from India, and he expressed his anxiety to Mawlānā Abul Ḥasan ʿAlī Nadwī, saying,

> Probably the Burmese students have departed. I am quite worried about them. I am also concerned about the inconvenience that they might face. I wish they had joined with me in two or three forty-day Tablīgh programmes. One could then hope for a lot of *barakat* (blessings from God). I do not see how they will be able to carry out the work with just the amount of understanding they gained before their departure (Ilyās 1952, 66).

Mawlānā Ilyās prepared detailed maps of the various districts of Mēwāt and planned the movement of the Tablīghīs according to them. He instructed the Tablīgh groups to submit written reports to the centre, summarizing the population of each village they visited, the distances between places, their routes and the names of the village heads (Qādirī 1971, 99). He was very specific about the places and the people who should be invited to a Tablīgh gathering, and he always made it a point to involve the local authorities.

Ḥasanī says that the Jamāʿat was very particular about the participation of the Chaudhrīs of Mēwāt in Tablīgh activities. Mawlānā Ilyās used to convene their meetings at the occasion of every Tablīgh gathering, and Mawlānā Yūsuf continued this policy carefully. One gathering of prominent *ʿulamā*, Mashāʾikh (the Ṣūfī leaders) and Chaudhrīs in 1944 consolidated Mawlānā Yūsuf's leadership at the beginning of his career (Ḥasanī 1988, 213).

Each Tablīgh public gathering requires that the city that has proposed to hold the *ijtimāʿ* first send a large *jamāʿat* to the centre in Niẓāmuddin. During their stay the members of the visiting *jamāʿat* listen to addresses and participate in various Tablīgh activities like *taʿlīm, mashwara, gasht* and *nuṣrat* (reinforcement). Thus they receive practical training for the work. Then, before an *ijtimāʿ* is held in a city the Tablīgh work is accelerated within and around that area (Ḥasanī 1988, 300).

The method and programme of the Tablīghī work is practiced by them ritually. Mawlānā Yūsuf detailed the work in one of his letters step by step, (Ḥasanī 1988, 758), which can be summarized as follows:

Local work: The work in a local mosque should consist of *gasht* (rounds) twice a week in the area, asking people to come to mosque. The goal should be for each local family to produce a volunteer to spend three *chillas* (each *chilla* being forty days) with the Jamāʿat. These two *gashts* should be organized in two different mosques in the locality. A session of *taʿlīm* (see below) should be held in the mosque daily.

Three-day outing: Each person should spend three days each month in the Tablīgh work. Each mosque should send three-day *jamāʿat*s to work within a radius of five *kōs* (a *kōs* is about three miles).

Chilla: Each person should spend at least one *chilla* with the Tablīghī Jamāʿat each year and three *chilla*s in his or her lifetime.

Gasht: *Gasht* (round) is a Tablīghī activity that starts by making rounds in the viscinity of a mosque, inviting people to it. A group going on *gasht* should not consist of more than ten people. These should be selected on the basis of their Tablīgh experience, although one or two novices may be added for training. Two to three persons should remain in the mosque to receive those sent there during the *gasht*. One person among the outgoing group is selected to be the *mutakallim* (speaker) of the group. These *gasht* rules are repeated by the participants before departing. The group should then say a prayer for the *gasht*. During the round, while the *mutakallim* is speaking, others should occupy themselves in *dhikr*, without looking at the addressee or other things. The talk should be brief and to the point. The subject should be how the life of the Prophet is the only model to solve all problems in this world and in the Hereafter. This work is difficult, but the Tablīgh provides an opportunity to learn and practice this method and creates an environment that makes it easier. After explaining the objective of his visit, the Mutakallim invites the person to come to the mosque in order to listen to the *bayān*.

Bayān (address), also called *khiṭāb* (speech): After mutual consultations, one person from the Jamāʿat is selected to address the gathering for *Daʿwa*. Speaking about this worldly life and the life in the Hereafter, the speaker highlights the positive and negative aspects of the two worlds. He then repeats the Six Points (see above *Chhe Bāten*), after which he invites the audience to volunteer to go out with the *jamāʿat*. He starts by asking them to spend three *chillas*, but then he lowers his request to shorter periods. This invitation is called *muṭālaba* or *taqāḍa* (demand).

Tashkīl: After the *muṭālaba* has been made, another person stands up to record the names of the volunteers. This person also makes remarks urging people to volunteer, but does not give a long speech. The audience is then divided into smaller groups and the members of the *jamāʿat* join theses. This process is called *tashkīl* (formation of outgoing *jamāʿat*), and the objective is to form one local *jamāʿat* and to establish a system of bi-weekly *gasht* and *taʿlīm* in the locality.

Taʿlīm: The *taʿlīm* session begins by stating the rules of *taʿlīm*, which are as follows: One should listen to what is read with complete attention, love and respect. One should perform ablution before taking part in the session. While sitting one should not recline on anything. The subjects of the *taʿlīm* are *faḍāʾil* Qurʾān (merits of reading the Qurʾān), *tilāwat* (recitation) and *tajwīd* (correct pronunciation of the Qurʾānic verses). The *sūras* (chapters of the Qurʾān) recited during the prayers are memorized. Difficult parts of the prayer are not corrected in public, as not every person can read them correctly, and these parts may be learned in private. In *taʿlīm* there should be no speeches; only the *faḍāʾil* books are read (see chapter 4). After reading, each person should rehearse the Six Points recounting them.

Mashwara (consultation, council): This is an important principle and institution of Tablīgh. It is also a training in discipline and group life. Every person must participate in the *mashwara*. It begins with a special prayer made after reciting the rules of *mashwara*. These are as follows: one should give his opinion only when asked, and with complete honesty and sincerity. One must not expect nor insist on the acceptance of his suggestion. If it is accepted, one should ask God for His forgiveness and pray for security against possible negative repercussions. If it is not accepted, one should thank God because, if followed, the suggestion might have brought such repercussions about. It is necessary to consult everyone on every matter. Decisions are not made on the basis of majority opinion—final decisions must be left to the *amīr*. When announcing his decision the *amīr* should not belittle those opinions that have not been accepted; rather he should thank everyone. All must obey the *amīr* (Ḥasanī 1988, 758).

The procedure of *mashwara* has been meticulously institutionalized by the Jamāʿat. At almost every step the *amīr* of a jamāʿat makes decisions in various matters after *mashwara* with his group. The *mashwara* plays a significant role at local, national and global levels in the form of *shūra* (councils of elders), who assist the three *amīrs*. Today this council has been assigned the role of the *amīr* as well.

Organizational Structure

The Tablīghī Jamāʿat maintains a loose organizational structure. Mawlānā Yūsuf clarified that, "We have not established any organization for this work. It has no office, register or fund. This is a duty of all Muslims. We have not instituted a separate association for this purpose as is customary" (Ḥasanī 1988, 731). The Jamāʿat does not, however, abide by this principle as a rule. In countries like Morocco, Belgium and France, where the Jamāʿat can operate only as a registered society, it has established itself as a structured organization.

The Tablīghī Jamāʿat prefers to work as a community, based on personal relationships. The Jamāʿat certainly keeps a hierarchical structure, but this is mostly loose and temporary. *Amīr* and *shūra* are the essential structural features, and they exist at every level of Jamāʿat organization. The Tablīghī Jamāʿat has two types of organizational structures. One, which is relatively temporary, applies to the organization of groups going out on *tablīghī* tour. Each group is also called *jamāʿat* to signify that it is a micro-representation of the Tablīghī Jamāʿat as a whole. It is structured like the main Tablīghī Jamāʿat organization. It chooses its *amīr* for the duration of the tour and an *amīr ṭaʿām* for the preparation of meals and other matters. The Tablīgh elders sometimes appoint this *amīr* when the group forms. The group may be further divided into various sub-groups, and each must have an *amīr*. Even the smallest group for *gasht* must have an *amīr*, a *mutakallim* (spokesman) and a *rahbar* (guide). The latter is a local volunteer, and not necessarily a full member of the group.

The second level of organization, which is relatively continuous, is territorial. This usually corresponds to the different levels of local administration, such as province (state), district, city, or village. Each city is divided into *mohallas* (neighborhoods). The centre appoints an *amīr* at each level, and the centre is usually located in the capital of the country. The central headquarters of the Jamāʿat are in Bastī Niẓāmud Dīn, Delhi, India. The leadership there has so far been limited to Mawlānā Ilyās's family. The two *amīrs* who succeeded Mawlānā Ilyās were closely related to him. Since the third *amīr's* death, the Jamāʿat has been led by a central *shūra* which consists of relatives of the three past *amīrs*.

Unlike other *Daʿwa* or missionary organizations, the Tablīghī Jamāʿat has no welfare or educational programmes, or formal training institutes for its workers. Members receive training by participating and spending time with the Jamāʿat and by residing in the centres of Niẓāmuddīn and Raiwind. New members from abroad are advised to come to Pakistan and India to stay for some time at the center. There are institutions of religious learning attached to the centers, as in Niẓāmuddīn (Delhi), India, in Raiwind (Lahore), Pakistan, and Dewsbury, England, but they are not considered part of Tablīghī Jamāʿat's missionary or training programme.

The Tablīghī Jamāʿat is in essence a grass roots movement. It draws its membership from all walks of life. Nevertheless, the Jamāʿat is very conscious that without the support of the influential and well-to-do, it cannot achieve its objectives. Mawlānā Ilyās launched the movement in a meeting attended by local *chaudharis* (village heads), and he always convened a special meeting of the *chaudharis* of Mēwāt in conjunction with Tablīgh annual gatherings. Outgoing *jamāʿats* are consistently instructed to first contact the influential people in any village or the city. Mawlānā Ilyās was overjoyed when influential people began to participate in Jamāʿat activities (Ilyās 1952, 31).

Tablīghī Jamāʿat differs with most *Daʿwa* organizations, too, in its emphasis on the principle of self-finance. The members and the *amīrs* receive no salaries. A Tablīghī going out on *tablīgh* tour is supposed to meet all of his own expenses. The Tablīghīs pay no contributions or fees to the organization, and are not allowed to accept any contribution or meals. The Tablīghīs do, however, contribute in kind and services at the time of large gatherings.

Conclusion

The Jamāʿat in its early stages was local, restricted to Mēwāt. Mawlānā Ilyās uses the word *bīrūn-i mulk* (literally, abroad, outside the country) in a letter to Miyānjī ʿĪsā. The editor, Mawlānā Abul Ḥasan ʿAlī Nadwī, explains in a footnote that it actually meant 'outside Mēwāt' (Ilyās 1952, 92). The fact therefore remains that, despite its transnational spread, the Tablīghī Jamāʿat continues to be parochially South Asian.

The Jamāʿat seems to have adapted itself to the local environment, at least in adopting various local names including "Foi et pratique" (France), "Jamāʿat al-Tablīgh wa'l-Daʿwa" (Morocco), "Tabligh Jamat" (South Africa) and "Jamaa Tablīghī India" (Malaysia). It has also used different names in India and Pakistan. The name Tablīghī Jamāʿat has now become most popular. In the beginning it was called "Taḥrīk-ī-īmān" (faith movement), "Jamāʿat," "Niẓām" (system), "Tanẓīm" (organization) (Ḥaq 1972, 45), "Dīnī Daʿwat" (Nadwī 1985), and even "Bhōpālī Jamāʿat" because some of its annual meetings were held in Bhopal.

Nonetheless, the Jamāʿat has rigidly followed Mawlānā Ilyās's method of Tablīgh. The few changes introduced by Mawlānā Yūsuf were only procedural. It appears that method itself is taken by Tablīghīs to be the message. Essays in this volume comment on this particular feature of the Jamāʿat as its weakness. They observe that the Jamāʿat has continued to follow the same strategies that were developed in Mēwāt. *Daʿwa* methodology has been employed in European environments where its message has become limited to a particular segment of society, and where it has little appeal for the educated.

Islam in Tablīghī Jamāʿat's message has been reduced to an aversion toward modernity, to a minimal and personal Islam, and to the Mēwāt paradigm of reform. The minimal Islam lays stress on performance of Islamic rituals, within which now the rituals of Tablīgh are included. This narrow worldview has simplified missionary work, but has also perhaps become an opaque lens that leaves the message of the Jamāʿat unclear and ambiguous. Before his death, Mawlānā Ilyās worried that the Jamāʿat was misunderstood as a movement for *ṣalāt* and religious rituals. The Jamāʿat has attracted millions of followers yet it has been unable to cultivate a religiosity among its followers, or to bring about change in communities where it has been working for years. Its focus on individual reform and faith renewal, without social concerns, has produced a strong sense of separation between personal and social morality. This does not seem to have been the vision of Mawlānā Ilyās.

Appendix I

Mawlānā Muḥammad Yūsuf's Speech

Bayān (public speech) is a part of the activities of the *ijtimāʿ*. It may be delivered after *fajr, ʿaṣr, maghrib* or *ʿishā* prayers. These are often long speeches, and are followed by equally long *duʿā* (prayer). Often they are very emotive and sometimes even sarcastic (see Kepel, Tozy, this volume). These speeches are frequently recorded and published, and there are several collections available. I have selected a speech that Mawlānā Muḥammad Yūsuf delivered at Raiwind, Pakistan three days before his death on 30 March 1965. This was his last public speech. Mawlānā ʿAbdul ʿAzīz Kalnawī recorded it and Mawlānā ʿAzīzur Raḥmān Bijnawrī published a summary in *Tadhkira Amīr-i Tablīgh* (Bijnawrī 1980, 238–248), which I have translated here.

After praising God and prayers for the Prophet, Mawlānā began his speech in the following manner, contrary to his usual practice.

You see I am not feeling well. I have not been able to sleep the whole night. Nevertheless I am speaking to you because I thought it was essential. Whoever understands what I am saying and translates it into action he will be rewarded with success by God. If he does not he will harm only himself.

The formation of this *Umma* is the result of a great deal of effort. The Prophet, peace be upon him, and his Companions, may God be pleased with them, worked very hard to build this *Umma*. Their enemies, the Jews and Christians, have been trying incessantly not to let Muslims remain one *Umma*, but rather divided into pieces. Now Muslims have lost their state of being an *Umma*. As long as they were an *Umma*, a few million of them were stronger than the whole world. They had not built up a proper house. There was no proper mosque. There was not even a lamp in that mosque. The first lamp in the Mosque of the Prophet was lit in the ninth year after migration. It was Tamīm Dārī, may God be pleased with him, who lit the first lamp. Tamīm Dārī accepted Islam in 9 A. H. By 9 A. H. almost the whole of Arabia had come into the fold of Islam. Several nations, several languages, several tribes had been forged into one *Umma*. When all of this had been achieved, only then was the lamp lit in the Prophet's mosque. On the other hand, the light of guidance that the Prophet had brought had lit the whole of Arabia and beyond. The *Umma* had been formed. Then this *Umma* arose, and wherever it went country after country fell to it.

This *Umma* was formed in such a way that none of its members was a partisan to his family, clan, party, nation, country or language. They did not look toward property, wife or children. Everyone looked only to what God and His Prophet said. An *Umma* is formed only when all relations and interests against the commands of Allah and His Prophet are disregarded. When Muslims were one *Umma* the whole *Umma* was shaken if one Muslim was murdered. Now hundreds and thousands are killed and we are not disturbed at all. *Umma* is not the name of a nation and the inhabitants of one territory; rather it is a joining of hundreds and thousands of nations and territories that forms *Umma*. Whoever regards one particular nation or territory as his own and others as aliens, he slaughters the *Umma* and cuts it into pieces. He destroys the results of the efforts of the Prophet, peace be upon him, and his Companions, may God be pleased with them. By dividing ourselves into pieces we have slaughtered ourselves. The Jews and Christians have done no more than slice an *Umma* that was already cut into pieces. Now if Muslims become Muslim again, then the forces of the world united against them cannot harm them at all. No atom bomb or rocket can eliminate them. But if they continue dividing themselves according to national and territorial loyalties, then I swear to God, your weapons and your armies shall not save you.

Muslims are suffering defeat all over the globe and dying because by eliminating the *Umma* they have destroyed the sacrifices of the Prophet, peace be on him. I am telling you these agonizing stories. All this destruction has happened because this *Umma* is no longer an *Umma*. They have even forgotten what *Umma* means and how the Prophet, peace be on him, constituted this *Umma*. To become an *Umma* and to deserve God's support of Muslims, it is not enough that Muslims perform prayers, hold sessions to remember God in *dhikr*, have schools and education. Ibn Muljim, who assassinated ʿAlī [d. 661], may God be pleased with ʿAlī, was so perfect in his performance of prayers and remembrance that when angry people wanted to cut out his tongue during his punishment, he asked them not to cut it so that he could continue chanting God's remembrance until the last moment of his life. Despite all this the Prophet, peace be on him, declared that ʿAlī's assassin would be the most cursed person of his *Umma*. As far as having education in the Madrasa is concerned, Abul Faḍl [d. 1602] and Fayḍī [d. 1594] too obtained it and to such a level that one of them wrote a commentary on the Qurʾān without using a dotted letter. Yet they were those who led [Indian Mughal Emperor] Akbar [d.1605] astray and destroyed religion. Therefore, how can the qualities, which even Ibn Muljim, Abul Faḍl and Fayḍī possessed, be sufficient to constitute an *Umma* and to deserve the hidden support of Allah.

[The two leaders of the *Jihād* movement in India], Shāh Ismāʿīl Shahīd [d. 1831] and Sayyid Aḥmad Shahīd [d. 1831], may Allah have mercy on them, and their followers, when they arrived in the frontier territory and people accepted them as their leader, Satan suggested to some Muslims of that area to remember that they were people from another territory. Why should they lead them? They organized a rebellion against them. Several of their followers were killed. Thus Muslims themselves destroyed the state of *Umma* on a territorial basis. As a punishment God installed the English in that territory. It was a torment from God.

Remember, words like "my nation," "my territory," "my clan," are factors that destroy the *Umma*. God dislikes such words to the extent that a great Companion such as Saʿd b. ʿUbāda, who committed a mistake in this respect, had to suffer consequences in this world. If his mistake were not rectified Muslims would have been divided into *muhājir*s (migrants) and *anṣār*s (supporters). Tradition tells us that he was killed by the *jinn* and people in Madina heard a voice whose speaker was not seen saying: "We killed Saʿd b. ʿUbāda, the chief of the Khazraj tribe. We targeted his heart with an arrow that did not miss." This event set an example and a lesson that God will destroy a person, even if otherwise worthy, if he harms the *Umma* on the grounds of nation and territory.

The *Umma* will come into being only when all classes without discrimination engage themselves in the work that Prophet Muḥammad has bequeathed to us. Remember that the things that destroy the *Umma* are wrongs committed in social transactions. When an individual or a class commits an injustice against another and does not give to others what is their due or hurts them, ridicules or insults them, then discrimination occurs and the state of *Umma* begins to break. That is why I say chanting *kalima* and *tasbīḥ* will not form the *Umma*. The *Umma* will be formed by reforming mutual transactions and social life, by giving others their due and by instituting respect. Sacrificing one's own rights and interests for others will form it. The Prophet, peace be upon him, Abū Bakr, may God be pleased with him, and ʿUmar, may God be pleased with him, constituted this *Umma* by sacrificing everything they had as well as by suffering and patience.

During the period of ʿUmar, may God be pleased with him, one day there arrived a sum of several billion Dirhams; consultations were held for its distribution. The *Umma* was intact in those days. The parties in the consultation did not belong to only one tribe or class, rather, they consisted of different tribes and classes that were considered elders and special persons because they had the privilege of the Prophet's company. They decided after consultation that the sum should be distributed in such a way that the maximum share be allotted to the Prophet's tribe, the next amount to Abū Bakr's and the next ʿUmar's. The relatives of ʿUmar were placed third in order. When ʿUmar, may God be pleased with him, was consulted, he did not accept the order. He said whatever we have got and are receiving is thanks to the Prophet, peace be upon him. Therefore only one relationship, affinity with the Prophet, should be the criterion for division. Whoever is closer to the Prophet, he should be given more than the others. The second, third and fourth place should be decided according to this order. Thus the maximum should be given to Banī Hāshim, then to ʿAbd Munāf, then to the families of Quṣayy, Kilāb, Kaʿb and Marra, respectively. In this order ʿUmar's tribe was placed very low and its share was reduced greatly. ʿUmar decided this and let his tribe stand far behind in the division of wealth. That is how this *Umma* was formed.

The foremost requirement for the formation of *Umma* is that everyone strives for unification, not division. There is a *ḥadīth* that can be summed up by saying that on the day of judgement a person will be brought out who will be punished even though he has performed prayers, paid *zakāt*, kept fasting, performed pilgrimage and participated in missionary work. The reason will be that some of his statements have caused a rift in the *Umma*. He will be told to undergo punishment for this statement that harmed the *Umma*. There will be another person, who will have fewer prayers, fasting and pilgrimage in his balance, and he will fear God's wrath for this, but he will be well rewarded. He will wonder what action has caused this blessing. He will be told that he had made a statement on such and such an occasion that prevented an imminent rift in the *Umma*, that he had thereby helped to unify rather than divide the *Umma*. All this reward for that one statement. The most frequent source of the formation and disruption of *Umma* is the tongue. The tongue unites hearts but it also breaks them apart. One wrong word spoken by a tongue can lead to quarrel and skirmish. One right word may unite and join hearts rent asunder. One must therefore have a firm hold on one's tongue. That is possible only if one is always mindful that God sees one at every place and every time, and listens to every word that we speak.

There were two tribes of Aws and Khazraj in Madina. They were at daggers drawn for several generations. When the Prophet, peace be upon him, migrated to Madina and the Anṣār [the supporters of the Prophet at Madina] accepted Islam, the enmity between those tribes came to an end. Thanks to the Prophet and Islam the Aws and Khazraj became friends. When the Jews saw this they planned to sow enmity between them again. In a meeting where persons from both tribes were present, a conspirator recited poetry alluding to their previous hostility. Both parties became infuriated. First they used hot words against each other, and then they drew swords. Someone informed the Prophet. He immediately came there and asked them why they were ready to shed blood when he was there. He delivered a short but compassionate speech. Both parties felt that the Devil had led them astray; they cried, and were reconciled. These verses were revealed on this occasion:

> O you who believe! Fear Allah as He should be feared, and die not except in a state of Islam (Qur'ān, 3:102).

If a person is mindful of God every moment and is fearful of His punishment and obedient to His commands, even the Devil cannot beguile him. The *Umma* will be saved from disruption and other evils.

> And Hold fast all together by the rope of God, and be not divided among yourselves. And remember with gratitude Allah's favour on you. For you were enemies and He joined your hearts in love, so that by His Grace, you became brethren. And you were on the brink of the pit of fire and He saved you from it (Qur'ān, 3:103).

This means to hold fast to God's pure Book and his faith together. That is, that with full collectivity and within a state of *Umma*, you hold the rope of religion together with others, and engage yourselves in this task. Do not divide into groups on the basis of nation, territory, language or some other consideration. Do not forget the favour of Allah, who eliminated the hostility and enmity that had existed in your hearts for generations and created love in your hearts and made you brothers of each other. You were fighting among yourselves and had reached the brink of Hell. You were about to fall when God held you and saved you from Hell. The Devil is among you. One solution is for you to form a group among yourselves whose only function is to invite to good and welfare and prevent evil and corruption.

> Let there arise out of you a band of people inviting to all that is good, enjoining what is right, and forbidding what is wrong (Qur'ān, 3:104).

There should be a group in the *Umma* whose only task and goal should be to invite others toward faith and all kinds of good, who continue working hard for faith and paving the way for good, who strive for prayers and remembrance of God. They should strive to achieve knowledge brought forth by the Prophet, peace be on him, and to save people from evils and afflictions. All this effort will keep the *Umma* as *Umma*.

> Be not like those who are divided amongst themselves and fall into disputations after receiving clear signs. For them is a dreadful penalty (Qur'ān, 3:105).

These verses refer to those people who create differences by following the devil and by following separate paths after receiving guidance. They will disrupt the state of *Umma*. Then God will punish them.

> They are those for whom there is a great punishment (Qur'ān, 3:105).

All that religion teaches and everything in it leads to unification and unity. Prayer unites, fasting unites. In pilgrimage people from different nations, countries and languages come together. Education sessions are for unity. Respect for Muslims, mutual love and exchange of gifts all aim at unification and lead to Paradise. On the day of judgement, the people who strove for such deeds will be beaming with light. On the other hand hatred, jealousy, backbiting, insult, ridicule and hurting other's feelings are all deeds that divide and break the society, and lead to Hell. The people committing such deeds will be disgraced on the day of judgement:

> On the Day when some faces will be white, and some faces will be black, to those whose faces will be black will be said, "Did you reject Faith after accepting it? Taste then the penalty for rejecting faith." But those whose faces will be white they will be in Allah's mercy, therein to dwell forever (Qur'ān, 3:106–107).

The verse means that those who have disrupted the *Umma*, or have committed deeds that led to divisions, they will rise from their graves on the day of judgement with black faces. They will be told that they have adopted the ways of unbelief after accepting Islam and Faith, and deserve to taste the penalty of Hell. As for those who took the right path, their faces will be lit up and glowing. They will be with Allah's mercy and in Paradise forever.

My brothers and friends! All these verses were revealed when the Jews tried to divide the Anṣār and caused their two tribes to confront each other. These verses have shown that division and dispute among Muslims are matters of unbelief, and have warned of the punishment in the hereafter.

Today, when the whole world is making efforts to disrupt the state of the *Umma*, the only antidote and solution is that you should dedicate yourselves to the efforts that the Prophet, peace be on him, taught. Bring Muslims to the mosque, where they should talk about faith. There should be circles for education and *dhikr* and consultations about undertakings for religion. People from different classes and languages should gather together on the pattern of the Prophet's mosque. Only then will the state of *Umma* obtain. Avoid those things, which give the Devil an opportunity to sow the seeds of disruption. Whenever three individuals sit together they should always remember that the fourth with them is God. When you are four or five, then always remember, that the fifth or sixth with you is God, who is present there and listening to every word. He is watching if we are talking about forming the *Umma* or about disrupting it. That we are not backbiting, or conspiring against others. This *Umma* was formed by the Prophet's blood and fasting, peace be on him. Now we are disrupting the *Umma* for our trivial concerns. Remember the punishment for disrupting the *Umma* is greater than for not performing Friday prayers. If Muslims gain the state of *Umma*, they can never be humiliated in the world. The power of Russia and America shall bow down to them. But the state of *Umma* will come only when Muslims abide by the command of "Lowly with the believer" (Qur'ān 5,57), namely, when each Muslim is lowly and humble to other Muslims. You have to practice this in missionary work. When Muslims have achieved the attribute of "Lowly with the believer," then they will be "Mighty with the unbelievers." They will be stronger against the unbelievers and will overpower them all, whether these unbelievers belong to Europe or to Asia.

My brothers and friends! Allah and His Messenger have strongly forbidden making statements that rend hearts asunder and that lead to disruption. If people begin whispering in groups of two or three, the Devil may create misunderstanding among the people. So this is forbidden and called Satan's handiwork.

> Secret councils are only by the Devil, in order that he may cause grief to the believers. But he cannot harm them except as Allah permits (Qur'ān, 58:10).

Similarly it is forbidden to ridicule, jeer at and deride others.

> Believers, let no man mock another man, who may perhaps be better than himself. Let no woman mock another woman, who may perhaps be better than herself (Qur'ān 49:10).

It is also forbidden to pry into someone's private concerns in order to find out unknown wrongs. It is forbidden to mention before others even the known wrongs of someone else. Backbiting is prohibited. Backbiting is defined as mentioning the real wrongs of a person to someone else.

> And spy not on each other, nor speak ill of each other behind backs (Qur'ān 49:12).

This ridiculing, derision, prying into privacy, and backbiting are all evils that create disunity and disrupt the state of *Umma*. All are prohibited. Respect each other and have regard for others because that has been emphasized. It is forbidden to demand respect from others, because it disrupts rather than unites the *Umma*. The *Umma* is formed only if each person resolves that he does not deserve respect. Therefore, it is not my right to demand respect but it is my duty to respect others. All others deserve respect and I must respect them and have regard for them.

Sacrificing selves and egos shall form the *Umma*. When *Umma* is formed, respect will be achieved. Respect and humiliation is not in the hands of Russia and America. It is in God's hands and He has rules and law for it. If a person, a nation, a family or a class follows the principles that promote respect, and acts upon them, God will promote them. Whoever performs deeds that are harmful to these principles, God will eliminate him. When the Jews, who are descendants of the prophets, did not follow these principles, God rejected them and disrupted their unity. The Companions of the Prophet, may God be pleased with them, were descendants of idol worshipers. But since they followed these principles God made them prosper. God has no relatives; He follows only principles and rules.

Friends! Devote yourself to the effort that the *Umma* of the Prophet, peace be on him, gains the state of *Umma*, and achieves faith and certitude; becomes an *Umma* that performs *dhikr*, *tasbīḥ* and *ta'līm*, that bows before God, that becomes a serving, forbearing, and respecting *Umma*. It does not become an *Umma* that derides brothers and colleagues, that pries into others' private affairs, and that backbites. If only one place begins to strive for this in the manner that it deserves, the whole world will follow.

Now you should strive to make people of different nations, regions and languages join in groups who abide by these principles. God willing, this effort shall lead to action in favour of a state of *Umma*. And God willing, the Devil the willful shall not be able to do it any harm.

Appendix II

Duʿā (Invocation, prayer)

Prayer in Tablīgh is a pedagogical device. It restates the basic tenets of Islam, Six Tablīgh Principles and Muslim creeds. Prayer at the close of an *ijtimāʿ* has special significance not only for Tablīghīs, but also for the general public. A large number of people, even those who are not part of the Tablīgh gathering, attend this event. In Pakistan, often the head of state and other high officials attend the prayer at the end of the annual gathering (*Ijtimāʿ*) at Raiwind. I have selected and translated the following prayer by Mawlana Muḥammad Yūsuf, who said it in the final session in Muradabad, held on 30 November 1964. (For a report on this meeting see Ḥasanī 1967, 353). The text of this prayer is found in Bijnawrī (1980, 249–257) and Ḥasanī (1967, 773–783). Bijnawri explains that this was reproduced from a tape recording. The prayer was said in two parts, Arabic and Urdu. The Arabic part consists mostly of Qur'ānic verses and *aḥādīth*. A careful reading of this text reveals some political overtones, and also concerns about communism, secularism, Jews and Christians.

After Salutations to the Prophet, peace be on him, the following prayer was recited loudly by Mawlānā Yūsuf, in Arabic.

Allah! There is no god but He—the Living, the Self-subsisting, Eternal [Qur'ān, 2:255].

Alif, Lām, Mīm. Allah! There is no god but He—the Living, the Self-subsisting, Eternal [Qur'ān, 3:1].

All faces shall be humbled before Him—the Living, the Self-subsisting, Eternal [Qur'ān, 20:111].

There is no god but You. Glory to You, I was indeed wrong [Qur'ān, 21:87].

O the only One, the Eternal, the Absolute, who begot none and nor is He begotten [Qur'ān, 112:2].

O the most Merciful! O full of Majesty, Bounty and Honour [Qur'ān, 55:27]!

O our Sustainer! Our Lord! Our Master! O our Creator! O the end of our desires! We have wronged our own souls. If you do not forgive us and do not bestow on us in Your Mercy, we shall certainly be lost [Qur'ān, 7:23].

O our God! Forgive us and turn to us Your Mercy, because You are the Oft-returning, Most Merciful [Qur'ān, 2:128].

O God! Forgive us. Have mercy on us. Pass by our ills that You know. Certainly You are the most powerful, the most kind.

O God! The Turner of hearts, turn our hearts to Your Obedience. O God! The Turner of hearts, turn our hearts to Your Obedience. O God! The Turner of hearts, turn our hearts to Your Obedience. O Changer of hearts, firm our hearts in Your Faith. O Changer of the hearts, firm our hearts in Your religion. O Changer of hearts, firm our hearts in Your religion. O God! Our hearts, our foreheads, the limbs of our bodies are in your hands; we do not possess them at all. Thus you do with us whatever you do. You are our Guard. Guide us to the right path.

O God! Show us the Truth correctly and support us to follow it. Show us Falsehood as falsehood and support us to avoid it. O God! Bestow on us Your Love, the Love of your Prophet, and the Love for those whom You like to be loved. Support us to perform deeds that bestow on us Your Love. O God! Make your Love the dearest of all things to me and make your fear the most fearful thing to me. O God! There is no comfort except what you have made comfortable and You can change difficulty into comfort whenever you wish.

There is no God but Allah – the Forbearing, the Generous. Glory is to God, the Sustainer of Great Throne. Praise is to Allah, the Lord of the worlds. I ask you for things that attract your Mercy and for the resolutions that attract your Forgiveness, for protection from every sin, return for every good deed, safety from every sin. Leave no sin of mine unforgiven, no worry unremoved, no distress unrelieved, no harm unlifted, no need that you have permitted unfulfilled.

O the most Merciful! To Yourself O Lord! Make us lovable. To ourselves make us humiliated. In the eyes of people, make us respectable. Protect us from bad habits. Support us in good habits. Make us firm on the right path. Help us against our enemies, Your enemies and the enemies of Islam. Help us O God! Do not help others against us. O God! Make us dignified, not desolate. O God!

O God! Increase us, do not decrease us. O God! Plan in favour, not against us. O God! Have mercy on us and do not empower over us those who are not merciful to us. O God! Open our hearts to Islam. O God! Make the faith dear to us and adorn us in our hearts. Make unbelief, sins and disobedience detestable to us. O God! Make us one of the rightly guided. O God! Guide us to the right path. The path of those whom You have rewarded, the Prophets, the Truthful, the Martyrs and the Pious. They are the best companions.

O God! Guide this *Umma* of the Prophet, peace be on him. O God! Teach them the Book and the Wisdom. O God! Reveal to them the right points in their affairs. O God! Make them inviter to You and to Your Prophet. O God! Make them firm in the faith of Your Prophet. O God! Support them to thank you for the Blessing that you have bestowed on them. Support them to fulfil their vows to you, which You have promised. O God! Support them against Your enemies and against their enemies. O God of Truth! Amen.

O God! Guide this city. O God! Guide this country. O God! Guide this government. O God! Guide all the people. O God! Guide all mankind. O God! Deal with the conspiracies of the Jews, the Christians and the Pagans. O God! Deal with those who are strong against Islam and Muslims. O God! Cut their reinforcement. O God! Take their power and their wealth. O God! Blunt their weapons. O God! Destroy them as you destroyed the people of ʿĀd and Thamūd. O God! Capture them in the manner of the powerful. O God! Expel the Jews, the Christians and the Pagans from the Peninsula of the Friend, Our leader Muḥammad, peace be upon him, the Peninsula of Arabia. [This sentence is repeated three times]. O God! Expel Judaism, Christianity, Zoroastrians, Communism and Polytheism from the hearts of Muslims.

O Master of Sovereignty! You give power to which You want, and take it away from which You want. You give strength to which You want and You humiliate whom You want. The good is in your hand. Verily you have power over everything. O God! Support the Muslims in the easts of the earth and the wests, with a just ruler and goodness and with obedience and following of the practices of the Leader of all the living. O God! Support them to do what you like and approve. Make their present better than the past. O God! Support Islam and the Muslims in the easts and the wests. O God! Make Islam and Muslims strong in Arabia and beyond.

O God! Make the word of Islam and Muslims supreme in India and adjacent countries. O God! Give us good in this world and in the Hereafter, and save us from the punishment of fire.

O God! We ask for Your Forgiveness and Protection, Success in this world and the Hereafter. O God! Make our end better in all affairs and protect us from failure in this world and from punishment in the Hereafter. O God! Have mercy on us by helping us to abandon sins forever as long as you keep us alive. O God! Help us to recite the Qur'ān, to remember you, to thank you and to improve our prayers. O God! Keep us away from evils, obvious and hidden. O God! Keep us, our children, our friends, our relatives, all missionaries (*muballighīn*) and students away from evils, both obvious and hidden. Keep us away from the forbidden, whenever and wherever and with whomever it is found to exist. Make a wall between such people and us. O God! We ask of the good that your Prophet Muḥammad, peace be on him, asked from You. We seek protection with you against the evil from which your Prophet Muḥammad, peace be on him, sought protection from You.

O God! We seek your approval and Paradise. O God! We ask you for Paradise and for the words and deeds that take us close to it. O God! We seek your protection against the Punishment of Hell, we seek your protection against Punishment in the grave, and we seek protection against the trial (*fitna*) of the Anti-Christ. We seek protection from the trials of life and death. We seek protection from places of sin and we seek protection with you against the death we find in retreating from your path. O God! Strengthen us as you strengthened Moses, peace be on him. O God! Strengthen us as you strengthened Moses, peace be on him. O God! Protect us as you protect a newborn. O God! Protect us as you protect the newly born. O God! Help us as you helped Muḥammad, peace be on him, and as you helped his Companions. [Repeated three times], O God! Give us good in this life and in the Hereafter. Save us from the Punishment of Fire. Our Lord! Forgive our sins, excesses in our affairs, strengthen our steps and help us against the unbelieving nations.

[The following recited in Urdu]
O God! Forgive our sins. O God! Forgive our errors. O God! We are at fault, we have erred, and we have committed sins. We are culprits. We have spent our whole lives indulging in our desires. O God! We kept the world before our eyes and were lured into it. We were attracted by its sight and became its seekers. We wasted all of our skills in its pursuit. O God! Forgive this great sin that we committed by distorting our efforts. Thousands of evils were created in us by this great sin. We lost the immense wealth existing within ourselves. O God! Distorting this effort in Your way is our great sin. We pray, forgive this great sin of the whole *Umma*. O God! Forgive this great sin of the whole *Umma* of the Prophet Muḥammad, peace be on him. We abandoned the efforts to which the Prophet Muḥammad, peace be on him, had guided us. We indulged in efforts from which the Prophet dissuaded us. O God! Distorting the direction of this effort is our greatest sin. We ask your particular forgiveness for this sin. Please forgive all those sins one by one, which we have committed by leaving the original effort. Forgive each of our acts of disobedience. Forgive each of our deviations.

O God! The way we earn our livelihood is the way of disobedience, our ways of spending are the ways of disobedience, and the way we live is the way of disobedience. O God! We are drowning in the ocean of disobedience. O God! We find no way out of this quagmire. How can a drowning person save himself? Only the One who cannot drown can save us. O God! We are all drowned. Only you can save us. O God! Save us from drowning in the ocean of disobedience. Save us by Your Grace, by Your Generosity. O God! Send to us your rope of Mercy and pull us out. O God! Take us out from the waters of disobedience and put us on the road to your obedience.

O God! Lead us to the summits of sacrifice. O God! Accept us for the efforts for religion. O God! Accept us all for the efforts for religion. O God! Accept the whole of *Umma* cent per cent for the effort for religion, for the effort for knowledge, for the effort for faith, for the effort for worship, for the effort for remembrance, for the effort for morals, for prayers, *ḥajj*, for fasting, for *zakāt*, and for the effort for all the obligations and rituals of worship to be on the pattern practiced during the days of the Prophet Muḥammad, peace be on him. O God! Support us fully in these efforts. O God! Eliminate malpractice in all departments of our lives. Eliminate malpractice in the ways we earn our livelihood. O God! Revive good deeds in our social life. O God! Eliminate malpractice in our social life. O God! Revive the deeds of justice in our social life. O God! Adorn us by good deeds. Save us from bad deeds.

O God! Since you have provided an opportunity to make effort for the profession of faith and prayer by means of this *tablīgh*, since you have enabled all our friends here to assemble together, to speak and listen to each other on your path, O God when you have provided a direction to this task, and have provided a direction to the movement for this task, O

God! Accept us all for the sake of your Kindness. O God! Train us all in a way that this movement earns your approval. O God! Train this order and movement with your Kindness. You are the Sustainer, You are the Trainer, You are the Purifier, and You are the Cleaner. O God! Accept this movement and revive the good deeds of earning our livelihood, eliminate the bad practices from our life at home.

[The rest of the prayer is said in a voice expressing extreme humility, intermittent with weeping and crying.]

O God! Bestow on us sincerity. O God! Bestow on us faith in Your Power. O God! Bestow on us faith and certainty. O God! Bestow on us faith in Your Promises. O God! Set our beliefs aright. O God! Instill in us the passion needed for this effort. O God! Create in our hearts love for the sacrifices that make human beings your friend, human beings that are made of a dirty drop of semen. O God! Extend your Grace that helped start this task to let it complete it. O God! Extract the love for this world from the hearts of those that have joined this task, extract from their hearts love for land and property, love for power. O God! Inculcate disinterest in their hearts from the plan (*naqsha*) of the world. Show them the reality of death. Bestow on them the wealth of sufficiency. O God! Give them the powers of sincerity, patience and struggle. O God! Give us the wealth of struggle that makes the inner self of human beings radiant and dazzle with your Light and Attributes, that opens the door to further promotions that human beings may reach the summit of virtues.

O God! The way You have started this work let it become a means of guidance for the whole world. O God! Make it a cause for the guidance for the whole of mankind, for all countries, and for all Muslims. O God! Accept our efforts for reaching all times, all nations and all countries. O God! Guide our companions, our relatives and friends of all of us, those who are engaged in this work. Give all of us the guidance that you give to the Mujāhidīn and to the *dāʿīs* (missionaries) and that you gave to Muḥammad, peace be upon him, and his Companions, the guidance and the sacrifice that you gave to the Prophet in the past and your friends. O God! Give us a full share of this guidance. O God! Fill our empty hands with your kindness. Fill our hearts with your grace, with your love. Issue to us a decree of guidance with your love. O God! Relieve us, the whole *Umma* of the Prophet (peace be upon him), from the hands of those who drag us astray from your path. O God! Transfer us to the hands of those who guide us.

O God! Relieve this *Umma* of the Prophet (peace be upon him) from the hand of the Jews, Christians, the pagans and the secular. O God! Make us to stand on the foundations laid by the Prophet Muḥammad, peace be upon him. O God! Correct our servitude, give us guidance, fill our hearts with the worth of Muslims and bestow upon our hearts your remembrance. Grant us disinterest in this world and give us guidance to live our lives according to the knowledge of the religion that we rely on. O God! Give guidance to all mankind; give guidance to the inhabitants of this country. O God! Give guidance on this path to the rulers and the ruled of this country, the minority and the majority of this country. O God! All human beings that are types of beasts and pythons and the humans that are predators and humans You have decided not to make humane, O God! Destroy them one by one, sundering their grounds apart; destroy their houses, take away blessings from them and punish them in such a way that the whole world witnesses the fact that whoever spoils his human nature, God changes his form and appearance. O God! Destroy all cruel and corrupt persons. O God! Give guidance to those whose guidance can render nations and countries guided. O God! Destroy those whose destruction will save nations and countries from destruction and corruption. O God! Bring injustice and cruelty to an end. Set up the environment of justice. O God! Be kind to accept these prayers of ours. O God! Let the loans of those who are in need among us be paid, fulfill the needs of the needy among us. Bless the sick among us with health. O God! Heal the eyes of those who suffer from illness. O God! Heal the illnesses of stomach. O God! Fulfill the prayers of all those who have made requests in this meeting. O God! Fulfill the needs of all those who have requested us to pray or who will request us in future to pray for them. Eliminate their worries. O God! Make this meeting the source of extreme goodness and blessing, guidance, favour, progress, welfare and success for all mankind and for the whole world. O God! Accept our prayers to your grace and kindness and accept with your grace those who have set their foot on your path. Amen.

CHAPTER TWO

TABLĪGHĪ JAMĀʿAT AND WOMEN

Barbara D. Metcalf

The Tablīghī Jamāʿat presents itself to outsiders with a wholly masculine face. A quietist movement of internal spiritual renewal, it is men who go from door to door in college hostels, men who approach other Muslim men to invite them to pray in airports, men who can be seen travelling in small groups by bus or train in Indian cities as part of their monthly or yearly sacrifice of time for proselytization or *Daʿwa*. It is men one sees in sub-continental cities, dressed in simple white loose pants, long shirt, and cap, modest bedding on their back, disappearing into a mosque where they will spend the night. Tablīgh originated in the sub-continent, but their networks now reach throughout the world, as this volume makes clear. What little has been written on these diverse movements invariably gives the impression that even in a movement so extensive, women barely exist.

It is, in fact, critics of Tablīgh who talk about women a great deal. Indeed, one sometimes thinks they talk of nothing else. In Westernized circles in Pakistan, for example, angry opposition is invariably articulated by criticism of what is taken to be Tablīgh "treatment" of women. Here are a string of examples:

A retired government official trained as a psychologist: "Tablīghīs treat women very harshly. A nephew of mine became a Tablīghī and basically starved and beat his mother. They treat their wives and daughters badly."

A professor, also a retired government official: "My neighbour, an active Tablīghī, went on a mission at the very time of his daughter's wedding. He was in Bangladesh and she was getting married. Who would leave at such a time?"

A Western-trained, university professor in his forties: "There was a case of a little girl abducted while her father was away on a tour. He would not even come back."

A young woman in development work: "In Karachi I went to condole with the widow of a close family friend. This was an open, pleasant family.... One of the sons, a bit older but always "*bhā'ī*" [brother] to me had become a Tablīghī. As I walked in he just walked out and didn't even speak to me. He keeps his wife hidden away. His mother said to me that now that this son was head of the family, she didn't know what would happen to her."

Opponents play on other themes. In Pakistan, some lump Tablīghīs with other religious groups and denounce all who would purport to tell people what is and what is not Islam. Others criticize Tablīghīs vaguely as lazy, fanatical, dirty and corrupt. More specific critics denounce their withdrawal from politics in favour of religious obligations at the cost of worldly affairs. But the theme that runs through many of these objections, and is particularly marked in the comments about women, is the assumption that Tablīghīs neglect what should be their basic responsibilities, whether toward their family or toward development. Thus, an MBA from Michigan State University (seated next to me on a PIA flight) grew angry on the subject of Tablīgh absenteeism; committed to economic growth and development, he would not give his subordinates leave to go on tour; when Tablīghīs came to his door "*mayn tālā lagā lētā hūn.* (I lock the door)."

A final comment from an opponent, not about women but articulating an issue of gender definition, strikes a somewhat different note. A journalist associated with the Jamā'at Islāmī (see Introduction, this volume) blamed Tablīghīs for corruption and for failing in their requisite duties. What bothered him most, however, seemed to be what he presented as gender confusion: Tablīghīs act female. He was distressed about the state of a friend's son, of particular concern since, he explained, his own son "had almost fallen into Tablīgh clutches." The friend's son, he continued, "now behaves abnormally. He acts like a Pakistani girl!" At this he bowed his head, pressed his knees together and folded his hands. "They become abnormal," he repeated. A colleague in the same office picked up the thread, speaking with more respect, but implicitly continuing the theme. "I have never seen a Tablīghī Jamā'at person lose his temper. This is astonishing given the way, for example, we used to react to them in the hostel when they would come around, especially during Ramaḍān, to invite us to come to the mosque. Normally, people in any religious sect will react very strongly if you oppose them." He was at once respectful and bemused. It is women who are supposed to be bashful, reticent, and non-confrontational.

That talk about women in relation to Tablīgh should be such a central theme is perhaps not surprising. Issues related to women have occupied a central space in public discussion of law and politics in Pakistan, particularly since the late 1970s. For many people, women have, quite simply, become a powerful public symbol of what Islamists call an "Islamic order." This is an extraordinary change in Muslim discourse, for while the control of women has always been important, the notion that women bear a special burden of embodying Islamic teachings and norms is new. An active, articulate professional class represented by movements such as the Women's Action Forum has, moreover, challenged the assumption that women should therefore be secluded and their activities highly constrained.

What, then, is going on in relation to Tablīgh? The question has to be answered along two lines. First, one must note that in contrast to the Jamāʿat Islāmī, for example, issues related specifically to women are in fact marginal in Tablīgh teachings and publications. There is nothing like the spate of publications on women associated with Mawlānā Mawdūdī or more recent writers like Sayyid Asʿad Gīlānī, one of whose texts I have elsewhere analyzed at length (Metcalf 1987). Second, despite their invisibility to outsiders, women are involved in Tablīgh and there are issues related to women that are specifically discussed. By exploring this participation and discussion, we can better address both the silence of Tablīghīs themselves on women and gender and, perhaps, the angry complaints of their critics in relation to women.

Women and Men in Tablīgh

The key teaching of Tablīgh enjoins proselytizing tours primarily on men. These tours are meant to transform participants in their fundamental relationships to other people, both men and women. We should not, therefore, be surprised that the resulting changes affect women as well as men. Rather than talk about "how men treat women," as the critics cited above ask us to do, we might simply look at some issues related to human interactions over all.

Tablīgh, as conceived by Mawlānā Muḥammad Ilyās (1885–1944), was meant to do nothing less than turn social hierarchy on its head. His movement assumed that any sincere Muslim could, by going out to offer guidance to other Muslims, in effect, undertake what had heretofore been the province of men distinguished by education, saintly achievement, and, often, notable birth.[1] That elevated role was, in a sense, to be confirmed by a range of protocols meant to foster a kind of mutuality and corporate identity in the experience of the tour.

To have any sense of how radical were (and are) the bases of human relations within the Tablīgh, one must recall the fundamental principles of Indo-Muslim society in which the Tablīgh took shape and continues to flourish. This society is defined above all by structures of subordination and hierarchy. From the earliest age both boys and girls learn the careful calibrations of age, gender, and birth, all displayed in a range of obligations, manifestations of deference, and expectations of respect in virtually every daily interaction. Children must learn forms of proper address and precise discriminations of grammar and diction in order to be considered well bred.[2] Boys are not only subject to the authority of elders within the family, but as they move into the public world they are expected to respond without question to the authority of teachers and spiritual leaders, authority commonly exercised through displays of corporal punishment and humiliation. Ultimately, the male will move into a role where these habits will shape relations to both superiors and inferiors in the workplace, where markers of status abound.[3] He will moreover expect and be expected to exercise authority over women in his household, at least over those junior to him.

What happens to such relations in the missionary tour? The tour consists of a *jamāʿat* of ten or so men who go out for an evening, a

---

[1] For the Indian origins of the movement see Ḥaq (1972), which is based on Nadwī (1983 [Urdu original written ca. 1948]). See also Troll (1985), which includes references to important Urdu sources. Also useful are articles in Lokhandwala (1971), especially Ziyaul Hasan Faruqi, "The Tablīghī Jamāʿat" (pp. 60–69), Mawlānā Saʿīd Aḥmad Akbarābādī, "Islam in India Today" (pp. 335–339), and Waheeduzzafar, "Muslim Socio-Religious Movements" (pp. 138–142). For the late nineteenth century origin of the Deoband movement, see Metcalf 1982.

[2] See Mawlānā Thanawī's *Bihishtī Zēwar* (Metalf 1991), first published at the turn of the century as a guide for girls and women to the reformist Islam that also produced the Tablīgh. The book is an excellent source for understanding hierarchy. See for example the sample letters in Book One, where a girl learns the appropriate diction for writing to superiors, inferiors, and equals; the content of the letters reviews such issues as appropriate names for elders and behaviour before them. At the same time the book points to the kinds of changes in transcending conventional hierarchy that the Tablīgh further develops.

The text is translated in Metcalf 1991.

[3] For a brilliant evocation of this hierarchic culture among the privileged *sharīf*, see Lelyveld 1978, chapter 2.

few days, or a prolonged journey. The tour is the occasion for a radical break with all the enmeshments of intense face to face hierarchies of family and work. That break allows the far-reaching change that was Mawlānā Ilyās's goal, for he was explicit that it was the journeyer, not the audience, who would be most significantly changed (Zakariyyā n.d.a., 23). Everything in the tour is meant to inculcate humility, not least the fidelity to prayer that renders a Muslim humble before Allah. Travel, moreover, encourages a state of permanent vulnerability and uncertainty in which, outside one's normal moorings, one learns to be dependent upon God. The humility, which is the movement's goal, is further encouraged by the priority given to proselytization so that each participant places himself continually in a situation that risks rebuff. He learns the limits of what he can do.

Beyond all this, however, a range of practices fosters a leveling among the participants, a leveling modified only by degrees of fidelity and faith. In a society, again, where dress is a clear mark of status and particularist identities, all Tablīghīs dress alike in the simplest garments. In a society where to open one's mouth is to betray the great hierarchic gaps in the society, above all that of English and vernaculars and, among the vernaculars, between elegant Urdu and simple language, all cultivate simple language. In a society that looks down on manual activity, everyone carries his own bag; everyone does the most menial tasks.

The very openness of the group further diminishes hierarchy. There are no criteria for membership or entry. Any Muslim who seeks to join is welcome in a way that is virtually unknown in highly institutionalized, highly stratified societies. No priority is given to intellectualism. Each member is seen to have the very same capacity for full participation by the simple step of embracing readily accessible teachings and committing himself to spread them. Each person by the virtue of being born a Muslim is assumed to be a potential participant worthy of respect.

Among those on a tour, the elimination of hierarchic distinctions is relentless. Decisions are made through a process of consultation known as *mashwara*. The group chooses the *amīr* himself. He ideally should be distinguished by the quality of his *īmān*, not by worldly rank: a peon can be an *amīr*. Indeed one senior full time worker in the Tablīgh in Pakistan, himself a retired civil servant, laughingly suggested it was better that a senior civil servant *not* be an *amīr* because then anyone of a higher grade would have difficulty accepting his leadership! There are echoes of Ṣūfī notions in the conviction that the least likely person may be one of the spiritual elect. Thus authority is, in principle, no longer based on outward attainments or birth.

Different roles are assigned to each member of a mission. Key to those roles, and to Tablīghī thinking generally, is the concept of service or *khidmat* (Qāsimī 1968, 14). Ideally, roles are shifted and a single person may act as teacher or preacher on one occasion but humble cook or cleaner on another. The movement's focus on divine reward motivates this service, as it does all else. Mawlānā Ilyās argued that to do service was in fact to attain two rewards, that of serving one's companions and that of freeing them to engage in Tablīgh (Zakariyyā n.d.a., 36). To cook and serve food, to nurse the ill, and to wash and repair clothes—all tasks male Tablīghīs learn to perform—are jobs particularly associated with women. Thus all Tablīghīs perform actions associated with the lower-born and with women.

Mawlānā Ilyās preserved in his papers the letter of a university graduate describing the *khidmat* of one *jamāʿat*'s *amīr*:

> [He] fulfilled his responsibilities as the *amīr* so well that we all felt very happy over it. I have not found any *amīr* of any *jamāʿat* more efficient and considerate. He looked after everyone's comfort throughout the journey, carried the luggage of others on his shoulders, in addition to his own, in spite of old age, filled the glasses with water at mealtimes and refrained from sitting down to eat until everybody had been seated comfortably, helped others to perform *wuḍū* on the train and drew their attention to its rules and proprieties, kept watch while the others slept and exhorted the members to remember God much and often, and did all this most willingly. For a person who was superior to all of us in age, social status and wealth to behave as the servant of everyone was the most unforgettable experience of the tour (Nadwī 1983, 150).

Tablīghīs ideally pay their own way: no one is patron and no one is dependent. Tablīghīs thus simply stand apart from all the elaborate transactional arrangements that organize so much of sub-continental societies (Metcalf 1994).

What about women? If the Tablīgh has flourished in societies known for their pervasive emphasis on hierarchy, it has also flourished in societies known for great attention to issues of gender. The Tablīghīs, like the Deobandīs generally, espouse an ideal of human behaviour, understood as that exemplified by the Prophet, which is gentle, self-effacing, and dedicated to service to others.[4] Men engaged in Tablīgh activity, whether rich or poor, are expected to develop a new way of relating to other people and a new standard of humility as exemplified in their learning to cook, wash their clothes, and look after each other. In that sense, the Tablīgh encourages a certain reconfiguring of gender roles, particularly in the experience of the missions. The gentleness, self-abnegation, and modesty of the Tablīghīs, coupled with their undertaking a range of activity associated with women's work, marks them as inculcating what may be core religious values but are also culturally defined as quintessentially feminine.

If men change, women change as well. Women, although expected to conform to rules of modesty and seclusion, are included in a common model of personal style as well as in a shared commitment to Tablīgh. The women enjoined as models in such cherished texts as the *Ḥikāyātus Ṣaḥāba* (in Zakariyyā 1928–1940) are celebrated for just what it is that men should also be: humble, generous, pious, scrupulous in religious obligations, brave in the face of persecution, and so forth. Moreover, just as men in the course of travel on missions experience some redrawing of gender roles as they cook and wash, in the same way women left at home may take on a range of previously male responsibilities. They sustain the household so that men can go out, thus earning themselves equal reward. As in reformist movements generally, women in this tradition are expected to become educated in religious teachings (Metcalf 1982; 1991).

Women are encouraged to engage in Tablīgh and to go out, so long as they do not mix with unrelated men. They are expected to engage in *Daʿwa* within their own sphere of women and family members.[5] Women's *jamāʿat*s do go out, accompanying their menfolk, but this is largely the exception. There are invariably *jamāʿat*s of women at the large annual meetings, settled amidst various homes where, as in one home I visited, furniture had been cleared out to allow for bedding to be spread on every side. Pakistani women described

[4] See the essay on the Prophet's character, given as a preface to a hundred tales of model women—in itself significant in that the Prophet is a model for women as for men—in Metcalf 1991, 255–258.

[5] See my introduction to Mawlānā Thānawī's *Bihishtī Zēwar* (Metcalf 1991), where I contrast this inclusive conception of women with the discussion of women by the Jamāʿat Islāmī, which elaborates a more differentiated view of women as "complementary to men" or even the "opposite sex."

visits not only from expatriates and other South Asians but even of women visiting from such distant countries as France.

Most important, and more common than such distant travels, are neighbourhood meetings for women which are occasions for the committed to assemble and for others to be drawn in. In some places these meetings are held daily; in others they are less frequent. Thus, although far less visible to outsiders, there is Tablīgh work for women, albeit on a distinctive pattern.

Two aspects of these activities are striking. One is that they offer an unusual opportunity for women to congregate. Among South Asian Muslims women are discouraged from even going to the mosque. Even in homes, they typically gather in large numbers only on occasions of marriage or death. Now in the Tablīgh they have regular occasions for congregational gatherings and common worship. In Karachi, for example, women meet on Fridays at the Makkī Masjid in the heart of the city for the hours between the noon and late afternoon prayer; when I attended a meeting there in July 1991 perhaps a thousand women were present. First a woman spoke, then a man (over a loudspeaker). The warmth, gentleness, and simplicity of the discourse was palpable as women were reminded of their responsibility for their own piety, for guidance to their family, and for support to those going out. In the final prayer, the speaker implored God for guidance, forgiveness, and mercy. Women listened, prayed, meditated, and, at the conclusion, chatted and visited as they gathered their wraps to depart. In these settings, certain women take on roles of leadership and guidance for others: "Doctor Āpā" in Bombay and "Āpā Qamar" in Karachi are well known. "Āpā," elder sister, suggests the simplicity of relationships and language that pervades the movement as a whole. As a "fictive" relationship, it suggests that leadership rests not on birth but on personal work and qualities.

In a sense, there are fewer differential opportunities for men in Tablīghī Jamāʿat than in more politically oriented movements because no one, neither men nor women, seeks out public roles in the society at large. If differences in public are made more comparable between women and men, so too differences may be flattened within the family. Tablīgh eliminates whole arenas of customary ritual and ceremonial life which have been the purview of women, all the customs and social exchanges characteristic of marriage for example. Participants in an annual meeting have described to me that marriages are celebrated there by proxy, dozens at a time. Marriage has typically entailed the enactment of elaborate interactions which bolster social relationships and interdependencies. Tablīghīs are, presumably, people who opt out of those social enmeshments.

Women's honour, then, would not be measured by how many and what sorts of people participate in ceremonies they organize, nor by the lavishness of the hospitality they offer. Instead, men spoke to me of the piety of particularly women, crediting them, for example, either directly or indirectly for involving them in the movement. Indeed, members of a *jamāʿat* of women whom I met were indignant when, hearing their stories, I suggested that it appeared that either husbands or fathers had introduced Tablīgh into the family. They insisted I was wrong and told stories of women companions who, like other women they knew, had first practiced true Islam and made sacrifices that ultimately influenced their menfolk. "Not that we are like them," they added:

> Our sacrifices of time, money, and leaving our children, sad as we may be, are nothing in comparison to them, and nothing in comparison to the opportunity we now have for uninterrupted obedience to Allah.

They told me of a woman who read aloud each night from the *Faḍā'il* collection of *ḥadīth* in the basic text of the movement (Zakariyyā 1928–1940; Metcalf 1993a) despite her husband's disdain. One night she did not pick up the book to read. Disconcerted, her husband asked why; she replied that she saw no reason to since he ignored it. He then commenced to read the book aloud himself.

Another touching story, told to me by the person involved, also exemplifies women's initiative. This man serves as the president of his local union as well as of his national federation. For several years his mother, to whom he was devoted, had faithfully attended a weekly women's *bayān* (discourse) in the movement's central mosque, and had frequently volunteered his name (as women are asked to do for their relatives) to go out with a *jamāʿat*. Because of the heavy demands and unpredictable hours of his job, he never went. In 1984 she died, and he took the loss very hard. His brother, a young man in his early twenties, was equally stricken, to the extent that his health declined and within the year he too was dead. At that point, this person, who had never been involved in the Tablīgh before (and was known, other people told me, as secular and a "leftist"), committed himself on the spot to go out for four months—and has never looked back, sustaining a full schedule of Tablīgh activities including leadership in the city council (*shūra*) of the Tablīgh, responsibilities for his large family, and his obligations as a labour leader.

As for relations among women and men, two people spoke to me of how the atmosphere in their household had improved due to Tablīgh. One young man, the father of two small children, criticized his society generally for widespread harshness, including physical punishment, toward children, and even suggested that in this respect behaviour in the West was more humane. In his own case, he felt that the personal traits he was honing in the Tablīgh had made his family life far more cooperative and harmonious. Another person said he was less likely to become angry with his wife, for example, over cooking, since he now knew how easy it was to do things like adding too much salt! The standard set for women's segregation from unrelated men, is, to be sure, rigorous.[6] But overall, one might expect greater mutuality between women and men. As relations based on status change, those based on gender change as well since the dominance of men over women is part of a larger hierarchical structure.

What of the issue of neglect and mistreatment of families and irresponsibility toward jobs? Participants present very different interpretations of their behaviour than do the critics. First, from his or her perspective, everyone should be engaged in Tablīgh. If women and children are an impediment to men in fulfilling this responsibility for men, men and children are equally an impediment for women. Mawlānā Muḥammad Yūsuf's (1917–1965) biography describes his frequent absences from his ill wife (Ḥasanī n.d.). But how is that absence interpreted? One recalls the spiritual forbear of many Tablīghīs, Mawlānā ʿAbdur Raḥīm Rāʾipurī, unwilling to let his dying son distract him from his disciples who had undertaken the *ḥajj* in his company (Metcalf 1982, 168). If one considers Rāʾipurī's life to be a positive model, Yūsuf's behaviour deserves praise, not condemnation.

Women should do no less. A talk given at an annual Tablīgh meeting thus reminded men that women also had a responsibility to Tablīgh and that men should not only not object to, but actually facilitate their participation, for example, by providing childcare (see Faust, this volume, observing the same point with reference to

[6] In the very limited circle of people I met, however, this did not preclude, for example, women attaining university level education or marriage of daughters to husbands settled in the West.

Germany). The speaker reminded his audience that the Prophet had said that women had the right to refuse to nurse should they want to; on that analogy, they certainly could decline to provide child-care for a task as important as Tablīgh.[7]

Mawlānā Muḥammad Ilyās is remembered as encouraging work among women from the very beginning. He turned first to the wife of one of the first Mēwātī students of the Madrasa at Niẓamud Dīn in New Delhi, Mawlānā ʿAbdul Suḥbān. She herself was "a very pious, pure, religious woman, adorned with purity, a person of understanding (*ṣāḥib-i fahm*) and judgement." She began work among women in Delhi, and, at Mawlānā Ilyās' instruction, formed a *jamāʿat* to go to Mēwāt, each member accompanied by a close male relative, a *maḥram.* Ilyās had sought the approval of other religious elders who were very worried that such activity was inappropriate and conducive to women's using Tablīgh as a pretext for license. He persisted, gradually winning the support of people like the respected Muftī Kifāyatullāh (Firozpuri n.d.b., 105–106; his *fatwā* is in Tirmidhī 1981, 8).

Women were to be lodged in a private dwelling where they would be secure. The rule was set from the very beginning that the house had to have an indoor toilet, a custom unknown in Mēwāt but now common, as one history writes "through the blessing of Tablīgh." As this example suggests, Tablīgh generalizes the customs of the respectable and perhaps the urban, here replacing the custom of nighttime trips to the fields with interior toilets. A recent pamphlet lists "conditions" and "principles" for women's work in Tablīgh, summarized below in an appendix.

Not only do women participate in Tablīgh, but also Tablīghīs would deny that women's interests are damaged when men go out. At the least, women gain merit for sustaining the household. When asked about their families, moreover, participants are likely to tell stories, like those collected in interviews by Muḥammad Ṭālib in this volume, that invariably tell of how at the very time that a participant absented himself for a tour, a family crisis—irresponsible children, an ill parent, a pending lawsuit—was transformed for the good. Clearly, critics and participants differ concerning what is in individual and family interests and what is the nature of family

[7] I am grateful to Syed Zainuddin, Aligarh University, for describing this and other experiences encountered when he attended a Tabligh *ijtimāʿ* in Dewsbury, June 1991.

responsibility. Tablīghīs do respond to some criticisms. Thus we find a work on issues of *sharīʿa* or normative codes related to Tablīgh begins with a letter from a revered disciple of Mawlānā Thānawī, Mawlānā Shāh Muḥammad Masīḥullāh Khān, setting for Tablīgh the same conditions as for *ḥajj* in terms of undertaking tours only if possible without debt or hardship to the family or other dependents (Tirmidhī 1981, 5–7).

By not idealizing women's domestic role, Tablīghīs, on the pattern of leading Deobandīs like Mawlānā Ashraf ʿAlī Thānawī, do not participate in the elaboration of a distinctive female specificity, characterized for example by a unique spiritual capacity and by a distinctive physical make-up. Modern Islamists like Mawdūdī share this latter perspective characteristic of broad trends in Victorian thought. Some Tablīgh writers seem to share it as well, utilizing a language of "opposite" or "complementary" sexes, with the woman as "queen" of the home and possessing a warmer, more easily influenced, temperament (Firozpuri n.d.b., 102–107; Metcalf 1991, Introduction). Nevertheless, the dominant attitude is in favour of emphasizing an essentially shared nature and shared responsibilities. Although this very preliminary essay suggests a uniform Tablīgh view, much more work is needed to differentiate attitudes about women on the part of Tablīghīs over time, as well as in regard to what may be different attitudes toward and interpretations of women's roles between women and men.

Talk About Women; Silence About Women

Finally, to return briefly to the question posed above: Why do critics talk so much about women, and Tablīghīs hardly at all? Given the distinctive ideals of behaviour held out by Tablīgh, it is perhaps possible to explain the anger felt by opponents in relation to women. In part, Tablīghīs pay the price for more aggressive Islamic movements and for governments that legislate Islamic norms. Tablīghīs are conflated with all those movements that tell other people what to do, even though Tablīghīs see themselves as the most gentle of reminders. Beyond that, however, Tablīghīs may be triggering more complex reactions, as the outburst about the "abnormal" Pakistani boy and the comments on Tablīgh passivity suggest. Some of the anxiety evident about the reconfiguring of gender roles in Tablīgh may come from people committed to greater differentiation between women and men. Such fundamental reconfiguring of gender roles, part of Tablīghī's larger devaluing of all that most of the society desperately seeks—wealth, success, rootedness—cannot but threaten those who stand outside. "Mistreatment of women" becomes a metonym for all that the simply dressed, non-instrumental itinerant implicitly undermines.

Why do Tablīghīs talk so little about women? Quite simply, the space given to explicit definitions of women's roles and women's natures expands to the extent that movements focus on the modern nation-state, and with notions of "citizenship." Jamāʿat Islāmī is a movement formed in concern for the institutions of society and state, a movement that examines Islam to find the principles of a social "order." From Mawdūdī (1939) to the present, the position of women and the nature of women have become ever more central, and women today are systematically depicted as essentially different from men and as playing a privileged spiritual role in the domestic sphere. These are ideas familiar from the Victorian West as is the very notion of "the opposite sex." Tablīghīs are not apologists; they are not interacting with the institutions of the state; they abjure all debates and do not even interact with other Muslim movements. They focus on practice, an arena where women and men are, fundamentally, on the same ground. Women ought to stay at home, but men, even while they travel the world, devalue the public realm, which they may enter. With the focus on practice and the depreciation of social forms, the lives of women and men in this movement overlap in significant ways. Eschewing society's social distinctions and ignoring the history forged in the quest for national identity in favour of a mythic history of pristine examples, Tablīghī silence on women's roles suggests the uniqueness of the story they tell, and attempt to live amid the competing stories and movements current in their societies today.

Appendix

Principles and Conditions for the Work of Women[8]

I. *Conditions*

1. Begin the work from houses where the women themselves are pious and eager for this kind of work or susceptible to being made eager.
2. Make arrangements for seclusion, even along the route to a home where there is a gathering for instruction. A *maḥram* should accompany the woman because this is an age of disorder (*fitna*).
3. If women form a *jamāʿat* to travel to another town, each should be accompanied by a *maḥram*, ideally the husband and, after him, the son, father, brother, maternal uncle, maternal grandfather, or some other *maḥram*.
4. A *jamāʿat* travelling away from home should be composed only of married women.
5. Go simply dressed, whatever jewelry or clothing may be in the house. Whether you are going to another house for a session for instruction or going on a journey, wear plain clothes and no jewelry except simple earrings. [The rule of simple, ordinary clothing also applies to men]. This protects you from danger.

II. *Principles*

1. The *amīr* of the women is the same as the *amīr* of the men.
2. The same council is responsible for consultation on the women's work as on the men's. The women should make some sensible woman their leader (*dhimmedār*) who can seek advice from the council through her *maḥram*. He can transmit her questions and communicate what is settled—just as in Madina the women chose Ḥaḍrat Asmā to be present with the Prophet. The details are given in the *Ḥikāyāt al-Ṣaḥāba* [in Muḥammad Zakariyyā 1928–1940].
3. Women should not give speeches.
4. Women should engage in book learning, reading and teaching the *Faḍāʾil* texts on Ramaḍān, *ḥajj*, *namāz*, *dhikr*, *tablīgh*, Qurʾān, and *Ḥikāyāt*. There is no particular order. The manner (*adab*) is to teach the texts respectfully and without long discussion. However experienced someone claims to be, and to have the last word from Haḍratjī, she should be silent. [Again, this is a rule that would also apply to men].
5. When a *jamāʿat* of women goes out, settle that each is accompanied by a *maḥram*. The *maḥram*s should regard this as an opportunity for themselves to follow the principles of the *jamāʿat* for instructions, rounds, and so forth. They should settle the women in a house inhabited by women familiar with the work. The house should have a bathroom or one should be built.

---

[8] Paraphrased and summarized from Muḥammad ʿĪsā Fīrōzpurī n.d.a., 107–111.

6. Make use of local men to inform the local women of the presence of the *jamāʿat.*
7. Use them again to spread word of their schedule, having arranged it with the experienced and responsible people of the place by means of the *maḥram.* If the local people are slow in getting the word out, summon them repeatedly, remind them, and work with them.
8. Organize a meeting of ordinary people (*ʿawāmm*), begin instruction, and encourage them to send their menfolk to meet the *jamāʿat.*
9. Have a talk at the end given either by one of the *maḥrams* or by some experienced local person to awaken the women's religion. Let them be told the reward of preparing their menfolk for sacrifice for the sake of invigorating religion. Then organize *tashkīl,* the identification of those who will make an effort to send their menfolks for Tablīgh. Women should write down the names of their menfolk, the time they should spend, the expenses they can meet, etc., and that list should be sent through a child outside to the men. At least four or five of the local experienced men should be present during this talk.
10. During the tour women should make arrangements to offer the canonical prayer, supererogatory prayer, Qurʾānic recitation, and litanies (*Namāz, Nawāfil, Tilāwat, Tasbīḥāt*) and to arise early so that they can pray for guidance for the *Umma* and all humankind.
11. Wherever they go, women should strive that local women make arrangements for instruction in their houses and, in consultation with the menfolk, hold a weekly *ijtimāʿ.*
12. This work on the part of women is easy but delicate. Women should continuously consult the *amīr* so that the many relevant rules are well known.
13. Women's meetings should be held in homes with suitable arrangements for seclusion. These should be homes where the women of the household are familiar with the work of Tablīgh, love the work and do it, and consider the opportunity to host meetings a kindness of Allah. They should be respectful to the sisters who attend. They should love simplicity. Remember that a woman's voice is also *ʿawrat,* a part of the body that needs to be concealed. For this reason in Tablīgh there is no permission for women to give a speech [but note reference in the essay above to women speaking in women's meetings].

CHAPTER THREE

CONSTRUCTION AND RECONSTRUCTION OF THE WORLD IN THE TABLĪGHĪ IDEOLOGY

Mohammad Talib

This essay explores Tablīghī ideology in the moment of its appropriation by selected Tablīghīs in the context of their societies. This sociological analysis delves into the terrain of consciousness wherein ideology mediates Tablīghī experiences of their world. The focus on mediation thus analyzes broad descriptions and evaluations charted in the entire repertoire of meanings and metaphors, images and ideas, emotions and affectivities pertaining to associations and attitudes of the Tablīghīs to the socially prescribed objects of meaning and attention.[1] As significant categories of Tablīghī consciousness, the repertoire is explored to provide the material for a dual construction of the world; first, a world which is representative of a Tablīghī's value-frame, and secondly, one which constantly negates it. While the latter is laid out as a moral critique of the world 'out there,' the former seeks to reconstruct it. Indeed, the unlocking of Tablīghī ideology for analyzing the construction and reconstruction of the world also explores how the process is circumscribed by the individual's encounters and experiences with the society in which he routinely lives. At the same time, we examine how the process unfolds as the individual struggles to intervene in the way the world exists, and to work out possibilities for such intervention, which the dominant society pre-empts by various concealments and constraints.

Preliminary Considerations

Before presenting the material, some consideration of research methods is in order. The research employed a qualitative method of

[1] This paper has benefited immensely, both theoretically and methodologically, from John R. Hall's insightful 1978 study.

participant observation; data was collected while participating in various activities of Urdu-speaking Tablīghīs who were randomly selected in various places in Delhi and U.P.

As the Tablīghī discourse is rich in metaphors, images and personal observations, the study employed what has been termed a mundane phenomenological method of free attention (Hall 1978, 247). The method requires a researcher to hold in abeyance any concern with formal tools of research and simply slip into roles and situations as they unfold during the course of Jamāʿat programmes. The method facilitated access to the ethos and culture which the Tablīghī ideology develops in the life of individuals in various segments of Indian society. The respondents selected for in-depth interviews were longterm Tablīghīs whose exposure to the ideology had been spread over a minimum of four *chillas*. They were also regular participants in the three-day *jamāʿat* that are organized every month in the mosques of their respective localities.

Any attempt to understand the Tablīghī world-view makes it an imperative to grapple with a more general epistemological problem of sociology. This is the difficulty in completely bypassing the phenomenological frame of the actor's orientation and representing the Tablīghīs' world in concepts and categories that are alien to them. The divergence between the truth that the Tablīghīs encounter, and the truth the social scientists seek to construct within the matrix of research, was sometimes so conspicuous that some Tablīghīs themselves expressed it in their own idiom. A general aversion to theoretical knowledge was once brought out succinctly: "Access to the truth we seek is routed not through *nuqūsh* (signs, knowledge) but through their *nufūdh* (implementation, practice)."

Another respondent found himself in a quandary upon being asked to share some experiences of the *chilla* from which he had just returned. "How do I tell you of my heart's heaviness and the restlessness of my soul?" he replied. In an instructive tone he added,

> Suppose you know nothing about an apple and someone describes it to you, then even the most brilliant description would tell you nothing about its taste. This is the weakest basis on which to develop one's faith. Here truth is news. In the trajectory of faith, it is known as *ghayr al-yaqīn* (faith bestowed by others). In the next stage you see an apple but haven't yet tasted it. Any description of its physical form would scarcely convey anything about how it tastes. The sight of an object is still far from the actual taste of it. Here truth is sight and the corresponding faith is *ʿayn al-yaqīn* (faith based on one's own observations).

> But in the ultimate stage, when one tastes an apple, one has a direct encounter with truth. Here truth is experience, and the stage is *ḥaqq al-yaqīn* (faith rooted in the direct encounter with truth).

The Tablīghī discourse ridicules and disparagingly rejects the dominant approach of understanding reality, which relies exclusively on "seeing is believing." The eye is limited to seeing the surface of an object, not its essence, its existing appearance and not its antecedent and ultimate reality. The eye cannot even see itself on its own. Obviously an eye cannot see anything in Allah's system, its angels, *ākhirat* (life hereafter), heaven, etc. A fetus's eyes cannot see what exists outside its mother's womb. A fish cannot see the world outside the pond. Similarly the things in Allah's system cannot be seen in this world but with eyes of *imān-wa-yaqīn* (faith and certitude) which are the only true eyes of a Tablīghī.

Observations and Descriptions

What follows is a brief presentation of the three studies of Tablīghīs encountered during the fieldwork, whose fluent discursive projection is comparable to the other respondents chosen in the sample. The first respondent is a small landowning farmer, the second a peasant-cum-carpenter, and the third a college teacher. The case study material is then integrated with observations and explanations collected from the remaining thirty-two respondents.

Case One: Abdul Azeem

Abdul Azeem [ʿAbdul ʿAẓīm], aged forty-five, is a peasant who owns approximately ten *bīghās* of land. He lives in a town called Azampur in Western UP. His ancestors were share croppers on land owned by the local *zamīndārs*, absentee landlords who monopolized ownership of land in a village. During his short life Abdul Azeem claims to have witnessed several upheavals and catastrophes in the little world around him. This gave him sufficient evidence to ground his faith in the omnipotence of Allah. He illustrated his argument by pointing out how the *zamīndārī* system produced landlords whose *ḥavēlīs* (palatial mansions), resources of wealth, servants and animals created an impression among people that their glory would never end.

> Do you know what happened over a period of time? As the *zamīndārī* system was legally abolished, their splendour burst like a bubble. Termites ate the wooden beams that supported the sprawling roofs, the walls collapsed under the weight of time. The real inhabitants of these dilapidated mansions are skylarks and bats. Doesn't this provide the required jolt to wake us up to the fact that the entire universe capitulates before Allah? We look for security in our land, material resources, family and business. But in the work of *Daʿwat* [*Daʿwa*] I have realized that my security lies in the deposits I make in the bank of Allah by working for *dīn* (through *gasht, chilla* etc.). This bank balance will never perish.
>
> Worldly resources that one possesses are either lost in the event of one's death or because of extravagance or misfortune. Every *paisa* (smallest currency denomination) that one spends in working for *Daʿwa* would multiply a thousand fold in the *ākhirat.* But if one goes there with empty pockets then one will really be in trouble as there will not be any means to earn wealth. What one spends on Allah's Will now are the true savings. Worldly resources (*māl*) never belong to anyone, these merely change hands. They are with me today; they will pass on to someone else tomorrow. They are never loyal to anyone. My real *māl* is that which I consume or spend for Allah. But my savings in worldly resources actually belong to their inheritors, usurpers or buyers. The interesting thing is that one laboriously accumulates wealth for those with whom one would not willingly share even a *paisa.* The irony is that one maintains an account of one's expenditure, but leaves it unaccounted for those who appropriate it after one's death. One saves due to a lurking fear that if one spends now one may need it against some greater exigency tomorrow. This fear is due to a disbelief in Allah, for one doesn't realize that He who sustains today will protect you tomorrow as well.

Abdul Azeem recalls the immediate precursor to his decision to go on a *chilla.* In those days he had lost a patch of land in a dispute with his brother over its ownership. In a state of depression, he met the *amīr* of a visiting *jamāʿat* to the village, and he told him how he had been robbed of land through a legal procedure, brought by his brother, no less. The *amīr* patiently listened and asked him: "How much land do you expect to receive in the *ākhirat,* the land that no one can steal?" Abdul Azeem quickly followed this logic and discovered during the *chilla* a world that he had not known so vividly. "Until then I believed in Allah's will, but my practice never reflected it. Moreover, in a short span of two years, after I began working for *Daʿwa,* I was able to buy four more *bīghās* of land. On the other hand, my brother suffered several family losses. Had Allah not been responsive enough? All that I can say is that He protects me from those who intend to harm me through no fault of my own."

I asked Abdul Azeem whether if by spending so liberally on Allah's will, he would not deprive his children (three sons and three daughters) of some of his savings. I suggested to him that a minimum of material support is necessary even for protecting one's *dīn* from the illusions of the world. "Have you thought about your children's future?" was my final question. Abdul Azeem remained unruffled, but paused a little before answering my battery of questions.

> I pray to Allah that they inherit from me what I lack so conspicuously. This is the wealth of character and morality which makes one distinguish between the legitimate (*ḥalāl*) and illegitimate (*ḥarām*). I can leave behind Qārūn's [Biblical Korah] treasure, but without knowledge of this distinction it can be squandered in just a few days time. But mere knowledge of the distinction is not enough; to observe it in practice with an alert mind is a more difficult proposition. Earning one's wealth through *ḥalāl* doesn't automatically guarantee that one will not spend it on *ḥarām* things. A *ḥalāl* purpose, such as building a house, may became a point of deviation where the same house absorbs the owner in its cosmetics to such an extent that one's attention is deflected from thinking and working for Allah. Prayers demand a heart emptied of the anxiety for worldly affairs. Owning too much in worldly resources implies owning too many anxieties. They worry you with numerous engagements and diversions. Perforce the time one ought to spare for one's *dīn* slips away.
>
> I am struggling hard that my children should be familiar with Allah's dictates and Prophet Muḥammad's life. If they practice what they teach, they will lead their lives without penury or dependency. I'll show you in my own village a number of people who were pauperized in no time, for they inherited material wealth alone, without *dīn*. Leaving behind *dīndār* (possessing *dīn*) progeny is better than leaving *māldār* (materially wealthy) progeny.

In a reference to the "future" in my question, Abdul Azeem commented that if one pursues the world for its own sake then one has no future. Nobody gets more in life than what fate ordains. But those who covet the world find their hearts filled with numerous engagements and diversions that perennially make them suffer from deprivation.

> If you own one mango grove now, you will feverishly strive to buy another tomorrow. If you possess one mountain of gold today you will burn your blood to secure two in the future. Is there an end to it? Yes, in one's death. It is the mud of the grave that satisfies the limitless hunger for material wealth.

> The real future lies not in the present world but in the *ākhirat*—a world whose life is perennial and where pleasure and fulfillment are real. The world and *ākhirat* are each other's counterpoints: like two co-wives they compete in seeking the common allegiance of their husband, the believer. The believer usually finds himself in a quandary. If one is kept in good humour, the other is automatically displeased. They are like the two pans of a balance. If one tilts downward, the other goes upward. They are like the two directions—east and west. If your proximity is to the east, you'll naturally be distant to the west. Like water and fire, they cannot coexist in a common heart. It is the strength of one's *īmān-wa-yaqīn* which enables one to recognize that the pleasures of the world contain the pain of this world as well as the *ākhirat*.
>
> The person who defines the ultimate purpose of life as the earning of material wealth constantly labours for it, and fills his heart with thoughts and plans to accumulate more and more. Such a person suffers from a perpetual fear of sliding into pauperism and deprivation. His earnings appear to him ever more insignificant. But if *ākhirat* is one's real purpose, then Allah bestows upon such a person an emotional poise that cleanses the heart from worldly worries. For such a person the conditions of his life and security become organized on their own, so that the world hankers for acceptance before such a person.

This relates to the belief that a person's quota of subsistence is preordained, and neither increases with extra effort or decreases with withdrawal. Like death at an appointed hour, the unalterable quota of life sustenance seeks the person.

This interview, which took place in installments, ended at a time when *ʿIshā* prayers (the last prayer of the day, an hour after sunset) was drawing nearer. Abdul Azeem instructed his sons to attend to the cattle (a pair of bullocks and a buffalo). He also allotted to them the duty to water the fields from the tube-well of the neighbouring landlord in successive shifts during the night. The children showed some reluctance to remain awake for part of the night. But there was hardly any option, for the supply of electricity for agricultural purposes was timed the same as *tahajjud* (between *ʿIshā* and *Fajr* prayer). The children were cajoled, and subtly coerced, into accepting their duties. And, at least for this little segment of reality, Abdul Azeem accepted the containing reality of the world in toto, and coerced his own children to do the same.

Case Two: Azam Ali

Azam Ali [Aʿẓam ʿAlī] aged forty-eight, hails from the small town of Rajabpur in Western U.P. He owns five *bīghās* of land, which supports his family's needs in vegetables, cereals and pulses. Ali's carpentry shop earns him money for clothing, house repairs, medicines, and also allows him to partake in exchanges and social reciprocities within the *birādarī* (clan).

When he decided to join a *jamaʿat* for one year, he closed his carpentry shop. It took him almost ten months to prepare himself before he could implement this decision. Surely, it was Allah alone, Azam Ali confessed, who enabled him to leave his home against multiple odds. His eldest son, Rashid, twenty-one years old, was a school drop-out, and was generally irregular in earning money for himself, even through unskilled work. Only when local orchards owned by big landlords were ripe in mangoes or guavas could Rashid make a living for himself by selling fruit in the neighbouring market. Two more adolescent sons were studying in a *madrasa* about five kilometers away from Ali's home. Ali laments that his sons are not mature enough to shoulder family responsibilities.

What made Ali become a regular participant in the Jamāʿat programmes? Ali always found in them reinforcement and elaboration of his religious convictions. The Jamāʿat people were exceptionally simple and sincere in their dealings. On being probed as to whether a year's absence from home was a loss to his family, especially when the children were still economically dependent, Azam Ali replied with equanimity that it was, on the contrary, a veritable gain. He explained that there was no other way to awaken his sons to their responsibility toward their family, their own life and above all the *ākhirat.* Ali recalls how his family was stunned when he declared his decision to invest one year to work for *Daʿwa.* The eldest son dared to ask him who would look after them, as the carpentry shop would be closed. Ali replied, no one but Allah. Ali read out to me a letter from his eldest son telling him how well his family was now doing. His sons were growing vegetables and wheat on their land. Neighbours were being especially considerate whenever their help was required. His son ended the letter by assuring him that everything was fine at home and requesting him to pray for the family and suffer no anxiety regarding matters at home. Ali explained in low whispers how Allah is always responsive to believers who sacrifice for Him. He added, "If you walk towards Allah, He runs to receive you (to protect you). Isn't it astonishing that my sons matured in my absence and learnt to be more responsible toward the family." A simple calculation is eluded, but the laws of the world and those of the *dīn* are remarkably different. He further added that working in the path of Allah is mandatory, as we are all indebted to Him for our being blessed so lavishly in so many ways. At this point, I ventured to ask Ali if his material condition was not a poor example of Allah's blessings. I further added that only a rich person had grounds to thank Allah for the blessings, not those who are living from hand to mouth. Clearly, Ali was unimpressed with a question that revealed my naivete regarding this complex matter. He clarified without offending:

> One needs to have an eye imbued with *dīn* to discern thousands of blessings that shower over living beings all the time, but which generally go uncounted. Even such blessings, as deep sleep, fresh water and uninterrupted breathing deserve gratitude. And these are common to both the rich and the poor. On the last judgement day, we will be held accountable if the piece of bread that satisfied hunger, the water that quenched thirst and the clothes one wore to protect the body have been received without gratitude to Allah.

Ali surmised that the world around us confuses us between what we need for survival and what we want as a resident in the world (i.e., the social group to which one belongs). The world, being morally degenerate, makes us want goods and resources which add to our conceit and make us so haughty as to forget Allah. We are constantly made to feel poor amidst plenty.

Ali confided how his association with the work of *Daʿwa* made him richer, since he could now cater to all his needs as well as his wants. This pronouncement of Ali required further examination, as, on the face of it, there seemed little sense in it. On further prodding to explain how he attends to all his wants, when he neither has abundant material resources or moral approval, Ali remarked wittily, "I attend to all of them by requesting some to wait for another day." He added, "Sometimes, I borrow from immediate needs to attend to a given urgency. I prefer this to borrowing from the *mahājan* (local money lender)." He gave the instance that on the wedding of his daughter he had extended a simple hospitality to the *bārāt* (bridegroom's kinsmen and friends), contrary to the standard set by the *birādarī* and other community elders. In the heat of criticism, people did not even spare Ali's association with the work of *Daʿwa*, stating that this had made him selfish and stingy. He could not convince them that he was answerable to Allah if he borrowed money from the *mahājan* to promote his pride, but he prayed to Allah, beseeching Him to change their hearts and asking for forgiveness if he had erred in the matter.

Case Three: Afaq Ahmed [Āfāq Aḥmad]

Afaq Ahmed, aged forty-two, has two daughters and one son. Afaq has been a regular participant in the programmes and activities of Tablīgh for the last ten years, and is a college teacher in a small town called Muradnagar in Western U.P. This brief sketch is an account of a small gathering consisting of Afaq's neighbours and colleagues, all incidentally Muslims but outsiders to the Tablīgh movement. Afaq was asked a number of questions by his fellow teachers about the Tablīgh movement, pertaining to their doubts, and their desires for clarifications and explorations. Afaq Ahmed's responses recapitulate the predominant beliefs and practices of a serious participant of Tablīghī Jamāʿat who confronts the world through the mediation of Tablīghī ideology.

Afaq was all too happy to be interrogated by his friends, since he felt that the doors of *hidāyat* [*hidāya*, guidance] might open at any time for anyone and, who knows, a person sitting in the gathering might receive it during their discussion. He was asked to explain why he spends so much time and money on Tablīghī activities and yet does not send his daughters to a good public school. They commented that the wife and children of a Tablīghī always suffer from the frequent absence of the family head. They added that were he to send his daughters to a public school it would cost him so dearly that he would soon forget his Tablīgh. Afaq replied that if it were really so, he would prefer not to forget Tablīgh. But the matter was deeper than its surface appearance conveyed. Afaq explained, "The public schools help induct pupils into the world at large and to be successful in every sphere of life. But have we ever thought about the nature of this success? It consists of a persistent acquisition of status, power and material wealth. But what would you do with it after you die?" Afaq further added,

> Whatever you accomplish in this world has to perish. But the life of *ākhirat* is never going to end. The choice is open to a wise man to run after shadows or to pursue real objects. This world is, for me, like a waiting room of a railway station. As soon as the train (death) arrives, I will have to board it. It would be folly on my part to forget the incoming train and instead involve myself in the decoration of the waiting room—to clean the room, put its furniture in order, purchase

> a wall mirror and an exquisite hanging picture. But where is my luggage and how do I board the train without any preparation? The train has to leave and my luggage is scattered. This is the plight of most of us when death knocks at our door. We are unprepared to receive it.

Afaq then recalled the original strand of thought and said that he is sending his daughters to learn Qur'ān, *Namāz* and other fundamentals of Islam. Only when the basic foundation of *dīn* has been laid may they be sent to school, private or state-run.

Afaq further asserted that it was not true that the time he spent in organizing and attending Tablīghī Jamā'at activities made his family suffer. On the contrary, his wife shared with him his concern to build an atmosphere wherein it becomes easier to abide by the dictates of Allah and Prophet Muḥammad's tenets for leading one's life. This concern is kindled each day when, after *'Ishā* prayer, the entire family listens to excerpts from *Faḍā'il-i-A'māl*.

Afaq was then asked if, through his belief, he is not turning himself into a recluse, given his contempt for wordly success. The questioner supported this query with an observation that Afaq forbids his daughters to attend birthday parties in the colony or cultural programmes organized by the college students and teachers. Afaq replied that most birthday parties provide a setting to display conceit and status as well as consumerism. Similarly the cultural programmes promote vulgarity and blind submission to degenerate culture. Above all, these events all invariably clash with the Tablīghī schedule of *Namāz* and recitation of Qur'ān.

Afaq did not agree that he was contemptuous of the world and its splendour or that he was turning into a recluse. He explained this by evoking a metaphor:

> Worldly successes and riches are like a venomous snake. If a person is skilled in handling it, he can extract its venom and to convert it into medicine to cure ailing people. But if the snake is handled clumsily, the person will be killed instantly and perhaps others within range of the venomous bite. Worldly status and wealth are like lush vegetation, pleasant to the senses only if lived in according to the restraints prescribed by the *sharī'at* [*sharī'a*]. But if the world is acquired without heed to Allah's dictates, then such a person will resemble a glutton who fills his stomach without the slightest sense of fulfillment.

Afaq Ahmad paused a little before extending the theme he had meticulously built:

> One must bear in mind that worldly riches and status are not intrinsically evil. Indeed, they have a number of merits and are instrumental in fulfilling various worldly and religiously pursuits. But in so far as they carry a streak of venom, one finds that the Qur'ān and *ḥadīth* usually admonish the believer to avoid indulging in them excessively. As it is difficult to walk across water without wetting one's feet, similarly one cannot pursue worldly successes and riches without contaminating oneself with the sins it breeds.

Another question thrown at Afaq was regarding his callous indifference to his father's ailing condition when he had left for four months in Malaysia with a *jamāʿat*. Furthermore, they said, he had spent ten thousand rupees on his travel expenses but hardly a *paisa* on his father's medical expenses. Afaq replied that his friends had heard of his father's ailment but not of his immediate recovery as soon as Afaq left for his Tablīghī tour. This recovery was so amazing and contrary to the doctor's expectations that Afaq considered it *ghaybī madad* (divine help). Afaq did not wish to make public mention of the ten thousand rupees, but surmised that even ordinary teachers in decorating their toilets usually spent a similar amount. With ten thousand rupees he was building a house in the *ākhirat*, a house whose spaciousness and comfort is unfathomable in this life.

> What we build in this world, a house, bank account, status, or name, are ephemeral. They are like vigorous and shining flora that grow during the monsoon, but then all of a sudden, due to some acute seasonal change, disintegrate completely, their particles scattered hither and thither at the mercy of a wandering breeze. Only a person grounded in *īmān-wa-yaqīn* knows that worldly status and riches are simply brief passing glories. What survives until *ākhirat* are a person's virtuous deeds, and they alone should provide the foundation for one's hopes.

Afaq finally commented,

> The ten thousand rupees are also being used to build a sanatorium on the earth, a moral order whose climate will attract the battered and tattered people who are suffering the wrath of God in the form of affluence, power, progress, and communication. In this sanatorium they will regain their lost spirits. This sanatorium is being built by thousands and millions of people, labouring day and night in the work of *Daʿwa*. The people in the sanatorium will love each other. They will work with pleasure, and sleep with contentment. No work will halt, no problem will grow. If a person has had an opportunity to rest under its trees for just an hour, he will refuse to return to the material world, which will look like a cobweb to be cleared.

Discussion & Analysis

The three case studies represent but three instances wherein Tablīghī ideology mediates and intervenes in particular settings. In the process, the general principles of the ideology, while addressing themselves to differing social and cultural scenarios, are concretized. A Tablīghī in this respect plays a crucial role as a mediator who appropriates the general categories of ideology, and invests new meanings in the objects and objectivities of a given situation. At the same time, the wide array of meanings and metaphors, symbols and signs, encounters and experiences pertaining to the microcontexts are also appropriated, to be classified and catalogued around the new templates of a Tablīghī world-view. The experiences of the common Tablīghī invite us to understand how the ideology, which is codified in texts (such as books, speeches, articles, booklets and audiocassettes), mediates the individual's encounters with his microworld. It is at this level that the general ideology comes into contact with an already organized social order and cultural setting, with a given constellation of objects of meaning and attention. The Tablīghī ideology, at this moment of appropriation, mediates insofar as it offers general principles to describe and evaluate the existing modes and manners of production and reproduction of the conditions and possibilities of life.

The three cases differ considerably with respect to three different narratives evoked in response to three not-so-similar sets of questions. Nevertheless, the three cases reveal rather vividly the underlying commonalities of principle and precept around which the world is encountered and experienced. The Tablīghī ideology is an intervention, insofar as it offers an alternative blueprint to reconstruct society through a radical remoulding of the individual. This is manifested in a common concern to forge a moral alternative at various levels of belief and practice.

While drawing upon the experiences of the three cases for the purpose of analysis, we shall weave in related material and observations collected from a total of thirty-five Tablīghīs interviewed at the *markaz*, in the setting of the *jamāʿat*, in the mosque after the *bayān* or *taʿlīm* following *ʿIshā* prayers, and at their respective residences. Most of the respondents reside in U.P., while the rest are settled in Delhi. They have many ancestral places of origin, such as Bihar, Orissa, Assam, West Bengal and Kashmir.

For many of these Tablīghīs, joining the work of *Daʿwa* has involved a major shift from life's compulsions and associations. The acquired way of life is a change in a broader sense, but in its details the shift consists of rejections and modifications of various components of one's existing way of life. There is somewhere in the mind of the believer, discursively expressed or silently lived, a long dialogue with the life which he now seeks to review and alter. The world outside the fold of *dīn* is morally disdained. The world's power and grandeur are grotesque and false, yet they present themselves to people as objects of ultimate concern. Abdul Azeem tells us how absentee landlords, despite their access to wealth and splendour, quickly became paupers. His brother, who became rich in land after winning it through litigation, eventually became impoverished. Ali's absence from his home, despite his being the only breadwinner, was a veritable gain to his family. The world's claims are unwarranted, its promises illusory. The security it posits in wealth, status and power seldom protect people from the states of penury, dependency or death. The world is deceptive insofar as its enchantments are never accessible to people. It is pursued for its own sake, it turns people into gluttons. A sense of fulfillment always eludes people in their achievements. The world could scarcely be worthy of much concern. It may be a waiting room but never the ultimate destination. The illusory appearance of inevitability and permanence bears no relationship to the tragic outcomes which confront people every now and then.

During the course of fieldwork, certain images of the world were recorded. The respondents appropriated these images from the standard texts of the Jamāʿat entitled *Faḍāʾil-i-Aʿmāl* (Zakariyyā 1990) or *Ḥayātus Ṣaḥāba* (Yūsuf 1960). But in their projection, these were not formal quotations made conscious of their location in the text. Rather, what seemed to impress the respondents most vividly was the appropriateness of the images in embellishing realizations of the Tablīghīs vis-a-vis their encounter with the world. The images provide the narrational and moral presentation of reality, out of which, in the subsequent derivation, the moral alternative is constructed. These images offer a medium for the Tablīghīs not only to organize their perceptions but also to express their moral disapproval toward that world which is routinely lived outside the fold of *dīn*. What follows are some selected images that particularly struck me for their salience and intensity of communication:

i) The world is a house of dishonour where the destiny of a settlement is destruction, its inmates enter their graves alone, its solidarity suffers from dissensions, its spaciousness breeds poverty, its abundance survives on labour, and its penury begets pleasure.
ii) The world deceives its lovers by decorating itself with a colourful costume. And, like the bride on the first nuptial night, it casts its spell on her lover to captivate his soul. But beware—this bride is a different one because it poisons its lovers in their trance. It kills them as it has so many of its lovers in the past.
iii) Prophet Muḥammad once came across a heap of garbage where stray bones and human skulls were rotting amidst decaying waste and tattered pieces of worn garments. He explained to his followers that the garbage heap was the world's ultimate destination. He elaborated that these skulls had once nurtured a mind that aspired to conquer the world. The human excreta, which now repelled, had once been colourful cuisine prepared with great pains, its aroma evoking a craving in people. The tattered costumes had once been worn by people to enhance their conceit. The bones were those of the horses upon which rode arrogant warriors. Surely, the world is not worthy of being held as a pinnacle of all concerns and desires.
iv) On the day of Qiyāmat (Resurrection) an old, hideous woman, condemned to hell, will be brought before people. Her eyes will carry a cruel tint and her crooked teeth will project outward. People will be told that she is (the personification of) the world.
v) In a diagrammatic presentation of the plight of man in this world, Prophet Muḥammad drew a square, which was divided by a line in the middle. This line extended a little outside the square. A number of small horizontal lines were shown emanating inward from the vertical walls of the square, ending half way to the middle dividing line. The middle dividing line represents the man in the world, surrounded by the four lines of the square that are his death. The little protrusion at the top of the square is his tall hopes, which attempt to outlive death. The incomplete horizontal lines are the trials and tribulations that constantly surround the individual without letting him escape. The *Umma*'s well being, according to the Prophet, lies in its faith in the *ākhirat* and disaffection with the world. Its degeneration would emerge from its unlimited aspirations for worldly honour and privileges.
vi) The plight of man-in-the-world is constructed through a com-

> plex imagery. A man is portrayed as one who, being chased by a lion (death), seeks refuge by holding onto a branch of a tree. But he is staggered to find that the branch bends over a pond where several crocodiles (graves) wait for prey with their mouths wide. The branch as a lifeline is being hollowed out by a woodpecker (ailments and anxieties which reduce life). The man hanging from the branch suddenly forgets his agony, as he tastes a drop of honey that falls from a beehive (worldly allurements) on the treetop. The world assumes attraction only in the moment of forgetfulness of the ineluctable damages, which can be repudiated by a systematic preparation (abiding by *imān-wa-yaqīn* during one's life) for the *ākhirat.*

The abominable images[2] of the world are certainly not an invitation to prepare oneself to renounce the world. They merely caution the believer that a constant vigil is required during one's engagement in the world to eke out a living. To stay inside its portals beyond the necessary time is to let oneself be captured by the world's deadly ways. A true believer stays in the world like a wounded patient who abides by the medical prescriptions (maintaining distance with the world) for quick recovery and swallows bitter medicine (engaging in the world strictly for survival) to pre-empt the spread of his disease.

Absolute trust in Allah's succour equips a Tablīghī to safely navigate the dark and deceptive alleyways of the world. A total submission to Allah's will not only bestow huge reserves of strength but also other resources which hitherto lay unrecognized and unrealized, such as deep sleep, or uninterrupted breathing. When a Tablīghī seeks Allah's proximity through a sincere observance of mandatory prescriptions (*farā'iḍ*) and *Nawāfil*, then such a believer is chosen as His beloved. In the state of love, Allah becomes the ear of the believer, his eyes, hands and feet. And if he supplicates he is blessed, and if he seeks shelter he is duly protected.

But Allah also puts one to a trial in order to ascertain if a blessing reinforces faith in the divine or promotes self-conceit. Similarly, in a condition of protracted suffering the person may complain of

---

[2] Editor's note: These images of the world and the general theme of the abomination of worldly attractions appear to have entered Tablīghī thought from its Ṣūfī background.

being degraded, as though he expected a better treatment. Only a true believer will realize that just as neither wealth nor status indicates honour, nor does a shrinking of resources prove one's degradation.

One Tablīghī's father suffered from a terminal cancer but this made the son turn to the *farā'iḍ* and *du'ā*, and he received from Allah an immense contentment of heart. Without this blessing, the family would have had to contend with two patients. Another respondent, a schoolteacher by profession, and the only breadwinner of his family, finds himself among family members who are extremely hostile to his engagement with the work of *Da'wa*. In an otherwise spacious apartment, he is relegated to a small room. But he is not alone in the room. With *Namāz, Tilāwat, dhikr* etc., he relates to Allah, and in turn, to a world larger than the one in which he lives physically. Although the world places many odds before a Tablīghī when he sets out to labour for *dīn*, Allah intervenes with a *ghaybī madad*, and the believer finds himself equipped with such mental and physical powers as to enable him to repudiate the adverse conditions. After all, there are innumerable instances in the experiences of a Tablīghī to warrant that, if one walks towards Allah, He runs to receive you. Afaq Ahmad found himself in a tight corner in choosing between spending money on a *chilla* and bearing the medical expenses of his father's serious illness. Allah was supplicated and was rapidly responsive. The Tablīghī could now opt for *chilla*, as his father recovered without medical treatment. In another instance, a Tablīghī reports that a *jamā'at* staying in a certain mosque in Bhopal found themselves untouched by the poisonous fumes that spread after the gas leak in the local carbide factory in December 1984.

In their intervention in the world, the Tablīghīs do not seek to struggle for control of the larger institutions and apparatuses to implement their programme of reconstruction. One worker in the fertilizer industry commented that the politics of the trade union were un-Islamic, as the union either aroused emotions or suppressed them. In the work of *Da'wa*, emotions are shaped and given a direction.

The Tablīghīs, however, do not propose to retreat from the world into a hermit-like existence. Instead, they engage in a moral struggle against the established order by living out a blueprint of an ideal life through the programmes of the Jamā'at. The basic concern of a Tablīghī is to demonstrate that the world can be "saved" from the fire of Hell if it becomes organized around the dictates of *Dīn*. A *Dā'ī* (a person engaged in *Da'wa*, a Tablīghī) acquires a true self-image while engaging in the work of *Da'wa*, and becomes conscious of the tremendous reserve of resources at his command. This point was explained by invoking the story of a lion and a donkey that were brought up together without knowing who they themselves were. One day, as they strayed to a nearby river, the lion sighted his image in water. The moment he sensed that he was a lion, he instantly pounced upon the donkey to tear him into shreds. The Tablīghī evoked another story to extend this metaphor to explain what will happen to the world when the lion wakes up to its true identity: all the false lions will be driven into oblivion. The Tablīghī explained that the false lion here refers to the donkey that is wearing the skin of a dead lion but considers itself a true lion. The reference is to a tradition in politics which seeks to draw false strength by capturing state power or other institutions in society (the dry skin of a lion) as a precondition for reconstruction of the world. But without working hard for *dīn* (an internal strength), the *Umma*, despite its growing numerical strength, will become like the foam of an ocean, lifeless in content. And if such a state continues then the *Umma*'s enemies will invite each other to devour them as though they were sitting near a *dastar khwān* (food table).

By their discursive presentation of experience our respondents intend primarily to familiarize the listener with Tablīghī ideology. It may also be a part of the recurrent exercise of building up an atmosphere for the reinforcement of conviction. But one is constantly reminded that the tongue is not as reliable as the body, which practices faith. After all, the exhortations and the expressions which the tongue conveys represent only the outer crust of faith. Ultimately, the reality to which faith refers is to be attended to in its own right, as primordially given and experienced in practice. It is this aspect of Tablīghī ideology that deepens into the province of emotions, affectivity, and body language. Tears are a more reliable sign of one's communion with divinity than an appropriately chosen expression. A *duʿā* interspersed with intense emotional outbursts by listeners is closer to the marrow of true worship than a forceful *bayān* which renders the audience spellbound. If a *duʿā* is a hair-raising experience, accompanied by a vigorous pounding of the heart and a copious flow of tears, then these are considered sure signs of acceptance by Allah. The oral narrative of Tablīghī ideology is replete with anecdotes and associations that convey the importance of tears in one's communion with Allah. Through tears the discursive content of ideology acquires existential moorings. One *ṣaḥābī* (a companion of the Prophet) is said to have been weeping while supplicating: the tears that rolled down his eyes carried a tint of blood. When asked about the agony that struck him so deeply, he replied that this was his repentance for not fulfilling his duty toward Allah. The blood in his tears ensured that they did not deceive and were truly authentic. A woman saint wished to weep during prayers till her eyes dried up of tears. And then her tears would roll in blood till her body drained out its last drop.

Conclusion

The conversion of an individual to Tablīghī cosmology is at the same time a transformation of his world. A *Dāʿī* fathoms pathways where there are none in the picture puzzle of the world, and declares certain confident routes to be either blind, as they lead you nowhere, or simply non-existent on the acquired map. In the communion with the divine, the Tablīghī discovers resources amidst acute scarcity, receiving solace which until then had lay shadowed under the bulk of a protracted anxiety. He experiences a sudden enlargement of life when it is actually shrinking in given spaces.

In an altered perception a Tablīghī inhabits the same world but with a radical difference. The world is now imbued with different attributes, new connections are forged, new exigencies recognized. The world is transformed in the eyes of a Tablīghī as it undergoes a massive rechannelling of signification into areas hitherto unrecognized and unregistered. Certain objects stand shorn of their meaning, while new constellation of objects are created.

As the Tablīghīs construct new meanings and alter their attention, the existing relations of the objects around which the world's wealth, status and power are predicated also stand altered. This involves a holistic change in cognition so that conventional ways of seeing the world are transformed. Similarly, the system of priorities and problems, obligations and options, which the society had harboured also undergo a dramatic change. A Tablīghī prepares a different timetable and recognizes different objects of relevance. His altered economics is no less conspicuous than his altered emotional commitments.

A conversion to Tablīghī ideology is an alteration in subject-object, signifier-signified relationships. It involves a cataclysmic change in the orientation of the signifier as well as a modification in the constellation of objects signified. The insistent world of power and prospect, of projects and projections, which virtually monopolizes the allegiance of human beings, is symbolically deprived of its efficacy.

The withdrawal of meaning from the world's province of status and power, the creation of new vistas in *Dīn-wa-Īmān*, a reconstruction of one's life according to the divine dictates and Prophet Muḥammad's precepts, are not merely a passage from one configuration of ideas to another. This is an intellectual journey. A little deeper into ideas is the substratum of conviction and faith, of passions and emotions. There are no better signs of one's encounter with truth than the tears that roll down one's face. Weeping during *duʿā* manifests and indeed epitomizes a gradual kindling of realization of certain deformations and deviance which one's life nurtured and abetted, yet quickly concealed from public view and personal reckoning.

When meanings are partially or wholly revoked, believers' perceptions are altered not only in ideas but also in their affective content (Sartre 1948).[3] The world that commanded major passions is now rendered an emotionally neutral reality. The strong affective charge of power and privilege, riches and resources, life and its longings is neutralized. The facticity of the world, which punctuated the script of the believer's life, its space and time, its priorities and possibilities, is constricted to an affective minimum. And, by the same token, the world's urgency is apprehended as though it can be interchanged, regarded as equivalent to exigencies and reference points which the world seldom recognizes but which become apparent to a disciplined and seasoned Tablīghī.

Faith manifests itself not only in projecting affective signification upon the world it constructs—it lives in the new world that it has just established. But this living is not marked by alienation, depersonalization or coercion. Submission to the Tablīghī way of life is preceded by a local history of wandering, of anguish, of an unsettlement which life experienced but which the soul could rarely articulate. With such a background, allegiance to faith was a step toward a settlement, a resolution. The believer's volition is so profound that the entire being, not merely a tiny fragment, participates in its network. It does so with such a passion and in such a manner that the attributes which the believer imparts to the world, and the qualities and standards which he has set up, are further enriched. The new world

[3] In analyzing the emotions in the Tablīghīs experiences this study draws upon Jean-Paul Sartre (1948).

is established with the deepest and most inward part of the believer's self. The new world resides as much inside of as outside of the believer's soul. This is the world which presents itself to, and is in turn derived from the believer, without distance or detachment.

Post Script

The sociological construction of the world in Tablīghī ideology employs at length the discursive narrative of the respondents' experiences or their involved reading of stories, and the complex of imageries from the Tablīghī lore. Occasionally, the narrative is interspersed with glimpses of social contexts which circumscribe the Tablīghīs' encounter with social reality, which exist independent of their ideological projection. This mode of representation portrays the moral construction of the world as it is and as it ought to be.

Further research is required to analyze those contexts of Tablīghī lives which limit and constrain the world projected by them. Moreover, the Tablīghī ideology is limited by the ongoing world-construction by other traditions of Islam. Tablīghīs are "looked at" by those who share their social space but not their ideology. This nonsharing is expressed in forms of indifference or serious disagreement and even opprobrium, and generates phenomenological processes that deserve study. A researcher seeking to explore Tablīghī ideology should also unravel the complex mediations (sacred or secular) which have a bearing upon practice. Surely, ideological claims are seldom consummated in conformity to the wishes of the proponents. A Tablīghī exists in a state of constant interaction with realities which enjoin different theories and practices. Other reality-defining agencies as well as constructions of the "world" compete with each other for Tablīghī attentions. When a Tablīghī endeavours to walk straight, the researcher must depict the various undulations of the pathway. Similarly, when a Tablīghī appears to listen to a "single drummer," the researcher should adequately portray the polyphony in the ideological voices with which he engages. We should work to portray a process, and not a product.

CHAPTER FOUR

IDEOLOGY AND LEGITIMACY

Muhammad Khalid Masud

Uses of the terms "revivalism" or "fundamentalism" lead one to believe that what is being revived are well-defined ideologies, principles, fundamentals or doctrines. But in fact the ideologies presented by the revivalist or fundamentalist movements are new constructions, and that is why their legitimacy is contested like any other ideologies. This chapter examines Tablīghī Jamāʿat's ideology from this perspective.

The Tablīghī Jamāʿat claims to revive the method of Tablīgh practiced by the Companions of the Prophet in early Islam, and Tablīgh literature justifies its ideology with reference to the Qurʾān and *ḥadīth*. Others have questioned this claim. This chapter first reviews the development of Tablīgh ideology with reference to the Tablīgh literature recommended by the Jamāʿat. It then summarizes the criticisms of this ideology and of the views of the Jamāʿat elders concerning various issues.

Viewing the Tablīgh literature, one cannot fail to conclude that the ideology of the Tablīghī Jamāʿat developed gradually from first, a general idea of religious duties (as defined in Mawlānā Ashraf ʿAlī Thānawī's books) in the early period, then to a socio-political programme (as reflected in Mawlānā Iḥtishāmul Ḥasan's writings), and finally to a spiritual revival of Muslim religious consciousness (as reflected in Mawlānā Zakariyyā's Niṣāb). There has been no official statement of ideology by the Jamāʿat itself. There is, however, what we call the Tablīgh literature. This includes, first, books written about the Jamāʿat by people associated with it. Second, there are a number of books that have been recommended by the Jamāʿat to the Tablīghīs for reading sessions. Third, there are available statements and letters by the movement's three *amīrs*. In addition, public speeches of the elders of the Tablīgh are available as books and audiocassettes. The following reconstruction is based on these sources, and I shall briefly introduce them before discussing their contents.

The Tablīgh Literature[1]

Mawlānā Ilyās was not in favour of writing about the Tablīghī Jamāʿat, probably because he believed that action and practice were the best methods to effectively change minds. Tablīgh was a matter of action. He also refrained from publicizing the Jamāʿat in the newspapers (Ilyās 1952, 48). The Jamāʿat believes that media cannot effectively change minds as it tends to project only what is customarily intelligible. Mawlānā Yūsuf explains that,

> It is necessary to avoid usual (*riwājī*) channels like newspapers, advertisement and the press for the publicity of this work, since the customary words cannot properly describe this significant work. This is an extraordinary work. The media, as an ordinary means, tends to reinforce the current ordinary customs in the society. It cannot explain this extraordinary work. The true forms of publicity are *gasht, taʿlīm,* and *tashkīl* (Ḥasanī 1988, 731).

Literature was nevertheless needed for study sessions (*taʿlīm*) and instruction for Tablīgh novices. In the beginning, the Jamāʿat used Mawlānā Ashraf ʿAlī Thānawī's *Ḥayātul Muslimīn* (Thānawī 1982), Muftī Kifāyatullāh's (d. 1952) *Taʿlīmul Islām* (n.d.b) and Mawlānā ʿAbdush Shakūr Lakhnawī's *ʿIlmul Fiqh* (Lakhnawī 1965), but they did not serve the purpose of the movement, probably because they focused too much on details about the code of life and laws. Until 1940, there was no prescribed syllabus for the Tablīghī Jamāʿat.

Several scholars associated with the Jamāʿat, like Mawlānā Iḥtishāmul Ḥasan Kāndhalawī, Mawlānā Abul Ḥasan ʿAlī Nadwī, Mawlānā Manẓūr Nuʿmānī, Iftikhār Farīdī, Mawlānā ʿĀshiq Ilāhī Mīrathī and Mawlānā Muḥammad Zakariyyā, began writing about the Jamāʿat and its teachings. Mawlānā Ilyās still preferred Mawlānā Ashraf ʿAlī Thānawī's books (see Introduction). He particularly recommended his *Jazāʾul Aʿmāl* and *Rāh-i Nijāt,* which spoke about the life hereafter and the basic duties of a Muslim. He also included Mawlānā Muḥammad Zakariyyā's *Chihl Ḥadīth, Faḍāʾil-i Namāz,* and *Ḥikāyāt Ṣaḥāba* (Ilyās 1952, 28, 92) which, although not specifically written for the Jamāʿat, were useful for motivational purposes.

Had Mawlānā Ilyās's letters been dated, we could establish the chronology of his recommendation of these various books and the

[1] English translations of citations from Urdu in this chapter are mine.

varying foci of subjects during this period. It appears that the lists of recommended books varied. First Mawlānā Thānawī, and then Mawlānā Zakariyyā and Mawlānā Iḥtishāmul Ḥasan, were his favourite authors. Two treatises, *Muslim Degeneration and its Only Remedy* (Kāndhalawī 1939) and *Faḍā'il-i Tablīgh* (Zakariyyā 1928–1940) by Mawlānā Zakariyyā, came to be recommended as essential reading for Tablīghīs (Ilyās 1952, 40). As other writings of Mawlānā Iḥtishāmul Ḥasan and Mawlānā Zakariyyā became available they replaced the older books, and finally Mawlānā Zakariyyā's books were adopted as the Tablīgh curriculum, with only *Muslim Degeneration* retained from before.

Mawlānā Abul Ḥasan ʿAlī Nadwī edited and published an annotated selection of Mawlānā Ilyās's letters under the title *Makātīb Ḥaḍrat Mawlānā Muḥammad Ilyās* (Ilyās 1952), and several editions of the *Makātīb* have appeared since. Mawlānā Manẓūr Nuʿmānī recorded the various statements of Mawlānā Ilyās during the last years of his life and published them under the title *Malfūẓāt-i Ḥaḍrat Mawlānā Muḥammad Ilyās* (Ilyās 1960). Similarly, Iftikhār Farīdī published a selection of Mawlānā's letters and statements in *Irshādāt wa Maktūbāt Bānī Tablīgh Ḥaḍrat Mawlānā Shāh Muḥammad Ilyās Ṣāḥib* (Ilyās 1989).

A selection of Mawlānā Yūsuf's letters were edited by Ayyūb Qādirī and published as *Muraqqaʿ Yūsufī* (Yūsuf 1967). Selections and extracts from speeches and statements by Mawlānā Yūsuf, Mawlānā Inʿāmul Ḥasan and other Tablīgh leaders are also available in their biographies, small booklets and on audiocassettes.

Mawlānā Iḥtishāmul Ḥasan wrote six books in a series under the title *Tabligh Kiyā Hay* [What is Tablīgh?] in 1944, while Mawlānā Ilyās was still alive (Kāndhalawī 1962), but they were published only later. The series consisted of the following books: *Islāmī Ẓindagī* (Islamic way of life), *Iṣlāḥ-i Inqilāb* (Reform of revolution), *Payām-i ʿAmal* (Call to action), *Dīn-i Khāliṣ.* (Pure religion), *Musalmānōn Kī Mawjūda Pastī Kā Wāḥid ʿIāj* (Muslim degeneration and its only remedy), *Iṣlāḥ-i Muʿāsharat: Asbāb-i Fasād Awr ʿIlāj kī Tadābīr* (Social reform: The causes of social corruption and ways of its treatment).

Mawlānā Muḥammad Zakariyyā wrote a series of books entitled *Faḍā'il-i Qur'an* (1929), *Faḍā'il-i Ramaḍān* (1930), *Faḍā'il-i Tablīgh* (1931), *Ḥikāyāt-i Ṣaḥāba* (1938), *Faḍā'il-i Namāz* (1939), *Faḍā'il-i Dhikr* (1939), *Faḍā'il Darūd* (1960), *Faḍā'il-i Ḥajj*, *Faḍā'il-i Tijārat*, and *Faḍā'il-i Ṣadaqāt.* He explains that he did not write the *Faḍā'il* series for the Tablīghī Jamāʿat. The first books written for this specific purpose were *Faḍā'il-i*

Tablīgh, and later *Faḍā'il-i Namāz*, both composed at the behest of Mawlānā Ilyās (Zakariyyā n.d.f, 196).

Tablīghī Niṣāb

The Jamā'at did not at first authorize publication of these books officially. Subsequently, however, the books written by Mawlānā Muḥammad Zakariyyā were officially adopted. They were collectively published under the title *Tablīghī Niṣāb* (Curriculum for Tablīgh); the first collective edition under that title was probably published in two volumes in 1955, and another in one volume in 1958. Metcalf (1993a) has emphasized the need for studying the chronology of the publication and translations of these texts.

The title *Tablīghī Niṣāb* was changed in 1985 to *Faza'il e-A'maal* [*Faḍā'il-i A'māl*] (The merits of practice). Some Urdu editions also include Mawlana Iḥtishāmul Ḥasan's treatise *Musalmānōn kī mawjūda pastī kā wāḥid 'ilāj*. All of Mawlānā Zakariyyā's Faḍā'il books were not, however, included in the *Niṣāb*. It is significant that the Delhi 1986 English edition of *Tablīghī Niṣāb* contained translations of the *Faḍā'il-i Ḥajj* and *Faḍā'il-i Ṣadaqāt* (Metcalf 1993a), but these were excluded from later editions. Similarly, *Tablīghī Niṣāb* (1983 Karachi reprint) included *Faḍā'il-i Darūd*, which was excluded from the English version of the collection because some Deobandī scholars in Pakistan decried its inclusion (e.g., Sakharwī 1987, 67).

The first English translation of the *Tablīghī Niṣāb* appeared in 1960, and a revised edition was published in 1980 by the Kutub Khāna Fayḍī, in Lahore (Raiwind). These translations were published in Delhi under the title *Teachings of Islam* (1985). A third revised edition was published in 1985 as *Faza'il A'maal.* The 1987 Karachi edition is a reprint of the 1985 Kutub Khāna Fayḍī edition. This same edition was reprinted in Dewsbury, England and in South Africa. A further revision in simple English was published in 1995 under the same title. The 1985 edition has also been translated into French, but French and Arabic speaking Tablīghīs often use Nawawī's *Riyāḍus Ṣāliḥīn* instead (see Tozy, Kepel, this volume).

Translation is a crucial process in the transmission of transnational messages. Concepts, vocabulary, style and content are all adapted and transformed in translation. The Tablīghī literature, most of which was written in Urdu, retains its Indian background, the town-based worldview, and Madrasa idioms in translations. The English and French idioms, grammar and style used in these translations, mostly produced by Tablīghīs themselves, often seem unfamiliar to native speakers (see Kepel, this volume), and this limits transmission to readers of that background (see Azmi, this volume).

One could even speak of the *Faḍā'il-i A'māl* as ethnic literature. The cultural worldview of this literature, even when translated, is ethnically limited. In that respect, it is not even South Asian. It is very much conditioned by the local cultural environment of the UP towns in which the authors lived. They were content with premodern life patterns and ideas, and they regarded modernity as a way of life hostile to them as *'ulamā*, and, therefore, a threat to Islam. They believed that modernized Muslims had forsaken them for worldly progress. These themes also predominate in their speeches and writings.

Faza'il A'maal *[Faḍā'il A'māl]*

Tablīghīs were advised to carry the edition of this work published in Raiwind, Lahore by Kutub Khāna Fayḍī (1980) with them on *tablīgh* tours (Bulandshahrī n.d.b). A photo offset copy was published as the first Pakistani edition in Karachi by Dārul Ishā'at in 1987 under the title *Faza'il-e-Aamal.* This "official edition" (Karachi 1987) comprises the following books, which are not paginated sequentially.

1. *Stories of Ṣaḥāba* (Mawlānā Zakariyyā's *Ḥikāyāt-i Ṣaḥāba*, translated by 'Abdul Rashīd Arshad, 272 pages). This book contains stories of the Companions of the Prophet, focusing on their strong moral characters. They are described as role models for Muslims. The following characteristics, which are also chapter titles, also allude to the qualities required of a Tablīghī: steadfastness in the face of hardship, fear of Allah, abstinence and self denial, devotion to prayer, piety and scrupulousness, self sacrifice, valor and heroism, zeal for knowledge, obedience to the Prophet, and love for the Prophet. The last three chapters narrate stories of women and children among the Prophet's Companions. Their inclusion in the book reminds the Tablīghī of the importance of including one's family in one's religious life.

The book employs a special style of storytelling that is probably in the tradition of *quaṣṣāṣ* (traditional storytellers), *wa'z* (sermons) and *tadhkīr* (reminders), where a story is followed by a discussion of its morals.

2. *Virtues of the Holy Qur'ān* (Mawlānā Zakariyyā's *Faḍā'il-i Qur'ān*, translated by 'Azizud Din, 120 pages). This is a selection of forty *aḥādīth* on the merits of the Qur'ān. It explains the etiquette of reciting the Qur'ān, merits of memorizing the Qur'ān and the role of the Qur'ān as an intercessor on the day of judgement. One section discusses the Qur'ān's impact on the rise and fall of nations. Citing the *ḥadīth* that God raises certain nations and demotes others with the Qur'ān, the author comments that those nations that translate the teachings of the Qur'ān into action are elevated in this world and in the hereafter. Those who disregard the book are ruined. The angels pray for the person who reads the Qur'ān and abides by it (Zakariyyā 1987, 557–558). The author explains that the Qur'ān protects its reader from various afflictions and calamities.

3. *Virtues of Salaat* (Mawlānā Zakariyya's *Faḍā'il-i Namāz*, translated by 'Abdul Rashīd Arshad, 112 pages). This book consists of *aḥādīth* describing the merits of prayer, sanctions against those who do not pray, merits of congregational prayer, devotion and concentration in prayer, and stories from the lives of the pious. The author follows the style of *ḥadīth* books, narrating the sayings of the Prophet and providing the last person in the chain of narrators going back to the Prophet. At the end of the narration he gives the sources of the *ḥadīth* and its status of authenticity. After citing the Arabic text of the *ḥadīth* and its translation, the author adds his own comments.

4. *Virtues of Ẕikr* (Mawlānā Zakariyyā's *Faḍā'il-i-Dhikr*, translated by Shafīq Aḥmad, 265 pages). This is a selection of Qur'ānic verses and *aḥādīth* about the merits of *kalima*, the formula of faith, and other formulae and phrases with which to remember God. Three chapters deal respectively with the merits of remembering God, Kalima Ṭayyiba, and the third *kalima*, namely the formula to glorify God. This book touches on numerous subjects favored by the Ṣūfīs. It contains mostly *aḥādīth* that provide incentives for reciting these formulas. The author comments that these formulae are easy to remember and to repeat, and that people waste much time in trivial chats. Shopkeepers as well as farmers can recite them without difficulty while doing their daily work and thereby earn invaluable wealth in the hereafter.

5. *Virtues of Tablīgh* (Mawlānā Zakariyyā's *Faḍā'il-i Tablīgh*, translated by Maẓhar Mahmood Qureshi and Khawāja Iḥsānul Ḥaq, 48 pages). This book, written in 1931 by Mawlānā Muhammad Zakariyyā at the behest of Mawlānā Muḥammad Ilyās, was designed, according to the title of the 1977 Urdu edition, to discuss "the significance of *tablīgh*, its rules and etiquette, and the duties of preachers and other people". At the top of the title page is an extract from a *ḥadīth* commanding believers to convey what has been received from the Prophet, even if it is a single verse. Listing seven Qur'ānic verses and *aḥadīth* relating to *tablīgh*, Mawlānā Zakariyyā discusses the subjects of self-reform, Muslim honor, sincerity, faith and self-criticism, respect for the *'ulamā*, and finally the importance of keeping company with pious people as part of the conception of *tablīgh.*

Mawlānā argues that *tablīgh* is not the duty of the *'ulamā* alone—every Muslim is obliged by the Qur'ān and *ḥadīth* to carry on *tablīgh*, enjoining good and forbidding evil. One need not be a competent scholar to be a preacher, one must only convey to others whatever one knows of religion. However, he urges Tablīghīs to keep company with *'ulamā*.

6. *Virtues of Ramadhan* (Mawlānā Zakariyyā's *Faḍā'il-i Ramaḍān*, translated by Maẓhar Mahmood Qureshi and Khawāja Iḥsānul Ḥaq, 80 pages). This book deals with the merits of Ramaḍān, the month of fasting, the historical significance of the month, and the practice of the Prophet, his Companions and other pious people during this month. There are special sections about fasting and two other rituals relating with Ramaḍān: *Shab-i Qadr*, the night of power, the night of the revelation of the Qur'ān, and *i'tikāf*, reclusion in a mosque during this month. The author's style is quite emotive and he employs poetry frequently to express his feelings.

7. *Muslim Degeneration and its Only Remedy* (Mawlānā Iḥtishāmul Ḥasan Kāndhalawī's *Musalmānōn Kī Mawjūda Pastī Kā Wāḥid 'Ilāj*, translated by Malik Haq Nawaz, 48 pages). This book addresses the problem of Muslim degeneration, traces its history, diagnoses the cause, and describes the method of *tablīgh* as a course of action to solve the problem.

Development of the Tablīgh Ideology

Mawlānā Muḥammad Ilyās

As we have said earlier, Mawlānā Ilyās had a statement prepared for the Jamʿiyyatul ʿUlamā-i Hind meeting in 1943. Ilyās (1985) explained that *tablīgh* (*Daʿwat, Daʿwa*) was important religious work that also guaranteed worldly welfare and progress. The ongoing debates among Muslims in India during this period raised the question whether progress and welfare was possible through adherence to religion. Some Muslims believed that progress was possible only by modernization of society and education.

The concepts of "progress" and "perfection" (*taraqqī* and *kamāl*) were popular subjects of discussion in the twentieth century. It was generally believed that the West had achieved the perfection and that progress meant following the ways of the West. Mawlānā analyzed these concepts and explained that the Muslim concepts of perfection and progress differed from those of other people. Prophet Muḥammad was the model of perfection, and progress lied in imitating his model.

Mawlānā explained progress as two levels of achievement: individual, and social or collective. Individual progress called for abiding by the laws and prohibitions prescribed in Islam. Collective progress meant the empowerment of society as a whole. According to Mawlānā, collective progress was achievable only by *Daʿwat*.

Mawlānā warned, "While enjoining others for good and forbidding evil, it is essential that in the beginning only those goods and evils are targeted which are agreed upon, upon which there is no dispute. Disputed and conflicting matters must be avoided" (Kāndhalawī 1962, 13).

There were two approaches to collective progress. First, to capture worldly power and achieve progress by the force of the government. This is not the method of the Prophets. The second approach was to follow the Prophet's model by first reforming the individual life. Mawlānā believed that "God in His Grace helped and guided him to this plan of action that is derived from the model of the Prophet and his Companions" (Kāndhalawī 1962, 16).

Mawlānā Ilyās, therefore, stressed *Uswa-i Ḥasana* (Prophet Muḥammad's life as a model for perfection and progress) and *sharīʿa* as the only way to progress. He insisted that the Muslim concept of rise and fall is quite different from, indeed opposite to, that of other peoples (*aqwām*). Progress for a Muslim lies only in his remaining faithful to Islam, and not in following other peoples. Mawlānā developed a plan of action that consisted of the method of *tablīgh* and basic principles, as discussed in chapter one.

Mawlānā Iḥtishāmul Ḥasan

It is difficult to distinguish between the ideas of Mawlānā Ilyās and Mawlānā Iḥtishāmul Ḥasan because the latter explained that *Payām-i ʿAmal* was in fact Mawlānā Ilyās's statement. It was first published as Mawlānā Ilyās's statement, but later Mawlānā Iḥtishāmul Ḥasan published it under his own name. Its contents are also repeated in his other books, for example, *Musalmānōn kī mawjūda pastī*. One therefore concludes that these are indeed Mawlānā Iḥtishāmul Ḥasan's ideas. One may say that Mawlānā Iḥtishāmul Ḥasan in his books developed further the ideas of Mawlānā Ilyās. Nevertheless, it is significant that a concern for Muslim society was more pronounced in Mawlānā Ilyās's thought, and in Mawlānā Iḥtishāmul Ḥasan's ideology, than is revealed in the present *Faḍāʾil Aʿmāl*.

Mawlānā Iḥtishāmul Ḥasan (d. 1971), a relative and a close associate of Mawlānā Ilyās, was affiliated with the Madrasa Kāshiful ʿUlūm. Mawlānā Ilyās also nominated him as one of his successors. He wrote on such political and social questions as the decline and fall of Muslims and the concept of progress. These questions were on the minds of every educated Muslim at the time. Mawlānā refuted the argument by the modernists that education and modernization were the only ways to progress. He explained that knowledge was never an objective in itself; rather the goal was to apply knowledge and its practice in one's daily life. The separation between religious knowledge and practice was illustrated by the gulf between Madrasa and Khānqah (Ṣūfī hospice)—the former stressing only knowledge, the latter only practice. Political power, so emphasized by modern Muslim writers, was not the objective but rather a means to achieve the objective.

There were two paths open to Muslims. They could either forget their past and follow other nations into an uncharted future. Or, they could return to the teachings of Islam and to the Prophetic period, which was a known and tested way of *sharīʿa*. Mawlānā was critical of the duality in Muslim education: modern education was fascinated with modernity and ignored Islamic heritage, while religious education was bereft of the realities of the day. Mawlānā wished that both could join hands, and noted that Muslims in the past had not been adverse to foreign sciences but had adopted them to their own civilization.

Mawlānā believed that there was no need to search for new methods.

> The Tablīgh did not aim to launch a new movement or found a new group. In fact, this very trend of innovation, group formation and sectarianism is the cause of our present disgrace. The purpose of this work [Tablīgh] is to revive the most ancient work to which all the prophets had invited (Kāndhalawī 1962 "Iṣlāḥ-i Inqilāb," 43).

This [Tablīgh] work does not aim to gain political power. The power belongs only to God. It was never the objective of the prophets or the believers (Kāndhalawī 1962 "Iṣlāḥ-i Inqilāb," 42).

Mawlānā Iḥtishāmul Ḥasan was critical of the impact of modernity and technology on Muslim society and their way of life.

> Modern communication technologies like the postal system and the printing press had facilitated the spread of short stories, novels and other forms of literature that were undermining religious values, and higher intellectual and moral tastes. They were leading to moral corruption and broken families. Moreover, products of modern technology like radios, gramophones, theatres, cinemas, and bioscopes were introducing this corruption into Muslim homes. They were particularly affecting women who were striving for more freedom and becoming addicted to new modes and fashions. Not only were women losing interest in good home keeping, but they were also tending toward extravagance (Kāndhalawī 1962, "Iṣlāḥ-i Murʿāsharat," 4).

Mawlānā Iḥtishām also analyzed degeneration in the wider senses of religious, social and political decline. He argued that up to the end of the thirteenth century Hijrī, Muslims had been the sole possessors of honour, dignity, power and grandeur.

Mawlānā found six causes for this degeneration. The root cause was the abandonment of the duty of "*amr bil maʿrūf wa nahīy ʿanil munkar*" (enjoining good and preventing evil). The Tablīgh movement aimed to revive this duty. He argued that the Qurʾān promises Muslims supremacy on earth, but that this is contingent upon faith (*īmān*). Degeneration had occurred due to the loss of faith and neglect of the duty of *tablīgh*.

> The continuous onslaught on Islamic faith and social structure by various foreign elements and forces has weakened religious sentiments. Muslims must act quickly to wrest the initiative from the hands of opposing forces and launch a strong counter-effort to revive the dead spirit of each and every Muslim in order to rekindle in him the love and attachment for Islam. Unless such steps are taken vigorously, the present state of complacency will spread deep and wide and Muslims may meet the fate of total extinction (in Zakariyyā 1987, 23).

Mawlānā Zakariyyā's treatment of the subject is entirely different from that of Mawlānā Iḥtishāmul Ḥasan. While Mawlānā Iḥtishām explains the need and duty of *tablīgh* rationally, Mawlānā Zakariyyā justifies it theologically. Supporting his arguments from the Qur'ānic verses and *aḥādīth* relating to *tablīgh*, Mawlānā Zakariyyā discusses the subject in terms of self-reform, Muslim honour, sincerity, faith and self-criticism. He lays obvious stress on respect for the *ʿulamā* and underscores the importance of keeping company with pious people, that is, the *ʿulamā*, as part of the conception of *tablīgh*.

Mawlānā Muḥammad Zakariyyā

Mawlānā Zakariyyā does not focus on the political decline of Muslims. He speaks rather about religious decline. The religion is under threat from Muslims themselves. The decline of religion is defined not only as neglect of religious duties, but also as indifference to religion and unconscious unbelief. Both the *ʿulamā* and laymen are disappointed; the former complain about the lack of an attentive audience, the latter lament the absence of guidance from the *ʿulamā*.

Mawlānā Zakariyyā focuses on the reform of one's own self. Preaching should not mean forgetting one's own duties. Preaching is never effective if one does not act upon what one preaches to others. The Mawlānā advises preachers to speak kindly to the audience and not to expose others in public. A preacher must be sincere to his cause; he should not aspire to fame or wealth. The Mawlānā advises preachers to show special respect to the *ʿulamā*. This advice is particularly significant because a lay preacher may criticize the *ʿulamā* for neglecting their duty. The Mawlānā defends the *ʿulamā*, particularly against the popular criticism of their frequent disagreements on religious matters.

The *Faḍā'il-i Aʿmāl* reflects Mawlānā Zakariyyā's world-view, which is markedly different from that of Mawlānā Iḥtishāmul Ḥasan Kāndhalawī. Mawlānā Kāndhalawī is aware of the problems of modernity and modernization and he deals with them in a logical manner, albeit as a conservative. Mawlānā Zakariyyā simply ignores these issues. His ideal is a Ṣūfī scholar, and this is what he wants the Tablīghīs to imitate. Unlike Mawlānā Iḥtishāmul Ḥasan Kāndhalawī, Mawlānā Zakariyyā treats degeneration only in a narrow sense of religious decline.

Opposition, Criticism and Issues

In the beginning, as we have seen, the *ʿulamā* were reluctant to support the Tablīghī Jamāʿat. The Jamāʿat first earned the support of the *ʿulamā* from the Deoband school, and gradually came to be identified with that school. The Brēlwī school (see Introduction) criticized the Jamāʿat for preaching Deobandī teachings, which they considered to have deviated from the practice of *Sunna* and Jamāʿat. ʿAllāma Arshadul Qādirī, an Indian scholar, wrote a detailed refutation of Tablīghī Jamāʿat in his book *Tablīghī Jamāʿat, Ḥaqāʾiq-wa Maʿlūmāt kē Ujālē mēn.* The book was probably published first in 1959, and by 1981 it had seen more than twenty reprints. His main criticism is based on two points: Tablīghī Jamāʿat's concept of prophesy and the Deobandī basis of Jamāʿat's *Daʿwa.* In Pakistan, a debate between the Tablīghīs and the Brēlwīs appeared in the daily *Nawāʾi Waqt* (M. Riḍwī 1978; I. Riḍwī 1979). Fayyāḍ Aḥmad Kāwish (n.d.) also wrote critiques of the Jamāʿat, but most of his objections against the movement were anticipated by Arshadul Qādirī.[2]

Mawlānā Mawdūdī visited Mēwāt in 1936 on the invitation of Mawlānā Ilyās, and he admired the work of the Jamāʿat in his editorial in the *Tarjumānul Qurʾān.* Later, however, he lost interest in the Tablīghī Jamāʿat, probably because he had launched his own Jamāʿat Islāmī. ʿAlawī writes that Mawlānā Iḥtishāmul Ḥasan corresponded with Mawlānā Mawdūdī for a long time, unsuccessfully soliciting his support for the Tablīghī Jamāʿat (ʿAlawī 1989, 28). The Jamāʿat Islāmī's criticism of the Tablīghī Jamāʿat is best summarized in two articles by Mumtāz Aḥmad (1986 and 1991a). Essentially, Jamāʿat

---

[2] For information on this point I am indebted to Mr. Mujeeb Ahmad (Rawalpindi) and Mr. ʿĀbid Ḥusayn Shāh (Chakwal).

Islāmī criticized the apolitical stance of the Tablīghī Jamāʿat. Later when there emerged an active freedom movement against the British, and still later when Muslim political parties began participating in *Jihād* movements in Afghanistan, Kashmir and elsewhere, the Tablīghī Jamāʿat was criticized more vehemently for its political indifference.

Ahli Ḥadīth, a religious group that opposed adherence to any school of law or to the Ṣūfī orders, formed a political party and began taking part in *Jihād* in Kashmir and elsewhere. They criticized Jamāʿat for its adherence to the Ḥanafī school and for its indifference to *Jihād.* This is best represented in Ṭālibur Raḥmān's book *Tablīghī Jamāʿat kā Islām* (1992). Recently, some Deobandī *ʿulamā* have also expressed reservations about the Jamāʿat. Muftī Sayyid ʿAbdush Shakūr Tirmidhī (1985) best explains their views.

These criticisms raised several issues concerning the ideology of the Tablīghī Jamāʿat. Let us briefly review some of these.

The Tablīgh Method

Ṭālibur Raḥmān (1992, 11), an Ahli Ḥadīth writer, has questioned the method of *tablīgh* saying that it is not supported by the *aḥādīth.* He particularly objects to the method of going out, because there is no mention in the *aḥādīth* about the Prophet sending individuals out for three or forty days to other towns or villages for *tablīgh.* He argues that an outsider who does not know the local situation cannot be an effective preacher.

Mawlānā Masīḥullāh Khān, a successor to Mawlānā Ashraf ʿAlī Thānawī, did not permit one of his disciples to go on *tablīgh.* He advised that "One should go on *tablīgh, gasht* or gathering only after first ascertaining that there was someone to look after the financial needs of the family in one's absence" (Tirmidhī 1985, 7). Muftī Kifāyatullāh, a well-known Deobandī scholar and a supporter of the Jamāʿat, explained that "*Tablīgh* of religion was a duty of every Muslim only to the degree that one possessed religious knowledge. Journey for *tablīgh* was thus not obligatory for everyone. It was permitted only for those who were qualified and had financial means to do it. Women were never required to go out of their homes in the best of the days. There appears to be no permission for the women to go out alone for *tablīgh*" (Tirmidhī 1985; Kifāyatullāh n.d.a, 2:10).

ʿAbdushakūr Tirmidhī, a Deobandī Muftī, concludes, after citing the above views, that the Jamā'at has gone to the extreme by making *tablīgh* obligatory for every Muslim. He observes that often the people who spend forty days with the *tablīgh* neglect the significance of other branches of religion and begin to criticize the *'ulamā*, saying that they are not doing the *tablīgh* work. (Tirmidhī, 1985, preface). He explains that journey for *tablīgh* is only commendable, not obligatory. Similarly, demand for *chilla* was also a religious extremism. The Tablīghīs were wrong to assign the duty of speech to people who were not qualified (Tirmidhī 1985, 97).

We need not go into the polemics of whether *aḥādīth* support the *tablīgh* method. The Tablīghī literature, for instance *Stories of Ṣaḥāba* and *Faḍā'il-i Tablīgh*, refers to several stories of the *Ṣaḥāba* going on *tablīgh* journeys. It would, however, be difficult to support the view that *aḥādīth* support the method of *tablīgh* in any detail, as practiced by the Tablīghīs. We have already seen in previous chapters that the method developed gradually in the early practice of the Jamā'at. Muftī Tirmidhī's criticism of the *tablīgh* method reflects the *'ulamā*'s conception of *tablīgh* and their precautions in this regard. The Tablīghī Jamā'at's conception of *tablīgh* differs from theirs in essence, since the Tablīghīs regard it a personal duty of every Muslim.

Da'wa and Prophesy

Al-Qādirī claims that the Tablīghīs considered Mawlānā Ilyās as no less than a prophet (Qādirī 1981, 47). He cites from Tablīgh literature to support his point, quoting Mawlānā Ilyās saying that the method of *tablīgh* was revealed (*munkashaf*) to him in a dream and that the dreams were part of Prophethood (Ilyās 1960, 51). Mawlānā Ilyās is further quoted saying that he was told in a dream that the meaning of the verse "You are the best people" was "You are sent like the Prophets to the people" (Ilyās 1960, 51).

It is difficult to conclude from these statements that either Mawlānā Ilyās or the Tablīghīs claimed that he was a Prophet. The terms *kashf* (revelation) and dreams are not used in the meaning of prophecy and prophethood.

The problem arises from the Jamā'at definition of *Da'wa* as originally a function of Prophets, which has now become the obligation of the Muslim *Umma* because there will be no prophet to come after the Prophet Muḥammad.

The Tablīghī literature, therefore, sometimes describes Mawlānā

Ilyās and his movement in a style similar to the biography of the Prophet Muḥammad, stressing the prevalence of evil, and God in his mercy deciding to send an individual to preach goodness. This is why the Tablīgh literature often compares Mēwāt with pre-Islamic Arabia. We reproduce a paragraph by Miyānjī ʿĪsā Fīrōzpurī to illustrate this point:

> When humans go astray, neglect observing their duties, indulge in immorality, forget the life Hereafter, and begin to believe in the creatures instead of the Creator, and associate success with material forms instead of action, it is a divine custom that Allah, out of sheer grace and kindness, decides to arrange for the guidance of humans from the unseen (*ghayb*). A person possessing the qualities of goodness and kindness is selected from among the people of the day. This person is taught the methods and principles of guidance through inspiration. He is told about how to put this guidance into practice. God sends His support with him. Since Muḥammad was the final prophet, these persons are called *mujaddid* [see Introduction, this volume] or *imām* (Fīrōzpurī n.d.c, 5).

Explaining the role of *mujaddid* and *imām* as a successor to the Prophet Muḥammad, he then defines Mawlānā Ilyās's mission in this context, saying,

> God's mercy and kindness outpoured to select Mawlānā Muḥammad Ilyās. He unveiled to him the methods and principles of guidance for today. This method of labor (*miḥnat*) for the application of this guidance came to be popularly known as *Tablīghī Taḥrīk.* The Mawlānā used to call it *Tahrīk Īmān*, or Labour for the reform of *Umma* (Fīrōzpurī, n.d.c, 5).

Mawlānā Ilyās also used to stress that God assigned him this work and revealed to him the method of *tablīgh.* It would be too literal to conclude from these statements that Mawlānā Ilyās or the Tablīghīs believe the Mawlānā to be a prophet. The Islamic tradition places *ʿulamā* as successors of the Prophet. It also accepts *mujaddids* to continue the work of the prophets.

Al-Qādirī does not seem to persue this argument too seriously because, according to him, the Tablīghīs do not have high regard for the prophets. He cites Mawlānā Ilyās writing to a Tablīghī, "When God does not want something to happen, howsoever effort the prophets make, an iota cannot be moved. When He wants, He can use a weak person like you to get something done which even the Prophets could not do" (Ilyās 1952, 107). Al-Qādirī concludes that the Tablīghī Jamāʿat was actually preaching heresy (1960, 153). His objection is apparently again too literal. The advice, in fact, seems to stress humility and to a Tablīghī is a reminder about human limits.

Sectarianism

A basic objection against the Tablīghī Jamāʿat, according to Mawlānā Arshadul Qādirī, was that it spread Mawlānā Thānawī's teachings, not Islam (Qādirī 1981, 54). He is very critical of Mawlānā Thānawī and cites several of his statement which he regards as objectionable. We have noted Jamāʿat's affiliation with Deoband and Mawlānā Ilyās's high regard for Mawlānā Thānawī. It must, however, be noted that although the Jamāʿat used Mawlānā Thānawī's books in the beginning, they were gradually replaced by other books. The reason probably was that the Jamāʿat's approach to *tablīgh* differed from that of Mawlānā Thānawī, who insisted that only *ʿulamā* were qualified to undertake *tablīgh*. Once again, some Deobandī scholars continue to differ with the Jamāʿat on this point.

Al-Qādirī also compares Tablīghī Jamāʿat with the Wahhābīs. He argues that the associates and members of the Jamāʿat like Ḥusayn Aḥmad Madanī, Mawlānā Thānawī, Rashīd Aḥmad Gangōhī, Mawlānā Zakariyyā, and Manẓūr Nuʿmānī had sympathies with the Wahhābī movement (Qādirī 1981, 75). He argues that, like the Wahhābīs in Najd, the Jamāʿat began on simple premises of faith, prayer and morals, but later took an extremist turn (Qādirī 1981, 89). He claims that the Jamāʿat reached an agreement with the government of Saudi Arabia in 1938 (Qādirī 1960, 92).

This criticism reflects Brēlwī ʿUlamā's general view that the Deobandīs were closely connected with the Wahhābīs. The conclusion that the Jamāʿat reached an agreement with the Saudi government in 1938 is based on the exaggerated statements in Tablīghī writings about their early achievements. Abul Ḥasan ʿAlī Nadwī, for instance, reports that in his first visit to Saudi Arabia Ilyās won sympathies of the king, his Shaykhul Islām Abdullāh b. Hasan and Shaykh Ibn Bulayhid (Nadwī 1946, 98–104). The Jamāʿat could not receive open clearance for *tablīgh* work from the Saudi government. As the severe criticism by the Salafīs and the Ahli Ḥadīth shows, these groups differed with the Jamāʿat on several basic issues.

Ṭālibur Raḥmān wrote his book on Tablīghī Jamāʿat primarily to warn the Ahli Ḥadīth against the objectives of the Jamāʿat, namely the spread of Ḥanafism, which, according to the author, is a crime in the eyes of God (1992, 10). Incidentally, the Jamāʿat, Deobandīs and the Brelwīs all follow Ḥanafism. Raḥmān wants to convince the Tablīghīs that by spreading Ḥanafism they are not serving Islam, but rather paving the way for *shirk*, idolatry (1992, 10). The book argues in detail with citations from the Tablīgh literature that the Jamāʿat preaches adherence to Ḥanafi Fiqh, instead of to the Qur'ān and *ḥadīth*. Like al-Qādirī, Raḥmān considers Jamāʿat to be spreading the teachings of Mawlānā Ashraf ʿAlī Thānawī (1992, 44–57). Also like al-Qādirī, he criticizes the Jamāʿat for believing that Mawlānā Ilyās was sent by God (1992, 56).

As we shall see later in this chapter, the Jamāʿat avoided sectarianism by focusing on *faḍā'il* (merits) instead of *masā'il* (problems), motivating for action by describing merits of the said practice and by excluding details of creed and practice from its purview. Mawlānā Ilyās wrote the following to his workers:

> You should make sure that our movement and Islamic *tablīgh* do not allow hurting someone's feelings, nor do we want to hear the words *fitna* and *fasād* (disturbance). You have called some people *bidʿatī* (heretics). You should avoid such words in future that incite disturbance (Ilyās 1952, 142).

The movement could not, however, extract itself completely from Ḥanafism and Deoband teachings since most of its early supporters belonged to Dārul ʿUlūm Deoband, Maẓāhirul ʿUlūm Sahāranpur, and Nadwatul ʿUlamā, in Lucknow. The Tablīghī Jamāʿat was criticized and opposed mostly by Jamāʿat Islāmī and Brēlwī scholars. Both Mawlānā Manẓūr Nuʿmānī (1980) and Mawlānā Muḥammad Zakariyyā (1972) replied to this criticism. The former belonged to Nadwa, the latter to Maẓāhirul ʿUlūm. The tensions between the Jamāʿat and the Brēlwīs in South Africa are analyzed by Ebrahim Moosa in this volume.

Two events will serve to illustrate how Jamāʿat takes a cautious attitude toward controversial issues, while still maintaining its stance.

Miyānjī ʿĪsā inquired regarding some religious practices common among some Mēwātīs. For instance, they held a formal ceremony and a feast at the completion of the reading of the whole Qur'ān, believing that the reward for this act transfers in favour of the dead. This practice was called *Khatm Qur'ān*. Another practice was *ṣalāt wa salām*, greeting the Prophet Muḥammad with salutations believing that he was physically present and witnessing the event (*ḥāḍir* and *nāẓir*). There were similar religious practices that the Deobandī ʿUlamā opposed as innovations in Islam, and they called their practitioners heretics. They argued that the belief in the Prophet being *ḥāḍir* and *nāẓir* amounted to denying that God alone was omnipresent and omniscient.

Mawlānā Ilyās replied,

> It is commendable to take part in Khatm as it has been a practice of your elders. However, one should be careful if there is a fear of resemblance with the *mubtadiʿīn* (heretics). Similarly, saying *al-ṣalātu wa'l-salām-u ʿalayka* (peace and greetings to you, O Prophet) is not allowed if one believes that the Prophet was present (*ḥāḍir*) and witnessing (*nāẓir*) the event. It is also not permitted if the act could possibly imply heresy. However, there is no harm if one says this involuntarily, overpowered by love for the Prophet. These are such sensitive matters that there is ample opportunity for Satan to corrupt one's faith. They are, therefore, quite dangerous (Ilyās 1952, 90).

A similar occasion arose in 1993. *ʿUlamā* in Bangladesh had launched a movement against the Aḥmadīs. They came to Mawlānā Inʿāmul Ḥasan and complained that since Tablīghī Jamāʿat never specifically declares any one a *kafir* (disbeliever), the Aḥmadīs take advantage. The *ʿulamā* proposed that the Jamāʿat should specifically call the Aḥmadīs *kāfir*. Mawlānā agreed, but advised the Tablīghī speakers to repeatedly use words in their speeches that stress that Muḥammad was *Khātam al-Nabiyyīn*, the last Prophet. They should also explain that if one did not believe him to be the last Prophet this amounted to disbelief in Islam (Rāshid 1997, 431).

In both cases the Jamāʿat avoided open confrontation on a sectarian level but continued to adhere to a particular school of thought, namely the Deoband.

Finances

Al-Qādirī also alleges that the Jamāʿat was paid by the British government and that the other Western powers continue to financially assist them in order to oppose communism. Referring to Mawlānā Ḥifẓur Raḥmān's statement in *Mukālamatus Ṣadrayn*, he argues that the Tablīghī Jamāʿat received money from the British government through Ḥājī Rashīd Aḥmad. This conclusion is based on a misreading of a Mawlānā Ilyās statement to which Mawlānā Ḥifẓur Raḥmān referred. We have already mentioned that Mawlānā Ilyās wrote to Ḥājī Rashīd Aḥmad that he had used to receive five rupees from the trust of Nawwāb Chhatārī (see chapter 1). Obviously, Ḥājī Rashīd Aḥmad did not pay this money, nor was the British Government involved. On the basis of the same source al-Qādirī claims that Mawlānā Thānawī was on the payroll of the British government (Qādirī 1981, 92). Such claims are generally based on suspicious evidence which is then exaggerated and presented as proof. Another such argument is Al-Qādirī's claim that the Jamāʿat is supported by such extremist Hindu groups as Jan Sangh and Mahasabha (Qādirī 1981, 104). He explains that in 1968 the workers of these parties assisted the Tablīghī Jamāʿat's in staging their annual gathering in Bita in Bihar, India. According to him, availability of such financial assistance alone could explain the heavy expenditures that were made on the salaries and funds for the *amīrs*, *madrasa*, kitchen and Tablīgh workers (Qādirī 1981, 107).

Daʿwa and Politics

The Tablīghī Jamāʿat is generally described as apolitical. That, however, should not be taken to mean that the Jamāʿat has no political vision. This issue may best be understood within the context of the debate among Muslims in twentieth century India. The majority of the traditionalist *ʿulamā* were of the view that Muslims should not take part in active politics. They believed that *Daʿwa*, which was an essential duty for the Muslims, was best served by *madrasas*. Mawlānā Ilyās found this method ineffective and instead opted for a mass movement. Other Muslims founded political parties and were otherwise active in politics. They thought that Tablīghī Jamāʿat's withdrawal from politics was harmful to the Muslim cause.

Mawlānā Ilyās believed, first, that the Muslim religious leadership was not trained for politics. Mawlānā Nadwī states that "Mawlānā had a fixed idea, rather the essence of Islamic history in his mind was that the *ʿulamā* had lost the ability to deal with political matters since they had possessed no political power for centuries" (Nadwī 1985, 250). Muslims should, therefore, give priority to *Daʿwa* over politics. He stressed that Muslims should first struggle to change their lives according to the principles of faith and religion (1985, 249).

The second reason why Mawlānā Ilyās avoided politics was perhaps to avoid confrontation with the government. This is illustrated by one of Mawlānā Yūsuf's statements. He explained that when Ḥasan al-Bannā, the leader of the Ikhwān al-Muslimūn decided to hold a rally of his followers in Egypt, Mawlānā sent him a message through his people not to do so. He advised him to continue his efforts for the revival of religion, and not to indulge in a show of his power—the government might use its force to suppress his movement. Comparing the Tablīghī Jamāʿat with the Ikhwān, Mawlānā Yūsuf said the Jamāʿat has been successful while the Ikhwān movement had been suppressed (Bijnawrī 1980, 64).

Mumtāz Aḥmad has recently analyzed this aspect of the Jamāʿat in detail. He explains why Jamāʿat Islāmī and other Islamists criticize the Tablīghī Jamāʿat for remaining indifferent on such crucial issues as framing an Islamic constitution for Pakistan in the early 1950s, Islam versus socialism in the 1970s, the anti-Aḥmadiyya movement in the 1950s and 1970s, and the Islamization movement of the 1980s (Aḥmad 1991a, 518). The Islamists accuse the Jamāʿat of having strengthened secularist forces indirectly. Mumtāz Aḥmad finds that Ayyūb Khān promoted Tablīghī Jamāʿat in Pakistan in the 1960s due to its apolitical stance. He claims that while the government harrassed Jamāʿat Islāmī, the Tablīghī Jamāʿat was patronized officially by the government "to neutralize the influence of the Jamāʿat-i-Islāmī and other politically active *ʿulamā* groups" (Aḥmad 1991a, 518, citing his 1979 interviews with Pakistani government officials).

Mumtāz Aḥmad observes that Jamāʿat's stance has gradually changed from apolitical to explicitly antipolitical. He ascribes three reasons for this. First, the traumatic experience of the partitioning of India in which millions of Muslims were massacred in India; second, the precarious position of Muslims in post-partition India; and third, the popularity of Jamāʿat Islāmī in Pakistan (Aḥmad 1991a, 522). According to him, Tablīghī Jamāʿat deliberately took an antipolitical stance in order to distinguish itself from active political parties and gain government support. We have already described how Mawlānā Yūsuf dealt with the situation in 1947 and afterwards. Other Muslim political parties, including Jamāʿat Islāmī in India, also had to change their political strategies.

Whereas Islamists regard Jamāʿat as antipolitical, the secularists and the nationalists considered Jamāʿat's work as negatively political. Nirmala Sinha argues that the Jamāʿat was promoting communalism. She observes that the synthetic Meo culture was in danger since the Jamāʿat was making Muslim males observe their own religion. The Muslim women were not observing Hindu customs, and Hindu festivals and fairs like Chuhrsiddh, that the Hindu and Muslim Meos had formerly observed together, were declining. Hindu gods were losing attraction for the Meos. On account of Tablīghī Jamāʿat, the Muslim Meos were developing contacts with other Muslims in India (Ali 1970, 37–42).

Hashim Amir Ali, an Indian sociologist, also criticizes the Tablīgh movement for excluding Meos as a community from other communities in the area. He argues that by observing Islamic injunctions such as avoiding interest transactions, Meos will no longer take part in the mainstream economic system and cooperative schemes that are so essential for the economic growth of the area. He is also critical of the Jamāʿat for discouraging Meo girls from attaining a modern education (1970, 44).

In a very broad sense, the Tablīghī Jamāʿat's work is, in fact, political. Making Muslims conscious of their separate identity and aware of their social obligations from a religious perspective ultimately serves a political purpose. It cannot, therefore, be concluded that Mawlānā Ilyās had no political vision and agenda. He was certainly opposed to secularism, which provides the basis for most modern political systems, and this meant that the Tablīghīs would not support secular political parties. He once remarked that the religion was under threat from two dangers. The first was missionary movements like Shuddhī, which were luring the illiterate into unbelief. The other danger was the secularism that accompanied Western rule and politics (Ilyās 1960, 62).

The political vision of the Jamāʿat becomes clear in the emphasis on *Umma* consciousness in the Tablīgh literature (see Mawlānā Yūsuf's speech, appendix one of chapter one). The Jamāʿat's criticism of modernization also reflects its political vision. Modernists were critical of the Jamāʿat's approach to modernity and insisted that the Western countries were models of progress and success. Mawlānā Yūsuf rejected this argument and asserted that the Western nations did not really want Muslims to progress. They were helping Muslim development only as far as it would serve their own purposes:

> The Prophet's lifestyle is based on cleanliness, simplicity and modesty. The lifestyle introduced by the Jews and Christians is founded on immodesty, lavish spending and luxury. You have begun to like the lifestyle of those that shed your ancestors' blood, disgraced them, and dispossessed them of their property and power. Now they are giving you aid the same way as you feed the chicken (Ḥasanī 1988, 714).

The political implications in this statement need no further elaboration.

ʿUlamā

We have already mentioned Mawlānā Ashraf ʿAlī Thānawī's Tablīgh activities. When he came to know of Mēwātīs going for *tablīgh* he was alarmed. He said, "The people are not ready to listen to the *ʿulamā*, what kind of *tablīgh* would these illiterate Mēwātīs be doing? This is not Tablīgh, it is a heresy (*dīn mēn nayā fitna*)" (Fīrōzpurī n.d.c, 23).

Mawlānā Thānawī and other *ʿulamā* believed that *Daʿwa* was their function and others were not qualified to undertake the responsibility. Tablīghī Jamāʿat insisted that *tablīgh* was the duty of every Muslim. Mawlānā Ilyās, however, could not afford to offend the *ʿulamā*. He sent one of the *tablīgh* groups to Kāndhala with instructions that a group of eight would go from Kāndhala to Thāna Bhawan, the seat of Mawlānā Thānawī. They were to first seek his permission to visit him. Mawlānā Thānawī agreed and invited them to Thāna Bhawan. According to the Tablīgh sources, he discussed and approved the work, commenting, "If one wanted to see the Companions of the Prophet one should see these people" (Fīrōzpurī n.d.c, 35). Mawlānā Nadwī (1985, 120) also mentions this story. One may find Mawlānā Thanawī's words exaggerated, but the story certainly shows how Mawlānā Ilyās valued the approval of the *ʿulamā*.

As we have already observed, Mawlānā Ashraf ʿAlī Thānawī's method of *tablīgh* differed from that of the Jamāʿat. Mawlānā Ilyās had a high regard for Mawlānā Thānawī's work but he believed that his own method was more effective. He observed that "Ḥaḍrat Mawlānā Thānawī has done admirable work. I wish that Mawlānā's teachings may be combined with my method of *tablīgh*. That way his teachings will become more popular" (Ilyās 1960, 50).

Mawlānā Ilyās expected that the *ʿulamā* would appreciate his work and would join him with enthusiasm. Mawlānā Nadwī recalls that Mawlānā Ilyās became worried when the *ʿulamā* did not pay due notice. Nadwī enumerates five reasons for their inattention. First, in those days several other movements had emerged and the *ʿulamā* were occupied with them. The Tablīgh was a quiet and constructive movement and therefore attracted fewer of the *ʿulamā*. Second, there was no publicity regarding the work of the Tablīgh, and so very few people knew about it. Third, the popular meanings of the word Tablīgh were a great hindrance. People considered it *farḍ kifāya*, and thus failed to appreciate its full import. Fourth, Mawlānā Ilyās stammered in his speech. When he explained his mission to the

ʿulamā he could not present it effectively. Finally, the simple Mēwātīs who were engaged in the Tablīgh work could not impress upon the *ʿulamā* the work's value (Nadwī 1985, 126).

Mawlānā Ilyās was unhappy with the role of the *ʿulamā* in the history of Muslim India. Once he remarked that Akbar had gone astray because he relied too much on the *ʿulamā*. He did not possess the ability and the qualification to choose between them. As a result, the Seekers of the World (*Ṭālibān-i Dunyā*) and competitors (*Mutanāfisīn*) surrounded him. When Akbar realized their selfishness and worldly greed he began to hate them all and abandoned them completely. The leaders of other religions came to dominate and a Dīn-i Ilāhī[3] came into being in place of Islam (Ilyās 1960, 101).

The Jamāʿat has deliberately encouraged non-*ʿulamā* to take an active role in Tablīgh activities such as *bayān* (public speech) and *taʿlīm* (reading sessions). Questions have often been raised within the Jamāʿat about this policy. Someone complained to Mawlānā Inʿāmul Ḥasan, the Amīr of the Jamāʿat, that the Tablīghīs often made mistakes during their readings of the Tablīgh books—it would be better if the *ʿulamā* were asked to read them. Mawlānā Inʿāmul Ḥasan advised that if an *ʿālim* were present he might be asked to read, but the *ʿulamā* should not correct the mistakes in public. They might apprise the reader of his mistakes in private, however (Rashid 1997, 430). This remark implies that even if an *ʿālim* is present he cannot assume the duty of reader unless invited by the *amīr*.

The *ʿulamā* have frequently criticized the Jamāʿat on this point. In a meeting in Madrasa Ḥusayniyya in Taoli, district Muẓaffar Nagar, UP, on 26 February 1968 a group of the Deobandī *ʿulamā* observed that the Tablīgh movement was undermining the position of the *ʿulamā*. The proceedings of this meeting, including a long statement by Mawlānā ʿAbdur Raḥīm Shāh, were later published under the title *Uṣūl-i Daʿwat-wa Tablīgh* (ʿAbdur Raḥīm 1968). Mawlānā ʿAbdur Raḥīm complained (1968, 46) that for over five years he had been drawing Mawlānā Yūsuf's attention to the fact that "Immature leaders [the illiterate preachers] of the Tablīghī Jamāʿat address the public whereas they are not allowed to do so by *sharīʿa*. They insist on

[3] Dīn-i Ilāhī, Mughal emperor Akbar, in 1581 introduced certain practices as a new understanding of Islam. They emphasized tolerance and concessions to other religions in India, particularly Hinduism. It adopted values like celibacy, dislike of animal slaughter and reverance for light. The Muslim orthodoxy condemned it as heresy.

the superiority of this work beyond limits" (1968, 52). He argued, "It is a pity that a person cannot practice as a compounder [a paramedical person] without a proper certificate, but the matter of religion is considered so frivolous that any person may stand up to speak. No qualification is required" (1968, 54).

Mawlānā Maḥmūd Ḥasan Gangōhī argued that even the Jamāʿat was divided on this issue. He said that Mawlānā Iḥtishāmul Ḥasan left Bastī Niẓāmuddīn Delhi to settle in Kāndhala because he had developed differences with the new Jamāʿat leadership concerning how to conduct *tablīgh* (al-Qādirī 1981, 173). Al-Qādirī further provides the following extract from Mawlānā Iḥtishāmul Ḥasan's book *Ẓindagī kī Ṣirāṭ-i Mustaqīm*:

> The present *Tablīgh* in Niẓāmuddīn is beyond my understanding. It is neither in conformity with the Qur'ān and *ḥadīth*, nor does it agree with the teachings of Mujaddid Alf Thānī, Shāh Waliullāh or other righteous *ʿulamā*. It is the duty of the *ʿulamā* participating in *tablīgh* to first bring this work into accord with the teachings of the Qur'ān, *ḥadīth*, *imāms* and the *ʿulamā*. I fail to understand how something that Mawlānā Ilyās considered only a *bidʿat-i ḥasana* [praiseworthy, but still an innovation], even if performed in strict accordance with its principles, can be termed as the most important religious work despite frequent violation of its principles these days (Qādirī 1981, 170).

It is unclear which aspect of Tablīgh the Mawlānā was criticizing. Mumtāz Aḥmad characterizes the approach of the Tablīghī Jamāʿat as "anti-intellectual" and refers to their "disdain for book knowledge" (1991a, 516). This characterization is partially justified, at least so far as Tablīgh views of available religious literature are concerned. These books are often too technical to be understood by a people the majority of whom cannot read. The *ʿulamā* are in fact writing for the other *ʿulamā*, and common people do not benefit from their knowledge. Tablīghī Jamāʿat, as a grassroot movement, cannot use these books. Furthermore, the Jamāʿat lays more stress on practice than on information, and the books usually provide details that are not conducive to action.

Faḍā'il/Masā'il

Tablīghī Jamāʿat's first priority was to avoid any sort of controversy, and there were several areas of potential conflict. One was the differences between various sects. Another was the varying interpretations put forth by the various schools of Islamic law. To avoid these areas the Jamāʿat decided to focus on principles and to leave out the details upon which the *ʿulamā* differed. The strategy was to distinguish between *faḍāʾil* (the discussion of merits and reward for a religious act) and *masāʾil* (the elaboration of rules and regulations for performance of those acts). There could be no difference on the *faḍāʾil*, but the various sects and schools might differ on rules and regulations. That is why most books in the Tablīgh literature focus on *faḍāʾil*.

Ṭālibur Raḥmān criticizes this *faḍāʾil*/*masāʾil* principle of the Jamāʿat. He says that the *faḍāʾil* literature is not based on authentic *aḥadīth*. He argues that when a layman is only taught the merits of an action and is not told how to perform an act he might be confused or might go astray from the right path (1992, 6). In fact, the Jamāʿat developed this approach mainly to motivate people to practice religion. People could perform a religious obligation according to whatever school they belonged. This approach agreed with the general nonconfrontational stance of the Jamāʿat.

Mawlānā Ilyās explained:

> *Faḍāʾil* have priority over *masāʾil*. *Faḍāʾil* produce certitude in the reward for deeds, which is a state of faith (*īmān*), and that is what prepares a person to act. The need for knowledge of *masāʾil* arises after a person is ready to act. We therefore grant more importance to *faḍāʾil* than to *masāʾil* (Ilyās 1960, 137).

Women

The attitude of the Jamāʿat toward female participation in *Daʿwa* reflects a conservative attitude of the *ʿulamā*. According to them, the role of women is limited to their homes. Their participation in *Daʿwa* is supportive and supplementary to that of men, not independent or equal to them. Mawlānā Ilyās remarked, "I say to women to support their menfolk in the work of religion. Let the men go out for the work of religion in peace. Share some of men's household responsibilities so that they can attend to the work of religion with a free mind. If women do not follow this advice they will become *ḥibālatush shayṭān* (conduits for evil) (Ilyās 1960, 104).

Mawlānā Yūsuf also believed in a limited role for women in *tablīgh*. He said, "Regarding *tablīgh* among women, only the following should be allowed: women should read and teach religious books. They should abide by the Islamic customs in their entirety and make their relatives conform to them also. They should send their menfolk out for *tablīgh* to learn about Islam. They can then teach the women what they have learned. Women should never be allowed to make *gasht*" (Ḥasanī 1988, 742).

Mawlānā Inʿāmul Ḥasan, too, favoured confining the women's participation in *tablīgh* to their homes: "In each house the women must engage themselves in prayer, *taʿlīm, dhikr* and recitation of the Qurʾān. But how can this be done? After consulting the male family members the women should gather together other women to perform these acts. Their *tablīgh* work must be confined within the limits prescribed by the Prophet." He added further, "The jurists (*fuqahā*) have ruled that gatherings of women are seldom free from disadvantages. A woman who cares for *tablīgh* should gather women at her house" (Rāshid 1997, 414–415).

Replying to the possible objection that the Tablīgh literature contained stories about women participating in *Jihād* and tending to the wounded, Mawlānā Inʿāmul Ḥasan explained that all of those stories belonged to the battle of Uḥud, when the injunction about *purdah* (veiling) had not yet been revealed. "A woman cannot be appointed as *amīr*. She is not a full witness, so how can she take the position of a judge" (Rāshid 1997, 454).

One can clearly see that the three *amīrs* adhered to the general views of the *ʿulamā* regarding the role and status of women. This does not, however, mean that women do not participate in the Tablīgh. The two studies by Metcalf and Faust in this volume show that women's participation is increasing. Both studies also describe how women feel about the restrictions the movement imposes upon them.

Non-Muslims

As explained earlier, the Jamāʿat does not aim to convert non-Muslims. Their focus on Muslims is so narrow that one can find little evidence concerning their attitudes toward non-Muslims. The term *kufr* in Jamāʿat discourse is used in a very wide sense to include everything from secularism, to atheism, to materialism (see the Tablīghī letters in this chapter's appendix). We have seen that the Jamāʿat arose as a Muslim response to Hindu Arya Samaj missionary activities and the Shuddhī movement. It did not, however, engage in polemics with Hindus nor did it try to convert them to Islam. It went only so far as to reclaim Muslims that had converted to Hinduism. Similarly, although one hears Tablīghīs speak about Christians in the West converting to Islam due to Tablīgh activities, Jamāʿat's *Daʿwa* is not addressed to them. However, one interesting incident indicates how the elders of the Jamāʿat view Christianity. Mawlānā Inʿāmul Ḥasan recalled that he received a letter from the Pope [Bishop?] from Sheffield. The letter suggested that they work together for a collective cause. Mawlānā said that the *shūrā* advised him not to respond, but he would have liked to have told the Pope that the Muslims already believed in ʿĪsā (Jesus) as a prophet. If the Christians and the Jews would accept Muḥammad as Prophet then the three religions could work together toward a collective cause (Rāshid 1997, 436).

Jihād

Daʿwa movements often define *Jihād* as one of the methods of implementing the Islamic principle of *Amr b'il maʿrūf wa nahiy ʿanil munkar* (enjoining good and forbidding evil). Tablīghī Jamāʿat also conceives of its *Daʿwa* within the framework of this principle, which derives its justification from a *ḥadīth* that prescribes the use of force to prevent evil. Frequently, *Jihād* is considered as the highest form of this method of prevention. In India, especially after British persecution of Muslims as perpetrators of *Jihād* in 1857, *Jihād* came to be defined more generally as effort and struggle, rather than as combat. Tablīghī Jamāʿat, neither a militant nor a political movement, tried to avoid any implications of confrontation, war or fighting. It chose to interpret *Jihād* and related terms like *nafar* within the broader meaning of action in the path of Allah. *Jihād* was the supreme act of sacrifice in this path. *Tablīgh*, too, meant sacrifice in physical as well as financial terms.

The Jamāʿat interpreted the physical movement for *tablīgh* as *Jihād*. The various terms used in the Islamic tradition to denote *Jihād* were adopted in the Tablīgh literature to denote the work of *tablīgh*. Mawlānā Ilyās compared the travel in *tablīgh* with *ghazwa* (a raid as part of *Jihād*), saying, "This travel has the same characteristics as that of *ghazwāt*, and therefore we hope to earn the same reward. Even though it does not constitute *qitāl* (physical fighting with weapons), it is still a branch of *Jihād*. It is lower than *qitāl* in certain respects, yet it is higher in other respects (Ilyās 1960, 66).

The Jamāʿat took this position at a time when one section of *ʿulamā* belonging to the Deoband school was actively involved in politics. Among them were Mawlānā ʿUbaydullāh Sindhī, who had organized Ḥizbul Anṣār (The party of supporters) and Junūdullāh (God's army) to establish Ḥukūmat-i Ilāhiya (Kingdom of God). Ḥabībur Raḥmān Khān Mēwātī narrates that once Mawlānā ʿUbaydullāh Sindhī complained to Mawlānā Ilyās, "You have transformed a brave people (Meos) into a cowardly lot." Mawlānā retorted, "No, I am preparing soldiers for your *junūd.* I am training these people in such a way that they will serve your and our interests alike" (Mēwātī 1979, 234). The remarks reflect different perspectives of the two *ʿulamā* concerning *Jihād.* Mawlānā Ilyās did not believe in militancy.

We have already mentioned Miyānjī ʿĪsā's remarks about "*Nafar fī Sabīl Allāh*" (going out in the path of God). The phrase is used in the Islamic tradition largely with reference to *Jihād.* The Jamāʿat adopted this phrase for the *tablīgh* work, especially for *khurūj* (going out for *tablīgh*). In the Islamic tradition *khurūj* meant rebellion, often armed. Miyānjī explained that *Nafar fī Sabīl Allāh,* in the meaning of *Jihād,* was a substantive institution of Islam, but not a Tablīgh principle. He compared the two, and said that *Nafar,* apparently in the meaning of call for *Jihād,* was applicable only when the necessity arose, whereas *tablīgh* was a perennial duty (Fīrōzpurī, n.d.c, 103). Similarly, *gasht* or *jawla,* which had militant connotations, were adopted for Tablīgh work and assigned different meanings.

The Jamāʿat has avoided participation in any militant conflict. Consequently, Jamāʿat has been criticized as indifferent to *Jihād.* For example Ṭālibur Raḥmān says, "The Jamāʿat invites people to Raiwind for the purification of their souls instead of sending them to Afghanistan for *Jihād.* The Jamāʿat has killed the spirit of *Jihād* by sword among the Muslims" (1992, 5). The title page of Raḥmān's book depicts the Jamāʿat with an illustration of a prayer carpet, a water pot for ablution, a rosary and a broken sword.

Ṭālibur Raḥmān also raises the issue of why the Jamāʿat has not been allowed to work in certain countries. In his view, this is because they take the sword from the hand of the Muslims and give them instead a water pot, prayer carpet and rosary (1992, 6). Raḥmān does not cite specific countries.

The Islamist movements simply cannot tolerate Jamāʿat's indifference to the Muslim sufferings at the hands of non-Muslims, and their lack of support for *Jihād* activities of Muslim organizations. Once an Arab leader asked Mawlānā Inʿāmul Ḥasan if the Tablīghīs had no sympathies with the Muslims in Bosnia and Kashmir. Mawlānā said,

"We do pray for them, although we do not specify them. We pray for all the wronged people" (Rāshid 1997, 435). This remark reveals the cautious attitude of the Jamāʿat regarding these issues.

Appendix

Tablīghī Views of Western Societies

I have translated two letters written in Urdu by outgoing Tablīghīs to Tablīgh headquarters in Delhi. They illustrate how a Tablīghī views the ideology of the Jamāʿat, particularly in the Western environment. Letters play a significant role in Tablīgh work. They provide constant contact between Tablīgh groups and between individuals and the centre. The outgoing Jamāʿats report their activities and experiences to the centre and the centre issues them regular instructions.

Letters by the outgoing Tablīghīs to the centre are often restatements of Jamāʿat rhetoric, yet they can also reveal a conception of *Daʿwa* in Tablīghī mind that is not apparent in the Tablīgh literature. They reflect passion, concern and hope for the conversion of non-Muslims in these countries, and offer comparative comments by Tablīghīs on the cultural, religious and general environments there. The political and economic aspects of the comments are particularly striking.

Bijnawrī (1980) has published several such letters. Ḥasanī also reproduces extracts from letters written by participants in the Manchester 1961 gathering, and one of them (Ḥasanī 1967, 508–510) is almost the same as the first letter translated below (Bijnawrī 1980, 137–141). No information is available on the authors of these letters, although their contents and dates are confirmed by other sources.

The second letter, from the United States (Bijnawrī 1980, 157–169), reports on Tablīgh work in American cities, including New York (August 1971), Boston, Detroit, Chicago and Washington D.C. Ḥasanī (1988, 513f.) refers to several such letters reporting Tablīgh work in America. Although none of these extracts matches the letter we have translated, all share a common style, content and perspective. All speak about promiscuity in Western culture, and refer to a lack of interest in Tablīgh among Arab Muslims. Their comments about Elijah and the Nation of Islam are also similar. One of the letters (Ḥasanī 1988, 527) compares Chicago with Qādiyān in India, where Mirzā Ghulām Aḥmad claimed Prophethood.

Letter no. 1[4]

Harbandan[5] UK
7 August 1962

Revered Ḥaḍrat Jī [Mawlānā Muḥammad Yūsuf].

Peace be on you and Allah's Mercy and Blessings.

Please forgive me for waiting for such a long time to write. I received your letter dated 2 Ṣafar [5 July 1962] through Mr. Munawwar Husayn. Your advice is certainly an antidote to the poisonous environment here. I shall do my utmost to act upon it. It is indeed very difficult to abide by Allah's commandments in this environment. However, God's support makes it easy.

I heard a *ḥadīth* from you, which meant something like the following: There will come a time when fornication will be common; it will be committed in public. A person, who will preach against fornication, asking the concerned person to fear God and not to do it in public, will be given the same reward as given to the Companions of the Prophet. Here young men and women kiss each other publicly on roads, in parks, on railway stations, even while sitting in railway trains. I have no courage to preach to them. Yet I feel worried at heart. There are several Pakistani and Indian brothers who, like others in this society, indulge in sex with women. People used to say that it was impossible to preach in London. Those who believe in human authorities other than Allah become victims of the environment. But those who believe in Allah have proved by their actions that this environment can be changed only by preaching Islam.

The meeting held in Manchester from 4–6 August 1961[6] established the fact that when work is done in strict accordance with the principles it becomes easy to travel on the path of this lofty religion by the grace of God, even in this polluted environment. The impact that this Manchester meeting had is impossible to describe. It seemed as if God was going to make us perform an important task, as if the time was getting closer when such humble persons would cleanse this dirty environment. Either God will bestow upon them this faith or no one will save them from destruction. The countries that we call big powers will be unable to defend themselves. Today all those great empires, which we once called the Dutch Empire or the British Empire, where the sun never set, are no more. Tomorrow the big power itself will take that turn. I wish our brothers who succumb to this environment would contemplate this fact. May Allah support us to face the challenge of the environment. In this Manchester meeting we saw some strange things. People in London wrote that they would start their journey by car on the morning of the 4th. The distance between London and Manchester is about

[4] Bijnawrī 1980, 137–141.

[5] I have been unable to identify this place.

[6] For reports on the Manchester gathering in August 1961 see Gaborieau, this volume. Ḥasanī (1967, 508) also reports on a Tablīghī *Ijtimāʿ* in Manchester without mentioning any date.

250 miles, with Herbandan 200 miles further on. I found it hard to plan how to travel alone. The train fare was around 55 rupees. I was not worried about the cost. The only worry was traveling alone.

On the morning of 3 August, at breakfast time, I spoke to Mr. Jarvis, a Christian. He said that he would be traveling to a place three miles further away from Liverpool. Although we never spoke of traveling together, around eleven o'clock that morning Mr. Jarvis came in his jeep and offered to set out before four o'clock and to drop me in Manchester. After that he would go on to Liverpool. I called Mr. Ghulam Sabir, the *amīr* of the Jamā'at in Manchester telling him that I would be reaching the mosque at 9.00 p.m. I reached Manchester with Mr. Jarvis within five hours. Some people were actually waiting for me in the mosque and were glad to receive me. We talked over some matters during the night. Three local persons accompanied me to spend the night in the mosque. In the morning a group joined us from Leeds. After performing *ẓuhr* prayer, we formed a group for making arrangements. We had just started coming out of the mosque when Mr. Munawwar arrived with his group from Birmingham. We continued our rounds. When we returned we found that a group of seventeen people had come from London by car. Four or five persons who could not come with this group were traveling by train, and one or two of them might not be able to come. There was also a group coming from Glasgow. Is this the annual meeting in Bhopal? No, it is a meeting in Manchester in England! Most participants are bearded, some are clad in English dress. Some are officers, some are businessmen, and some are medical doctors, scientists, and students. There are old men and children. Some were born in Britain. Some have come from Madina the Enlightened. Some have traveled by train, some by car and some by caravan. What are these preparations for? Why are they gathering? Why have they come to a mosque, leaving their homes? These are the people who have left their homes even in this environment. They have come to promote God's authority. They have come to refresh their faith and share it with others. So where are those people today who used to say that it was not possible to preach in London, England?

They prayed to God after coming out of the mosque. After the *Maghrib* prayer they held discussions. The group from London told us how, when they were praying on the grass at the side of the road on their way to Manchester, the English would stop their vehicles to see what was going on. It was only the spectacle of prayer that impressed them. About sixteen persons came from Bradford and encouraged everyone. Among them was a Ṣūfī who teaches *ḥadīth* there. He has accompanied a group and explained in his speech that during two years in this country this was the first time he has traveled for the sake of preaching. There were three or four among them who had memorized the Qur'ān, and others were Qur'ān readers. Most were people who were anxious to see the religion flourish. The group from Bradford informed us that the English have started Urdu-language prayers in their schools so that Muslim children would learn something about Christianity. Muslims themselves have established schools for their children in the mosques in Glasgow and Leeds. The speeches in this meeting were full of passion.

After the meeting, people were asked to volunteer for three sequences of forty days. Mind you, this demand for three sequences of forty days was being made in London, not in Mēwāt. We also requested people to go to Aligarh University. This demand for three sequences of forty days seemed unrealistic because it meant an expenditure of several thousand rupees, but it is Allah who makes it possible for anyone to serve religion. The following persons volunteered for a four-month period in a place which lies 6000 miles away and whose environment is detrimental to faith: Ibrahim Nasimullah and Rashid Alam from London, Muḥammad Azim from Manchester, Ghulam Hussein from Bradford, Muḥammad Ishaq from Glasgow, Niaz Muḥammad and Dewanjee from London and Zamanul Haq from Leeds.

Other people volunteered to work for one week and three days. The book *Ḥikāyāt-i-Ṣaḥāba* was read after the '*Ishā*' prayer and people went to bed after. The six principles were explained after the *fajr* prayer, and then we again went to sleep because the nights here are very short. We had breakfast in the morning, then we went for rounds. Discussions were held between Ẓuhr and ʿAṣr. The people coming from British Guyana spoke in English. There was someone from South America who explained the six principles in English. More people volunteered to work in the path of God.

The people from Leeds returned in the evening. In the morning the group from Bradford and British Guyana also returned. The group from London and Birmingham went out to spend Monday, 6 August, in Coventry. When departing, people embraced each other and cried. It was a sight worth seeing, these people who had undertaken this global task so strongly resolved at heart and with prayers on their lips. People began departing by car and by train. They spent some time making rounds in Coventry and began their journey at six o'clock. My friends dropped me at Herbandon. The train fare from Manchester to Herbandon costs three rupees but I had to pay only three and a half shillings, which is about two and a half rupees. These are really matters which are hard to believe. It shows that Allah has decided to employ us for the work of guidance.

I wish the sleeping Muslims would wake up even now. I wish that our lives were spent according to the true religion. Blessed are those who undertake this work. May Allah save sinners like us for the sake of these blessed people. Amen. That is all. Peace be on you.

Your Servant
Rafiq Ahmad
[Dr. Muhammad Rafiq Siddiqi, Alig.]
(Written down by Mushtaq Ahmad)

Letter no. 2[7]

Flint [Michigan, U.S.A.]
2nd September 1971.

In the name of God the Powerful and Excelled.

Revered Ḥājī Ṣāḥib[8] and other friends!

Peace be on you and Allah's mercy and pleasures.

I hope that you are well. I have already written in detail about developments here. Now I would like to add that our group arrived in America in two or three groups. In the beginning only two persons arrived, then four and later another four. We worked in New York until 23 August.

New York is one of the biggest cities in the world. It is certainly the biggest city in America. Its total population is more than eight million, consisting of a large number of people from all nations and races. The population in America is divided in such a manner that in big cities there are people of black races who are called Afro-Americans. They are more numerous. In addition, there are other people coming from other countries. The white Americans live in the villages [suburbs] outside the cities. There is no difference between facilities in villages and in cities. I have observed after coming here that man has made great efforts in manufacturing things, and by these efforts he has produced great refinement, but abundance of this kind does not provide prosperity. I came to know that in spite of abundance of material goods there exists hardship, poverty, ignorance and worries, to say nothing of commercial activities that are additional worries.

In short, thanks to God, the fact has become quite clear that we people are quite happy and content in our country despite the scarcity of things. Satisfaction, comfort, love, regard of others, manners, sympathy, sharing of sorrows, sacrifices and smiles are nowhere to be seen. If ever they are there, they are unreal. Abundance is useful, only so long as one is well and healthy and able to earn one's livelihood. When one is disabled, one becomes valueless. There is no concept of family life. Children stay with their parents until they are thirteen or fourteen years old. After that, girls go out searching for their own place to live and boys search for their life partner. Parents spend their time playing with dogs and animals. If they have no money left, it is common to take refuge in welfare. This is a general picture of life. If one falls sick, he goes to a hospital where no one comes to see him. If he dies, there is no one to mourn. Even relatives receive the news of his death after several weeks.

Life is very difficult and very hard. If you do not work whole-heartedly for eight hours daily it can put you in much trouble. You can depend on insurance for a few days, then you become dependent on welfare. There is apparent glitter but within there are great afflictions. Life is very costly. The

[7] Bijnawrī 1980, 157–169.

[8] The letter is probably addressed to Ḥāji Arshad. See Gaborieau, this volume, about Ḥājī Arshad.

old have their separate hostels like the handicapped. In these welfare institutions, they spend the last days of their life like dependents. The capitalist system has complete control over their lives. The masses do their utmost to earn their livelihood. Whatever they earn goes back to the capitalists's pockets in one way or another. The necessities of daily life are manufactured and sold by the capitalists. There are no small shopkeepers. There are only employees in the shops. No doubt cars are cheap; everyone is forced to keep a car in view of the life pattern here. Petrol is also quite cheap.

Travel by railway train is very costly. Very few people travel by train. Train journeys are therefore only a matter of pleasure. People travel by their own cars on long trips. Railway trains are very comfortable but travel by buses is cheaper. Buses are of a high quality and very comfortable. Travel by air is also cheap; the airfare costs only a little more than the train.

The one virtue in these people is that there is no adulteration in anything. The food items are pure and cheap in relation to the income. You can find all types of meat. Only *dhabīḥa* [meat of an animal slaughtered according to Islamic injunctions] is not available. The Jews do not consume food prepared with lard. They prepare everything separately for Jews. Usually lard or the fat of animals not slaughtered according to Islamic teachings is used for the preparation of bread, but food items prepared for the Jews do not use this kind of fat. These foods are called *kosher.* The Jews consume only meat if slaughtered according to their own method. Their slaughtering method resembles that of Muslims. I have heard that Muslim scholars have declared such meat permissible but I have not confirmed this.

Those Muslims who are a little more careful consume only *kosher* meat. Those who are not careful eat almost everything. We do not eat even *kosher* meat, eating only vegetables if possible. We slaughtered chickens to eat. Only lentils or vegetables are available. All spices are available. *ghee* [clarified butter] is not available. You do find butter, olive and other cooking oils. By the grace of God, all other food items are available in abundance. Running hot and cold water, gas, cheap electricity, telephones, high quality roads and other facilities are available to everyone, but there is no contentment. God has given them all the worldly things. Looking at them, one's faith in the following verses of the Qur'ān become stronger: "When they forgot what they were reminded we opened upon them the gates of everything until they become happy with what was given to them. Then we caught them suddenly while they were dumbfounded" [6–44].

Now these people have started taking pride in these worldly blessings. God's seizure can be postponed if the work of *Daʿwa* is undertaken. It is certainly a punishable act if one disobeys God after receiving so many blessings. I wish someone would make them understand this fact. The difficulty is that Muslims themselves are so much impressed and engrossed with this glitter that they have forgotten their own roots. Whereas the Qur'ān rules very clearly: "And let not thine eyes overlook them, desiring the pomp of this worldly life and do not obey him whose heart We have made heedless to Our remembrance who follows his own lust and whose case has been abandoned" [Qur'ān, 18:28].

The Jews are in full control of life in this country. It is they who control capital, newspapers, radio, television and other things. They can influence public opinion. Everyone is forced to obey them. Discrimination is quite obvious. The black races were brought in as slaves in the beginning. All the laborious work was assigned to them. They were exploited to the maximum and were deprived of education and other means of development. Consequently they are in the same position as that of untouchables in our country. No religion could bring justice to them. Legally slavery has been abolished and the Constitution gives them equal rights, but practically they are subjected to the maximum discrimination. Their living habitat is dirty and they suffer from a serious inferiority complex. The result now is that they are totally fed up with this system and are rebelling against it intellectually and practically. That is why they are inclining towards Islam. These people are converting to Islam in large numbers. Taking advantage of this psychological action, and basing his message on protest against racial discrimination, a person by the name of Elijah Muḥammad has started a Black Muslim movement. This person appeared in the shape of a reformer in the beginning, then he claimed Prophethood and now pretends to be God. We take refuge in Allah from all these things. The famous boxer Muhammad Ali Clay is one of the believers. He has a large circle of followers. These people are militant and quarrelsome. Elijah has gathered a great deal of money in this manner. He owns an airplane and a big palace. He leads an isolated life. A very notorious criminal Malcolm X became his follower and converted millions of people to Black Islam. He stayed for some time in Egypt and Hijaz where he came to know the reality of Islam. Then he became a staunch Sunni Muslim. He wrote a book against Elijah and converted a large number of people to Islam. Elijah's followers killed him after a few days. To Allah we belong and to Him we shall return.

Very few new people are now following Elijah. Several of his followers are accepting Islam. Two of his sons have returned to Sunni Islam. In addition to black Americans, white Americans are also feeling disillusioned by modern developments. As a result the new generation wishes to be free from all kinds of social bondage. They want to solve their mental problems by accepting secularism, where they will be free to use opium, drugs, music and other measures of promiscuity. Consequently these people are being exploited. We have observed that the people in America are not intelligent. Their intelligence level is quite ordinary. They rush after every new thing. They are turning to deviations and a mindless life, leaving all their comforts and luxury. For us there is a lesson to learn, that we would prefer this message (*Daʿwa*) to sleeping. The white youth are adopting hippyism in great numbers. Leaving their comfortable houses, they wander everywhere in search of satisfaction. They are suffering from mental confusion. This is the best time for spreading and working for *Daʿwa*.

Everyone pays a large share of his earnings in taxes and insurance premiums. Everyone has to contribute from his income a specific amount to insurance. The capitalists run insurance companies. A capitalist manufactures a car and then sells it and insures it. As a result a car, which appears to be inexpensive, becomes a liability requiring payments in the form of insurance. Apparently everyone believes that if there is an accident he will receive money from the insurance company. The fact is that it is his own money that he is receiving back. Similarly some amount is deducted for medical insurance each month. Again, these are capitalists who manufacture medicine, and who establish hospitals in order to hide their capital. When someone falls ill, this insurance money covers his expenses for only up to fifteen days. After that, the capitalist provides loans on interest and thus in the end money comes back finally to him. Medicine is very costly. Welfare institutions treat only the poor. The real purpose of such institutions is to hide the wealth. Usually a thousand dollars are spent on the birth of a child, and similarly a thousand dollars at the time of death. The government raises and nurtures illegitimate children. There are large numbers of such children. They are born in hospitals and for months their parents are not allowed to visit them.

Thefts, dacoity and murder are committed in full daylight. Pornography, evil doing, drunkenness, consumption of interest and pork, and similar illegitimate activities are part of general life here. There is no concept of sin and nobody thinks of the hereafter. They indulge in activities in public which even animals do not commit in our society. They have no morals, no fear of God and no fear of other people. Their moral decline has led them to the last possible depth. Here there is nothing left but God's punishment. But God will not punish them until the final argument by *Daʿwa* is completed.

The Muslims who have arrived here are lost in this colourful life and the apparent glitter; far from the mission, oblivious of God, and neglectful of the life of the Prophet, peace be upon him. They are influenced by these morally depraved human beings who are themselves on the road to Hell. They are working hard to convert this world into a furnace. The position of the Arabs is particularly pitiable. They are oblivious to their origins and are influenced by the local [secular] trends. They have established Islamic centres here and there. Yet they are embarrassed to call them mosques. Every type of luxury and comfort in worldly terms has been provided in these centres. They gather together in the afternoons on Sundays. They have no concern for prayers. In certain centres where there are pious people some Islamic features are visible in this total darkness. There are some servants of Allah who continue their efforts to keep the lamp of religion alight. By the grace of God there is some hope of success. I had in mind to report details of the work but unconsciously I have ended up reporting upon the environment here.

We worked in New York until 23 August, meeting people of all classes. A large number of people from our homeland are here. They paid much attention to what we were saying. New York is like a country in itself. It is the largest seaport. It is very important and most international institutions are situated here. Muslims are scattered in various quarters. New Muslims are very passionate and have the courage to learn and adopt the ways of the Prophet Muḥammad, peace be upon him. Most often new Muslims keep beards. They have prayer signs on their foreheads. They wear caps or turbans on their heads, long shirts and several of them wear *shērwānī*. They are eager to learn. I wish there were someone to teach them. A large number of them came to us daily and brought other new people with them. On average almost one person daily accepts Islam, even though no missionary work is reaching them. Whoever accepts Islam follows it steadfastly. However, I fear that due to the absence of institutions of learning and the lack of a proper system of training there may sprout thousands of islams. The reason is that these people study English translations of the Qur'ān and Mishkāt Sharīf [*Mishkātul maṣābīḥ*, a collection of *aḥādīth* by Khaṭīb Tabrīzī] and start acting upon what they understand from them. Those among them who have come back after spending some time in Tablīgh in another country or have traveled with Tablīgh groups stand out on account of their faith, actions, morals and knowledge, thanks be to God.

Leaders are arising in great numbers among the new Muslims. This has some danger. But by the grace of God, and thanks to the Tablīghī Jamā'at, some have gained some understanding. The Jamā'at can handle this development temporarily, but the problem must be solved permanently. It is essential that experienced people should offer sacrifices by sending groups to this country continuously. Otherwise God will take us to task. Firstly, these people wish to come into the fold of religion and there is no one to invite them. This nation is standing on the threshold of Islam. I wish there were some people who could work among them here without being influenced by worldly things. The chain of groups coming here should not break. It requires a great effort to provide education to these new Muslims and to guide them in the right direction. Their education and training is the greatest problem. Tablīgh is the only way to join them together; otherwise it is feared that they will be divided into thousands of sects.

Some of these people are very serious. They are very softhearted. They fully abide by what very little they are told; whatever you teach them they follow. They have a real passion for learning. They are very careful about their prayers. Several of them stay awake studying at nights. There is a great thrust for learning Islam. It is essential that full attention is paid to them. Some of their women folk observe *purdah* and wear the *burqa'*. Others, even though they do not wear the *burqa'*, cover their hair and their bodies properly. Most of these people have asked their women folk to resign from their jobs. These people are planning to come to our country. Two young persons are preparing to come for a full religious education. Perhaps they will return with us. They will first spend four months in *tablīgh* and then they will join some *madrasa* to acquire religious education. Their passions are remarkable. They appear to be a clear demonstration of the Qur'ānic verse: "If you turn away He will exchange you for another nation and they will not be like you" (47:38).

Most of the new Muslims are young people. Their parents and other relatives are non-Muslim. They are suffering from all kinds of opposition and difficulties. This reminds us of the early period of Islam, although it is not as hard as it was in those days because in this society every person is completely free. Some responsible people are also joining us. There is a weekly two-day holiday, so every week one group goes out of New York. Thus groups have been visiting Philadelphia, Elisabeth, Jersey City, the Bronx, Queens and other places. In these groups local new Muslims join people from our country and gather together twenty or thirty persons. Sometimes even two groups go out in a week. Our true effort was to establish our work as a permanent local feature. By the grace of God, in New York and some other cities, we have started two rounds on Saturdays, daily education in mosques, five congregational prayers daily, and outings for three days a month and forty days a year. Several people have committed themselves and begun work. Several friends spend the night with us. We divide our groups into three sub-groups.

We went out to Boston, which lies about 300 miles from New York. We stayed there for about eight days. There are some Muslim teachers and students and some government officials at Harvard University. This university is counted among the best in America. Throughout America, people from our country, wherever they are settled, care for religion, at least to some extent, despite the difficult situation. They do make preparations for Friday prayers. This helped us a great deal in our work. We reached people who had already gathered. Quincy is a small place near Boston. The Arabs have established an Islamic centre there. We stayed in that centre. I have already written that the conditions of Arabs are generally poor. They are careless about religion and deviate from Islamic teachings. They have established clubs in which all they do is drink and gamble. Besides Arabs, Muslims from Iran, Yugoslavia and Albania are also of this type. Only those Arabs who have been associated with Ikhwān in Egypt, or who have come from our homeland, have sentiments for religion. By the grace of God, now the youth coming from our country are least interested in the lifestyle here. Most of the young are leading a careful and clean life. They are also inclined towards the work of *Daʿwa.* Some of them join *tablīgh* groups and then fly back as far as 2000 miles to their place of work. These people are also careful about *dhabīḥa.* They have good sentiments. May Allah accept them all for the work of the survival of religion and bless them with progress in the two worlds. Amen!

The rounds here can be described in the following manner. People either bring cars, or we have to use the subway for long distances. The subway is underground train. One group went to Washington D.C., Philadelphia and Baltimore. After consultation with all of these people it was decided how the work of *Daʿwa* should be promoted in America, starting with a consultative meeting. This meeting was held in Detroit from 27–29 August. We arrived in Detroit on 24 August. The new Muslims are here in large numbers. People gathered on the twenty-seventh and twenty-eighth. About forty concerned people gathered from Chicago, Washington D.C., New Orleans, Raleigh, New York and Philadelphia.

Some of them had flown 2000 miles by plane. They participated in consultation. A plan for the whole year was prepared. Local people expressed their willingness to spend forty days or three sequences of forty days in addition to shorter periods of time. It was a unique gathering. It was probably the first gathering of its kind in the history of America for the revival and promotion of the faith of the Prophet, peace be upon him. May God accept it and may He deepen the roots of this mission in this country.

Yesterday we arrived at Flint. This place is at a distance of seventy miles from Detroit, which is in turn 700 miles from New York. Today we are returning to Detroit. From there we shall go to Cleveland on Saturday morning. A three-member group has been dispatched to Chicago and its environs for work there. This group will come back to New York on 20 September. On 7 September we shall go from Cleveland to Washington D.C., the capital of this country. After staying there for about a week we shall go to Baltimore, and then via Philadelphia we shall, God willing, reach New York on 20 September. This country needs work. We have very little time at our disposal. The work here requires a great deal of patience and steadfastness. The opportunities are open. If Muslims take the right direction, the whole nation will be able to accept Islam. Arriving here we realize how much wrong we have done to the faith of the Prophet, how we have neglected the spreading of this faith. The whole *Umma* is now suffering for it. The whole *Umma* is humiliated. The *Umma* is divided because Muslims have abandoned missions. There is no one now to look after its affairs. We have attracted God's punishment because of our bad deeds. The situation is so perilous that there is only one way left for the *Umma* as a whole: to turn to God and repent. Otherwise humiliation and affliction are engulfing it and no one can save it. There is only one way out:

> But Allah would not punish them as long as you are amongst them, and God will not punish them as long as they ask His forgiveness (8:33).

All of us should repent before God and seek His forgiveness individually and collectively, to remedy present day loss. The elders and the wise also recommend this way out. The great sin on account of which the whole *Umma* is suffering is our disregarding the effort to spread the faith. It is essential that all the people collectively repent for this great sin and heinous crime. We should plan for collective repentance and prayers. Forgiveness must be asked for the errors and wrongs done so far and resolution be made that from now on no stone should be left unturned in the preaching of Islam. Otherwise, believe me! We cannot prosper in this world by abandoning Allah's religion. How shall we face the Prophet in the Hereafter? How are we returning the efforts made by the Prophet and the sacrifices offered by his Companion? Results are obvious. After spending our whole lives, we are still where we started.

Disregarding religion we fight amongst ourselves for worldly interests. How can we deserve Allah's mercy? The situation calls for serious deliberation and weeping. It is time for fear. I am not simply telling a tale; this is not just rhetoric. We are surrounded by very serious problems. We do not know when God will withdraw His mercy. Then we can only repent, nothing else can be done. Reason calls on us to postpone our individual interests and set out for long distances and for long durations to make efforts on behalf of Allah's religion; we must beseech Allah in all humility.

We must arrange for a weekly gathering at each place, for night vigils in which we pray *tahajjud* and prayers, two rounds a week, with daily education. Individually, we shall resolve to perform supererogatory prayers, *tahajjud*, recitation of the Qur'ān, rosary, the special prayers of *tawba*, and *ḥāja*. Gatherings of women should also be planned to introduce these efforts. We should beseech Allah, continuously.

I hope this letter is not considered insignificant and read only for the time being. It is hoped that due importance will be given to this letter. It is very difficult to write in a letter what I want to say and convey the worries that I feel. I pray to God that He gives us all concern for religion and that we may appear successful before the Prophet of God. Amen. Please remember us in your special prayers. May Allah shield us from all kinds of evil, bestow on us sincerity and accept us for the work of revival and progress of his religion. Amen. My greetings to all and request for prayer. If I have been disrespectful to you elders in any way, please forgive me. Without meaning to, the letter has become too long. However, some very essential matters have been addressed in it. Please do not destroy it, I will collect it on my return.

Yours obediently
Servant and Seeker of Prayers
Shujāʿat

PART TWO

TABLĪGHĪ JAMĀʿAT
A TRANSNATIONAL MOVEMENT

CHAPTER FIVE

THE TRANSFORMATION OF TABLĪGHĪ JAMĀ'AT INTO A TRANSNATIONAL MOVEMENT[1]

Marc Gaborieau

The Tablīghī Jamāʿat operated under two limitations in the beginning. First, it operated only within the Indian subcontinent (then undivided British India). Second, the Jamāʿat preached only to people who were already Muslim, at a time when proselytism by Muslims among non-Muslims was politically sensitive. Until the late 1970s, many observers believed that the work of the Jamāʿat remained confined to South Asian Muslims, a view that has persisted among some people until recently (e.g., Agwani 1986, 46–47).

From the late 1970s on, students of Islam around the Indian Ocean (Nemo 1979, 632; 1983, 77, 96, 212–214), in the Maghreb (Tozy 1984) and in Europe (Kepel, Dassetto, this volume) reported that the Tablīghī Jamāʿat was gaining ground in Reunion and in Morocco, and had become a leading Muslim missionary organization in countries like France, Belgium, and Britain, where it had long been active. Far from being limited to South Asia, the movement had extended its work to the entire world. Scholars also drew attention to the fact that the Jamāʿat no longer aimed only at helping Muslims to strengthen their faith; it also tried, often with success, to convert non-Muslims to Islam. The two limitations initially imposed by Mawlānā Muḥammad Ilyās no longer prevailed.

How did this dramatic change come about? Anwārul Ḥaq had noticed that after the death of Muḥammad Ilyās, under the leadership of his son and successor Mawlānā Muḥammad Yūsuf (see Gaborieau 1992, 19–20), the movement began to address non-Muslims and to expand out of South Asia. Ḥaq listed thirty-four countries

[1] This essay has grown out of my interest in the Tablīghī Jamāʿat which I have maintained since 1985–1986 when I chose the movement as the theme of my seminar on South Asian Islam in the École des Hautes Études en Science Socilaes in Paris (Gaborieau 1986a; 1987b; 1990, 356–357; 1992, 12–13).

where the movement had spread, but supplied no details about when and how it reached them (Ḥaq 1972, 162–163, 186).

The Urdu biographical literature of the movement in fact provides a great deal of information about the way it spread abroad. The object of this essay is to present and analyze this information. Our questions will be the following: What are these sources? Which period do they cover? What do they teach us about the aims of those who expanded the movement? What information do they provide about the chronology of this expansion? Which classes of South Asian Muslims participated in this work, and which classes of people were addressed in the countries where the movement spread? How successful was Tablīghī Jamāʿat's spread? I will address these questions and the present state of our knowledge, and try to assess and highlight those areas that require further research.

Sources[2]

This essay draws upon three kinds of sources: biographies of Mawlānā Muḥammad Yūsuf, institutional and biographical literature produced by the Nadwatul ʿUlamā of Lucknow, and oral information provided by Jamāʿat workers.

Biographies of Mawlānā Muḥammad Yūsuf

A detailed biography of Muḥammad Yūsuf by Sayyid Muḥammad Thānī Ḥasanī was first published in 1967 in India (Ḥasanī 1967). The author is related to Sayyid ʿAbdul Ḥayy Ḥasanī (1869–1923) and his two sons ʿAbdul ʿAlī (1893–1961) and Abul Ḥasan ʿAlī Nadwī (d. 1999) (Nadwī 1983, 34; Khān 1984, 454). The Ḥasanī family has, since 1915, managed the Nadwatul ʿUlamā (see Introduction, this volume, and Nadwī 1983, 278ff.; Khān 1984 passim).

More than one third of Ḥasanī's book (274 out of 783 pages) is devoted to an account of the spread of the movement to the various parts of India (Ḥasanī 1967, 300–355 chapter 6), to West and

---

[2] I am grateful to Khalid Masud for providing me with a copy of Bijnawrī's work (1980), and for data he collected from a senior Tablīghī worker in Islamabad about the chronology of the first pedestrian *jamāʿats* sent abroad. This data is presented as an appendix to this essay.

East Pakistan (Ḥasanī 1967, 356–386 chapter 7), to countries situated along pilgrimage land and sea routes, including the Arabian peninsula (chapter 8), its spread by travel on foot (chapter 12, particularly 548–552 and 555–574), to the other Arab countries (chapter 9), to Afro-Asian [*sic*] countries (chapter 10) and to the industrialized countries of Britain, the United States and Japan (chapter 11). The chapter order is not chronological but geographical, and it betrays a world view where South Asia comes first, and then Arabia, which is set apart from the Arab world. The rest of the world is divided into underdeveloped Afro-Asian countries and developed countries.

A shorter biography was written at the end of 1965 by ʿAzīzur Raḥmān Bijnawrī (Bijnawrī 1980, 19–20). An entire chapter of this book (chapter 8) is devoted to the spread of the Tablīghī Jamāʿat outside of South Asia, particularly in Britain, Japan and America. The author was closely related to the Tablīghī movement and knew Mawlānā Muḥammad Yūsuf personally. He wrote this book with the approval of Muḥammad Yūsuf's family, and it was prefaced by Mawlānā Iḥtishāmul Ḥasan Kāndhalawī (1906–1971), the premier historian and ideologue of the Jamāʿat (Masud 1994). Bijnawrī's biography offers little of significance beyond Ḥasanī's.

Literature About Nadwatul ʿUlamā

Two books concerning the history of the Nadwatul ʿUlamā and the life of its head, Abul Ḥasan ʿAlī Nadwī, contain additional information about the Tablīghī Jamāʿat. Written first was *Kārwān-i Zindagī*, an autobiography of Abul Ḥasan ʿAlī Nadwī. Its first volume covers the period from his birth in 1914 to 1965. It gives an account of the part taken by the Nadwa in the spread of the Jamāʿat in Arabia and other Middle Eastern countries in 1947 and 1951 (Nadwī 1983, 326–394).

The other book is the official history of the Nadwatul ʿUlamā (Khān 1984). Its second volume presents an account of these same events from the viewpoint of the institution, particularly during 1930–1961 when Sayyid ʿAbdul ʿAlī Nadwī was its head. His younger brother, Sayyid Abul Ḥasan ʿAlī, who was to succeed him and other members of Nadwa, became increasingly involved in the work of the Tablīghī Jamāʿat from 1940 on, and helped it spread to the Arab countries from 1945 to 1952 (Khān 1984, 308–460 passim). Lacunae in these sources can be partly filled from oral traditions collected from Jamāʿat workers (see apppendix).

Scope of the Sources

The scope of these sources is limited in two ways. First, these books are biographical and cover only the lifespan of their subjects. Except for the autobiography of Abul Ḥasan ʿAlī Nadwī (four vols. to 1990), all were written posthumously. Thus the official history of the Nadwatul ʿUlamā stops at the death of Sayyid ʿAbdul ʿAlī in 1961, and presumably the next volume will appear only after the death of the present head of the institution, Abul Ḥasan ʿAlī Nadwī. Similarly, a detailed history of the spread of the Tablīghī Jamāʿat after 1965 is provided in the biography of Muḥammad Inʿāmul Ḥasan (Rāshid 1997), and biographies of Mawlānā Yūsuf cover only the period between 1944 and 1965.

Secondly, these sources were not written independently. Oral information and Bijnawrī's biography of Muḥammad Yūsuf both express the views of the Tablīghī Jamāʿat. The other books were written and published under the auspices of the Nadwa, which played a leading part in spreading the Tablīghī Jamāʿat and also in recording its history. Although the latter reflect a slightly different point of view, these sources are not really independent of each other. And since Ḥasanī's book, the most detailed account of the spread of the Tablīghī Jamāʿat abroad, emanates from the Nadwa, our knowledge is limited mainly to the views of the Nadwa and reflects only internal perspectives. These sources are understandably biased, and we still lack an independent analysis that would complete and correct them. Keeping these limitations in mind, let us draw upon these sources to construct a picture of the spread of the Tablīghī Jamāʿat.

Tablīghī Jamāʿat and Mawlānā Muḥammad Ilyās's Policies: Continuity or Discontinuity?

During Mawlānā Ilyās's life, the Tablīghī Jamāʿat movement was restricted to British India, and preaching was confined to Muslims, at least in principle. Cases such as that of ʿAbdur Raḥmān Mēwātī (d. 1945), who is credited with the conversion of one thousand Hindus (Gaborieau 1992, 6), were exceptions. However, under the leadership of Mawlānā Yūsuf, these limitations were no longer observed. First, within two years of taking office, Mawlānā Yūsuf sent preaching teams to Arabia and England. His biographers state repeatedly that preaching to the whole world, including non-Muslim countries, was the movement's aim. Second, after 1944 Yūsuf lifted the ban which his father had imposed on preaching to non-Muslims (Ḥaq 1972, 163–180). Can we conclude from this double departure from Mawlānā Ilyās's practices that there was a change in the movement's policies and objectives?

Mawlānā Ilyās had already planned the spread of the movement beyond South Asia. He himself had briefly carried it to the Ḥijāz when he went there in 1938 for his last pilgrimage with his son Yūsuf, whose first pilgrimage it was (Ḥaq 1972, 91–94, 99; Ḥasanī 1967, 182–183; Nadwī 1983, 326). The extension of the Jamāʿat after 1944 thus appears as the fullfillment of a plan initiated by Mawlānā Ilyās, not a new policy.

Nonetheless, one may wonder whether the work proceeded in the same spirit. Many indices lead us to think that it did. Like his father, Mawlānā Yūsuf insisted that preaching concentrate on the essentials of the faith, and that involvement in politics should be carefully avoided. This point is stressed repeatedly in Ḥasanī's biography. For instance, Muḥammad Zakariyyā (1898–1982), who was both an uncle and father-in-law of Muḥammad Yūsuf and of Inʿāmul Ḥasan, and a great doctrinal authority of the movement (Gaborieau 1992, 20), wrote in a letter to one of the first preaching teams going to Saudi Arabia that, "It must be clear that this movement is not interested in any way in the politics of the kingdom" (Ḥasanī 1967, 414). He blames the failure of the Muslim Brothers in Egypt on their involvement in politics (Ḥasanī 1967, 429), and the success of the Tablīghī Jamāʿat in East Africa is explained by its aloofness from politics: "The reason for this favourable reception is that the Tablīghī teams never entangled themselves in local politics or tribal alignments. They only worked to preach and teach the basic principles of Islam, the righteous acts and the morality of the Prophet" (Ḥasanī 1967, 471–472). More generally the rule was to avoid any kind of controversy whatsoever (Ḥaq 1972, 177).

Muḥammad Yūsuf went beyond the two rules set out by his father. First, he increased the required duration of time for preaching:

> Yūsuf was more exacting than his father. Ilyās had required his workers to start with a three-day tour every month, followed by a forty-

> day tour or *chilla* [forty-day retreat] annually, and topped by three *chillas* in succession, once in a lifetime. Yūsuf recommended further stages such as three *chillas* every year to be gradually raised to six months in a year. Then came the crowning act when one devoted four months every year to earning a livelihood, and the remaining eight months to preaching tours" (Agwani 1986, 47, quoting Fīrōzpurī n.d., 9; see also Ḥaq 1972, 163).

But this does not deviate from the spirit of Mawlānā Ilyās's work. Only the second point, namely preaching to non-Muslims, seems to be a real departure. I have found no explanation in the sources as to why it took place. We might speculate that Muḥammad Ilyās forbade preaching to non-Muslims because during his time, in British India, it was a politically sensitive issue. Preaching to non-Muslims became possible only with the change of political circumstances in the Indo-Pak subcontinent, and with the spread of the movement to other parts of the world where conversion was less controversial. Explained in this manner, this second change was also not a real departure from the spirit of Muḥammad Ilyās's work.

Chronology

We shall first try to reconstitute a chronology of the spread of the Tablīghī Jamā'at to various parts of the world on the basis of the details contained in the biographies of Muḥammad Yūsuf. Then we shall examine the questions about strategy.

The Decision to Spread the Movement

The decision to extend the movement outside South Asia was made soon after the election of Muḥammad Yūsuf as its head during the first general meeting (*ijtimā'*) held at Muradabad, U.P., north of Delhi, on 14–16 January 1945 (Ḥasanī 1967, 231; Bijnawrī 1980, 133). It was during this meeting that the new leader announced preaching teams would be sent to countries like Syria, Iraq and Egypt (Ḥasanī 1967, 233–234). More generally, it was decided to extend the movement to foreign countries, in particular to Britain:

> One of the greatest religious works of Muḥammad Yūsuf was that, from the very beginning of his tenure of office, missionary work (*tablīghī kām*) in foreign countries was started.... It was at the Muradabad

meeting that he initiated his call to spread [Tablīghī Jamā'at] to foreign countries" (Ḥasanī 1967, 245–246).

First Missions and Delays

The spread actually started in 1946 when teams were sent to Ḥijāz and Britain. This beginning was a modest one because of the uncertain political situation in South Asia, and the demand for Pakistan. The partitioning of India in August 1947 and the troubles and massacres which followed delayed the work considerably. It was not until 1948 that, with a fresh mission to Ḥijāz, the extension of the Tablīghī Jamā'at truly started.

Tentative Chronology

The organization of the Tablīghī Jamā'at inside South Asia is beyond the scope of this essay, but let us recall that while spreading elsewhere the movement had also to consolidate its hold over the subcontinent. Until 1944, the Tablīghī Jamā'at remained mainly concentrated in U.P. and in the Panjab, with later extensions to Karachi and to Bhopal. After 1947, from its headquarters in Delhi, it built a network all over India, as well as beyond the newly demarcated borders in East and West Pakistan. In the East (now Bangladesh) a centre was established in Kakrail mosque in Dhaka proper, and another in Tongi near Dhaka (Mohsin 1983, 234–235; Hours 1993, 70, 137–139). In West Pakistan (now Pakistan) a center was established at Raiwind near Lahore (Ḥasanī 1967, 360).

The chronology of the extension of the Jamā'at outside the subcontinent is not given outright in the biographies. As noted, the only available systematic account, Ḥasanī's book, is arranged geographically rather than chronologically, and dates are not always provided. Accounts are most often quotations from the letters of "missionaries" who were sent abroad (see the appendix of chapter four, this volume). Dates are often missing from these excerpts or are incomplete (dates and months, but not years). Most of these gaps, however, can be filled from oral accounts, and we know the dates of the arrivals of the first teams.

If we calibrate the various dates given in the books and from oral sources we find that the spread of the movement between 1946 and

1965 proceeded roughly through eleven steps, some of them taking place simultaneously in different directions.

1) *1946–1951: Pilgrimage Routes and the Arabian Peninsula.* This is the best-documented area, which we will often cite to illustrate our analysis. The extension to these places was planned by Muḥammad Yūsuf, we are told, as soon as he became the head of the movement. But it was launched only in 1946 by letters sent to all the branches of the movement (Ḥasanī 1967, 389–390). The first preaching groups started out, by boat and on foot, in 1946 (Ḥasanī 1967, 393–394). From 1948 onwards teams began to arrive in Arabia every year. "To do work among the pilgrims and the immigrants, Muḥammad Yūsuf made a rule of sending teams every year. Various teams left from Hindustan and Pakistan on pilgrimage on foot or by boat. Most who went stayed for one year. Work went on continuously and the number of [Tablīgh] workers kept increasing" (Ḥasanī 1967, 400). This missionary work, traveling along pilgrimage routes by boat, had become fully organized by 1951. It was complemented by teams that toured the Arabian Peninsula on foot, or even came on foot from Pakistan through Iran, Kuwait and Qatar. Seventeen teams traveled from South Asia to Arabia between 1953 and 1965 (Ḥasanī 1967, 548).

2) *1946–1962: Britain.* According to Ḥasanī (1967, 247–248), the first mission sent to London in January 1946 was comprised of: Zakir Husayn (who later became the President of India), a certain S. Muḥammad Rāḥat ʿAlī Riḍwī, who was then studying for the diploma of the Royal Aeronautical College at Bletchley, and the famous ʿAbdur Rashīd Arshad Peshāwarī. The latter was popularly known as Arshad Ṣāhib (d. 1963), and was an engineer from Peshawar, who would later be active internationally (Gaborieau 1992, 9). The first team from Pakistan to Britain was sent in 1952 (on the work of Jamāʿat in Britain see Faust, this volume). Two letters reporting the progress of the movement there are dated 1961 (Ḥasanī 1967, 407ff.) and 1962 (Bijnawrī 1980, 137–141) The latter is translated in the appendix to chapter four of this volume.

3) *1946 and 1951: Arab Countries.* Implanting the movement in the Arab world was considered an important development. Having consolidated its roots in the Arabian Peninsula, the Tablīghī Jamāʿat could now spread systematically to other Arab countries (Ḥasanī 1967, 426–470). Egypt, Sudan and Syria were visited first in 1951.

The chronology of Tablīghī Jamāʿat's introduction into other Arab countries is not given in Ḥasanī's book, but from the history of the Nadwa—which was instrumental in opening these contacts—we can surmise that the first visits to the Maghreb (Tunisia, Algeria and Morocco) and to the Near East (Jordan, Iraq, Lebanon and Palestine) took place during 1951–1952 (Nadwī 1983, 326–394; Khān 1984, 419–420; for Morocco, see Tozy, this volume).

4) *1952 and 1962: Southeast Asia (Malaysia, Burma and Indonesia).* A team is reported to have been first sent from Pakistan to Malaysia and Singapore in 1952, but systematic coverage of Southeast Asia seems to have started in 1962 (Ḥasanī 1967, 478–485). It is interesting that these countries, despite being very near to India, were visited so late.

5) *1954: United States.* The first Pakistani team was sent to the United States in 1954, according to information collected by Khalid Masud. A letter reporting the progress of the Jamāʿat in America is dated 1971 (Bijnawrī 1980, 157ff; see translation in the appendix of chapter four, this volume.). No other date has been found in the sources.

6) *1953–1954: Turkey.* According to the information collected by Khalid Masud, the first Pakistani team went to Turkey during 1953–1954.

7) *1956: Japan.* The first Pakistani team was sent to Japan in 1956. The first date given for a team from the Indian side is 1958 (Bijnawrī 1980, 147). Arshad Ṣāḥib completed the first Japanese translation of the Qur'ān in 1962 with the help of a Japanese, Ḥajjī ʿUmar Mītā, who had converted to Islam while travelling in China (Bijnawrī 1980, 141, 147, 148).

8) *1956: East Africa and Indian Ocean.* Ḥasanī mentions the following countries or places as being visited in these years: Kenya, Uganda, Tanzania, Malawi, Zambia, Mozambique, East Africa, Rhodesia, South Africa, Mauritius and Reunion (1967, 488–449). Note that these areas, which played such an important part in the movement's later extension to continental Europe, were explored rather late (for South Africa, see Moosa, this volume).

9) *1958: Afghanistan.* The introduction of the Tablīghī Jamāʿat into Afghanistan, a country which borders on Pakistan, was also surprisingly late (Ḥasanī 1967, 472–478). Does this reflect a gap in our knowledge, or was this delay due to the traditionally strict control

by the local government of religious affairs? Or could it have been due to the prevalence of Russian influence? We do not know.

10) *1961–1962: Continental Europe.* Teams of Jamāʿat workers began arriving on the European continent, including Yugoslavia (presently Bosnia Herzegovina) and Western Europe, in the 1960s. According to oral accounts, the first Jamāʿats from Pakistan were sent to these areas between 1961 and 1962. Tablīghī activity was also being carried out in Europe during this period by workers in London (Bijnawrī 1980, 136; for France, Belgium and Germany see, respectively, Kepel, Dassetto and Faust, this volume).

11) *1961–1962: Nigeria and West Africa*: Ḥasanī reports that the earliest Tablīgh activity in this part of Africa began during 1961–1962 (Ḥasanī 1967, 493).

In summary, by 1962, that is to say eighteen years after Muḥammad Yūsuf took charge of the movement, a worldwide network had been established stretching from Tokyo to Chicago.

Strategy

From this data we can draw some inferences about the strategy devised by Muḥammad Yūsuf and his followers. Two points immediately come to mind. The first is that the movement spread from three centers: South Asia, Arabia and London. The most important bases of the movement remained in South Asia, where people from other parts of the world would come for training. Formally, the historical headquarters in Niẓāmuddīn, in Delhi, remains the main base where the *shūra* of the Tablīghī Jamāʿat resides. The importance of Raiwind in Pakistan as a decision-making center is said to be growing. We know very little about the functioning of the Tablīghī Jamāʿat in Bangladesh that would help us to appraise the strategic importance of the headquarters at Kakrail and Tongi, in and near Dhaka. The holy cities of Arabia, Mecca and Medina were made into a second centre for the propagation of the movement. Finally, from the start an effort was made to build a third centre in London, in the heart of industrialized countries.

The selection of these three centres—and this is our second point—is indicative of a strategy. The first priority was to have a centre in the Holy places in order to establish contacts in the Arab countries, and more generally in the Muslim world, through pilgrims. The second priority was to build a bridgehead in London. The leaders of the Jamāʿat may have thought that power over the other parts of the world remained in Europe, and that a strong centre there was necessary for spreading the movement. It is perhaps also important that science and engineering students who were attending European schools were the first there to be attracted to the movement. Expanding to Afro-Asian countries was considered only after the movement was consolidated in these three main centres. Afro-Asian countries were reached last and very late, considering their geographical proximity and their long historical connections with India.

The Roles of South Asians

Who were the people who helped the movement spread outside of South Asia? Were they mostly South Asians? And if so, to which classes did they belong? Let us now explore these questions.

Tablīghī Jamāʿat Members from South Asia

Biographers never fail to state that the initiative for sending teams abroad and establishing permanent centres came from South Asia, ultimately from Muḥammad Yūsuf and his close mentors and associates.

People of the movement most often carried out the missions themselves. While I have not yet collected all the names and biographies of those who worked in the various areas of the world to see if any patterns emerge, I can make two observations from what I have analyzed. First, volunteers for trips abroad were recruited from all across the subcontinent. The 1947 boundaries that separated India from Pakistan were irrelevant; even if Muḥammad Yūsuf had chosen to keep the old historical headquarters in Delhi, South Asian Muslims were still considered to be a community with a particular responsibility to extend the movement abroad. When reporting about the teams sent to other countries, the biographers stress again and again that they came from "India and Pakistan" (*Hind wa Pāk*).

Second, not everybody went everywhere. Of course most would go to Arabia, as the place of the pilgrimage, but for the other countries there seem to have been specializations. These may have been due to some degree to geographical proximity; those who went to the Indian Ocean were naturally Gujratis. But specialization seems to have been related more to training—as we shall see presently, those who led missions to Arab countries were learned in Arabic. The same appears to have been true for missions to Western countries: both Ḥasanī and Bijnawrī stress in several places the key role of ʿAbdur Rashīd Arshad, alias Arshad Ṣāḥib, whom, we have already mentioned, was a Peshāwarī who had a Western education and was an engineer (Ḥasanī 1967, 549). He first went to London in 1946, and then to Japan, where he stayed for two and a half years (Ḥasanī 1967, 252–254 n. 4; Bijnawrī 1980, 141ff.). He was later called back and then sent to the United States. He finally got an appointment in Saudi Arabia as an expert on the installation of automatic telephones. There he spread the missionary work and looked after local South Asian workers (Ḥasanī 1967, 401–402). He died in a car accident in Mecca during *ʿumra* in 1963–1964. He was considered a martyr by his biographers, and is buried near the tomb of Imdādullāh Thānawī (1817–1899) in Mecca (Gaborieau 1992, 9).

Nadwa Graduates

Among the missionaries who came from South Asia, the graduates of the Nadwatul ʿUlamā played a conspicuous role because they were learned in Arabic. They are reported to have established contacts in the Arab countries. The accounts of their roles vary in our different sources, however. The history of the Nadwa states that in 1948, and in 1951–1952, the head of the institution, Sayyid ʿAbdul ʿAlī, sent his younger brother, Sayyid Abul Ḥasan ʿAlī Nadwī, and several graduates on extensive tours of Arab countries to learn more Arabic, establish intellectual links, and to do "missionary work" (*Daʿwa/tablīgh*). The last was mentioned only in passing (Khān 1984, 419–420). But in his autobiography Abul Ḥasan ʿAlī Nadwī more explicitly connects these trips to the Middle East with the extension of the Tablīghī Jamāʿat outside of South Asia (Nadwī 1983, 326–328). In Ḥasanī's biography of Yūsuf, the initiative for this tour is not ascribed to the Nadwa but rather to Yūsuf himself. He asked the Nadwīs for help because Tablīghī Jamāʿat members did not know enough Arabic to converse with or convince the scholars of the Arab countries. Abul Ḥasan ʿAlī Nadwī wrote and printed a booklet in Arabic to explain the objectives of the Tablīghī Jamāʿat, and distributed it in the Near East, and Nadwa graduates worked as interpreters. In 1949 the group was joined by the famous Sulaymān Nadwī (d. 1953) and Manẓūr Nuʿmānī Nadwī. Finally, Sayyid Abul Ḥasan ʿAlī Nadwī was appointed leader of the Tablīghī Jamāʿat in the Ḥijāz. The Nadwa acted for a time as an important intermediary between the Tablīghī Jamāʿat and the Arab elite (Ḥasanī 1967, 406–418, and chapter 9, particularly 430–451).

Local South Asian Communities

Before reaching the local populations, Tablīghī Jamāʿat first aimed at a more accessible target: migrant South Asian populations. As the movement started its spread along the pilgrimage roads on the way to the Ḥijāz, the Jamāʿat workers first preached to pilgrims in South Asian railway stations, ports, airports, on boats, and finally in the Holy cities of Arabia. Next they targeted South Asians who had settled as immigrants (*muhājir*), merchants (*tājir*) or as workers in Arabia (Ḥasanī 1967, 398–402). This same pattern was repeated almost everywhere in the world, in Britain, America, Africa and Southeast Asia.

Does this mean that the work of the Tablīghī Jamāʿat was confined to South Asians who had migrated abroad? A recent observer wrote: "Most of the preaching teams are sent out on the invitation of Indian immigrants abroad and the preaching work is confined to them" (Agwani 1986, 14 n. 1). Is this really true? The following section attempts to answer that question.

Local Populations: Authority and Hierarchy

The observation that the movement's work was confined to reaching South Asians may have contained some truth in the beginning. But that seems to have changed by the end of Mawlānā Muḥammad Yūsuf's life, by which time the Tablīghī Jamāʿat claims to have reached local populations (*maqāmī bāshindē*; see Ḥasanī 1967, 403). We shall first address what Jamāʿat workers say about this phenomenon, and then assess the validity of their claims.

A Hierarchical Vision of Muslim Society

Chapter 8 of Ḥasanī's book, which deals with Saudi Arabia, is the most detailed on this topic (Ḥasanī 1967, 387–425). On the basis of this information, we can analyze how work with local populations is conceived, and the strategies adopted for the various classes. We find that the population is classified and approached according to their place in the local social hierarchy, just as Mawlānā Muḥammad Ilyās did in Mēwāt when he first contacted the local authorities. Similarly, in Saudi Arabia due respect was given to local authorities and every effort made to gain their favour (Ḥasanī 1967, 413–414). Aloofness from politics does not mean ignoring political authorities; these have to be respectfully acknowledged. Beside the authorities, the population is divided into four classes, arranged in a hierarchy which betrays the point of view of the *ʿulamā* who wrote the accounts. A similar view of society is also briefly outlined in the other biography of Muḥammad Yūsuf (Bijnawrī 1980, 133–135).

The Classes Contacted by the Jamāʿat

The accounts are not equally precise, and more work needs to be done on this topic, but the following system of classifying target populations emerges from an initial inspection of the sources.

1) *The ʿulamā*. In Muslim countries *ʿulamā* must be contacted first (Ḥasanī 1967, 410–417). As we have seen in Arab countries, this was done through local leaders and graduates of the Nadwatul ʿUlamā, who already formed a network in the Middle East. For instance, in Morocco first contacts were made through Taqiyud Dīn al-Hilālī al-Marākashī, an Arabic teacher at the Nadwatul ʿUlamā in Lucknow from 1930 to 1933 (Khān 1984, 415–417). He first supported the Tablīghī Jamāʿat (Ḥasanī 1967, 463–467), but later became its strong opponent (Tozy 1984, chapter 4, 335ff.). The same approach was adopted in non-Arab countries. In Iran, Malaysia and Burma first contacts were made through *ʿulamā* who had studied in India (Ḥasanī 1967, 481, 482, 549). Where there were no such links, as in Indonesia, Jamāʿat workers complained of their difficulties working where they did not know the language and where *ʿulamā* could not act as their intermediaries and interpreters (Ḥasanī 1967, 478).

2) *Lay intellectuals.* The next targets were lay intellectuals who had influence over the masses:

> In every country, among the educated classes, the most influential groups are the intellectuals and writers who can change the morals of a country with their pen. If they have a passion for religion, they can contribute to the spread of religion. . . . in Ḥijāz there are many *literati*. It was necessary to make Tablīgh known to them. So in 1950 [the first step was taken . . .] (Ḥasanī 1967, 415–416; see also 413).

There is here an echo of the leaders of the Nadwa who always emphasize the role of intellectuals in Muslim societies.

3) *Merchants (Tājir).* Merchants are always praised for providing funds and taking part in missionary work. The role of merchants was particularly conspicuous in the Indian Ocean and East African regions where they were the main vectors of the expansion of the Tablīghī Jamāʿat (Nemo 1983, 212–214). Elsewhere, although they are mentioned, it is hard to find any details about their missionary activities. Our sources, written by the *ʿulamā*, do not seem to value merchants and their efforts.

4) *The common people.* As I have stressed elsewhere (Gaborieau 1986a), the common man is an even hazier figure than the merchant in literature of the Tablīghī Jamāʿat which is written by the *ʿulamā*. Social distance is maintained, and the writings display no familiar knowledge of the popular classes.

But here and there the common people of the various countries are mentioned. For instance, in the Ḥijāz, preaching tours in various quarters of towns and villages are narrated, but nothing is told beyond the place names. As for the Bedouins, derogatory remarks (in the same wording as comments on the Mēwātīs) are made about their religious ignorance. The same tone is found everywhere, be it in Nigeria, when speaking about local Maliki Muslims (Ḥasanī, 1967: 493) or in the United States. In the latter, when Jamāʿat workers encountered some Black Muslims led by Elijah (transcribed as ʿAlī Jāh in Tablīghī accounts) Muḥammad in Chicago and elsewhere, they considered them not as orthodox Muslims but as kinds of Qādiyānīs (i.e., Aḥmadīs) because some of their leaders claimed a share in prophecy (Ḥasanī 1967, 527; Bijnawrī 1980: 160).

The local people whom Jamāʿat workers contacted were usually Muslims who were either indigenous, as was the case in Africa or

Indonesia, or were immigrants from countries outside of South Asia, as in Britain or America.

Work Among Non-Muslim Populations

Surprisingly enough, little is said in the Tablīghī literature about the conversion of non-Muslims to Islam. From the biographies of Mawlānā Muḥammad Yūsuf it is difficult to know how much energy was spent on converting local people and what the results of such efforts were. One may wonder whether there has been much change in this area since the death of Mawlānā Muḥammad Ilyās. According to Muḥammad Yūsuf's biographers, the emphasis is still on working with Muslims.

Cases of conversion are mentioned specifically with reference to Tablīgh work in the United States and Japan. In the former, special attention is given to Black people but little detail is provided on the conversion process (Bijnawrī 1980, 160ff.). Perhaps the most interesting account is in Arshad Ṣāḥib's letters detailing his experiences in Japan. He analyses the motivations of the converts, and describes the organization of the Japanese convert community in Tokyo, with its own mosque and cemetery. He also speaks about the translation into Japanese of the Qur'ān and of the *Hikāyāt-i Ṣaḥāba* of Muḥammad Zakariyyā Kāndhalwī (1898–1982) (Bijnawrī 1980, 142–156).

An Emphasis on Results

The literature produced by the Tablīghī Jamāʿat is always anxious to proclaim that the preaching tours obtained wonderful results (*natā'ij*). The accounts are written in a militant style and can be summarized as follows: "Thanks to Allah all obstacles were lifted; people were greatly impressed and joined our movement *en masse*." Unfortunately, I was unable to locate in the accounts of Ḥasanī and Bijnawrī any precise data or even estimates concerning the strength of the movement in a given place, at a given time. The only proof of the participation by local people is that in the time of Muḥammad Yūsuf some had already adopted the habit of coming to the Tablīghī Jamāʿat headquarters in Niẓāmuddīn in Delhi from various parts of the world:

> Since preaching teams went continuously to Arab countries, taste and enthusiasm for Tablīgh grew in various circles of these countries. And at the invitation of Indian teams, traders and workers started coming to the Tablīgh headquarters in Niẓāmuddīn, and to travel to various centres, towns and areas (Ḥasanī 1967, 348, see also 341–343).

The first coming of Arabs to Tablīgh headquarters in India can be dated to 1962. Similar statements are made about other areas, but when those peoples began coming to India cannot be dated with any certainty. In East Africa: "Some people devoted their life to Tablīgh and kept coming to the Centre of Niẓāmuddīn" (Ḥasanī 1967, 488). In Britain, local "Muslims got interested in Tablīgh, they traveled to Hindustan and Pakistan from where they came back very impressed" (Ḥasanī 1967, 511). Similarly, three Muslims from Detroit, in America, "went to our country [India] and learned the art of Tablīgh" (Ḥasanī 1967, 525).

Conclusions and Questions

We can only guess that the pattern of Tablīghī work and success we see after 1980 was already in place between 1946 and 1965, including the recruiting of local Muslims who were then sent to India for training. But the work does not seem to have gained much momentum, for it did not attract the attention of external observers. That is to say, the Tablīghī Jamāʿat was not yet a mass movement by 1965; it became such only after that date.

Further questions then arise: Was it just a matter of time and was success gained by continuing the work in the same way? In other words, did Inʿāmul Ḥasan, who assumed leadership of the Jamāʿat after 1965, follow the same policy as his predecessor? Or did he inaugurate a new policy which might account for the emergence of the Tablīghī Jamāʿat as a major Muslim organization worldwide? Or perhaps this tremendous success was due to external factors which were not present before 1965? Or were all of these factors, or even others, at work? The material explored in this essay only partly explains the transformation of the Tablīghī Jamāʿat into a transnational movement between 1944 and 1965. We glimpse only the beginnings of a process, not its fulfillment. For a full understanding we will need to more closely explore the period from 1965–1980, and for that, more sources will first have to be located.

A drawback to the sources analyzed here is that they do not take precedents into account. Tablīghīs always speak and write as if they were the first South Asians to send missions abroad, though they were not. The earliest and best documented case is that of the Aḥmadīs, who in the beginning of this century established a truly universal missionary movement which, by 1920, had begun sending preachers to West Africa, America and the Soviet Union (Friedmann 1990, 22–31). Indeed, it seems that it was this group that first popularized the word *tablīgh* in South Asia (J.M.S. Baljon, personal correspondence). In the 1940s Mawlānā Mawdūdī—who, incidentally, had links both with the Tablīghī Jamāʿat and the Nadwa between 1938 and 1943—and his organization, the Jamāʿat Islāmī (founded in 1941), also built a transnational network which covered both Muslim and Western countries (Gaborieau 1986b). Did the Tablīghī Jamāʿat capitalize on these previous experiences? Or did it start something completely new? A serious study of the Tablīghī Jamāʿat must address these questions.

Appendix

*Chronology of the First Pedestrian Jamāʿats Sent Abroad**

The following table shows the dates when the work of Tablīgh began in various countries with the dispatch of groups travelling on foot to that destination. It marks the year, the destination, and whether the *jamāʿat* originated in India or Pakistan.

Year	Destination	From	Description
1946	Hijaz	India	First from India
1946	Egypt, Sudan, Syria	India	First *jamāʿat* to its destination
1950	Hijaz	Pakistan	First pedestrian *jamāʿat* from Pakistan
1951	Egypt, Sudan, Syria	Pakistan	First from Pakistan
1952	Malaysia, Singapore	Pakistan	First from Pakistan
1952	USA	Pakistan	First from Pakistan
1952	England	Pakistan	First from Pakistan
1956	Japan	Pakistan	First from Pakistan
1956/1957	Turkey	Pakistan	First from Pakistan
1961/1962	France	Pakistan	First from Pakistan
1962	Western Europe, Yugoslavia	Pakistan	First from Pakistan

* Source: Personal communication by a senior Tablīgh worker to M.K. Masud in Islamabad on 10 June 1993.

CHAPTER SIX

CLOSE TIES AND NEW BOUNDARIES: TABLĪGHĪ JAMĀʿAT IN BRITAIN AND GERMANY[1]

Elke Faust

The Tablīghī Jamāʿat has challenged the existing model of centre and periphery within the Islamic world.[2] The fact that the movement spread to Europe successfully underlines its transnational character and should be analyzed as a special topic.

The first *jamāʿat*s (mission groups) arriving in Europe from South Asia in the late 1940s apparently found little interest among the small local Muslim communities already living there. With the fresh waves of immigrants in the 1960s and early 1970s, however, a new potential emerged which enabled the Tablīghī Jamāʿat to build a dynamic network of adepts and sympathizers. It is said that they played an important role in leading Muslim minorities of several European countries conscious of the need to foster religious life. During the 1980s the Tablīghī Jamāʿat developed into one of the strongest Islamic movements in some regions.

The assumption that *jamāʿats* travel to distant places during their *Khurūj fī Sabīl Allāh* (going out on the path of God) without having a particular address to turn to, may be true in exceptional cases, but this is not the rule. For the recruitment of new members, the Tablīghī Jamāʿat depends upon established networks of traders and

---

[1] Acknowledgements: I wish to thank Jamal Malik for his kind help and comments on this paper, and Barbara D. Metcalf, Christian W. Troll, Muhammad Khalid Masud and Marc Gaborieau for providing me with unpublished material. I am also grateful to T.N. and all other German "Tablīghīs" for their personal confidence and for giving me insight into their lives. I have not provided the names of my interlocutors so as to protect their anonymity.

[2] The historical background and ideology of the Tablīghī Jamāʿat is well known thanks to the works of Anwārul Ḥaq (1972), Nadwī (1983), Troll (1982), Gaborieau (1986a), Aḥmad (1991a) and Metcalf (1993a). Yet, in comparison with other contemporary Islamic groups, there has been little research done on the Tablīghī Jamāʿat. This is probably due to its apolitical stance on the one hand, and the prevailing perception of India as being on the "Islamic periphery" on the other. For the center-periphery model see Eickelman and Piscatori (1990b) and Malik (1997).

scholars. What are the mechanisms of Jamāʿat's spread in Europe? What is the social base of the Tablīghī Jamāʿat there? Which segments of society have been active in, or sympathetic to this faith movement that brings about radical change in the lives of individuals? And finally, what structures were established by the Tablīghī Jamāʿat? The following essay considers these basic questions in regards to two European countries: Britain, with its large Indo-Pakistani population, is contrasted with Germany, where the vast majority of Muslims are of Turkish origin.

The European Setting

When considering the Tablīghī Jamāʿat in Europe, one must pay special attention to the broader phenomenon of Islam in Europe, which is both complex and dynamic.

After the Second World War most Muslims came to Western Europe as workers following in the footsteps of receding colonialism. Young men traveled from the newly independent countries to the former colonial "motherlands" as skilled and unskilled workers for the industry that was recovering after the war. Immigration was encouraged by recruitment, but when the economic situation of the industrial nations improved official recruitment of foreign workers ended. Laws were made to stop immigration on a longterm basis. In England this process had already started in the early 1960s; other European countries followed suit in about 1973 or 1974. One decade later the restrictions were so strong that immigration of workers to Europe almost came to an end.

There are nevertheless a relatively large number of Muslims—some second and third generation residents—living in Europe.[3] It is assumed that the demand for Islamic institutions among Muslim inhabitants grew when families of these immigrants began to join them in the 1970s, a process that led to the more permanent settlement. The education of Muslim children, for instance, became (and remains) a pressing need. Public schools have been a field of

---

[3] By the end of the 1980s Muslims in Europe numbered almost 7 Million: 2.5 Million in France, 1.7 million in Germany, 1 Million in England, and 300,000 in the Netherlands and Belgium. Today the number of Muslims in Germany is estimated at between 2 and 2.5 Million. It is difficult to find exact figures because in most European countries there are no statistical surveys done according to religious affiliations. A first overview and bibliography on Islam in Europe was given in Dassetto 1994.

tension between Muslims and their co-residents in almost every European country. With the increase of social and racial conflicts, a multitude of Islamic movements emerged among the Muslim immigrants, filling a cultural vacuum with a unique symbolic system (Schulze 1990, esp. 31ff.). These movements represent all facets of Islam, ranging from purely religious to politico-religious movements. They vary from organizations emerging specifically in response to the needs of European Muslims to European branches of home-based associations. In addition to competing with each other both at home and abroad, Islamic movements must represent "Islam" more broadly vis-a-vis non-Islamic publics:

> Organizations are in competition with each other both for resources and for adherents, and a balance has to be found between legitimisation by distribution of benefits (dependent on access to resources) and legitimization on Islamic grounds (namely, the Qur'ān, consensus and/or line of succession) (Nielsen 1995, 127).

In the European field of competition the Tablīghī Jamāʿat has succeeded in disseminating its ideology of reviving a puritan and practical Islam. Members are engaged in establishing mosques and *madrasas*, supplying Muslims with ritually slaughtered meat, and serving other social interests. The basic activity of the Tablīghī movement, *Khurūj fī Sabil Allāh*, mirrors the situation of immigrants in the diaspora who have traveled to unknown places. At the same time, it recalls Islamic doctrines like *ḥajj* or *hijra*.

> Muslim doctrine explicitly enjoins or encourages certain forms of travel. . . . Travel of several kinds is therefore significant for Muslim self expression, and travel is of course informed by the cultural and social contexts in which Muslims are located (Eickelman and Piscatori 1990, 5).

Although the social situation of Muslim immigrants today is similar throughout Western Europe, the popularity of the Tablīgh differs between countries. In Britain the movement spread successfully among Indo-Pakistani immigrants, while in France it gained access to the Maghrebi community. Gilles Kepel has noted the presence of the Tablīghī Jamāʿat in these countries before Islamist groups spread through the mid-1980s (Kepel 1987).

The early presence of the Tablīghī Jamāʿat and its role as a pioneer for Islamists has been noticed by scholars in the Maghreb (for Tunisia see Magnuson 1991; for Morocco, Tozy 1984 and Ḍarīf 1993). Magnuson (1987, 78) suggested that the spread of the movement in Tunisia was partly due to immigrant adepts coming from France. It has also been said that there are close ties between French Tablīghīs and those in the Maghreb and other African countries like Senegal and Zambia (Diop 1994, 153). In Spain, Belgium and the Netherlands the Jamāʿat became popular among the Maghrebis as well (For Spain, see Aguer 1991; for Belgium, Dassetto 1988; for the Netherlands, Landman 1992). Although there seems to exist a close network of Indo-Pakistanis on the one hand and Maghrebis on the other, the Turkish community in European countries remained largely inaccessible to the Tablīghī movement.

The first address for Tablīghī adepts in Britain was London. When passing through the city's immigrant quarters one may notice the presence of Tablīghīs displaying literature in Islamic bookstores. The central Tablīghī mosque in London, the Markazī Masjid, was established in a former synagogue (Metcalf 1996, 113). But from the 1980s onward Dewsbury (Yorkshire) became the movement's most important center in the western diaspora. There, approximately 8,000 to 15,000 adepts from all parts of Europe assemble at the large *ijtimāʿ* (gathering) that is held each Christmas.

Close Ties: Britain as a Center of the Tablīghī Jamāʿat

Before moving to different parts of the Arab world, *jamāʿats* came to Britain (Gaborieau, in this volume). The reason for this priority lay in the close ties that resulted from British colonial rule in India that led many people from the Subcontinent to the colonial "motherland." Increasing immigration of Pakistanis and Indians to England took place after independence in 1947. British citizenship included all citizens of the Commonwealth and the state granted full legal status to immigrants. A policy of containment followed. In the years leading up to 1971 the government issued a series of immigration acts which resulted in a differentiation of "white" and "black" Commonwealths. Terms like "race" and "ethnic group" found their way into modern British legislation. The aim was to construct a multicultural society where minorities lived together with equal rights irrespective of their cultural differences. This process found an institutional expression in the *Race Relations Acts (1968 and 1976)* which gave legal and financial support to minorities, and promoted a policy of "colour consciousness" and "communitarism" (Kepel 1996, 143ff.).

The majority of immigrants in England originate from the Punjab, Gujarat, and Sylhet in Bangladesh. Nearly all Sylhetis, more than half of the Punjabis, and one fifth of the Gujrātīs are Muslims. Altogether, Muslims form the largest religious denomination among South Asian immigrants.[4] There is tremendous competition among the many Islamic movements who have arrived in Britain from the subcontinent like Ahli Ḥadīth, Jamāʿat-i Islāmī and the Aḥmadiyya. However, the Deobandīs (Metcalf 1982) and Brēlwīs (Lewis 1994, 81–89) are considered to be the strongest. The Brēlwīs have a more local tradition of popular Islam and its sympathizers congregate around individual *pīrs*. The Deobandīs seem to be organized differently; their networks of institutions and personal connections are closely tied to the Tablīghī Jamāʿat. One likely effect of the diaspora has been that links between Deobandīs and Tablīghī Jamāʿat are probably more evident in Britain than in South Asia.

The Deobandī Network

Bradford, a small British industrial town which became famous for the Rushdie affair, has a large Muslim population. Its lively network of institutions reflects all facets of Islam in Britain, with the expected political and social implications. Out of thirty-nine Muslim institutions, twelve mosques and two seminaries are associated with the Deobandī School (Lewis 1994, 57, table 3.1).[5] Different ethnic groups dominate these, and Urdu is their *lingua franca*.[6] The first mosque, the Howard Street Mosque, was established in 1959 and called the Muslim Association of Bradford. It has a pre-eminence among Deobandī mosques and is used by the Tablīghī Jamāʿat as a center in Bradford. The first *ʿālim* of Howard Street, Luṭfur Raḥmān,

---

[4] British minority studies often elaborate upon ethnic affiliations because of the assumption that immigrant community building follows parochial relations like caste, sect or descent more than nationality. The community life of immigrants living in England is said to be determined by a system of reciprocal kinship relations (*jātī/birāderī*). Religious affiliation can be a powerful mobilizer, but tends to be short-lived and motivated more by current events. See Ballard (1994, 4, 20).

[5] There are other Deobandī seminaries scattered throughout Britain, for instance *al-Jāmʿia al-Islāmiya* and *The Islamic Institute* at Nottinghamshire.

[6] Seven are dominated by Pathans and Punjabis from Pakistan, four by the Surati community from Gujarat in India, and three by Sylhetis from Bangladesh (Lewis 1994, 89). Lewis points out that "The influence of Gujaratis in the religious life of Bradford Muslims is disproportionate to the small communities actually settled in the city" (1994, 204).

held for twenty years the office of the president of the Jamʿiyyat-i ʿUlamāʾ Briṭāniya (JUB), a national umbrella organization of Deobandīs in Britain formed in 1967. Luṭfur Raḥmān is a Murīd of Yūsuf Motāla, the principal of one of the seminaries, the Dārul ʿUlūm at Bury, founded in 1975. Yūsuf Motāla himself studied in India at the feet of Muḥammad Zakariyyā (Gaborieau 1992, 20)—it was Zakariyyā who encouraged his novice to establish a seminary in England (Lewis 1994, 91f.).

The vice-president of JUB, Mawlānā Naʿīm, teaches at another Deobandī seminary at Dewsbury. Unlike the apolitical stand taken by the Tablīghī Jamāʿat, the JUB functions as a supporter of Muslim political interests in England, trying, for example, to obtain official recognition for Islamic family law in Parliament. The JUB also works against *shirk* and *bidʿa*, aiming mostly at the Aḥmadiyya movement and Shīʿī groups (Lewis 1991, 97).

In order to counter generational conflicts, Deobandīs are trying to motivate young Muslims who have grown up in England to study at one of the local seminaries. This is desirable because of their greater familiarity with British language and culture. In 1989 Maḥmūdul Ḥasan, a son of Luṭfur Raḥmān, a graduate of Bury, and the first *ʿālim* educated in England, was appointed to a mosque in Bradford. For his Friday sermon he uses, among other books, a multi-volume Qurʾān commentary written by the Deobandī scholar Muḥammad Shafīʿ (d. 1978) from Pakistan. Both the Bury and Dewsbury seminaries recommend this commentary. Moreover, all Deobandī institutions of the region read the *Tablīghī Niṣāb* (Metcalf 1993a; see also chapter four, this volume). Because of his bilingual skills, Maḥmūdul Ḥasan teaches Islamic topics to Muslim children in the English language, using textbooks like *Lessons from Islam* by Kifāyatullāh (d. 1952).[7] In comparison to those of his father's generation, Maḥmūdul Ḥasan takes a more liberal view toward questions of sexuality and contraception. When he receives questions beyond his competence he passes them on to a specialist of Islamic Law, Ismāʿīl Kachhaulwī, who was appointed head of the Institute of Islamic Jurisprudence, UK in Bradford in 1988 by Deobandī scholars. Kachhaulwī—successor of Muḥammad Zakariyyā—works together with two local *muftīs* who are employed at the seminaries of Dewsbury and Bury. The

[7] On him see Khalid Masud in Gaborieau 1992, 14f.

specialists draw up *fatāwā*, with statements of the problems of British Muslims. The collection of these *fatāwā* "provide a unique window into the day-to-day concerns of British Muslims" and could be valuable to other European countries also (Lewis 1994, 117ff.).

In 1990, the first graduate of Dewsbury was allowed to preach in Bradford mosques. Both seminaries provide Islamic institutions in Britain with a potential staff grown up and educated in England. In this way they contribute to the independence of British institutions. This process of autonomization has been approved by the British government and since 1985 a local educational body has been giving financial support to some students. Fifteen students were financed at each seminary in 1990 (Lewis 1994, 91). Both seminaries are closely connected to the Muslim institutions in Bradford. Each mosque has a number of students at both seminaries and groups are sent to the weekly Thursday meetings of the Tablīghī Jamāʿat held at Dewsbury. *Jamāʿats* depart from there almost every weekend and find quarters in the mosques of Bradford.

The Islamic Institute at Dewsbury

The Dārul ʿUlūm or Islamic Institute is located in a quarter of Dewsbury called Seville Town. This quarter is primarily populated by immigrants and has the typical character of a multi-cultural suburb: Indo-Pakistani shops, mosques and *madrasas* are installed in small British suburban houses. Out of this busy quarter rises a large complex of buildings, the Markazī Masjid and the Dārul ʿUlūm. In these the European center of the Tablīghī Jamāʿat is located. The members have founded a formal association called Anjuman-i Iṣlāḥul Muslimīn, U.K.

Ḥāfiẓ Patēl, the *amīr* of the Tablīghī Jamāʿat in England, functions as the *amīr* of Europe as well as the head of the seminary at Dewsbury, although he has not been educated as an *ʿālim*.[8]

[8] When I visited the Tablīghī center in January 1996 I met a German student, T.N., studying at the Dārul ʿUlūm. My experience stands in contrast to that of some other Western researchers; Tablīghīs in Britain as well as in Germany have always treated me in a friendly manner. Although my visit at Dewsbury was not announced, I was allowed to enter the office, which is reached by passing through the yard of the complex where generally only men stay. I had a short conversation with the man in charge, who tried to explain to me in short but flourishing words the main

The Tablīghī Jamāʿat itself recruits students for Deobandī seminaries through its national and international networks. Because a large number of students come from all parts of Britain and from other countries, boarding facilities have been added to the Dewsbury seminary, founded in 1982. The Deobandī Institute at Nottingham has created separate classes for its foreign students: "Due to a student intake from various overseas countries, a separate class has been formed for students with English as a second language" (Islamic Institution n.d., 7).

While all students at the Dewsbury seminary participate in the activities of the Tablīghī Jamāʿat, their syllabus is not directly concerned with the movement.[9] The education to become an *ʿālim* at Dewsbury lasts for seven years, preceded by a period of three years for *ḥifẓ* (memorization of the Qurʾān) and "private school" classes attended by almost half of Dewsbury's 300 students. The thirteen- to sixteen-year old students are expected to learn a minimal British syllabus. For this reason the curriculum is complemented by a teaching plan that complies with the standards of the British school system, even though the *ḥifẓ* class is the focal point of the "private school." During the morning program pupils learn the correct pronunciation of the Qurʾān (*tajwīd*) and improve their skills in Urdu. The basic Urdu text is the *Taʿlīmul Islām* of Kifāyatullāh. As in the *ʿalīm* course, Urdu is the language of instruction during morning lessons, while English is the medium for afternoon lessons, when "worldly topics" (*dunyawī*) adapted to the British standards are taught (history, geography, social sciences, law, mathematics, English, general science and Urdu). In 1989 it was possible to earn a formal British graduation in four of these subjects.[10] At the Islamic Institute in Nottingham, in addition to secular curriculum and *ḥifẓ* and *ʿālim* courses, formal education in computer science is also provided (Islamic Institute n.d., 11).

---

ideas of the Tablīghī Jamāʿat. He also emphazised that the Tablīghī Jamāʿat is in Britain directed only at Muslims.

[9] Paraphrased from a personal letter of T. N. to the author, Dewsbury, 28 March 1996.

[10] Philip Lewis opines that there is little coordination between the morning and afternoon lessons: "Students, in the morning and afternoon, live in two unrelated linguistic and cultural worlds" (Lewis 1994, 93). The Department of Education and Science drew up a "Report by HM Inspectors on the Institute of Islamic Education" in Dewsbury 1986, criticizing its methods of learning for its mere repetition (Lewis 1994, 94).

Whereas the "private school" provides lower-level personnel for British Muslim institutions, the religious leadership is educated in special *ʿālim* courses.[11] The syllabus of Nottingham compared with that of Bury, which has been analyzed by Philip Lewis, and remarks of my informants, confirm the perception that the curricula of British Deobandi schools are in their essentials similar to that of Maẓāhirul ʿUlūm, Sahāranpūr, where Muḥammad Zakariyyā was the principal and Muḥammad Ilyās, the founder of the Jamāʿat, taught before he dedicated himself to the Tablīghī mission. This syllabus goes back to the famous "Dars Niẓamī," a curriculum composed by the Farangī Maḥall in the eighteenth century.[12]

Generally the *ʿālim* course at the Islamic Institute begins with Arabic grammar and syntax, *Sīrat* (life of the Prophet), and study of the early history of Islam by means of Urdu textbooks. Arabic is the medium of instruction during the lessons on basic Arabic literature and language. Grammar and syntax, literature and language continue during the second year, complemented by exercises translating Arabic passages into Urdu, Fiqh lessons from selected Ḥanafī text and *tajwīd*. In the third year, the students are taught in the different disciplines of Arabic language including rhetoric, and also study *tafsīr* and basics of Islamic jurisprudence. Study of the life of the Prophet and recitation of the Qur'ān continue. Selected *aḥādīth*, and translation of half of the Qur'ān from Arabic to Urdu, complete the syllabus. The next year students are taught in classical Arabic literature and rhetoric, Islamic jurisprudence, *ḥadīth*, *tajwīd* and elementary principles of logic. They also translate the second half of the Qur'ān. In the fifth year differences between classical and modern Arabic are studied, and a Ḥanafī textbook on the terminology of *ḥadīth* studies is introduced. In addition the following works are taught: the Qur'ān commentary *Tafsīrul Jalālayn* by al-Suyūṭī (d. 1505) (Brockelmann 1943, 2:138), *Mishkātul Maṣābīh* of al-Tabrīzī

[11] A private school for girls provides the Deobandī institutions with female staff. Since 1984, seventy girls have studied at the Howard Street mosque. In 1987 a boarding school, the Madīnatul ʿUlūm al-Islāmiyya, was established first at Shenstone, Kidderminster, then moved to Bradford in 1992. At the boarding school girls may take an *ʿālima* course lasting five years. Graduation enables them to teach *dīniyāt* (religious studies) to women and girls (Lewis 1994, 100). The school has international students as well, including German activists from Frankfurt.

[12] For a detailed analysis of the history and content of Dars-i Niẓāmī, see Malik 1997.

(Brockelmann 1943, 1:448), *Hidāya* of al-Marghīnānī (d. 1197)[13] (Brockelmann 1943, 1:466) and *Al-ʿaqāʾid* of al-Nasafī (d. 1143) (Brockelmann 1943, 7:969). The year ends with *kalām* and *tajwīd*. In the final year the students read and translate all six *ḥadīth* selections, and *Al-Muwaṭṭāʿ* of Imām Mālik Ibn Anas (Brockelmann 1943, 1:184, and *Supplement* I:521f.).

Citing the requirements of the new environment, Lewis criticized this curriculum for its strict adherence to the reformist Deobandī tradition, and its lack of any comprehensive study in Islamic history and philosophy, not to mention British history and politics. Nevertheless, Lewis acknowledges that there were a few innovations, such as the introduction of a book on Arabic language written by Sayyid Abul Ḥasan ʿAlī Nadwī (d. 1999),[14] and the rule that every student had to write a thesis of 10,000 to 15,000 words in Arabic, Urdu or English, a method borrowed from al-Azhar. Recently the principal of Bury recommended to some students that they continue their study at a British University in Arabic language, law or Islamic studies (Lewis 1994, 135ff.). But after final examinations students generally attend a University in Pakistan or India, the University in Medina, or al-Azhar in Cairo.

The main difference between the seminaries of Bury and Dewsbury is the latter's strong tie with the Tablīghī Jamāʿat, though there is also close cooperation with Bury. Students at Dewsbury devote a minimum of one weekend per month, a part of their holidays, and a whole year at the end of their study, to the Tablīgh work, crossing all regions of Britain on their tours.

The nearby towns, Leeds for instance, are often visited by *jamāʿats*, whose influence on Muslim populations has increased in recent years. One of the adepts at Leeds, who started Tablīgh in 1956 in Burma, is also engaged in local social politics. He is a chairman of the Leeds Muslim Commonwealth and participates in a police forum called West Yorkshire Police Authority (Geaves 1995, 15f.).

---

[13] Translation from Persian by Charles Hamilton, *Hedaya or Guide: A Commentary on the Mussulman Laws*, first published in 1791.

[14] Abul Ḥasan ʿAlī Nadwī, the head of the Nadwatul ʿUlamāʾ, was important in the dissemination of Tablīghī ideas in the Arab world. His institution today is in close touch with the international network of the Tablīghī Jamāʿat, even though there is a competition for the support in the Tablīghī Jamāʿat between the Nadwa and the school of Deoband in India. For a history of the Nadwa see Malik (1994).

Islamist Criticism on the Tablīghī Movement

The extensive presence of the Tablīghī Jamāʿat in Britain is also reflected in Islamic discourse. Due to its lack of political activism the Tablīghī Jamāʿat in Britain is sometimes criticized by other Muslim organizations. A 1989 issue of the journal *Trends*, published by the Young Muslims UK, a youth organization of the Jamāʿat-i Islāmī, replied to a letter to the editor by explaining that,

> *Daʿwah*, the Tablīghī way, is correct but is limited to a very few personal aspects of life; that is, it is incomplete. *Daʿwah*, according to Sunnah, is to invite to complete submission to Allah, which includes organised social, economic and political struggle to establish the Islamic way of life. The Tablīghī way lacks this most important aspect of Islamic *Daʿwah* (Trends 1989, 13).

This statement represents a typical criticism of the Tablīghī Jamāʿat by Islamists who want to establish an "Islamic state" (see chapter four, this volume).[15] The Jamāʿat, they argue, by giving preference to the change of the individual over the change of political structures, favours a separation of religion and state (*dīn wa dawla*) that was unknown to Islam. Due to their competition to recruit sympathizers and adepts in Pakistan, the Jamāʿat Islāmī has had a critical attitude towards the Tablīghī Jamāʿat for a long time.[16] Its founder, Abul Aʿlā Mawdūdī (1903/1904–1979) was impressed by the Tablīghī Jamāʿat in the early 1930s, but later became one of its strongest opponents:

> There is no sense in applying a Christian-type mission to invite people to Islam. Even one million publications calling for adherence to Islam and screaming at the people day and night that they should be afraid of God would not help. What is the practical use of emphasizing again and again the validity of Islam at all places and times? Our time requires us to show the practical virtues of Islam in the real world. Repeating constantly that Islam has all the solutions, does not solve the materialistic problems of the world. The virtues of Islam should lead to a . . . practical ruling system, the impacts of which are noted by the people, and the fruits of which are reaped by them. We are living in a world grounded in conflict and struggle. Sermons and

---

[15] For an example of the criticism of an Arab (Jordan) Islamist, see the analysis of Maḥmūd Sālim ʿUbaydāt (1989) in my Masters thesis (1996).

[16] For comparative analyses of Jamāʿat-i Islāmī and Tablīghī Jamāʿat in the South Asian context see Aḥmad (1991) and Troll (1994).

> warnings will not change the way of this world, only revolutionary fighting will (Mawdūdī, n.d., 15; trans. by E.F.).

The apolitical stand of the Tablīghī Jamāʿat has been questioned by other scholars as well, who consider it to be hiding its true political aims in order to protect itself from repression (Gaborieau 1996). There is much competition between the Tablīghī Jamāʿat and other Islamist groups, and there are differences between their ideological approaches and working methods.

Another controversial point is whether the Tablīghī Jamāʿat tries to convert non-Muslims. A British Muslim writer deplores the failure to do this. He states that the Tablīghī Jamāʿat confines its mission to Muslims only, even though Islam needs new converts. According to this author, Tablīghī adepts are not educated in the proper way to meet non-Muslims in an "evangelistic style": "Converting a non-Muslim is not a matter of telling him or her to accept Islam because it is better than their religion. It needs convincing skills, sufficient command of language, knowledge of the other person's religion or ideology, as well as missionary skills" (Raza 1991, 72).

The Tablīghī Jamāʿat in Britain aims in the first place at Muslims who have little knowledge of Islam. These are often second and third generation immigrants. How far the missionary work has succeeded in converting "Muslims by name" into Tablīghī adepts, or what factors attract an individual to the ideology of the movement, are still open questions. At present, quantitative comparisons between various Islamist groups are not available. However, the Tablīghī Jamāʿat, embedded in the Deobandī network, is one of the most important Islamic movements in Britain.

New Boundaries: Germany, the Remote Territory

The position of the Tablīghī Jamāʿat in Germany is quite different from that in Britain. Some thirty-five years ago (about 1965) a small circle of Pakistani students in Frankfurt came into contact with the Tablīghī Jamāʿat. *Jamāʿats* from Pakistan crossing the European continent were seen in different German cities around this time, but the exact date when the Tablīghī movement established a branch in Germany is uncertain. We do know that Tablīghī Jamāʿat has been working in Frankfurt continually since 1980, and that a womens' group has been holding meetings regularly. The latter began first as a group providing a venue, specifically for female converts to exchange ideas about Islam.

In Germany the Tablīghī Jamāʿat membership remains small although its network covers twenty to twenty-five German cities. Adepts live in urban centers with high Muslim populations like Cologne, Frankfurt, Munich, Saarbrucken, Hannover, Hamburg and Berlin, and also in smaller towns like Eichstatt.

The German members I was able to establish contact with were all academics, but my interlocutors ensured me—and it proved to be true during the meetings I attended—that there are German Tablīghīs among different classes of the Muslim population.[17] The adepts are also heterogeneous in national background. This may explain the limited success of the Tablīghī Jamāʿat in Germany relative to other European countries. This is not to say that the Tablīghīs are less active in Germany, but they operate in different ways, to which we now turn.

The German Field

In Cologne the members of Tablīghī Jamāʿat established its *markaz* in Ehrenfeld, a quarter with a large Turkish Muslim population. In Ehrenfeld a multitude of Islamic groups, as well as secular and atheist circles of Turks and Kurds, have set up their centers, mosques and offices.

Except for Berlin and the industrial Ruhr region, the Cologne area has the highest concentration of Turkish "guest workers" in Germany. Germany's history as a colonial power differs from its European neighbours. However, recruitment of cheap labour from Muslim countries remained popular to aid in the economic recovery after World War II until the government stopped immigration in 1973. Turks in Germany play a role similar to that of Indo-Pakistani immigrants in Britain and Maghrebis in France. But while neighbour

---

[17] As far as I know, until now there has been no material available about Tablīghī Jamāʿat in Germany. The following is based on my own field study using narrative interviews and participant observations. Strict separation of the sexes meant that I could attend only women's meetings, although I did interview male activists. My two male informants both were engineers of Pakistani origin, while my female interlocutors were both social workers who have converted to Islam. I also corresponded with T.N., a prospective German *ʿālim* who is currently studying at Dewsbury.

governments have attempted to integrate immigrant population by giving them a formal status, Germany has always maintained a conception of citizenship as grounded in "blood and soil." The result is, that although more than 30,000 Turks are born in Germany each year, they are not granted even basic civil rights; their de facto immigration to Germany is denied by official policy.[18] Because it has no general representative body, "Körperschaftsrecht" (corporate law) does not recognize Islam. Muslim communities must usually be registered associations in order to become formally recognized. To control the religious activities of Turkish nationals, the Turkish government in 1985 set up the headquarter of the Diyanet İşleri Türk İslam Bi̊rli̊ği̊ (DITIB) at Ehrenfeld as a branch of the Turkish Department of Religious Affairs. After some years the DITIB also provided Turkish staff for most Muslim institutions in Germany (Gür 1993, 18f.).

The activities of the Tablīghī Jamāʿat in Germany are essentially the same as everywhere else and therefore need not be detailed here. Every Thursday evening (*shab-i Jumʿa*) there is an open meeting at the *markaz* in Cologne that is generally attended by forty to fifty persons ranging from strict followers of the Jamāʿat to first-time participants. At the *markaz* people talk about *dīn* and religion, perform their prayers and listen to the *bayān*, a public speech that is given at each meeting. Typically, each month seven to ten persons form a *jamāʿat* to undertake a *khurūj* from Cologne to a farther or nearer place. During the *gasht* (round) in Germany adepts visit institutions that are frequented by immigrant Muslims, such as Turkish teahouses. This requires knowledge of the terrain, not only with regard to the localities but also to the lifestyle of local Muslims. For their mission Tablīghīs adapt their language to the Muslim immigrants. I heard an adept explaining the idea of God counting good deeds on the Day of Judgement by referring to a "current account"; the good deeds are put into an account like money. With metaphors like these, adepts allude to the situation of most Muslims in Germany, living as immigrant workers in what they see as materialistic society.

In addition to Thursday meetings, the core of Tablīghī Jamāʿat in Cologne, of five to ten men, forms a *shūrā* (consultative body), that meets on Tuesdays to discuss organizational matters. Each month the *amīr* of Cologne is chosen from this body. At Frankfurt the core

[18] For a comparative study of citizenship see Brubaker 1992. Bade 1994 gives a critical review of German "foreigner" politics.

is comprised of approximately fifteen persons who, in 1989, established the first German formal association of the Tablīghī movement called Anjuman-i-Islāḥul-Muslemeen Deutschland e.V. The similarity of its name to the British association is not accidental—the chairman of the German Anjuman (I'll call him Mr. N.), one of the leading adepts of the German Tablīghī branch, together with his family, represent a link to British Tablīghīs and to branches elsewhere.[19] He was born in Pakistan and has been living in Germany for many years, married to a German convert. The family N. is in charge of the transnational contacts of the German Tablīghī Jamāʿat, and has a home telefax to facilitate world-wide communication. In general, however, Tablīghīs defer the use of modern communication technologies in favor of face-to-face relations.

The three sons of the family N. are studying at the Dewsbury seminary. The eldest, the twenty-three year old T.N., grew up near Frankfurt and studied at a secondary school before he started the *ḥifẓ* course at Dewsbury. Five years ago he decided to study at the Dārul ʿUlūm to become an Islamic scholar:

> At the beginning I had only the intention to take a Qur'ān course to learn the Qur'ān by heart. After that, I thought, I would return to Germany to finish secondary school and study at a University. There were fields that interested me, like medicine. But after finishing the course, when I was seventeen years old, I thought about my future. I was conscious that I knew little about Islam and that in general very few people know and practice Islam in its true form. There are many physicians, doctors and scientists in all fields, but people knowing true Islam are few (trans. by E.F.).[20]

If his plans do not change, T.N. will return to Germany after finishing his education—probably in two years—and become one of the few *Imāms* who have grown up in Germany or been educated in a European country. He is already authorized to lead the night prayers at German mosques during Ramaḍān, for it is a duty for all *ḥāfiẓ* students of the Dārul ʿUlūm to practice the tasks of an *Imām* and to recite the entire Qur'ān from memory in thirty days during Ramaḍān. In 1996, T.N. spent time at the Pakistani Center in Hannover for that reason; in 1997 he traveled to Japan with a *jamāʿat*.

[19] One brother of Mr. N, a Tablīghī activist, lives on his own in Denmark.
[20] Quoted with permission from a personal letter from T.N., Dewsbury, 28 March 1996.

Because the majority of Muslims in Germany are of Turkish origin, T.N. plans to learn the Turkish language. If he gains access to Turkish Muslim institutions he may contribute to their independence from the DITIB and "wild *hojas*" (traditional religious teachers), and therefore promote the process of autonomization of Muslims living in Germany.

Up to now the Tablīghī Jamāʿat has had little influence among the Turkish community in Germany. It had already established a section in Turkey in 1967 through the work of Muḥibbullāh Işıklar, who became acquainted with the movement in Pakistan, but it remained marginal (Çakir 1990, 248). There is at least one *Jamāʿat markaz* in Istanbul, and another in Adapazar, northeast of Istanbul. Indeed, German Tablīghīs sometimes read the Turkish translation of *Faza'il-e A'maal* [*Faḍāʿil Aʿmāl*] aloud in their circles.[21]

According to my informants, it is Pakistanis, Bangladeshis, and Arabs who are most interested in the Tablīgh, but its spread among Turkish people has been only gradual. At present there are ten to fifteen Turks among the Tablīghī adepts in Cologne, a very small number compared to the memberships of some Turkish organizations: The Avrupa Millî Görüş Teşkilatları (AMGT or IGMG), for example, in 1987 already had 19,000 registered members, and the Islamic Union (Cemaleddin Kaplan), a more radical section that broke away from AMGT, counts about 2,000 members (Binswanger 1990, 45). It may be that the network of Turkish Islamic organizations and associations already working in Germany fullfill the religious, ideological and social needs of Turkish minorities.

In 1996, the Cologne section of Tablīghī Jamāʿat established an association called Daʿwatul Ḥaq International e.V. Paragraph two of its formal statute reads as follows:

> The association actively supports basic and secondary education of Muslim children and youth, and further education of Muslim adults in the religious field . . . The association grants importance to this because more and more young people are maintaining a distance from religious values and moral ideology because religious education is neglected at their parents' homes and at school, and therefore they are driven to criminality, drug abuse and alcohol. The association takes care of social fringe groups by giving them the opportunity to integrate into our society (trans. by E.F.).[22]

---

[21] Muhammed Zekeriyya Kandehlevi, *Fezail-i Aʿmal. Amellerin Faziletleri* Istanbul, nd.
[22] Statute of Dawatul Haq International (Der Weg zur Wahrheit), e.V., Köln 1996.

Does this mean the movement undertakes a kind of social welfare, or "cure of souls" programme for uprooted youth? Or is this merely a strategy to facilitate official matters like getting visas, as one reads in the following: "There will be invitations to people from abroad who are devoted to the aims mentioned. Their lodging and travel, entry and departure will be guaranteed by the association" (trans. by E.F.).[23] Although the statutes of both German Tablīgh associations are similar, there is one notable difference: Daʿwatul Ḥaq Cologne extends the religious aims contained in the statute of Anjuman Frankfurt to social aims.

Both statutes are alike in rejecting political ambitions and cooperation with any political group or party. The Jamāʿat does not cooperate officially with any Islamist organization, nor does it publicly participate in umbrella unions to promote Muslim interests. The Tablīghī approach regarding socio-religious issues is that members must act as individuals; due to the lack of their own network of institutions, adepts may pray at mosques that are linked with other organizations. Sometimes Tablīghī members even recommend the propaganda material of other Muslim unions. One example is a booklet *Was ist Islam?* by Muḥammad Aḥmad Rassoul, published by the "Islamische Bibliothek" that belongs to the IGMG institutions at Cologne. Representatives of Islamic groups in Germany stated that they did not even know whether Tablīghī members used their mosques, but that they had been acquainted with them as individuals for many years. Only the press centre of the Aḥmadiyya Muslim Jamāʿat at Frankfurt openly deplored the fact that Pakistani Tablīghī members worked in committees against their movement. Tablīghī adepts responded to my questions about the Aḥmadiyya movement by explaining that Aḥmadīs were not Muslims at all.

Though there is formal recognition of the Tablīghī Jamāʿat's associations, the *markaz* in Ehrenfeld recently was closed by the police due to infighting among Muslim groups. Local Tablīghīs were unable to find new facilities in Cologne right away and therefore felt handicapped in their activities. The old *markaz* was established in a flat owned by a number of Turks, among them a leading adept of the German Tablīghī section.

The members of the Tablīghī Jamāʿat in Germany are diversified in their national and social backgrounds. One gathering at Cologne

---

[23] Statute of Anjuman Iṣlāḥul Muslemeen Deutschland e.V., Frankfurt 1989.

was visited by four Turkish females, one Moroccan, two men from Kasachstan, two German converts, four Pakistani women and a mother and daughter from Bangladesh. The father of the Bangladeshi family was a journalist and an interpreter, while other husbands were pensioners, industrial workers or unemployed. Another meeting in Frankfurt was visited by ten female participants: six German converts, one Indian, one Tunisian and two Arabic-speaking women probably of Maghrebi background. Besides the immigrants there is another segment of German Tablīghī membership that has been little noticed: converts of binational Tablīghī families. They make up nearly all of the German female converts.

Due to the small number of Tablīghīs in Germany, there is no *amīr* for the whole country. Rather, a few men form a Shūrā, comprised of *amīr*s of the main German cities, and some "brothers," as they call each other, meet every three months to coordinate the nation-wide network. At this *shūrā*, topics of transregional relevance are discussed and the nation-wide *ijtimā*ʿ is organized. This large meeting is held twice each year for three days at a large mosque or cultural center in a main German city like Hamburg, Munich or Stuttgart. In 1996 the meeting was attended—according to my informants' estimates—by about 600 people from Germany and abroad. Female adepts do not participate, and their activities are limited as much as possible to the private sphere. The main activity for female Tablīghīs in Germany is the *taʿlīm* a meeting held on the first Sunday of every month.

The Activities of Female Tablīghīs

While other German Muslim women are "veiled" by a simple scarf, if at all, Tablīghī women are heavily veiled. The converted Tablīghī women who I met at Frankfurt were all wearing a long black *chador*, some leaving their faces and hands uncovered, others covering their entire body. Some women told me that because of the clothing they often are assumed to be foreigners, for example from Saudi Arabia or Iran. The non-converts (immigrants) among the female adepts are usually veiled less strictly, reflecting the various types of veils of their home countries. For example, Turkish women wear a multicoloured scarf. It is noteworthy that the appearance of male adepts is more uniform; they all wear a beard and the typical South Asian *shalwār qamīz*.

Accompanied by their husbands, women come to the meeting-place of the *taʿlīm*, the private home of one of the participants. To start, the rules for the meeting are explained, ranging from having sincere intention (*niyya*) to sitting in a special position. Further, it is indicated that during *taʿlīm* angels are present who inform the blessings of God (*baraka*). After having created in this way the atmosphere of sacred space, one participant starts reading aloud from the collection *Faza'il-e-A'maal [Faḍā'il Aʿmāl]* of Muḥammad Zakariyyā, translating it from an English or Turkish edition into German. Passages are chosen by the readers which are appropriate to the upcoming events. If the time of pilgrimage is approaching, for example, passages from *Virtues of Ḥajj* (second volume of *Faza'il-e-A'maal*) are read. In the course of the gathering the rules of etiquette (*ādāb*) of the Tablīghī Jamāʿat are explained, following strictly the model of Prophet Muḥammad.[24] For a more comprehensive study on etiquette, especially for women, the Tablīghī Jamāʿat recommends the study of *Bihishtī Zēwar* by the Deobandī scholar Ashraf ʿAlī Thānawī.[25]

The first part of the *taʿlīm* is carried through by the women themselves, who assign the task of reading or explaining the rules of *ādāb* to younger participants in order to build their self-confidence. For instance, one twenty-three year old daughter of a Kasachstani adept living at Cologne was visiting an Islamic boarding school at Bursa in Turkey. It was she who led the *taʿlīm*, introducing the Six Point Program of the Tablīghī Jamāʿat (see chapter one, this volume) and reading from the *Faḍā'il Aʿmāl* in Turkish and Arabic with a German translation. Despite the movement's international composition in Germany, Tablīghīs do not face serious translation problems and often demonstrate innovative approaches to this multicultural context. The women's communication with the men, who during the gathering sit next door, is maintained through small children. Nevertheless, there is a problem of childcare; because of the noise of children it is hard to concentrate for long periods of time. Female adepts confided to me resentfully that actually it was the husband's duty to look after the children during the women's *taʿlīm*. Though the public face of the Tablīghī Jamāʿat appears male, due to strict separation of sexes,

[24] Both the rules of etiquette and the six-point-program are explained by Mawlānā ʿAshiq Ilāhī (1983).

[25] See the English translation and interpretation by Metcalf (1992).

female adepts call for their rights in the private sphere as an expression of emancipation.

After finishing the reading, the women listen to the *bayān*, delivered by a man. The *bayān* is usually transmitted by means of a loud speaker placed in the middle of the room, but Tablīghīs improvise when there is no transmitter, perhaps using a megaphone or simply hiding the male behind a curtain; a sort of *ḥijāb* in reverse. The language of the *bayān* depends on the speaker's mother tongue, but it is usually held in Urdu or Arabic, with a simultaneous German translation.

The contents of the *bayān* generally correspond to the listeners' social situation and predicaments. On the one hand it alludes to technological progress and the material orientation of the West, where ethical and moral values are said to have lost their place. This is contrasted with the need to return to true Islamic values and to call other Muslims to the right path. On the other hand, a *bayān* may be composed to fit the particular situation of women: In one I heard the speaker saying that God will give precious presents in paradise (*jannat*) to those women who say their prayers regularly. If they live according to Islamic rules, and if they take care of their husbands and children, God will grant them a good life in this world, too, by sending his angels (*malā'ika*) and his charity (*raḥmat*). The speaker continued by citing a *ḥadīth* and telling stories of the wives of the Prophet, their poverty and their readiness to make sacrifices. Concluding this comparison, the speaker then commented that we are rich and have many material things like food and clothes, and that it is not therefore a deprivation to send husbands *fī Sabīl Allāh* (on the way of Allah).

The *bayān* usually ends with a prayer, *duʿā*, and a request to the women to make *niyya* (intention) for their husbands. For this purpose one woman goes around with a piece of paper on which the participants inscribe their husbands' names. There is a choice of *naqd* and *niyya*, the former, "cash," meaning the immediate readiness to go out for *khurūj* the next weekend, the latter meaning an intention to make *khurūj* in the future. There is also the possibility of voting for a women's *jamāʿat*. In this case a woman may go out on a *khurūj* for forty days, accompanied by a male relative (*maḥram*, meaning her husband, her brother or her father). During the journey women *jamāʿats* do not stay at the mosque overnight, but with private families. Female adepts practice *khuṣūṣī gasht* only; they visit only private families. Because of the expense involved in female *khurūj*, a women's *jamā'at* starts out from Cologne only every two months, traveling for a maximum of three days.[26]

Conclusion

The urge to organize Islamic associations may increase in a diaspora situation, particularly if the new environment is negative or unsympathetic. Islam represents distinction of a higher moral value in a society where Muslims are mainly immigrant workers who belong to lower classes threatened by social poverty and discrimination. Many Islamic movements capitalize upon this situation, among them the Tablīghī Jamā'at. The movement sets the scene for Muslims in Europe to practice their religion, and it gives them a way to express their identity.

The Tablīghī Jamā'at defines itself as "Islamic," and hence operates as a transnational movement, but the recruitment and mobilization of new members takes place primarily on the basis of national, regional or ethnic identities. Among the Tablīghīs in Germany no nationality has an overwhelming majority, although the main adepts are mostly of Pakistani origin. The reason for the minimal Tablīghī Jamā'at impact on Turkish Muslims may lie in the international composition of German adepts themselves. We may conclude that the national composition of the Tablīghī following within the diaspora reflects the movement's strength in Pakistan. The movement's lack of success among Turkish people, especially in Germany but also in Belgium and the Netherlands, corresponds with the marginal place of Tablīghī Jamā'at in Turkey. Likewise, with regard to the worldwide network of the Tablīghī Jamā'at, Britain represents the crucial link between the Subcontinent and Europe.

Besides the immigrants of Western countries there is a further social group within the diaspora: the converts. Female converts told me that their husbands felt a positive change in themselves when their wives started Tablīghī activities, because while the women were on their journeys husbands were forced to do the housework. One female adept reported that in the beginning of her marriage there

[26] The material is derived from participant observation during two visits to *ta'līms* at Frankfurt on 31 March and at Cologne on 7 July 1996.

were many problems due to cultural differences—once they almost decided to divorce. Living according to the rules of an "authentic Islam"—which meant to her following the example of Muḥammad—this lady succeeded in improving her family situation. She believed that she found this "authentic Islam" in the rules of the Tablīghī Jamāʿat. At a micro-level, the Jamāʿat may in this way contribute to improvement and harmony within individual relationships. However, at a macro-level the Tablīghī Jamāʿat aims above all at recruiting new adepts. This is why its methods are adapted to the social situations of local immigrant Muslims. We witness a higher degree of coordination within the regions of the diaspora than in the country of origin. Finally, within the European setting the Tablīghī Jamāʿat must compete with a variety of ideologies, religions and sects. In this "supermarket of world views" the movement must sell itself well. A female adept put it in a nutshell: "It is a fight for each soul."

CHAPTER SEVEN

SEQUENCES OF A QUEST: TABLĪGHĪ JAMĀʿAT IN MOROCCO

Mohamed Tozy
Translation: Muhammad Khalid Masud[1]

Tablīghī Jamāʿat was introduced as Jamāʿat al-Tablīgh wa'l-Daʿwa (JTD, henceforth called the Jamāʿat) in Morocco at the beginning of 1960 by Pakistani Muslims. Officially, the Moroccan branch of the Tablīghī Jamāʿat came into existence on 6 July 1975, when its statutes were framed and when an old church was purchased and converted into al-Nūr Mosque to accommodate the Jamāʿat.

This essay studies the Jamāʿat neither because it is the most important or most promising phenomenon according to the theory of religion, but rather because it is the case most open to sociological investigation. It differs from secret religious groups that restrict providing information about themselves for security reasons. It also differs from mystic groups whose activities are difficult to describe; the reconstruction of an esoteric environment is always awkward, with rare exceptions. These differences in no way diminish the importance of Jamāʿat as a case study.

Theoretically, the Jamāʿat appears similar to other religious actors to the extent that its actions are re-enacted daily, putting into practice a plan for a civil and religious society dedicated to the revival of the Prophetic tradition. It operates within the framework of a modern association, enabling it to seek legal protection should the need arise.

In practice, however, the Jamāʿat manifests uniqueness at various levels. It embodies a very particular, although common, vision of Islam. It displays the characteristics of a 'reformist tradition' as it explains and justifies its actions with reference to the Qurʾān and

[1] Translators note: I am grateful to Mohamed Tozy, William R. Roff, and Ms. Miryam Ghalmi for reading and improving upon the script of my translation from the original french at several stages.

Sunna. The *murshid* [*amīr*] stresses the importance of recreating the life of the Prophet and his companions on a popular level, which essentially avoids the schisms and disagreements that might threaten the official interpretation of the Sunna. It is a popular regeneration because it allows mobilization of a strong pedagogic tradition, one that brings together instructions about daily practice, and makes them available to people who belong to a very low rung of society. Indeed, it responds to the needs of a people who are mostly illiterate.

The Jamāʿat operates within an international network. This not only offers an opportunity for comparative study of it in different Muslim countries, but, more importantly reveals the channels that link Moroccan Tablīghīs with other Muslims, particularly those within migrant populations (Kepel 1987).

We will not concern ourselves with the hypothetical linkages suggested by such terms as "sleeping partners," "the CIA conspiracy," or "reactionary forces," for two reasons: first, the movement does not employ propaganda techniques that require significant financing or otherwise demand affiliation with governments. On the contrary, it calls for self-financing through the mechanism of group solidarity. Secondly, states may nurture ambitions of purging these associations, as is so often the case, but at this level of belief and religious mobilization it becomes difficult to determine legally who is the manipulator and who is manipulated. Several governments have paid a high price for their audacity in persecuting such movements.

The Jamāʿat offers a unique example of a religious group that is entirely regulated by laws of association, under a *Dahir* [*ẓāhir*], a decree issued by the Sulṭān of Morocco on 15 November 1958 and later modified by another *Dahir* on 10 April 1973. The movement uses the traditional circuit of private mosques to cover the entire country.

Our analysis in this essay deals with three points in turn: first, defining the identity of the Jamāʿat according to theories of religion; second, analyzing the philosophy of the Jamāʿat; and finally, describing its activities in Morocco generally, and in Casablanca in particular.

This paper is the result of a continuous three-year observation. I deliberately call it an "observation" rather than an "inquiry" to avoid the implication of formal research. I was often obliged to undertake my research (in the double sense of the term "research," applicable to one's self as well as to the other) first as an insider and a participant in the activities of the Jamāʿat, and second by raising questions in terms of the classical analytical categories of the sociology of religion (such as numbers, followers, geographic origins and age-groups).

Theory

The Identity of the Jamāʿat

The purpose of including the Jamāʿat in a comparative register that refers to a general theory of religion is not to compare the system with a super system of reference. Neither is it an attempt to impose upon it some sort of ecumenism. Rather, I aim to explain the significance of universal concepts by showing a spectrum of solutions found for a given problem by different societies.

The question posed here is at once pretentious and simple. It is pretentious to the extent that it seeks to go beyond a Manichean vision reflecting two opposing positions. According to this vision, Islam is either a "specific" religion, and all views about its current of thought must be reducible to its own dynamics, or, on the contrary, Islam is only a crude product, following the model of other monotheistic religions. At the same time, the question is simple in the sense that, as far as inquiry is concerned, it is entirely limited to studying the lives of a group for the purpose of constructing a typology of a universal call, in Weber's sense (Seguy 1972, 71–104).

This inquiry will lead us, without subscribing *a priori* to one or another theory, to try to show (a) in what way the group studied is comparable to the different "churches" which recognize other revealed religions, and (b) how it distinguishes itself, in so far as the existence of the Jamāʿat is dependent on the theoretical availability of Islam—that is to say its capacity to express its divergence within the framework of an Orthodoxy.

Conversion in the Monotheistic Tradition

There are many typologies of Christian sects, but they only rarely (Desroche 1955–1956, 395) go beyond statements of sect/church opposition. They seldom propose a theoretical framework that takes into consideration the organic and existential singularity of a sect. Such a view could allow comparison of the experiences of sects belonging to different religions.[2]

[2] The French translation of the work of Wach (1955) appears to have been conditioned by the reorientation of studies of the French school of sociology of religions. The school seems to have begun taking a close interest in the problems of sects in a profound manner only from the beginning of the 1960s.

An article by B. Wilson (1963) offers an example of this approach. The author, without lingering on the Weberian opposition of church and sect, devotes himself to describing American reality and proposes a classification of seven categories of religious sects of which we will be concerned with only one: the conversionist.[3] This is a typical (fundamentalist) evangelical Christian sect. Its reaction to the world consists of suggesting that the world is corrupt because men are corrupt. If one can reform mankind one can change the world. The characteristic activities of this type of sect are revivalism and public preaching. The dominant tone in the atmosphere of the group is emotional, but not mystical (ecstatic). In the case of Christian sects, the most valued sects are those that encourage the preaching of gospels to the entire world. Such a sect greatly resembles the Jamāʿat, since both share key characteristics: active dynamism, pietist fervour and easy availability (i.e., a relatively open character).

The Position of the Jamāʿat in the Islamic Environment

In writings about Islamic sects, several terms have been used to express their separateness (sectarianism). From an early date Islam knew of *firaq* (sing. *firqa*) and *aḥzāb* (sing. *ḥizb*), and condemned more or less violently those departing from *jamāʿa* (collectivity of Muslims), which embodied the best sense of the *Umma*. It is in order to avoid such stigma that the Jamāʿat has chosen the name it has. Their recourse to the concept of *jamāʿat* justifies itself by its polysemic character, which makes it possible, thanks to that circumstances, to call even a group of four people *jamāʿa*.

(i) *Hostile Environments and the Jamāʿat*: The Jamāʿat is a community of persecuted faithful who conserve and defend the Islamic tradition from a position of weakness (*istiḍʿāf*). The concept expresses the force of solidarity (cohesion) necessary for the survival of Islam in a society where Muslims are a minority and which is governed by a power that is either non-Muslim or is influenced by non-Muslims. It highlights the obligation of vigilance, which is a duty of all Muslims.

The fact that Jamāʿat began in India, where Islam often competes with other religions, partially explains why "revivalism" and "conversion" are so important for the Tablīghīs.

[3] The categories are (1) missionary, (2) revolutionary, (3) pietist, (4) manipulationist, (5) miraculous, (6) reformist and (7) utopian.

(ii) *A Community of the Faithful*: The Tablīghīs narrate several *aḥādīth* supporting their conviction that they are the inheritors of the legacy of the original *jamāʿat* (*ṣafwat aṣḥābun nabī*), the companions of the Prophet. They advance this definition to dispel any accusations that they are creating a schism (*firqa, fitna*). The Tablīghīs exalt the virtues of group action, such as praying in a group (*ṣalātul jamāʿa*) and preaching in the group. This way of life is associated with the concept of the obligation to spread Islam.[4] Equating the concepts of *jamāʿa* with the community of the majority has helped the Muslim Brothers (al-Ikhwān al-Muslimūn, see appendix one, Introduction, of this volume), in another context, to demarcate boundaries (*ḥadd*) between those who are on the right path among the active believers, and others.[5]

(iii) *Jamāʿa (party) and Jamʿiyya (association)*: In modern Arabic usage, the term *jamāʿa* (party) is semantically close to the term *jamʿiyya*[6] (association) which reflects the strategic necessity of registering under the protection of the law, and especially the inability to escape state control without the risk of becoming clandestine. The term *jamāʿa* is used principally in connection with power politics. The statutes of the *jamaʿiyya* are invoked whenever the protection of law is necessary for the survival of the association.

Each time an official obstructs preaching, the Jamāʿat confronts him with its statute of a legal association, stating precisely that their activity is public, not secret. In 1982, the Ministry of Awqāf threatened to take over control of the Jamāʿat mosque. To avoid this, the

[4] A companion explains this urgency of group action in these terms: "Imagine my friends in what darkness we would have been thrown if the first companions had tried to perfect their Islam as individuals, by themselves, without engaging in the salvation of humanity."

[5] Sayyid Quṭb wrote on this subject saying, "The question in essence is that of unbelief (*Kufr*) and belief... Indeed people are not Muslims, as they proclaim to be, as long as they live the life of *Jāhiliyya*... This is not Islam, and they are not Muslims. Today the task of the call is to return these ignorant people to Islam and make them Muslims all over again" (Quṭb 1978, 258).

[6] The term *jamʿiyya* has a modern connotation of society or association, which contradicts the Jamāʿat claim that it is not a formal organization. This title may be easily misunderstood as indicating a cultural or social association. [Editor's note: This explanation raises further questions. The author has in mind the modern Arab usage. It is interesting to compare the usage of this term in India and Egypt. In the former, the official organization of the *ʿulamā* was called Jamʿiyyatul ʿUlamā Hind, and Mawlānā Mawdūdī named his organization Jamāʿat Islāmī; both are political parties. In Egypt, on the other hand, when all political parties were banned, the Muslim Brotherhood was allowed to continue because it called itself a *jamʿiyyat*, not a *jamāʿat*].

Tablīghīs transformed the first floor into offices of the association. This allowed them to claim half of the mosque as the property of the association, regulated by the decree of the Sulṭān relating to public freedom, making annexation by the ministry impossible.

(iv) *Jamāʿat—Group*: In the internal operational network of the Jamāʿat, the term *jamāʿat* has acquired a precise double meaning. It is an organic unity. Each time it takes the name of a locality, it expresses a level of organization in that network. Thus, for example, as a structural unit, a certain local unit of the Jamāʿat would be a district unit of its organization at the level of the Muslim World as a whole. The concept of *jamāʿat* at each level demonstrates forcefully the organic continuity of the Jamāʿat and its capacity to transcend national boundaries. One may thus notice that the *jamāʿat* of Ain Chok (a local neighbourhood) is a subdivision of the *jamāʿat* of Casablanca (city) which is in turn a part of the *jamāʿat* of Morocco (country) which itself is only a fraction of the transnational Jamāʿat.

The Jamāʿat is an active unit because the term means a group that goes out for preaching. A group or *jamāʿat* is identified with reference to its activity, namely by referring to the duration of an outing (three days, ten days, one month, etc.) of the group and its destination (Morocco/abroad). The activism of the Jamāʿat is expressed in its function of *Daʿwa*. This function justifies the withdrawal from the world as a Tablīghī leaves his home, family and children and in a sense withdraws from the world, though temporarily, and retreats himself in *Daʿwa*. The purpose of this 'withdrawal' or 'retreat' is to repair the damages inflicted by worldly indulgence. The Tablīghīs make use of the parable of the dry-dock to explain the *khurūj* that contains the risk of being condemned by orthodoxy.

> Man is a ship in trouble in a tumultuous sea. It is impossible to repair it without taking it away from the high seas where the waves of ignorance and the temptations of temporal life assail it. Its only chance is to come back to land to be dry-docked. The dry-dock is the mosque of the Jamāʿat.[7]

This parable explains not only the reformist/conversionist objective of the *jamāʿat*, but also the manner in which this objective is to be achieved. To recover his moral strength a Tablīghī must live in the

[7] A *morchid* offered this explanation to the author in September 1981.

jamāʿa, isolated from the corrupt world, for at least three days each month, forty days each year and four months continuously within his lifetime.

Analysis

The Philosophy of the Jamāʿat

The term philosophy is inadequate to describe the positions or principles adopted by the Jamāʿat. Its leaders and even its followers refuse to theorize their practice. In contrast to Mawlānā Mawdūdī, who theorized the practice of *Daʿwa* for the Jamāʿat Islāmī, Mawlānā Ilyās left no written work on its theory. That is why Mawlānā Mawdūdī, more than Mawlānā Ilyās, influenced most of the modern movements of *Daʿwa*, without necessarily being a party to them. The Tablīghī Jamāʿat exclusively addresses Muslims, although it can also be proud of its positive balance sheet of conversions.

The Jamāʿat believes in the principle that individuals must be changed before society is changed. According to Morchid [Murshid], "Muslims have been taken over by a whirlwind." The temptations of Satan are numerous, yet Muslims are basically good; they only need help to become model Muslims. It is not a question of converting them but of reminding them of their ignorance.

The Four Opportunities in the Life of a Tablīghī during an Outing

The "outing" must become a routine in the life of a Tablīghī. It may take place in the locality of his residence (and in that case it coincides with his daily life, and does not go beyond three days per month), or it may be a longer outing to other cities of Morocco or to a foreign country.

In Casablanca, the Jamāʿat is divided into four autonomous organizations by city quarters or areas: *jamāʿat* ʿAin Chok, *jamāʿat* Sidi Barnoussi, *jamāʿat* Sidī Uthmān, and *jamāʿat* Ḥayy al-Ḥasanī. Every *jamāʿa* works within its own constituency. Members leave to spend only three days each month in Mosque al-Nūr (in the locality of Beausejour). There they organize outings to make rounds in any part of the town. During these outings, the Morchid of the local autonomous *jamāʿa* is responsible for organizing the preaching. The heads of other localities can organize outings in their own constituencies when it is their turn to spend the day in their area.

The ideal for each Tablīghī is to perform a grand tour which will take him to India, Pakistan and finally to Mecca. Stories of these outings nourish Tablīghīs' evenings when they are not travelling. Often examples of Indian *jamāʿat* are cited. Each year the groups go out to all four points of the compass to meet in Mecca to perform pilgrimage together.

As one of the numerous *morchids* in Casablanca noted, the primary objective of the outing is development of the individual; preaching comes later. The *jamāʿat* mobilizes all the pedagogic skills to realize this objective during the outing. It is justified as a *hijra* (migration) which literally means to leave one's home to devote oneself to *Daʿwa* and to *dhikr*, even if it is in a local mosque.

Once a Tablīghī has decided to depart, he severs all his contacts with relatives. From now on, the leader (*morchid, amīr*) of the outing takes him totally in his charge. This active retreat tends to realize four objectives, framed in terms of obligations:

(i) *The Obligation to Teach and to Learn*: Here teaching and learning refer to an initial level of the skill of extemporaneous speech. The Tablīghīs insist that man's character is imperfect and it is necessary to improve it. One learns best by listening to others.

The Tablīghīs sit in a circle, which has a double symbolic significance. It is a *dāʾira*, of which the points of circumference are the Tablīghīs themselves facing the centre occupied by a divine presence. It is also a *ḥalaqa* (ring) of a symbolic chain, which constitutes the force of the *jamāʿat*. Access to the circle implies respect for the ritual of purification about which the *morchid* never forgets to remind the Tablīghīs. They must perform ablutions, use perfume and perform two *rakʿats*. During the *taʿlīm* sessions, one learns the merits of actions of piety, the rules of *Daʿwa* and the essentials of the Qurʾān.

(ii) *The Obligation to Serve*: The Tablīghīs engage themselves in serving other followers, for example by cooking and preparing hot water for ablution. While the Tablīghīs look after their own needs, they also serve the local people.

(iii) *Obligation to Worship (ʿIbādāt)*: *ʿIbādāt* can be translated roughly as canonical obligations to God. The Tablīghīs insist on prayers, *dhikr* and reading of the Qurʾān. This is where they come closest to the

Toroqis (*al-ṭuruqī*: the followers of a Ṣūfī brotherhood). Prayer becomes a means to transcend difficulties. A Tablīghī learns to give his prayer an emotional charge such that it becomes operational in his daily life. In contrast to the Toroqis, there is among Tablīghīs no distinction between levels of status. The Jamāʿat is a community of brothers. The *morchid* is not fixed, but rather there is a rotation between the old hands. Oldness is measured by the number of outings undertaken, and especially by their duration. One outing of four months to Pakistan gives one a great deal more power than those who have done their outings only in Morocco.

(iv) *Obligation to Practice Daʿwa*: *Daʿwa* is the crowning of the whole process of formation or training. It consists of four varieties:

(1) *Al-Daʿwatul ʿĀmma* (General): This is the normal function of the *jamāʿa*, and is directed to all Muslims. During his development, a Tablīghī learns first of all to preach at home. His training in public speaking begins when he accompanies an experienced Tablīghī on the *Daʿwa* rounds. These rounds are planned very precisely in the programme, and are held on every Thursday during the week. The groups scatter to several mosques in the city, each setting itself up in a mosque between the *ʿAṣr* and *Maghrib* prayers. The *amīr* speaks about the virtues of the Prophet, and reads from *Riyāḍus Ṣāliḥīn*.

Next to the "Life of the Companions of the Prophet" (*Ḥayātus Ṣaḥāba*), the *Riyāḍus Ṣāliḥīn* enjoys second place in reading sessions. Its merit lies in its apparent nonsectarian and orthodox presentation. The book is a classic work by Shaykh al-Nawawī and has been reprinted many times in Casablanca since 1980.

Readings from the book serve to open an informal talk on the necessity to reform society and especially to "convert" the people to "good religion." The talk concludes by proposing to the faithful present (those who have not gone out with the *jamāʿat*) to go out and call upon the people around the mosque and talk to them about their religious problems. To consolidate the response to the talk, the *morchid* forms into two-man preacher-groups (each with one old man and one new man) who go out inviting people to perform the next prayer (*maghrib*) in the mosque.

The conversations with the people are quite simple. Do you pray? If the person says yes, he is invited immediately to come to mosque by citing the virtues of praying in congregation (*ṣalātul jamāʿa*). If, on the contrary, the person responds in the negative, certain verses of the Qur'ān and a *ḥadīth* are recited about the obligation to pray. Sometimes the invitee reacts violently, but the Tablīghī always responds gently. A Tablīghī learns quickly to control himself even when he is attacked. In this respect one of the typical stories that the followers repeat among themselves at the mealtime is about a certain very active *morchid.* Before induction into the *jamāʿat,* he was approached by a Tablīghī. He reacted violently and slapped the Tablīghī's face. The Tablīghī remained very calm and thanked him saying, "The Prophet endured treatment that was worse than this (referring to Prophet's mission to Ṭā'if when he was attacked by the children of the village where he had gone preaching)." Shaken by this reaction, the person began asking forgiveness from the Tablīghī, who responded, "It is not up to me to forgive you, it is up to God because you have slapped his image. Come to the mosque and ask His forgiveness." Since then the man has never left the *Jamāʿat.*

Immediately before the prayer, when all the believers are there, one Tablīghī gets up and recites the *bayān* (the Jamāʿat manifesto speech). The speech is very brief. After defining the objectives of the Jamāʿat, the speaker invites the people to visit the headquarters of the association, reminding them that it is the duty of every Muslim to visit each other: "We have come to you as brothers, you should visit us too. We will wait for you on Thursday each week at the mosque in Beausejour."

(2) *Al-Daʿwatul Khāṣṣa* (Selective): Contrary to the general *Daʿwa,* in which meetings take place at random, the special *Daʿwa* starts by preparing a list of the people who are available in the area, or in the locality where a Tablīghī works. The leaders choose a person who would be useful for the cause of the Jamāʿat, and the Tablīghīs visit him with a view to recruiting him eventually into the Jamāʿat. Generally, the *ʿulamā'* are the preferred target of this *Daʿwa.* Tablīghīs try to win an *ʿālim* over and endeavour to invite him each time they have an opportunity to do so. This has a double advantage: first, it provides the *jamāʿa* a shelter against the eventuality of religious condemnation, and second, it enlists a qualified person who can stand guarantee for their practice.

(3) *Daʿwa for* reminding: After the speech on Thursday (*bayānul jamāʿa*), the *morchid* poses two questions: Who is ready to devote to God four months in his lifetime? Forty days? Ten days? Three days? One

hour? Secondly, he asks: Who offers himself to devote time in the future?

Groups are formed on the basis of the duration of the outing, with an old hand as their head (*amīr*), who decides what preparations are to be made and where to meet.

Each time a believer promises to go out with the *jamāʿat*, his name is written down in a notebook maintained by the *morchid* in charge of the locality where the volunteer resides. If the *morchid* notices that the volunteer has not fulfilled his promise, he sends two persons to contact him at his home. Every *morchid* of a group has a notebook in which he writes the names and addresses of the Tablīghīs and their programmes of outing (the location of their preaching, date and time). The *morchid* who stays permanently at the headquarter mosque must know where to find each *jamāʿat* each hour of the outing, if not each individual follower.

(4) *Daʿwa* for training and aprenticeship: Every Sunday one *jamāʿat* composed of new and old Tablīghīs makes rounds of hospitals and visits the patients. The purpose of the visit is essentially to train the novice, but it aims to reach the patients as much as the Tablīghīs themselves.

This rigorous practice involves for the Tablīghīs great self-control. They do not wish to convert this faith potential into an immediate political alternative, or at least not to turn it into an open criticism of society. Many Tablīghīs do not support this stance of waiting and prefer to join the ranks of activist political associations and parties.

The membership of Jamāʿat is renewed continuously, a fact of which the leaders of the Jamāʿat are conscious, and this has turned the Jamāʿat into a kind of crossroads for future Islamists.

Remodeling Behaviour

The Jamāʿat's training and practice is based on a two-point programme: (1) one objective, namely sanctifying daily routine, and remodeling behaviour; and (2) one programme—total control of the novice. Each gesture and each act performed by a Tablīghī must be productive, that is to say, it must mean bringing the believer nearer to eternal salvation. The life of a Tablīghī is a permanent ritual, and his conduct is regulated in its minutest detail so that it conforms in every detail to the life of the Prophet.

This Prophetic tradition, lived in an intense manner, signifies at one and the same time involvement, as well as development of a different identity. It provides the novice an opportunity to belong to a specific community, one which has chosen the path of preaching. This involvement implies a battle for which the novice is initiated and prepared in minutest detail.

Appendix

Tablīgh Manners

The following is an account of my first night spent in the mosque Al-Nūr (Beausejour) during a three-day (14–17 April 1983) outing. I was instructed about table manners and the etiquette of going to bed, according to the Tablīgh code.

(A) *Table Manners*
Everyone brought his own food for a collective dinner because it was the first night. The team that should have cooked meals had not yet been appointed. There was no table, but instead an eighty-centimeter long plastic mat, called *sufra*, spread between two rows of novices. Before the meal, an older Tablīghī reminded the participants of the etiquette of the Prophet regarding table manners (*Ādābul mā'ida*). The *morchid* chose an experienced person (a young man about thirty years old who was a teacher at a secondary school in Casablanca) to introduce me to good manners. The *morchid* took me aside and told me:

> The outing for the glory of God has many hardships. Satan lies in wait for good believers. It is therefore essential to remain vigilant, following in letter and spirit the example of the Companions of the Prophet, so that all of our acts are tuned into acts of worship. There are rules for each act, which are based on the Prophet's example. These rules are not new. They are part of daily Moroccan life from long past. But their teaching in the practice of the *jamā'at* gives them a new meaning: they become sacred. The Tablīghī has a feeling of participating in a great project for installing the Prophetic spirit eternally.

1. When you wish to eat, do it with your right hand, and sit in one of the three positions in which the Prophet sat: first position: sit straight, legs crossed; second position: one leg folded inside under the pelvis, the other folded outside; third position: on one's knees (as one does for the prostration (*sajda*) with buttocks resting on heels.
2. Say the *basmala.*
3. If the food is hot, one must wait until it cools and say, "God Almighty, bless what we eat and spare us from the torments of hell." When the food is cold, one must say, "God Almighty, bless what we are eating and give us more."

4. One must eat from in front of oneself, starting from the edge of the dish, chew slowly, serve one's table neighbour, eat with three fingers (thumb, index and big finger) because those who eat with only two are arrogant, and those who eat with five are uncivilized.
5. One must drink in three sequences, hold the container in the right hand, drink and swallow, take a breath away from it, repeat the same act a second time, then a third time; drink only to quench your thirst.
6. After eating, one should say "Thank you O God who satisfied us and gave to us our fill."

(B) *Etiquette of Going to Bed and Getting Up*

1. Before going to bed one must perform ablution, turn one's head toward *qibla* (Mecca), dust one's bedding, (if it is light, one should raise it with two hands and shake it, if it is heavy one should clean it by wiping it by hand on the upper side), read the following three chapters of the Qur'ān three times: Al-Nās, Al-Falaq, and al-Fātiḥa, lie down on the right side and say the following prayer: "God Almighty. Take my soul close to your throne."
2. Upon getting up, stay on the bed for a moment, blow into your hands and pass them all over your body and then say the following prayer: "Glory to God who revived me after my death."
3. If one has bad dreams during the night, one should blow out to one's left side and pray: "God Almighty, protect me from what I see, and make sure that this bad dream does not affect my religion or life," and do not tell anyone. If it is a good dream, it must be told to the believer who one loves the most.

Other daily aspects of life are regulated in the same detail. The Tablīghīs have rules for the market, for bathing, for visiting the graveyard and so on to the extent that a Tablīghī in the midst of the group finds himself profoundly different from those outside the group. He meets others with the conviction that he is chosen and protected from all surprises because all his movements conform to the code of ethics of the Prophet. The outing, when contrasted with the real life of a Tablīghī, gives an impression that he lives in a community that is perfectly synchronized and free from all conflicts.

CHAPTER EIGHT

TABLĪGHĪ JAMĀʿAT IN BELGIUM[1]

Felice Dassetto

During the past twenty years a number of Muslim religious groups have emerged in Belgium. Among them, the Tablīghī Jamāʿat stands out as the strongest and most effective.[2]

To describe the organization of the Tablīghī Jamāʿat in Belgium, one could use the image of concentric circles. At the centre is located true Islam, viewed as a personal attitude in perfect imitation of the initial prophetic era. Moving outward from this centre there are different levels of adherence, reaching finally a position of "exteriority" in relation to the "centre," with respect to Muslims, or of "otherness" with respect to non-Muslims. These multiple circles represent a global interpretation which constitutes the worldview of the Tablīghī Jamāʿat [Jamāʿat al-Tablīgh]. The organization of the Tablīgh approaches each of these circles in a simultaneous yet varied manner by deploying different resources toward each.

The Tablīghīs in Belgium intend to, and do, place themselves at the very heart of orthodox Islam.[3] They develop their specific activities

[1] Editor's note: This essay has been adapted from Dassetto 1988.

[2] This study is based on survey material collected between 1980 and 1984 during research on all of the organized forms of Islam in Belgium, and on a study of the legal statutes of the mosques. It also draws on the author's participation in Tablīgh activities and on interviews he made between 1984 and 1986 with Tablīgh leaders both in Belgium and from India, as well as new and old members of the Tablīgh in Belgium.

[3] It would be interesting—even if one knows from the start that it is an unending activity—to extend the analysis of the morphology of the religious organization to comparisons with the religious forms identified by the sociology of Christianity (See Tozy, this volume). Tozy (1984) compares the Tablīghīs with the model of the conversionist sect identified by Wilson (1970). If this comparison is legitimate from the point of view of a developed religious activity—although pietist sects also may be a useful point of comparison—it is less so from the perspective of the relationship between the religious organization and the surrounding religious environment. From this perspective, the Tablīgh would be more related to the category of movements of "protest within" as identified by Wach (1955). Examples are the Franciscan movement in the Christian Middle Ages and the contemporary charismatic renewal.

without rupture or separation from orthodoxy. Regarding the continuity of Islam, they suggest a cyclical interpretation of its history. After the missionary expansion of Islam during the early caliphate periods, came the period of consolidation in the times of the empires, followed by a period of decadence. Only at the beginning of this century did Muslims begin to review the shortcomings of the present status of Islam, the reasons for its degradation, and the consequences for society. For the Tablīghīs, the renewal of Islam is accomplished mainly through personal adherence to the founding principles and to emulating the life of the Prophet and his followers.

The Belgian Tablīghīs defend a practical Islam in contrast to the excessive intellectualism that they perceive in other movements. Their activities are based on a few simple rules: to have faith in God, to pray, to act with modesty, to learn the word and transmit it, to follow the right way, and to receive all believers. These are the virtues of pious Muslims, accompanied by the idea of the transmission of knowledge and invitation to believers.[4] Belief in God is translated into a strong projection into the otherworldly life and expectations after death. This can be deduced from expressions such as: "Here there is just earth" and "Life is a prison." There are prohibitions that must be adhered to.

This total faith is extended into the attitude toward politics, which is as neutral as it is radical. The Tablīghīs call themselves apolitical. They even say that it is prohibited for them to take part in politics. Since politics cause divisions in Islam, their reference model is derived from the origins of Islam. But the very radicalism of their faith and their models of reference are powerful critiques of existing political systems, particularly those claiming to be Islamic. One finds, therefore, that, far removed from power by virtue of their position in society, the Tablīghīs challenge the legitimacy of political systems without attaching themselves to any of them. They go to the heart of the problem of power in "Muslim" countries without touching it.

Prayer governs the life of the Tablīghīs. Their mosques are among the most visited, and in the topology that we have constructed they belong to the category of devotional mosques (Dassetto and Bastenier

[4] We speak here, in a general sense, of the Tablīghīs. It is a first approach. Our hypothesis, developed in the following section, is that the "Tablīghī" is shaped by a complex organization which is structured around forms of belonging and different religious and ideological references.

1984, 79–83). Seeking religious knowledge and transmitting it constitutes another rule of the Tablīghīs. Seeking the knowledge of Islam, as opposed to merely engaging in repetitive and conformist religious practice, is their response to the general ignorance among the common people on the one hand, and excessive specialization of religious erudition on the other. From this knowledge emanates the duty to call Muslims to practice it by missionary activity. This duty is incumbent on each believer as a continuation of the successful prophetic activity by the Prophet.

Individual modesty, moral improvement and openness to all believers are rules which guide individual attitudes and characterize the overall atmosphere of Tablīghī mosques. In this way, the Tablīghīs emerge as pious Muslims.

Organization

The Tablīghīs aim to enroll members who will adopt the Tablīghī principles as particular modalities, but modalities which are not separated from adherence to Islam. This adherence is generated by the secular society, particularly in the socially and culturally more marginal sectors. The Tablīghīs maintain a distance from political and religious authorities and exercise a certain autonomy. Tablīghī activities do not aim at a simple reproduction of existing religious fields, but rather are innovatory and expansive and do not hesitate to engage new social and geographical areas. A consequence of this is that the Tablīghīs must handle, from an organizational point of view, a large amount of uncertainty. In addition, there are multiple realms to consider, in view of the different social, political, and religious environments in which prospective members work.

My hypothesis is as follows: the Tablīghīs have created a complex organization which is capable of handling at one and the same time all relations within these multiple environments. It remains faithful to the objectives and missionary principles established by the founder, and it makes use of the human resources provided by the secular society, which also constitute the human material considered by the founder to be the targets for Tablīghī action.[5]

In sum, it seems that the success of the Tablīghīs has resulted not

---

[5] The concepts used in this context rely on works in the sociology of organizations

only from the appropriateness of the structure and function of the organization in relation to the goals it has set, but also from the fact that its structure and the function are juxtaposed to the objectives—this means that the organization of the Tablīgh is both its means of action and its aim. Moreover, since the organization uses values and human resources, which at the same time constitute the target of its activities, its very principles hold a capacity for self-expansion.

Managing Visibility

The Tablīghīs manage their relationship with the "exterior" (non-Tablīghī Muslims) and with "others" (non-Muslims) in Belgium using common means which are primarily aimed at their visibility, namely their appearance in the eyes of law, and their transparency to other Muslims and to non-Muslims. The relationship with the outside is entrusted to particular persons in a relatively exclusive way. Public relations are handled by persons who belong to the more intimate circles of the Tablīgh, the only people permitted a total knowledge of the organization. These men belong at the same time to the inside and to the outside, and are the legitimate spokespersons for the way in which the Tablīghīs define themselves.

The Tablīghīs also group themselves within formal organizations, often in the statutory form of non-profit organizations constituted according to Belgian law (abbreviated as ASBL). The law does not require that an organization be constituted as an ASBL; it could just as well exist as an informal organization. However, since the very beginning, the Tablīghīs have preferred to constitute themselves as non-profit organizations[6] in order to be visible, and perhaps to legitimate and assure their presence.

The first Tablīghī ASBL was founded in 1975 under the influence of the then *amīr* of Belgium, a Moroccan immigrant who had joined

---

and particularly on the analytical framework proposed by Touraine (1973, 277–293) and the work of Crozier and Friedberg (1977), as well as Etzioni (1971). Further on we shall use concepts proposed by Merton (1957).

[6] The constitution of an ASBL is based on statutes framed according to the law of 27 June 1921. Formally, an ASBL should be established by founding members (a minimum of three) adopting statutes which have been drawn up privately or before a lawyer. The statutes should state the objectives of the association, its competence, the modalities of the designation of the general assembly, and the functions of the general assembly and of the administrative board. The statutes are placed with the *Moniteur Belge* for publication, where all amendments should also be lodged.

the Jamāʿat by going to Bangladesh on a tour at the end of the 1960s. The mosque registered by this organization, one of the first mosques in Belgium to receive legal status, is still the centre of Tablīgh in the country.[7] The years 1975–1980 appear in retrospect as years of establishment but without visibility; but this began to bear fruit from 1980 onwards. Between 1980 and 1982, six mosques in Brussels were constituted as ASBLs with names and statutes identical to those of the first mosque. The year 1982 saw an important step in the internal life of the Tablīghīs when a large international meeting was organized in Charleroi. After 1983, five other mosques were constituted, one in Brussels and the others in Wallonia and in the Flemish region. Altogether twelve non-profit organizations were created during a ten-year period. They were given relatively simple statutes and sufficiently general aims so as to avoid all sectarianism and specific strategies.

It is interesting to note that in order to manage visibility three modifications have been made in the statutes of the original mosque. First, over the years, we can observe a desire to limit the possibilities of non-Muslims observing what goes on in Tablīghī ASBLs. In keeping with the law at the time, which prescribed that three-fifths of the founders of an ASBL be Belgians, there were in fact nine Belgians among the fifteen founders. As such, they also belonged to the general assembly (*shūrā*), but progressively and tacitly they were moved aside, and they are no longer called to meetings. Some of the newer ASBLs did not include any Belgians among their founding members.[8]

---

[7] The founding of this ASBL followed closely on the adoption of the 1974 Belgian law which recognized the temporal aspects of the Islamic religion in the same way as it does for the Catholic, Jewish and Protestant religions. Incidentally, by coincidence, during the year 1975 the Tablīghīs in Morocco also officially proclaimed the statutes of their first mosque Al-Nūr in Casablanca, which had the same name as the mosque in Brussels (Tozy 1984).

[8] This was inconsistent with the law at that time. The officials of the *Moniteur Belge*, accepted and published the statutes, while recognizing that they had no legal value since the association had been illegally constituted. The Moroccan Amicales had an analogous situation. The Aliens Act of 1984 changed the situation, since foreigners who had lived in Belgium for at least five years acquired the same status as Belgians. A kind of fiction was thus established for some years between the immigrant community and state officials, both pretending that they were dealing with legally established associations. This did not have serious implications since there were, to our knowledge, no situations where the legality of the associations was put to the test. This was symptomatic of the "social weariness," not to say rupture of communication, during these years between the Belgian community, particularly the state machinery, and the immigrant population, particularly the Moroccans.

Turkish and Moroccan ASBL mosques, by contrast, continue to include Belgians. Sometimes even municipal or Catholic authorities appear among their founders. It would appear, therefore, that the Tablīghīs wanted to become official and to become visible, but that they have also used all means available to minimize their visibility to the Belgians and Muslim outsiders.

Whereas the first statutes were very brief and vague concerning the internal rules of operation of the associations, time witnessed a gradual introduction of rules that, firstly, allowed a strong concentration of authority in a small group of leaders (constituted mainly by the permanent nucleus of the Tablīgh) and, secondly, established a mandatory monthly contribution of at least 500 FB as a criterion for membership. In addition, a 1984 modification of the statutes introduced a change of objectives for the mosques. Initially, these were expressed in a rather simple way: "To promote the Islamic faith and the teaching of the Qur'ān to Muslims" (section 2 in the statutes of 1975). At present, following an amendment of 16 January 1984, these objectives have been extended to include, in addition to religious activities, self-help, social and cultural activities, and the teaching of Arabic as distinct from the Qur'ān. Moreover, the targets of these activities are no longer only Muslims in Belgium but also those living in other European countries.

By means of the controlled use of special persons for external relations, and by statutory changes, the Tablīghīs have shown, during their short official history in Belgium, that they want to control their public visibility. If one can say that they have nothing to hide, it may also be said that everything cannot be seen and heard. This is due firstly to the fact that they understand the importance of managing their autonomy. Secondly, their differentiated visibility, which is part of their missionary strategy, and the organizational structure of concentric circles, are relevant factors. Moreover, legal status was initially a way to become visible and to receive social and legal legitimacy for their activities. Over the years, at least in the main mosque, it seems that this legal status has been transformed into a tool for the administration of an organization which has specific objectives.

Managing Representativeness

The modification of objectives in the statutes of the central mosque of the Tablīghīs from 16 January 1984 indicated a development in the strategy of managing Muslim representativeness and the visibility of the Jamāʿat, particularly with respect to the Centre Islamique et Culturelle de Belgique as representative of Muslims in Belgium. After having constructed a forceful consensus in a certain number of mosques, and having centralized the administration of the main mosque (1984), the governing nucleus of the Tablīghīs elaborated a strategy to take over the central administration of Islam in Belgium and thereby attain hegemony over Islam's relationship with the Belgian state and with public opinion. To accomplish this, the Tablīghīs institutionalized their movement by giving it an organizational form that makes them appear to be the best representatives of the Belgian mosques. They have succeeded in projecting a strong image of their own representativeness.

In fact, the Tablīghīs were behind the creation, in February 1985, of a Fédération des Mosquées et des Associations Culturelles et Islamique de Belgique. This is a rather pompous title for an association of a limited number of responsible officials from various mosques, many associated with the Tablīghī Jamāʿat, all located in Brussels. It is certainly an exercise in image production. The objectives of the federation are extensive: to defend the resident Islamic community in Belgium; to organize and promote the teaching of Arabic and the Qur'ān as well as of Islamic culture, particularly by the creation of Islamic schools; and to nominate *imāms* and to supervise the administration of member mosques.

One factor behind the inception of this Federation was a longstanding discontentment with the director of the Centre Islamique et Culturelle de Belgique, who was its founder and had held his position since 1969. The founding of the Federation was partly a veiled expression of an institutional opposition to this centre, one that had been voiced also by other associations and federations in the past, but with little success.

The Centre Islamique et Culturelle de Belgique, an outgrowth of the powerful Muslim World League, occupies a large mosque established in a building provided by the Belgian State in 1969. The Centre has received legal status as an international organization according to Belgian law. Its administrative board includes representatives of the Arabian ambassador. Although the legitimacy of this Centre is questioned by many, it has acquired power in the context of the mosque, the education of *imāms*, and the nomination of teachers. This power derives partly from the considerable funds put at its disposal by the League. To this should be added that it is the centre of the section of the League with the task of promoting the creation of mosques in Europe. But the place occupied by the Centre Islamique in Brussels on the Belgian scene derives also from the fact that it is, up to the present and with some hesitation, the only official counterpart to the Belgian state with respect to the effects of the law of 1974. This law recognizes the "temporal character of the Islamic religion" in the country (see Dassetto and Bastenier 1984, 165–190). The Tablīghīs see the Muslim World League as a body external to the immigrant populations. In short, it does not express, according to the Tablīgh, the people's Islam. Here the Tablīghī Jamāʿat can be seen as representing an oppositional and critical strategy which advances gradually and efficiently.

The Federation began by organizing popular pressure through submission of a petition to the president of the Centre Islamique, the ambassador of Saudi Arabia, asking him to dismiss the director. This petition, according to the Federation, was signed by tens of thousands of Muslims. There were also threats of a street demonstration. After three months of prevarication, the director of the Centre was dismissed and his assistant, a Saudi *ʿālim*, succeeded him. The Federation then adopted an attitude of collaboration with the new director.

The Federation makes itself indispensable to the new leadership of the Centre Islamique by adopting an interlocutory and mediating role in negotiations with the Belgian state. By intelligent use of the media, it has succeeded in appearing to the public and to the Belgian authorities to be the sole organized representative of all mosques. Thus, by means of the Federation, the Tablīghī Jamāʿat has become a force that cannot be ignored by the Muslim establishment.

An incident in 1986 allowed the Federation to confirm this role for itself in the eyes of public. On Sunday, 20 April, Arab associations organized a demonstration against the American attack on Libya. This demonstration, which the Tablīghīs did not officially participate in, was transformed, to the surprise of its organizers, into a manifestation of strong Islamic sentiments. This caused great concern among the general public and in the Belgian media, where it became front-page news. Subsequently, the spokesman of the Federation appeared before the Belgian people as a proponent of a non-fundamentalist viewpoint (Dassetto and Bastenier 1987).

The Tablīghīs have succeeded in working their way upward from a relatively marginal position in the Islamic religious field through the use of a favourable relationship of forces. Key here has been their clever use of the opinion-making process in Belgian society. The future, and particularly what emerges from the government's creation of a Supreme Council for Muslim religion, will tell if the Tablīghīs can succeed in maintaining their newfound position. They will have to deal with the Belgian state directly, competing with other Muslim protagonists on the ground. The outcome is uncertain since it may concern aspects not only of daily life but also of the rights and operations of institutions.

However, in the organizational and institutional reality of Belgium, the Tablīghīs have proved to have better administrators and more knowledgeable people, than other Muslim groups. The weakness of the Tablīghīs lies in their intellectual inability to weather a sustained encounter with political forces and alternative Islamic experts. One cannot exclude the possibility that, aware of this weakness, they will not attempt to extend their influence beyond the domain of the mosques, particularly as regards their organization. This would still give them considerable power, while leaving the other fields (for example teaching and higher education) to the authorities of the Centre Islamique. The Tablīghīs may eventually return to their marginal position, maintaining a hostile attitude toward the Centre Islamique.

Managing the Following

The relatively expansive character of the Tablīghī Jamāʿat, expressed in the increasing number of mosques in their zone of influence, and in their relatively high number of adherents, may be attributed to their ability to manage multiple followings while maintaining cohesion. The innermost zone of the Tablīghīs—relatively secret and regarded with a mixture of favour, awe and respect—consists of a group of persons who, strictly speaking, are the only people called true Tablīghīs by the entire group. This nucleus is composed of two subgroups. One is a small number for whom Tablīghī Jamāʿat is almost a permanent career. The other are self-employed, receive disability or old-age pensions, or, most frequently, are unemployed.

Let us look at the nucleus in more detail. Those at the heart of the Jamāʿat exhibit similarities with classic brotherhoods. They constitute the real leadership of the movement. When there are differences of opinion, they have the final say. This permanent and quasi-professional group has strong international connections—they constitute an international circuit bringing Tablīghīs to Delhi, Bangladesh, Pakistan, Mecca, and other countries where they are established.

The other circle around this small nucleus is made up of those for whom being a Tablīghī is a rather temporary state, lasting for a minimum of one year and perhaps renewable. All members of this group, and only they, are engaged in external missionary activity according to fixed rules which are described by M. A. Ḥaq (1972, 142–166) and M. Tozy (1984, 320ff.). They operate according to a detailed time schedule: once a week, three days per month or three months per year.

From the perspective of membership, adherence to the real Tablīgh is flexible and dynamic: it is possible to enter, leave, and move around. This circulation makes it possible, incidentally, to tell outsiders that "The Tablīghīs are not numerous; there are 200 at most in Belgium," because this means only the total number of persons having Tablīghī status at any one time.

To be a Tablīghī means, above all, to undergo re-Islamization by imitating the daily life of the Prophet and his Companions, by having a strong mystical experience and, of course, by missionary action. The imitation of the Prophet and his Companions is practiced by meeting in a Tablīghī mosque in a circle; those who can attend are limited, and are separate from ordinary believers. It is an egalitarian circle but its rules give it a hierarchical order. The final authority is held by the permanent nucleus. For each mission, temporary authorities are created. Equality and the prophetic social order are experienced simultaneously at the heart of the Tablīgh.

The emulation of the daily life of the Prophet is expressed not only by leading a poor and simple life, but also in the regimentation of each act of behaviour, both in the physical aspects of life and in relationships with others. This emulation is translated into a kind of permanent mystical state and results in a missionary activity that is carried out not only by way of speech, but also through personal appeal. The Tablīgh nucleus tries to demonstrate what the life of the Prophet and his followers was like and thus to show what the realization of true Islam might be.

The nucleus of the Tablīgh thereby not only realizes the missionary target; but also serves as a reference point for the other circles which turn to it; it mediates the references to the Prophet. If in its missionary activity it has the function of appeal, then inside the Tablīgh it has the constant function of reactivating aims. Those in the Tablīgh nucleus no doubt have a strong and marked experience. By regulating behaviour, and through its effects on the individual, the Tablīgh functions like a veritable total institution in the manner described by Goffman (1961). It differs, however, in that it is possible to leave it without sanctions. Furthermore, Tablīgh membership does not constitute a physical separation from the social world, but rather is a means to a real and symbolic penetration of it.

To understand Tablīghī Jamā'at we must also understand the satellites to the nucleus. A Tablīghī mosque (i.e., either a mosque where the Tablīgh nucleus is physically present and considered as a group of reference, or mosques that are centres for planning a strategy for dealing with the outside world), are frequented by many believers with varying degrees of commitment to Tablīgh. They include simple believers who have left the Tablīgh, who, while they retain nostalgic memories of their experiences, wish to detach themselves somewhat.

Our main interest in this context is the group which exists as a preliminary to Tablīgh and also as a satellite to its nucleus. The Tablīgh satellite is strongly attached to the totality. It unambiguously belongs to the Tablīgh system and therefore shares the benefits of Tablīgh dynamics. This is seen, first of all, in physical participation. For example, many believers participated in a big meeting in Charleroi in 1982 which was organized by the Tablīgh nucleus and by those in charge of external relations. It brought together for four days more than fifteen thousand people from various countries. This was a symbolic adherence to the principles of the Tablīgh nucleus. At the same time, it was almost a kind of presocialization into the Tablīgh style of novitiate.

Most importantly, from the point of view of the management of followers, the Tablīgh satellite fulfills functions of its own, and thus justifies itself to its followers. It allows people not only to place themselves within the symbolic space of the real Tablīghīs—which is of the prophetic companionship which they reactivate—but also to enjoy the beneficial atmosphere which results. The satellite, which presupposes a management of the followers by means of the regulation of time and constant discussions, fulfills essential functions for the members and justifies its attachment.

The regulation of time is based on the temporal organization of prayer. This seems to replace the temporal order of work. It is, in fact, unemployed adult males who constitute the majority of Tablīgh satellite members. To pray according to the temporal rhythm of the Prophet allows a life structured in a way similar to a working life, when viewed in relation to family members, wives and children. It seems that adherence to the Tablīgh may give unemployed men, more than others, a measure of legitimacy and perhaps a revindicated authority which may otherwise have been destroyed by unemployment and low income. Their legitimacy is also being eroded by the coming of new generations, girls and boys who reject the symbolic and cultural system of being their parents.

This is related to the way in which the Tablīgh appears to be a powerful arena for discussion. It is inappropriate for the satellites of the Tablīgh to launch themselves into exterior missionary activity; this is reserved for the core. Instead, one may observe among them extensive discussions which amount to a veritable cognitive bricolage. Verses from the Qur'ān are mixed with *ḥadīth* from the Prophet, as are pious or miraculous stories, para-scientific interpretations, daily events lived, heard about or seen on the television news, or even fictional films or television programs. These messages are diffused, thrown back and repeated, resulting in a total reinterpretation of the environment into an Islamic key. It is simultaneously Occidental and Christian, and carries the meaning of unemployment and the failure of the migratory project. At the same time, these men proceed to master the implications of the process of settlement, particularly regarding relations within the family and between the sexes. And it is in the family nucleus, particularly with respect to women, that the first attempts to establish what is presumed to be an Islamic order appear. These priorities are a result both of the re-Islamization process and of the lack of opportunity to realize Islam elsewhere. This process is also manifest in the schools, to which girls are sent with their heads covered, and where it is requested that girls and boys be separated in the swimming pools.

At the same time, the discussions provide opportunities to test the value of arguments, to construct a cohesive discourse, to enrich the meager heritage of references to the founding texts, to purify the view of the Islamic world from unorthodox elements and to construct gradually the orthodox Tablīgh. These discussions, moreover, provide opportunities for public speaking. All these qualities are useful in real missionary activity. But what seems to arouse the interest of the Tablīgh satellites most is the fact that the discussions allow everyone to be a conveyor of the word. The duty to speak about the message and later to announce it is also an affirmation of the speaker's identity. One can understand the rewarding and consoling character of this for people who are socially and intellectually marginalized. This also suggests the potentially revolutionary character of the Tablīgh for the dominant Islamic order.

Conclusion

The Tablīgh consists of different groups which have both a relative functional autonomy and a functional integration, and thus manage adherents in differentiated ways. This complex organization, capable of dealing with multiple segments of the social environment, seems to be a major asset for the Tablīgh when it comes to survival and expansion. Their major weakness is a lack of intellectuals who can respond to new environmental elements in Western and industrialized countries. This weakness is common in transplanted Islam, but it seems to strike the Tablīgh particularly hard.

The Tablīghī Jamā'at could therefore become, after this initial period of expansion, a residual organization, destined to cater to the needs of the Muslim population which has left the labour market for good. If no changes take place in the system of references, it could provide special satisfaction only to uneducated men of the first immigrant generation, or the less-educated second generation.

The constraints of this system of references partly hide the strengths of its symbolic system, that which is furnished by the heart of the Tablīgh—this is the reference group which is constantly in motion and which refers to the symbolism of the Prophet and his Companions. The question is, will this system of symbols be capable of anticipating and creating new missionary practices and new systems of reference based on social actors whose interests are decisively oriented to Western and industrialized contexts. At present this seems unlikely. To do so would perhaps appear as a sectarian deviation from the Tablīgh—given the strength of the transnational regulation of the core of the Tablīgh from the headquarters in Delhi.

Until the end of the 1980s we observed an increasing influence of institutionalized Tablīgh over transplanted Islam, particularly regarding the institutional handling of numerous mosques and of relations with the Belgian state. Today we are undoubtedly witnessing a diffusion of the Tablīgh influence to an increasing number of mosques. In the middle of 1990 the influence of the Tablīghīs began a general decline. A new generation of leaders and more modernist organizations have assumed leadership in the Belgian world of Islam in relation to the Belgian state.

CHAPTER NINE

FOI ET PRATIQUE: TABLĪGHĪ JAMĀʿAT IN FRANCE

Gilles Kepel
Translation: Muhammad Khalid Masud[1]

Foi et Pratique (Faith and Practice) is a major French branch of Tablīghī Jamāʿat, a pietist movement that has played a decisive role in reaffirming an Islamic identity among the Muslim population of France. In its methods and levels of preaching it responds quite adequately to the needs of the less educated and most numerous classes of the Muslim population. It preaches an Islam that is simple to understand and practice but that demands a significant personal investment by the faithful. These people suffer from a great loss of identity, and are torn between the daily life of factories in France and the seasons of the Aures in Algeria. They suffer from a growing conflict between their wives whose hands are red with henna and their school-going daughters who are clad in blue jeans.

France appears to them as a country without morals, and French as a language without rules. To them, therefore, the Tablīgh movement offers a discipline in life and thought, a spiritual direction that provides a sense of one's existence completely oriented toward salvation. It is the imitation of the Prophet Muḥammad that constitutes the touchstone against which a follower tests his faith. He spends his life according to a set of codified rituals that have been worked out to the minutest details of steps and movements. No act for a Tablīghī is gratis or random. For each occasion he must recite a prayer to God, so that every action in life, be it most obliging, harmless, or of little significance, finds its place in the semantics of the Islamic legal system.

---

[1] Translator's note: This chapter is a translation of part of chapter 4 of Gilles Kepel's *Les banlieues de l'Islam* (Paris: Editions du Seuil, 1987), pp. 177–209. I acknowledge with thanks the permission granted by Editions du Seuil for translation and publication of this material. I am also grateful to Gilles Kepel who reviewed and corrected my translation.

Foi et Pratique in France, an association registered under the law of 1901, has existed legally since April 1972, but the first missionaries of the Tablīghī Jamāʿat appeared in the Hexagon in the late 1960s. In the interval of about forty years between the foundation of the movement in India and the arrival of its preachers in France, the corpus of its doctrine was elaborated and the technique of preaching was developed in such a manner that they were particularly suitable to this area.

The circumstances of the movement's creation and its objectives help explain its success; it is considered today among the foremost Islamic associations on the globe, but it remains relatively unknown to the West.

Although very little is known about the great axis of space and time along which the movement grew, one nevertheless observes on various occasions a mechanism that conforms to the sixth principle of the Jamāʿat and which is included in several texts composed by the movement's leaders (Gaborieau 1986a; for Morocco see Tozy 1984, and this volume; for Belgium see Dassetto 1987a, and this volume). This mechanism is called *khurūj* (outing). Going out has a dual purpose: to reinforce the group's cohesion, and to focus the efforts of the followers on attracting new supporters. Those who go out are instrumental to bringing in new followers. A short outing operates within a limited area, for example going out from Mosque Omar on the street of Jean-Pierre Timbaud in Paris to the prayer hall of a building for immigrant workers in a suburb. A longer outing takes followers from different regions of the Hexagon, where the Muslim population is settled, to neighbouring European countries. These European outings are mostly to Dewsbury in the United Kingdom, where an Islamic college is situated. Dewsbury is the European centre of the movement (see Faust, this volume). A long outing may be even a journey to India and Pakistan where the followers visit the Jamāʿat's schools of training at a higher level. In the other direction, France is the destination of numerous Tablīghīs coming from abroad, most notably from India and Pakistan. They exercise moral influence on the French branches and function as arbiters or controlling authorities, depending upon the needs of the movement.

The Grafting of the Jamā'at in France

It was during such an outing that the preachers of Tablīgh first arrived in France in 1962. A group of missionaries came from the subcontinent at the invitation of a student from India known among the Tablīghīs in France as Sanaullah [Thanā'ullāh]. He was a brilliant university graduate and a student of brain surgery, a discipline regarded as very prestigious throughout the Muslim World today.[2] The first mission had no local impact. In the language of the Tablīghīs, it received no *nuṣra* (local help)—a term referring to the warm welcome offered by the inhabitants of Medina to the Prophet and his Companions when they migrated from Mecca and found refuge in that city. The missionaries returned empty-handed. Sanaullah spent another six years preparing the ground until finally a second mission arrived in 1968. This time grafting was successful and a Tablīghī branch began to produce results in the Hexagon. The implantation in France was quickly followed by the dispatch of new followers to the subcontinent to receive proper ideological training. Besides Muslims of immigrant stock in France, French converts to Islam (at the hands of the Tablīgh) also go on long outings and become efficient intermediaries between Tablīghīs and French society.

In 1969 the Tablīghīs took part in the creation of the Association Culturelle Islamique, an Islamic religious organization. They participated in its activities at the Belleville mosque until, after a dispute, they parted ways to install themselves at Clichy during 1970–1971. In 1972 the group acquired a vast tract of land in this same Paris suburb at Madame de Sanzillon Street. This became the headquarters of the association that registered itself in April in the prefecture of Hauts de Seine as "Association Musulmane Foi et Pratique," under the law of 1901. This group began to enjoy the best location on a French Islamic landscape that had lacked associations and places of worship. Ten years later, this status had assured the association a solid position, a network of efficient connections, and an excellent information system throughout Muslim areas in the Hexagon.

At that time, the land in Clichy was still largely wasteland, and the plot in the backyard of the mosque in Paris, managed by Si

[2] I had the opportunity to confirm the reference to brain surgery with Shaykh Kishk, the famous Egyptian preacher. See *La prophet et pharaoh*, ch. 6, "Shaykh Kishk's Preaching."

Hamza Boubakeur, was only partially and superficially developed. The World Muslim League had not yet established an office in Paris. Algeria did not consider its hold on Muslims in France an issue of central significance requiring direct control. Among the other Islamist groups only AEIF (Association of Muslim Students in France) enjoyed any success, and that limited to its student activities. Thus Foi et Pratique could dig deeper, very quietly.

In 1973, soon after Clichy, the movement built Abu Bakr mosque at the corner of Jean-Pierre Timbaud Street on Belleville Boulevard in Paris, in a small old building whose improvised prayer halls could accommodate about 500 faithful. Later other mosques were built in the suburbs—in Creteil, Goussainville, Mantes,[3] Corbeil-Essonne and Creil—and in other towns in the provinces where textile industry attracted concentrations of unskilled immigrant labour, notably Le Mans, Lyon, Marseille, Roubaix, Sochaux, Montbeliard, Mulhouse and Rouen. In Paris, the movement established two more important mosques: Ali Mosque on the Faubourg-Saint-Denis in Sentier, and, in 1979, Omar Mosque at Jean-Pierre Timbaud Street. Because of its size (it can accommodate 1500 persons) and its outreach (its neighbourhood is an orthodox Islamic area), this last is the grand mosque of Foi et Pratique. It is here that the *amīr* of the association, M. Muḥammad Ḥammāmī, a former Tunisian mason about fifty years old, preaches every Friday. This is the point of departure and destination for most of the outings taken by followers.

The Jamāʿat in Paris

A Friday in Jean Pierre-Timbaud Street

On Friday, Jean-Pierre Timbaud street attracts large numbers of Muslims from Paris and its suburbs. Coming for prayers there gives them an opportunity to do their shopping at Islamic stores on the street. These stores are mostly concentrated along the route between the entrance to the metro station Couronne and the mosque. This is also a valuable location for booksellers, food sellers and, above all,

[3] It is not the mosque on Denis-Papin street, but a very modest mosque in this suburb.

butchers. Since the inauguration of Omar mosque, indigenous French shopkeepers whose shops are situated on the path of the faithful have been continuously approached to give up their leases. Although some have resisted, the Islamization of the shops has progressed impressively. During the first half of 1986 alone, at least six such shops were opened. This phenomenon is not as spectacular as the transformation of entire commercial streets that has occurred in the area of the Avenue de Choisy into Chinatown, but it follows a parallel economic logic.

In Belleville renovation of the area not directly on this street led to the departure of the worker population who had provided the vote bank for the local communist party, together with their favourite customers. They left typically French shops which were mostly old. Certain "French" cafés on Jean-Pierre Timbaud street still retained the smoky, low quality of the pre-World War II period, indifferent to the changes and new fashions that transformed their counterparts into copies of London pubs. The French butcheries, selling guts and horsemeat and catering to low-income customers, were the first to be redeemed and transformed into Islamic butcheries.

Although there is hustle and bustle throughout the day, on Friday the peak hour for Muslim customers is towards midday, before the congregational prayer. The time of the sermon of the *imām* at the end of the prayer is set for the convenience of workers who have a noon break. Friday is spent entirely in pursuing the Tablīgh programme. The *dhikr* sessions and recitation take place in the morning, followed by readings from different texts used by the movement. The call to midday prayer marks the axis of the day. The mosque by that time is fully packed with an ethnically mixed crowd in which the Maghrebis dominate. It also includes large numbers of West African and other Muslim minorities; people from Comoro Island, Mauritania, Reunion Island, India and Pakistan. Superficial observation, however, might give the mistaken impression of social homogeneity. Modest clothes, with diverse external marks, indicate that the believers assembled here are probably labourers. Certainly they are neither students nor rich Levantines living in better quarters. Another striking factor is age, for one notices that most of the people gathered here are around forty years old; the youth of the second generation are not significantly present, even though their number has increased since the mid-1980s.

On one particular Friday, 21 February 1986 an orator spoke at 1.00 p.m. after the call to prayer, before the sermon of the *imām*. This orator is a former Tunisian pop-singer, whose cassettes still constitute the stock-in-trade of merchants of Arab music from Bellevilles to Gabes. His warm voice, velvet eyes and broad accent must have broken, at the time of his glory, many a heart in Sidi-Bou-Said. Today, thanks to the Tablīgh, he is back to Islam. He has dedicated his talents to the service of God, to the application of the fifth principle of Tablīgh.

"Are we true believers?" he questions the gathering. An entirely rhetorical question. "Not at all" is the obvious answer. "Because instead of submitting ourselves to God and His Prophet, we have submitted ourselves to our desires and lusts. The true believer is one who fights against these desires mercilessly to discipline himself according to the example set by Prophet Muḥammad." But how to measure the truth of one's belief?

"The only criterion that God has given us is outing (*al Khurūj fī Sabīl Allāh*). To go out preaching the word of God and to test our belief will permit us to cultivate this discipline. It will teach us to fight against our desires and eventually to go to Paradise with certainty. We ask all the brothers present here to stay with us after the prayer in order to listen to the word of God. And why not sign for outing and preaching?"

A small group will be formed which will return to Jean-Pierre Timbaud street. On lucky days numbers increase. From the street they disappear into the entrance of metro station Couronnes to reach the prayer hall in a building inhabited by immigrants in the suburb. But at the moment everyone is holding his breath. Muḥammad Ḥammāmī, the *amīr* of Foi et Pratique Association, the regular preacher at Fridays at the Omar mosque, has taken the microphone.

This person, small in stature, clad in typical Tablīghī costume, adorned from time to time by a red-and-white *keffieh*, has been shaking from the very beginning due to his extreme nervousness. Skipping words, with multiple movements of the lips, speaking breathlessly, he alternates between howling and murmur. The structure of his speech, the syntax and level of language are based mainly on some Tunisian colloquial dialect. The contrast is all the more striking for a person whose ears are accustomed to listening to the eloquence of the Egyptian Shaykh 'Abdul Ḥamīd Kishk. Shaykh Kishk could treat the most trivial moral and political themes in his sermon with extremely inflammatory words, in a classical rhetoric that he had learnt under the columns of Al-Azhar.

No flowery style in Jean-Pierre Timbaud street. This is due not only to the fifth principle of Tablīgh, that prohibits the display of knowledge, but also because a listener who was little or less Arabised, would sit unmoved if the orator employed a classical Arabic style. The speaker adapts the quality of his sermon according to the level of its public reception. Frequent repetition is a stylish technique that our preacher is fond of. Those believers who cannot understand well or could not identify the verse of the Qur'ān or the Prophet's saying the first time during the sermon have two or three more opportunities to listen to several literal elaborations, expressed in dialect and in a vocabulary reduced to a dozen or so words. Finally, M. Ḥammāmī combines bodily gesture with his voice. The mimicry, frowning, head shaking, finger pointing and interjections that he frequently uses are precious additions to his presentation. Apparently the *imām* succeeds in achieving what he desires. As the sermon comes to an end the style of delivery becomes more and more rapid. In order to reach its climax the words are swallowed. The rhythm prevails over the meaning of phrases which are no longer more than parts of propositions sliced or juxtaposed. The rhythm accelerates for some minutes, and then there follows an invocation to God, praying for protection and mercy for the believers[4] (Carré 1986, vol. 2; see also the appendix to chapter one of this volume on *duʿā*).

The sermon recalled briefly here was delivered at around 2.00 p.m. The prayer halls on all the floors of the Omar mosque were packed; more than 1500 persons had assembled there. The theme of the sermon was the futility of this world in respect to the last judgement. Nothing in it was original; it consisted mostly of the common themes of preaching. However, the sermon was concerned with addressing those Muslims of modest origins who had migrated to a non-Islamic country in order to improve their standard of living, under the imperative of the most urgent need, but who had undergone in the host country thousands of inconveniences. The art of the preacher consisted in explaining this by relating it to the terms

[4] Etienne and Tozy present an analysis of a *khuṭba* on the model of Shaykh Kishk, in Carré and Dumont 1986.

of work here, and then suggesting a radical therapy to put the principles of Tablīghī Jamāʿat into practice.

The Sermon at Omar Mosque

M. Ḥammāmī told his audience that God protects the believers from this world and offers them the hereafter. To those whom He dislikes, He gives money, power, and business in order to punish them.

> Whereas those whom God loves, He gives them nothing, nothing except piety, fear of God, the *dhikr* day and night, prayer, and the habit of reciting the Qurʾān at night at a time when people are asleep. [Only *dhikr*, the constant remembrance of God, appeases the heart].
>
> Nothing else, nothing at all. You say that a woman gives you comfort. This is all punishment. You say that children make you happy. Not at all. They are all torment. Is it then money? Business? [inflections of voice] Is it power of being a minister or a president? Punishment and more punishment! There is nothing in this world but loss, except for those who believe, do good deeds, enjoin the truth and are patient. Others, they are all lost. That mighty person? Lost! That merchant? Lost! That rich man? Lost. That engineer? That director? Lost. They are all lost except those who believe . . . All these are lost, lost, no matter if they own cars and furniture. No matter if they have women and children, cinemas and videos at home, and wine and women . . . and . . . yes, all that. They will be in immense pain when they meet God. He will be angry with them, and they will go directly to the fire of hell without any mercy. And there you see these are the things that fascinate a Muslim today. . . .
>
> Listen, therefore, carefully. Open your eyes. If you are sensible, detach yourself from this world, or otherwise this is what will happen. You miss your prayers to earn wages in this world here. There are people who come to me and say, "My brother! I am not allowed to say my prayer during work." You are not allowed to do what? Work or prayer? Who is he who provides you subsistence? Eh? When you are here with us you tell us it is God, but to your boss you say, "Boss! I will give up prayer so that you are not angry with me." Oh well, wait for the wrath of the Master of heavens and the earth.

The efforts for this world produce nothing valuable, explains Ḥammāmī. The success that appears to be dazzling and enviable hides the worst moral miseries.

> Now, there are people who go to the moon! And after that? There are more suicides in America than anywhere in the whole world. Every year more than 80,000 persons commit suicide there! That is the country that you find great and that you want to imitate! Oh son! For

> God's sake, it is a despicable country . . . Why are there more than eighty thousand people who hang themselves? This is because they have not found comfort in this world. Because they are farther from God. That is why they commit suicide. Nevertheless, the people whom we admire in social life are not the ones we should praise.
>
> Now, today, who are those whom Muslims regard as reasonable persons? I am not talking about unbelievers, nor about the hypocrites, only Muslims. Well, son! Here is an advocate, a despicable minister, and a director. These are the persons whom one believes to be reasonable. On the contrary, one who remembers the Qur'ān by heart, who spends his night praying, who goes out on the path of God, who calls people to God, one who performs *dhikr* day and night. That one? He is a dervish! Dervish! Very soon, one will learn. One will see with one's own eyes. It is the dervish who will enter paradise before everyone else. One will see the "reasonable" man going to the fire of Hell before anyone else. . . .
>
> To sever one's connections with this world and to prepare for the future life implies an immediate awareness. How many superficial Muslims say that they will pray and will pay *zakāt* after Ramaḍān, then after Muḥarram, and then after such and such *hijrī* month. Then death overtakes them. Instead of paying *zakāt*—for the collection of which a box has been placed near the exit in the mosque—they had deposited the cash in the bank; this cash will become debt on the day of judgement. One must never put off till later one's commitment to Islam, which is total and complete, assuming all the consequences of this delay, as seen by the preacher: "Hein! You say you have no time to come to Friday prayer. You cannot recite the Qur'ān because your business does not allow you. You who do not come to mosque, who cannot put fear of God in your daughter or son. You who do not ask them to say prayers, you whose wife goes out naked, you whose daughter goes out naked. Have you ever contemplated how you will find yourself before God? Someone said to me, "The women must work so that we should help each other against the adversity of this world." I told him, . . . You make your women work? And you are a Muslim; you are not a Christian, a Jew? They are the people who make their wives and daughters work! Let him be a Christian, be a Jew. He cannot be a Muslim. Not at all. It is the Christians and Jews who come to Muslims seeking work for women. When must a woman work? If she is bored, let her spin the wool, cook at home, yes . . . but going out to join men, to greet them in factories, offices, well, well! All are worries, and more worries . . . She goes to work! And with whom does she work? With angels? With whom?

The remedy for this life of moral dissoluteness, as painted by M. Ḥammāmī in the darkest colours, is very simple. Life must be regulated according to the model of living established by the Prophet, to conform strictly to the programme of Tablīgh. A gradual detachment from the connections with this world, by means of prayer, *dhikr*,

ʿilm (the knowledge of God), and 'going out' will lead the true believer finally to the peace that the spirit longs for. Family, job, social position and material well-being are only faint illusions.

This brief analysis of this type of preaching brings into relief two complementary themes: (1) rejection of the world and its temptations, and (2) longing for the world hereafter. But, in this case, the rejection of the world translates itself into a situation that questions the ideas and values of Western society. These immigrant labourers whom M. Ḥammāmī addresses find themselves immersed in this society. The yearning for the hereafter transforms itself into the reaffirmation of moral categories that belong to a very conservative frame of reference. This reaffirmation, furthermore, is only the first step towards total re-Islamisation of daily life, which is the objective of Tablīgh movement.

Immigrant Muslim workers have come to France primarily to earn money. Their migration, first of all, reduces them to a status of "homo economicus," which governs a number of their attitudes. Absolute priority is given to work and to saving money. If they can bear this way of living, which is loaded with constraints, it is because they see social mobility at the end of the tunnel. They expect well-being for themselves and for their children. Success is considered inherent in certain professions that ensure economic security: business, medicine, engineering, management, and ministry . . . M. Ḥammāmī recites the list breathlessly like a litany, qualifying each with matching pejorative adjectives. Thus 'minister,' *wazīr* in Arabic, is inevitably flanked by *ḥaqīr*, despicable. One cannot render fully the rhyming effect of Arabic pair-words in translation. He wishes them all to Hell. It may appear skillless for a preacher to snub the simple aspirations of his audience so brutally. But the explanation undoubtedly lies in that the listener himself only half believes in his dreams of social mobility, because most often he has been unemployed. One out of every three active Algerians in France is unemployed. When one is actively employed, one can hardly come to mosque on Friday, as it requires long hours beyond the lunch break. Moreover, this phenomenon is not peculiar to the Omar mosque. Prayer halls throughout the Hexagon are places for social encounters where one meets other unemployed Muslims.

These unemployed workers are the favourite targets of the preaching of Tablīgh. On the one hand, they have experienced, in the worst possible manner, the effects of the reversal of all the values in which they had believed—they have thus become a melted waxen mass on which this piety movement can stamp its seal of 'principle.' On the other hand, they also have their time entirely at their disposal, and the Tablīghīs may mobilize them in *dhikr* and soon in *khurūj*, to go out for the propagation of the faith.

Yet, in the congregation assembled at Jean-Pierre Timbaud there are also many who do have jobs. It is they that M. Ḥammāmī addresses when he tells the anecdote of a man who abandons prayer for work so that the boss will not be angry (and who thus incurs divine rage). But, it must be noted, our orator does not suggest any way out of this difficulty. He is happy to insist on the similarity of all the values closely related to work with activities that do not aim at serving God alone.

We find therefore, an indictment against the material values of Western society by M. Ḥammāmī. In this indictment France figures only in the character of a 'boss,' or as a copy of the American original, also reduced to a table of suicide statistics. Once the culpability of those who attach themselves to this world is demonstrated, there is an opportunity to make a vigorous plea in favour of the reconstruction of the Islamic identity of believers.

Placing his listener in this situation, the *imām* begins reaffirming the basis of the traditional morality of the society to which his listener belonged before migration. It is in this sense that one understands the anecdote of a man who lets his wife go out 'naked' and work outside her house. According to the sermon, this man cannot be called a Muslim. He can only be a Jew or a Christian or some similar creature. The implications are important. The Muslim population in France is highly sensitive about the status of women. Very often the honour of the head of family is at stake if one of the ladies of the house is seen on the street dressed like a European. But women, particularly young girls, insist on wearing blue jeans or casual dress like their colleagues at school or at work. This pressure is extremely painful for a husband and father, and all the more so because they are ill equipped to resist it except by means of coercion and authority. In part this is because they are not yet French enough, are illiterate, and depend on their children to fill out papers for social security or medical care. To these people the world appears upside down. They do not know how to address their children. It is to them that M. Ḥammāmī hammers away at fundamental injunctions that would put the universe on its feet again. If you let the women of your family go out naked, you are no longer a Muslim, you are only a Christian or a Jew. One may notice in that ethical reconstruction the affirmation of the absolute superiority of Muslims to the rest of humanity, who are non-believers. Similarly, true believers are superior to those who are Muslims only in name. The latter are hypocrites (*munāfiqūn*). The boss, whom to please one does not go to pray, is visibly put in his place, the place of an ungodly person who is inferior in God's eyes. From then on, one does not consider oneself an immigrant worker who serves a foreman, but instead regards oneself as a true Muslim who finds himself in the same situation that was described by the founder of the piety movement, Muḥammad Ilyās: "It is an undisputed fact that as long as Muslims remain faithful to their religion, they will be respected by all." *Ikrām*, respect is the fourth principle of Tablīgh.

Bag and Baggage

After the sermon, the rows of the faithful begin to disperse. One compact group, however, stays behind. M. Ḥammāmī or one of his deputies reads to them from a text, always taken from a guide book of the Tablīghī Jamāʿat, a selection of *ḥadīth* entitled *Riyāḍus Ṣāliḥīn*, the Garden of the Pious Believers. This selection, collected by Imām Nawawī (d. 671/1273), classifies *ḥadīth* according to themes. For example, the Book of Dress contains what the Prophet did or said on this subject; the Book of Sleep tells how one must sleep in imitation of the Prophet, and so forth.

A Tablīghī earnestly follows as literally as possible the injunctions in *Riyāḍus Ṣāliḥīn* (Nawawī 1985). This is in a proper sense his handbook. He refers to it on all occasions in order to know how to behave or what prayer to recite. Thus, to understand why the Tablīghī dress as they do one only needs open the book to the *Kitābul Libās* (Nawawī, 324ff.). The first chapter is entitled "White dress is recommended; red, green, yellow and black are permitted. Similarly, cotton, linen, coarse hair, and wool are allowed but not silk." The chapter then explains two Qur'ānic verses.

> O children of Adam! We have descended upon you the dress so that you can cover your nudity (7:26).
>
> And He made for you garments to protect you from heat and also the garment to protect you from violence. Thus He completes His favours on you that you may submit to His will (16:81).

Then the chapter narrates an authentic saying of the Prophet: "Dress yourself in white, this is because it is the purest and the best colour, and cover your dead with a white shroud." It also records testimonies of the Companions of the Prophet, who saw him wearing garments in other colours and the above-mentioned fabrics. Another chapter deals with the proper length of shirt, dress, and the end of turban that one may let fall down the back, and the prohibition against taking pride in one's clothes.

In brief, the *Garden of the Pious Believers* provides for the Tablīghī answers to all of his practical questions in daily life, and helps him to regulate his life closely in imitation of the Prophet. It is his code of conduct. It determines the practice of Muḥammad with plentiful injunctions. Thus, it tells the Tablīghī which prayer to recite on departing on a journey, entering one's house, sitting at the table, and so forth. Most of all, it is replete with prohibitions that cover almost all possible human acts, ranging from religiously deviant conduct such as the worship of graves, to the very smallest physical actions of humans that have social significance, for instance, easing oneself in the passage or urinating in standing water. This book that provides obligatory norms serves as the most reliable guide for believers to the last judgement, an efficient bulwark against the lawlessness of society—French in this case. This anthology has been chosen by the Tablīghī Jamāʿat on account of two main qualities: firstly, because it can be used as a handbook, and secondly, because of its small size—each *ḥadīth* is preceded only by the name of the first narrator. Thus it is ideal for taking on outings.

While the preacher comments on one of the chapters of the *Garden of the Pious Believers*, volunteers for outing regroup themselves. Friday is a particularly proper day, because it allows working people to accomplish their outing during the French weekend (Saturday-Sunday). The duration of this outing may vary from a few hours to several months, depending on a person's physical and intellectual availability.

Those offering themselves are grouped according to the duration that they have volunteered to spend on outing. Everyone carries his own cash, bedding, some pots and pans, and a copy of *Garden of the Pious Believers*. The group is called a *jamāʿat* (showing that it reconstitutes on the microcosmic level a community of believers). They elect their *amīr* (leader) chosen for his known piety and for his experience as a Tablīghī. They also elect a guide who is familiar with the terrain and responsible for planning the route to be followed. Before departure, one old hand addresses outgoing volunteers, reminding them of the purposefulness of their act, which is registered as the sixth principle of Tablīgh. Time as well as money will be spent during this outing on the path of God. One must force oneself to spend one's life scrupulously imitating the Prophet, methodically accomplishing the ritual prescriptions, not speaking about money or other subjects that are futile or mundane (the seventh principle). A mosque or a prayer hall is chosen which will operate as a base, around which rounds of Tablīgh will take place. They will head for the stairs of HLM (low price apartment buildings), for restaurants, pavements or the dwellings where Muslims live a hard life.

The mosque where the group will spend one or two nights is never selected at random. The organizers of the mosque would have ordinarily requested the person in charge of Foi et Pratique to send *jamāʿat* to them. Often when the prayer hall is situated in a building of immigrant workers, permission from the manager of the building is sought beforehand. The association has in fact very good relations with the authorities.

The Tablīghīs presume themselves to be invited to all the prayer halls in France. Probably a positive affirmation is necessarily implicit; an outright refusal would be wrong. In the early 1980s, the evidence in all cases suggests that the flow of outgoing groups was never-ending at Jean-Pierre Timbaud. For all associations, which were at their formative stages, which lacked everything and were searching for exemplary books on preaching, Foi et Pratique established itself as an almost indispensable example. It supplied religious services at a time when the Muslim initiative in France had just begun.

After traversing the distance from the Omar mosque to the prayer hall, and after saying proper prayers at the time of departure, at the time of boarding the metro, in the train going to suburbs and on arrival at their destination, the group accomplishes the outing. Now they negotiate with the hosts who have invited them and settle down in the premises. Consultation (*shūrā*) is held for the division of work. One of the members is charged with *taʿlīm*, the transmission of the knowledge of God with the help of readings ftom the *Garden of the Pious*. One or two other members are assigned practical work (cleaning the mosque, cooking, etc.). Everyone has a duty, turn by turn, to read *ḥadīth* after the five daily prayers. Others will make rounds in the neighbourhood of the mosque. They will go to the shopkeepers and to the various apartments of the building, inviting Muslims to come to where the group is staying.

On returning from this round, one of the members delivers a

speech (*bayān*). He recalls the objectives of Islam; man was created and lives on earth only to return to the path of Allah. The first objective of a Muslim, explains the speaker, is to practice his religion. Those who have come out for Tablīgh propose to the people gathered there that they rehearse collectively practicing Sunna by spending one or two days in complete imitation of the Prophet.

Before prayers in the evening, stories of the pious companions of the Prophet are read. They are drawn from the work *Ḥikāyātus Ṣaḥāba* (Stories of the Companions) written by Mawlānā Muḥammad Zakariyyā. After saying the prayers they dine together, recalling and practicing the *ḥadīth* that describe the table manners of the Prophet. If one is not very tired, one stays awake invoking the name of God (*qiyāmul layl*); otherwise one goes to bed as the Prophet of God did, head turned towards Mecca and cheek pressed against the right palm.

Getting up one hour before the dawn prayer, the members of the group hold a fresh *shūrā* and decide a plan of action for the day. One will do one's best to locate Muslims who are very sincere and who can be brought to the Omar mosque so that they may become missionaries of Tablīgh.

The Strength and the Weakness of the Tablīghī Jamā'at

The Tablīghī Jamā'at was established quite early in the Muslim areas in France, and is devoted to a very structured ideology and technique of preaching and conversion to accepted virtues. The movement is recognized to have discovered the tone of speech that the Muslim population in France expected to hear at the particular juncture of the 1980s. The decade was notable for several dramatic phenomena. First, a transition from a situation of immigration that was "provisional and hard" to another where settlement on French soil was inevitable but risky. The arrival of women and children confronted Muslims with the institutions and norms of the host country. Still further on, the tensions in the employment market struck unskilled migrant labour harder than most. The crisis of identity that developed in this context was compounded by a general breakdown of the values of the home country. Their countries of origin were themselves going through critical times marked by a loss of trust by the civil society in the states that had emerged after independence. In this context, it was all the more difficult for immigrants settled in France to identify with the ideals that were officially current in their home countries. The expatriates were the embodiment of slavery and corruption in the eyes of intellectuals and national leaders back home. On the other hand, French society was understood through representations that combined opacity of function with a fascination/repulsion toward the modes of consumption. But, in the context of the transformation of the apparatus of production, where the spectre of unemployment was a daily menace for less qualified immigrant workers, the charm of consumption changed into permanent frustration. These were additional factors of instability. It became necessary, therefore, to construct a new set of references that would allow a revival of a sense of meaningful existence in a universe struck by "lawlessness." For this they looked toward Islam.

One of these causes was the failure of other identity models evoked for this purpose to explain the existing cultural gap. According to Muslims in France, existence of Islamic cultural foundations was a prerequisite for the construction of their identity. Such foundations had not yet been established, and the Tablīghīs were the first to do so. The immigrants thus found among the Tablīghīs, for the first time, someone to stabilize the ground and lay solid foundations for Muslim identity. Although this great task appears to have been completed, the movement appears to lack the ability for further advancement.

In its ideology as well as in practice, the Tablīgh, whether in Mēwāt or Belleville, has targeted people that suffer from deep disorientation, ethical crises and loss of direction. The "lost" ones find in Tablīgh a controlling framework that allows them to escape from social deviations like drug addiction or juvenile delinquency. It is also necessary to look for the causes of the success of the movement among marginalised French youth, who encountered Islam through Tablīghī intermediaries when they lived a disillusioned life in the period after 1968. They lived within guru cults in the fumes of reefers. From this perspective, Tablīghī Jamāʿat's insistence on the congregational dimension of their activity was primeval. The new followers were taken by the hand, re-educated to the rhythm of *dhikr* sessions and, above all, by the outings. These activities reintroduced them to a communal life, and a sense of responsibility and participation.

Nevertheless, from the moment one is transformed into a "praying machine"—an expression used by a former Tablīghī—the movement offers no other perspective. Indeed, the follower hates all political activity. Obeying the express orders of the founder, Mawlānā Muḥammad Ilyās, he leaves thinking and studying to the *ʿulamā*.

For rejecting the demand to change the social equilibrium of their followers by effective political mobilization against governments which do not apply God's laws, the pietist movement is criticized by Islamic radical groups practically everywhere it operates. They are reproached for playing the game of status quo politics. In the subcontinent, in Pakistan and India, Mawlānā Mawdūdī's followers attack the Tablīghī Jamāʿat all the more sharply because its popular success is incommensurably superior to their own (Aḥmad 1986, 73–74; also in Aḥmad 1995, 71–72).

Mumtāz Aḥmad also points out that in India, "The secular government of Mrs. Gandhi" did not place any restrictions on exit visas or on currency allocation for Mawlānā Ilyās's followers, whereas the activists of the Indian branch of Jamāʿat Islāmī saw traps appearing under their feet.

> Taking an indifferent and neutral stance during a decisive conflict between Islam and anti-Islamic forces deprived the Islamic forces of the potential reinforcement that could have come from the big contingents of the Tablīghī Jamāʿat and, as a consequence, helped the cause of the anti-Islamic forces (Aḥmad 1986, 73–74).

This attitude is shared by active Islamist groups in North Africa and by their branches in France. Thus a Tunisian Islamist militant does not hesitate to tell us that when the immigrant workers return home with smuggled goods they are certain to find the eyes of custom officials upon them if they were affiliated with the ruling New-Dastur party. But if they can prove association with the Tablīghī Jamāʿat they are sure that their entire baggage will be free from custom duties. Polemics aside, one can hardly doubt the existence of excellent relations between the authorities (whether in the north or south of the Mediterranean) and the Tablīgh leaders; it is no secret. One need not go far to find the causes. The fact has been underscored by Mumtāz Aḥmad that as long as one spends one's day in prayers, *dhikr* and journeying, one does not participate in political activities that are considered subversive, and one does not participate in various Islamist movements.

This report accounts only for the short time that a Tablīghī spends with the Jamāʿat, even if the constant flow of recruits to the Tablīghī tends to obscure this fact. In effect, the movement is a sieve, indeed, a strainer. Once re-Islamised by the Tablīghīs, those who have no inclination to become a prayer machine distance themselves from the Jamāʿat and look for activities that are intellectually and politically more dynamic. The diverse rival groups of Foi et Pratique in French Islam are well aware of this. Among the congregation assembled on Friday in the Omar mosque, for example, police spies and touts have discrete but sure places. However, in France, as distinct from their countries of origin, the rivalry of Islamist groups who have relatively little influence outside the student milieu is less menacing to the Tablīghī Jamāʿat than is the very effective politics of religious control practiced by Algerian authorities through the intermediaries of the Central Paris Mosque, which remained under their control from 1982 to 1992.

CHAPTER TEN

WORLDS 'APART': TABLĪGHĪ JAMĀʿAT IN SOUTH AFRICA UNDER APARTHEID, 1963–1993

Ebrahim Moosa

Introduction[1]

The first effects of the Tablīgh movement were felt in South Africa less than three decades after the founder Mawlānā Muḥammad Ilyās (1885–1944) died in India. Today, the Tabligh Jamat [Tablīghī Jamāʿat] in South Africa is perhaps the strongest and fastest growing Muslim religious movement in southern Africa. The demise of white colonial rule in Zambia, Malawi, Botswana, Angola, Mozambique and Zimbabwe signaled the dissipation of the European presence in this sub-region. The end of European prestige did not mean the decline of Christianity. It did however, create the social space for Islam to flourish in the form of Tablīgh evangelism. In South Africa, apartheid rule tolerated only those forms of cultural and religious activity which did not threaten white political hegemony.

Islam arrived in South Africa from the Malay Archipelago as far back as 1658 with the earliest Dutch colonizers (see Moosa 1993, 27–59 for a detailed background). In 1860, Muslims from the Indian sub-continent arrived as indentured labourers under British rule. Isolated from the rest of Muslim Africa by the high visibility of Christianity, Islam in southern Africa has since the mid-twentieth century experienced a growth in visibility, largely as a result of Tablīgh activities. Today Muslims number well over 500,000, with some unofficial estimates suggesting one million followers. Although Muslims of Malay origin did proselytize among indigenous inhabi-

[1] I gratefully acknowledge the assistance of a University of Cape Town Research Grant, which made this contribution possible. I would also like to thank Jane Parry for her assistance, which saved me from several infelicities. The remaining mistakes, needless to say, are mine alone.

tants in the eighteenth and nineteenth centuries, there have been no discernable trends of significant conversion to Islam in the twentieth century.

The first adherents who arrived here three centuries ago hailed from the Indonesian archipelago and the Kurumandel coast of India, and found ethnic integration hard to resist. Conversion of "free black" slaves to Islam promoted ethnic and social assimilation. Thereafter, the conversion to Islam of some Afrikaners (persons of Dutch origin) further extended the scope of integration. The Indic religious consciousness that early immigrant Muslims brought with them from the East in the seventeenth century soon domesticated itself to the African context. It is nevertheless noticeable that the dominant leitmotif of Islam at the Cape remains its underlying Malay-Javanese character. Over a period of three centuries there have also been influences from the Middle East, ranging from the period of the Ottoman Empire to latter-day Egyptian and Saudi influences. The latter are transmitted by means of South African *ʿulamā* who are trained abroad.

The beginnings of the Tablīghī Jamāʿat in South Africa were inextricably tied to the fortunes of descendants of so-called "passenger Indians" who arrived in the provinces of Natal and Transvaal toward the close of the nineteenth century. Between 1830 and 1870 the effects of British capitalism in the colonies spawned the mass emigration of some two million Indians from the Indian sub-continent. Some of them paid their passage to Africa rather than being indentured, and subsequently became the mercantile class among Indians. Muslims among them hailed from various parts of pre-partition India, but mainly the Surat, Kathiawar and Bharuch districts of the state of Gujarat, and from the Kȯkan area of Maharashtra State. They served as traders in the rural areas of what is today known as the Kwazulu-Natal region, the three Transvaal regions (northern, eastern and western), and the Pretoria-Witwatersrand and Vereeniging (PWV) region which includes the metropolitan areas of Durban and Johannesburg.

History

Early History

While Islam in East and West Africa spread at the hands of Arab traders (Mazrui 1985, 817–818), in South Africa the "conversion" of diaspora Muslims to Tablīgh-Islam took place through descendants of Indian traders. They were the first to respond to the call of the Tablīghī Jamāʿat there. By "conversion" here is meant, not a conversion from one religion to another, but rather a "deliberate turning from indifference or from an earlier form of piety to another" (Nock 1933, 6–7). This is precisely what the teaching of the Tablīghī Jamāʿat inspires, a meticulous commitment to the fundamentals of faith and an unquestioning loyalty to prophetic authority (*Sunna*).

Interestingly, the first South African contact with the Tablīgh movement was not with its headquarters in India, but with Saudi Arabia. The reason for this detour was that soon after the coming to power of the National Party[2] and the advent of apartheid in 1948, Indian immigration to South Africa was halted. The white minority government was reluctant even to give visas to Indian visitors. Furthermore, contact between South Africa and the Indian subcontinent was severely restricted after India and Pakistan took a strong adversarial stance towards Pretoria's racist domestic policies and enforced a cultural boycott against the country.

By the 1960s, the Tablīgh movement, under the leadership of Mawlānā Muḥammad Yūsuf (d. 1965), the son of Mawlānā Ilyās, saw the annual pilgrimage (*ḥajj*) to Mecca as an ideal opportunity to promote his missionary work (see also Gaborieau, this volume). Given the large number of pilgrims at the holy cities, Tablīgh activists worked hard to gain new recruits among them in order that they might spread the simple content of this fledgling movement in their respective countries.

Local Founders

One of the earliest participants in South African Tablīgh work recalls that his first exposure to the activities of the Tablīghī Jamāʿat occurred

---

[2] This party was ousted from power in the historic April 1994 elections and was succeeded by the African National Congress, led by Nelson Mandela.

in the 1950s. An Indian, remembered only as Hafez Soojie (Ḥāfiẓ Sūjī), was on a visit to his Gujrātī-speaking relatives in South Africa. Feeling compelled to share his understanding of Tablīgh Islam he initiated the first *gasht* by taking a group of people to a mosque in the Johannesburg suburb of Roodepoort.[3] Although there was no continued activity after the departure of Hafez Soojie, the first seeds of the movement had been sown.

In 1962, a businessman from Umzinto in the Natal province, Ghulam Mohamed Padia, a Muslim of Indian descent, was exposed to the activities of the Tablīghī Jamāʿat during a pilgrimage in Mecca (Cilliers 1983). Before returning home to South Africa he spent four months (three *chillas*) abroad, visiting the movement's headquarters in Delhi where he learned the methods of Tablīgh instruction. Thereafter, Hadji-Bhai Padia, as he is better known, became the movement's most influential pioneer in South Africa. At first there was opposition to his activities. The local Umzinto community felt that religious instruction and propagation were best left to qualified *ʿulamā*. However, the sympathetic attitude of the *ʿulamā* of the Deoband school soon legitimated the activities of the Tablīghī Jamāʿat.

The main participants in the initial Tablīgh activities were businessmen of Indian descent whose ancestors had come from the Surat area of modern India. Gradually, the movement was successfully attracting individuals from other subethnicities which make up the range of Muslims of Indian descent in South Africa, such as the Urdu-speaking community from Hyderabad, Daccan, Memon speakers from north Gujarat, and later, Kokani speakers from Maharashtra. By the 1970s the Tablīgh movement had also made inroads into the Western Cape area, where it gained adherents among Muslims from the historical Malay and "coloured" (mixed race) communities. Among Muslims of African and European descent, the Tablīgh movement had little appeal.

Growth

In 1966, three years after Tablīghī Jamāʿat's inception in South Africa, the first nationwide gathering (*ijtimāʿ*), attended by some 300 persons, was held at Ladysmith, in what is today known as the Kwazulu-Natal region. Thereafter, the size of the annual gatherings

[3] Interview with Mr. Rashid Patel, 29 December 1993.

became an index of the movement's strength. In the mid-1970s annual Tablīgh gatherings became an important fixture in the country's religious calendar, and Muslim activities in particular. These gatherings attracted thousands of people and necessitated elaborate and detailed organization. The numbers at the Tablīghī Jamāʿat's *ijtimāʿ* eclipsed those at the annual convention of the Muslim Youth Movement (MYM), an event which was subsequently abandoned due to declining support (Tayob 1992, 101–124).

A range of factors account for the large-scale gravitation of Muslims towards the Tablīgh movement. Firstly, the Tablīghī Jamāʿat represents a type of Islam with a Ṣūfī orientation, which has an attraction for Muslims of Indian ancestry. The common group identity and ethnicity which a section of the converts to Tablīgh share with the geographical roots of the movement, namely India, provide a natural religious "home" in a "symbolic" diaspora.[4] In an alienating environment such as South Africa, the natural gravitation of diaspora communities towards ethnocentrism is hardly surprising. Nevertheless, it would be reductionist to suggest that ethnocentrism is the only factor contributing to the appeal of Tablīgh-Islam.

Secondly, the theological commonality between the Tablīghī Jamāʿat and the school of Deoband is critically important. The theological seminary of Deoband (see Introduction) has significant credibility among a section of the South African Muslim community, namely the descendants of Indian immigrants. At least three *ʿulamā* associations, the Jamʿiyyat al-ʿUlamā of both Transvaal and Natal, and Majlis al-ʿUlamā of South Africa, are pro-Deoband, and thus provide legitimacy to the discourse of the Tablīgh movement. Even though not all *ʿulamā* are Tablīgh adherents, it would be rare to find pro-Deoband *ʿulamā* who actively oppose the Tablīgh movement. The hegemony and authority which the Deobandī *ʿulamā* exercise in at least five regions—the PWV region, the three Transvaal regions and the Kwazulu-Natal region—contributes significantly to the growth of the Tablīghī Jamāʿat there.

[4] I am not asserting that South African Muslims of Indian ancestry consider India to be their home. Many of them belong to families that have been here for more than four generations. The younger generation in particular has little in common with Indian and eastern culture. The same applies to Muslims of Malay-Javanese descent. Yet, that there is a symbolic connection with India, Malaysia and Indonesia cannot be denied. For this reason, I chose to call it a symbolic diaspora, not intending thereby the Jewish connotation of diaspora.

Another factor that boosted the fortunes of the Tablīgh movement was the participation of graduates from the two pro-Deoband seminaries in Newcastle, in the Kwazulu-Natal region, and Azaadville, in the PWV region. Both of these seminaries actively encourage their students to participate in the Tablīgh movement. Once they qualify as *ʿulamā*, most of them vigorously further the goals of the movement from the mosques and pulpits which they occupy. A sizeable number of these graduates are from the Cape and they have made a noticeable impact on the Cape landscape by extending the influence of the Deoband School.

Opposition to the Tablīgh movement comes mainly from two segments of the Muslim community. The first is those who are commited to what can be called "folk Islam." Among the two main strains of folk Islam in South Africa, the Brēlwī school of thought (see Introduction, Metcalf 1982 and Sanyal 1990) has a sizeable support-base in the regions of Kwazulu-Natal, the PWV and the Cape. The other strain is the vintage Islam of the Cape, which carries elements of Southeast Asian Sufism. The second segment to voice its opposition is comprised of the youth, student and politicized sectors of the Muslim community, and the neoconservative *ʿulamā* of the Cape who align themselves to religious trends in the Middle East. Examples are those associated with Al-Azhar University in Cairo, and with pro-Wahhābī Saudi Arabian institutions such as the Islamic University of Medina and Ummul Qurā in Mecca.

Those who do not readily associate with the Tablīghī Jamāʿat are the neoconservative *ʿulamā* of the Muslim Judicial Council (MJC), who constitute the leading *ʿulamā* council in the Cape region, and members of the youth and student associations and politically activist groupings, like the Call of Islam and the Qibla Mass Movement (Le Roux and Jhazbhay 1992, 85–100).

These latter groups do not, however, overtly criticize the Tablīghī Jamāʿat. Thus it would seem that the Tablīghī Jamāʿat has managed to neutralize opposition in some instances where it has failed to gain allies. However, the opposition towards the Tablīghī Jamāʿat evident in the second group is mild compared to the hostility of the Brēlwī group (Jamālī 1987).[5]

[5] A full-length tract by Haḍrat ʿAllāma Arshadul Qādirī of Calcutta, translated by Professor Naʿīm Jamālī (Jamālī 1987), is evidence of the vituperative debate between the Brēlwī movement and the Tablīghī Jamāʿat.

In 1987 this hostility was exacerbated by an incident which had tragic consequences. A group of Brēlwī supporters decided to hold a *meelad* (*mīlād* or *mawlid al-Nabī*: birthday of the Prophet celebration) in one of the halls of Azaadville, home of the Madrassa ʿArabiyya Islamiyya seminary. Some prominent teachers at the seminary were also highly placed within the ranks of the Tablīghī Jamāʿat. After failing to obstruct the Brēlwī group's plans, the Tablīgh followers, spearheaded by the seminary leadership, decided to express their outrage at what they considered to be the *bidʿa* (heretical) practice of the Brēlwīs. They decreed their own activity to be a religious cause demanding of belligerence—*Jihād* against its opponents. Scuffles and pandemonium broke out as the two groups clashed, and one person was killed.

Islam in the Western Cape region,[6] where it has a longer history than in the rest of South Africa, is of a more diverse character. Muslims in this region are mainly of Indonesian, Malay and, to a lesser extent, Indian ancestry. Given the diversity and indigenous acculturation of Islam here, it is not surprising that the Tablīghī Jamāʿat has been relatively less successful. Furthermore, among a large section of the Kokani speaking Indian community in the Western Cape, Brēlwī influence is significant and there is resistance to Tablīgh encroachment. However, for many working class Malay and "coloured" Muslims, the Indianisation of their Islam is also an index of socially upward mobility. The demonstration effect of Tablīgh Islam, consisting of a dress code, beard and other ritualistic tenets, as well as the *charismata* that the Tablīgh movement offers to individuals, makes it an attractive prospect. A survey of Tablīgh activists indicates that the movement holds greater attraction for middle-aged persons, many of whom have for most of their lives not been devout in terms of observing daily rituals. They experience a new kind of religiosity in Tablīgh work. Elements of atonement and compensation for their lack of prior piety, plus the espousal of a new identity, make Tablīgh-Islam particularly attractive. The profile of Tablīgh adherents ranges from students, to blue-collar workers, to businessmen to profession-

[6] The previous four provinces have been redivided into nine regions under the new dispensation in South Africa, effective since April 1994. The Transvaal has been divided into the Pretoria-Witwatersrand and Vereenigng (PWV) region, Northern, Eastern and Western Transvall. The Cape into Northern, Eastern and Western Cape, etc.

als the latter mainly in the medical profession). At the same time, the turn-over of Tablīgh activists is high. Although a core group remains dedicated to Tablīgh work throughout their lives, the average individual is a fervent activist for only some five to ten years. Thereafter, the person may become an active sympathizer, or, most often, a passive sympathizer.

Among women, the Tablīghī Jamāʿat has cultivated an extensive constituency in South Africa (see also Metcalf, and Faust, this volume). Female family members or other women are often converted to the movement, but the majority of female converts are the spouses of male activists. Women have their own circles and operate from homes. Their activities are similar to those of men, with an emphasis on regular weekly *taʿlīm* (teaching circles) where they are exposed to literature that promotes zeal for virtue as defined by the instructional manual approved by the movement. This remains the *Tablīghī Niṣāb*, literally translated as Evangelical Curriculum, (now re-titled as *Faḍāʾil-i-Aʿmāl*; see chapter four, this volume) but better known as the *Teachings of Islam*.

Activities

Tablīgh activists travel frequently within cities and over the length and breadth of South Africa. Operating on austere budgets, they sleep in mosques and share food communally. Meager resources are stretched to optimum levels to allow activists to reach as many people as possible during evangelical travels. The movement's major strength is its access to grassroot communities and the recruitment of neophytes takes place particularly at the level of evangelical visits (*gasht*) to fellow Muslims on an individual basis.

There is a remarkable global uniformity in the format of Tablīgh *modus operandi*. Functions are divided into national, regional and local levels. In every locality and region one mosque is identified as the headquarters (*markaz*) of Tablīgh activity. On weekends, from Friday evening until Sunday, localities send groups of men to the regional headquarters, from where they are redeployed to spend time in targeted areas. *Daʿwa* work entails doing evangelical work on a voluntary basis and traveling at personal expense within a country as an itinerant lay preacher. Some Tablīgh activists also go abroad.

In this way, lay persons are trained to articulate the ideas and message of Tablīgh, and specifically to meditate on their own experiences of faith (*Īmān*). The entire programme is designed to make the individual an active participant in the dissemination and teaching of religion, a task that was previously assumed by the *ʿulamā*. Missionary zeal, combined with individual empowerment, bolsters the confidence and religious identity of persons who would otherwise consume religion passively. The religious experience gained through the intense exercise of prayer, a commitment to mission and the sanctified living environment of mosques, results in the Tablīgh activist discovering a new self-identity.

Ideology and Discourse

Tablīgh discourse projects the movement as Noah's ark, with its simplistic but attractive inference: whoever boards the Jamāʿat is saved, and those who fail to do so are doomed. Observation of Tablīgh workers has shown that they display all the characteristics of "conversion" (Snow and Machalek 1984, 167–190; Staples 1987, 133–147). The rhetorical indicators of Tablīgh "conversion" are that the adherents adopt a new discourse steeped in Islamic metaphor; they espouse an ideal and purist universe with its attendant discourse and paraphernalia. All events and happenings are causally attributed to God alone. The convert adopts a master attribution scheme which states that success can only be achieved if there is an unflinching commitment to the commands of Allah, meaning ritual piety and imitating the prophetic lifestyle. These range from the personal and customary habits of the Arabian Prophet to his religious practices. In emphasizing the claim that "success" is only attainable by imitating the lifestyle of the Prophet of Islam, the Tablīgh movement closely resembles a "prosperity cult."

To describe the Tablīgh movement as "cult" or "sect," however, risks distorting the sociological analysis. The Tablīghī Jamāʿat does have an unconscious sense of community (Wilson 1982, 103), but adherents also see themselves and their religious experiences as unique and incomparable to those of people outside the group (on this point see also Tozy, this volume). Their belief that their experiences are unique results in Tablīgh activists suspending analogical reasoning. This means that they are unable to compare their own experiences with similar, if not identical, Buddhist or Christian encounters. However, they can easily identify with an Islamic past dating back centuries. The most persistent analogical metaphor in Tablīgh discourse is identification with the Companions of the Prophet (Ṣaḥāba). It is therefore not surprising that *Teachings of Islam* contains hagiographic accounts of the Companions and well-known religious personalities, especially Ṣūfīs. Committed Tablīgh activists embrace the mission of the movement in an uncompromising manner. After conversion, many activists adopt an attitude that all their social interactions should lead to recruitment and the furtherance of the aims of the movement.

It is perhaps the accessibility and simplicity of the Tablīgh teachings that give the movement its greatest appeal. Every activist aspires to reach and share the prophetic *charismata* which is believed to be transmitted by means of strict emulation (*ittibāʿ*) of the Prophet, a notion which lies at the core of Tablīgh teachings. Its famous programme involves a commitment to the Six Points (see chapter one, this volume).

The International Connection

The affluence of the most visible ethnic group in the Tablīghī Jamāʿat, namely Muslims of Indian descent, allows the South African chapter to engage in extensive international work. South African groups regularly visit all neighbouring states and have been instrumental in the success of the movement in Zimbabwe, Zambia, Malawi, Mauritius and Mozambique. Prior to 1990, easy access to countries north of Zambia was restricted because of South Africa's pariah political status in the international community. With the country's readmission into the international fold, the Tablīgh movement there is expected to increase its activities in sub-Saharan Africa at large. In the past, the South African chapter concentrated its efforts in South American countries such as Brazil and Argentina, as well as parts of North America and Britain.

Tablīgh Ethos

The bulk of Tablīgh participants on their first international outings visit India and Pakistan, especially the main centres in Niẓāmuddīn in New Delhi and Raiwind in Pakistan. For it is on the Indian subcontinent that Tablīgh initiates are subjected to the proverbial baptism by fire. The unique living conditions of the sub-continent test the individual's ability to make *mujāhada*—a voluntary mental and physical ability to endure. *Mujāhada* is not an entirely novel concept to Tablīgh since it is more fully developed in Ṣūfī literature.

Many aspects of the Tablīgh movement are an attempt to bring about a synthesis between esoteric tendencies of the orthodox Ṣūfī orders (Ṭarīqa) and exoteric juridical practices (*sharīʿa*). Although this synthesis is characteristic of the school of Deoband, it also reflects the close association of the founder, Mawlānā Ilyās, with the more prominent figures of the Deoband school such as Rashīd Aḥmad Gangōhī and Khalīl Aḥmad Sahāranpurī, both of whom were Ṣūfī mentors (*shaykh*) as well as religious scholars. Many seasoned South African Tablīgh activists take *bayʿa* (oaths of spiritual initiation) with the prominent mentors of Taṣawwuf associated with the movement. The late Mawlānā Inʿāmul Ḥasan (1918–1995) was a *shaykh* of the Naqshbandī order (Ṭarīqa), and had several South African disciples. Mawlānā Muḥammad Zakariyyā (1898–1982), the author of the *Teachings of Islam* [*Faḍāʾil Aʿmāl*], also generated a substantial following among Tablīgh workers in South Africa. The ordinary Tablīgh routine introduces the lay person to a moderate discipline of daily oral remembrance (*dhikr*) of the Divine, a feature enthusiastically embraced by new activists. In short, the goal is to create missionaries who are inspired by a sober Sufism that will not clash with the demands of the law (*sharīʿa*). In summary, it would be fair to say that the Tablīghī Jamāʿat adheres to mainstream Sunnī practices and symbols of a moderately puritan kind which are conducive to pan-Islamic and transnational ideals.

Method of Work: Differences and Changes

At its very inception in South Africa, the leadership structure of Tablīghī Jamāʿat consisted of a national leader (*amīr*), with provincial *amīr*s in the previous provinces of Transvaal, Natal and the Cape. The Cape is the oldest seat of Islam in southern Africa, where the largest concentration of Muslims is to be found. But it is there that the Tablīgh movement is weakest. Despite nearly three decades of continuous work in this province, the Jamāʿat has failed to capture the imagination of Cape Muslims as it has elsewhere in the country. However, the Tablīghī Jamāʿat does command more support than other Muslim organizations in the Cape. A complex set of reasons, including the diversity of Islamic trends, ethnicities and class differences, account for the Jamāʿat's lack of success in the Cape. Islam there is a confluence of heterogeneous influences and no hegemonic force can claim to command the loyalty of all its Muslims. The majority of Cape Muslims have a mixed ethnic ancestry.

In the Cape, the Tablīghī Jamāʿat abandoned the practice of a single regional *amīr* after a leadership crisis in the 1980s. In an unusual precedent, the leadership issue became a matter of serious acrimony and politicking within Tablīgh circles. This contradicted the Jamāʿat's claim that it is free from the flaws and bureaucratic strictures found within other Muslim organizations which follow Western management styles. In the other regions, the Jamāʿat has a more coherent leadership, given the close affinity between the ideology of the Jamāʿat and the socio-cultural proclivities of its target audiences.

Impact on Society

One of the most visible aspects of the Tablīgh movement is its ability to promote a routinized Islam in a conservative guise. By "routinization" I mean the regulated discipline of especially religious rituals, which become the main preoccupation of a group. In the case of the Tablīgh it is more than just being ritualistic—for them rituals are the very fulfillment of Islam. By "conservative" I mean that preservation of tradition rather than innovation is the major thrust of the social expression of the religion. Every act, practice or idea is referred to an *ur-text*, the prophetic model, as visualized within the very specific confines of Tablīghī-Islam.

One of the direct results of the Tablīgh movement has been the introduction of rigid segregation between the sexes in those social spheres and institutions where the influence of Tablīghī Islam is dominant. A completely veiled (*purdah*) female is the definition of an ideal woman in the Tablīgh ethos. However, there is also a tolerance for women wearing *ḥijāb*, where the entire body except the face is covered. In order to cater to the increased demand for sexual segregation of Muslim women, several single-sex Muslim private schools have mushroomed in the last decade. Since there are no sexually segregated facilities at the level of tertiary education, many young Muslim women are forced to pursue post-secondary education by means of distance learning at the world's largest correspondence university—the University of South Africa.

The legitimation of the Tablīghī Jamāʿat by the pro-Deoband *ʿulamā* in South Africa in the 1960s, which led to the public acceptance of their role in religious life, has paid handsome dividends to the *ʿulamā*. Today the Tablīghī Jamāʿat is the most zealous purveyor of the Deoband school in theology, law and other aspects of ideology. The influence of the Deoband now extends beyond its original settings in the Northern, Western and Eastern Transvaal, PWV and Kwazulu-Natal regions.

Political Quietism

Tablīgh conservatism is not restricted to religious and gender matters, but extends to politics as well. Although Tablīgh spokespersons constantly emphasize that their mission is not to dislocate people from society and their professions, a commitment to the Tablīghī Jamāʿat inevitably has the effect of detachment from mainstream society, and of political isolation. Given their focus on eschatological matters and concern for personal salvation, the social and political ethos of Islam is not just neglected but ignored. In the South African context, except for self-confessed right-wing religious groups, virtually all significant religious denominations and movements except for the Tablīghī Jamāʿat demonstrated their abhorrence for the political system of apartheid.

Religious determinism is a noticeable feature of Tablīgh ideology. In fact, Tablīgh discourse explains the plight of millions of black people under the yoke of apartheid in the very deterministic language of Islamic theodicy. It comes perilously close to saying that apartheid was a divine visitation upon the people of this land due to their sin and disobedience to God. The belief is that when all Muslims follow the ritual obligations of Islam with sincerity and obedience then God will change the material conditions of people. During the dark years of racial discrimination, Tablīgh ideology found it prudent not to question the morality of the apartheid state and its attendant practices of racial discrimination.

The political quietism of the Tablīghī Jamāʿat, especially in conflict situations, can perhaps be traced to a specific type of Ṣūfī ethos that it embraces. In this Ṣūfī tendency the emphasis is on a Ghazālian-type of personal salvation. This is evident in the movement's six-point programme, which has negligible social content. Unlike expressions of militant Sufism, such as that practiced in the Sokoto Caliphate of ʿUsmān dan Fodio (1754–1817), in the Mahdiyyah of Muḥammad Aḥmad (1845–1885) in the Sudan, or by Sayyid Aḥmad Shahīd (1786–1831) in India, who all attempted to establish a socio-political order based on Islam, the Tablīgh focus is on the individual. In the Tablīgh movement the ideal of a socio-political Islam is not advocated. There are obvious advantages to this strategy. An emphasis on the individual makes Tablīgh-Islam amenable to the concept and status of religion in secularized societies, where religion is relegated to the personal or private sphere. Certain strains of political Islam which espouse socio-political ambitions among Muslim communities in the West, and the Middle East for that matter, are under regular surveillance by nervous governments, with occasional subtle restrictions on their activities. To date, Tablīgh activity has not been subject to such scrutiny and has had relatively free movement in the West and no significant opposition from Muslim governments.

The phenomenon of a personalized religion may explain why Tablīgh activity was acceptable in some Eastern bloc countries such as Hungary and Yugoslavia during the closing years of communism. A private and individualistic Islam is less of a threat to an autocratic state, which must devise strategies of appeasement of its more religious citizenry. Similarly, under successive apartheid regimes, evangelical groups, including the Tablīghī Jamāʿat, had no restrictions imposed on their activities. On the contrary, the apartheid state readily offered assistance to conservative evangelical groups as part of its counter-revolutionary strategy. By contrast, liberation theologians of all persuasions and their allies abroad were closely monitored—some of them had to suffer imprisonment and torture for their convictions.

Tablīgh activists are either hostile or indifferent to political Islam. The Tablīghī Jamāʿat engages in sustained propaganda to discredit the ideologues of the Pakistan-based Jamāʿat Islāmī, the Egyptian-based Muslim Brotherhood and the Iranian revolution. They hope to curb their influence on local youth and student organizations. Since the Tablīgh movement sees itself as the genuine torchbearer of Sunnī Islam, opposition to these politically motivated Muslim groups has a theological basis. In the case of the Jamāʿat Islāmī, the doctrinal *bona fides* of its chief ideologue, Abul Aʿlā Mawdūdī, are deemed suspect and hence undesirable for Muslims in South Africa. The Tablīghī Jamāʿat dismisses the Brotherhood for its lack of religious propriety. Most Brotherhood proponents adopt European attire and fashionable beards as opposed to the statutory dress and untrimmed beards demanded by Tablīgh standards. The revolution in Iran is clearly an anathema because it is believed to be Shīʿa-inspired.

Conclusion

In South Africa the Tablīghī Jamāʿat has proven to be a very successful religious movement in terms of its own objectives, and it has made an impact on local Islam. Depending on the vantage point of the observer, it is viewed as the very fulfillment of the ideals of Islam in the form of personal piety and the search for salvation, or as a movement which reduces Islam to mere rituals and adds to the intellectual stupor and social decline in Muslim social life. Some opponents go further and charge the Tablīghī Jamāʿat with conspiring against Islam.

The mileage that the school of Deoband has gained out of its links with the Tablīghī Jamāʿat in the South African context, in terms of its own spread and authority, is unmistakable. The fortunes of the Deoband School in this region will to a large extent follow that of the Tablīghī Jamāʿat.

It has been observed that "conversion"[7] to the Tablīgh ideology paves the way to a personalized religion. In seeking to satisfy an inner spiritual need, converts may not always value the role of community in which government and socio-political organizations play a vital role. In South Africa, Tablīgh activists displayed an apolitical attitude during the apartheid era. Some critics of the Tablīghī Jamāʿat argue that this apolitical stand was itself a political posture of defending the status quo. However, as South Africa enters into an era of full secular democracy with a strong market economy, in

[7] Richard Bulliet (1979, 128–129) writing in the context of conversion to Islam in medieval times, made two pertinent observations that may be relevant to the notion of "conversion" as used in this essay. Firstly, that conversion almost inevitably leads to the weakening of, or dissolution of centralized government; and, secondly, the conversion process in and of itself gives rise to a clash of interests between elements of the population that convert at different times.

which the state will not be hostile to religion but treat it as a private concern, there remains a strong possibility that personalized religion will fit [or "mesh"] comfortably with the new political order. It may just be that personalized religion *a la* Tablīghī Jamāʿat is Islam's answer to the rapid, market-orientated liberal democracies of the twenty-first century.

CHAPTER ELEVEN

A MOVEMENT OR A *JAMĀ'AT?* TABLĪGHĪ JAMĀ'AT IN CANADA

Shaheen H. Azmi

Introduction

This essay focuses on the entry of the Tablīghī Jamā'at into Canada, and reviews its activities and impact there. Islamic movements that seek to be a force in the Muslim immigrant communities in the West, especially in North America, face two pivotal longterm challenges. First they have to meet the problems of internal cohesion engendered by the encounter of Muslims from a multitude of parochial backgrounds. Secondly, they face the external challenge of minority status within the context of a militantly secular culture and society, which is highly corrosive to traditional, totalistic conceptions of a religion such as Islam. This essay will focus on the nature of the Tablīghī Jamā'at's response to these challenges, a response that may suggest the prospects for the movement's survival among the Muslim immigrant communities of the West.

In order to examine the entry of the Tablīghī Jamā'at into Canada in greater detail, this essay will concentrate upon Tablīgh development and activity in the single urban center of Metropolitan Toronto. Toronto is not only the home of Canada's largest concentration of Muslims, but has also been the major centre of Tablīgh activity for all of Canada and arguably for all of North America. The experience of the Tablīgh movement in Toronto's Muslim community should, to varying degrees, reflect their experiences in other Muslim communities across Canada.

Background: The Muslim Community in Toronto

In the early 1960s, the Muslims in all of Canada numbered no more than a few thousand. Most of them were Lebanese, Syrian, and

Albanian immigrants who had come during the post-war period. It was only then that immigration from Asia and the Middle East allowed the Muslim population to grow at a rapid pace (Abu-Laban 1983). Many initially came as students, and some chose to stay on as immigrants after completing their studies. By the late 1960s, the Muslim community in Metropolitan Toronto numbered somewhere in the hundreds, the largest portion being from India and Pakistan.

By the 1981 census (Rashid 1985) there were over 98,000 Muslims in Canada, with the largest concentration of over 30,000 living in Metropolitan Toronto, and another 20,000 living in the heavily populated region surrounding Toronto known as Southern Ontario. Almost two-thirds had come as immigrants after 1970. The flow of Muslims migrating to Canada continued unabated throughout the 1980s, and it is quite likely that their numbers are now almost 200,000, with more than a third, or almost 80,000, living in Metropolitan Toronto.

Muslim immigrants have come from virtually all parts of the Muslim world, and from Muslim minority communities in other countries, particularly the Caribbean. According to the 1981 census, over 35 percent at that time had come from Asia, of whom more than half were from India and Pakistan. Almost 30 percent came from Africa, most being South Asian immigrants from Tanzania, Uganda, and Kenya. Thus, although Muslim Canadians come from a wide variety of individual countries, their ethnic make up is much less diverse. In Metropolitan Toronto today most Muslims are of Indo-Pakistani origin (over 42 percent), and another major segment is of Arab origin (25 percent). Large international refugee movements in the 1980s have no doubt diversified Canada's Muslim population further—especially in Metropolitan Toronto where most refugees chose to settle—but this has not substantially disturbed the predominance of Muslims of Indo-Pakistani origin.

Reflecting their diversity of origins, the Muslim community in Canada has been highly diversified in terms of religious practice and doctrinal understanding. The full range of expressions of the Islamic tradition is present in the general Muslim population, especially in the Toronto area.

Divided as they are along doctrinal and ethnic lines, it is not surprising that the Muslim community in Toronto is highly fragmented. Despite their large numbers, Muslims therefore remain relatively unnoticed there, for unlike many other sizable communities in the city, such as the Jews and various European nationalities, Muslims, even in terms of their ethnic subdivisions, have been unable to ghettoize. One explanation is that many earlier Muslim immigrants, who were inspired by economic reasons to come to Canada (Abu-Laban 1983), pursued proven patterns of 'success,' adhering to established secular patterns of employment and association in Toronto. Consequently, Toronto Muslims live scattered throughout the metropolis and their religious institutions are more or less invisible, functioning basically as weekend drive-in facilities.

The Muslim community in Toronto has so far been unable to transcend parochial differences relating to ethnicity, language, place of origin, and doctrinal affiliation, and most are content to organize on the basis of ethnicity. Tablīghī Jamāʿat is one of the very few Islamic movements that have attempted to unite Muslims on the basis of a trans-ethnic Islamic message. It is unique because, transplanted from the Muslim world, it was tied to the fortunes of the Indo-Pakistani Muslim community. A review of its development in Metropolitan Toronto will show that, regardless of its apparently trans-ethnic religious message, the rise of the Tablīghī Jamāʿat in the city was due more to the immigration of so many of its supporters from the Indian Subcontinent, rather than to the success of its call to Muslims in Canada.

The History of the Tablīgh Movement

Origins in North America

The origins of the Tablīghī Jamāʿat in North America cannot be dated in exact terms. *Jamāʿats* (small groups of Tablīgh workers) were sent to North America as early as the late 1950s. They came from India or Pakistan, where they were recruited and selected to travel to North America. Invariably, these *jamāʿats* were led by individuals who could speak English. The first *jamāʿats* headed for the major cities of the United States. In opening up a new area the Tablīghī *jamāʿats* were ready to stay in motels and venture into urban concentrations in search of receptive mosques, of which there existed only a few, belonging mostly to Black Muslim groups. Where no mosques existed, a search would be made for Muslims living in the area. University campuses were often a good place to find them. Where nothing else was available, *jamāʿats* would make use of telephone directories. Each successive *jamāʿat* that came would benefit from the experience of the previous ones, and might avail itself of the support of receptive local Muslims, some of whom in the early days were Black Muslim converts.

Origins in Metropolitan Toronto

The Toronto area was opened to Tablīgh activity in a manner paralleling the efforts in the U.S. Again, events are difficult to date precisely. However, sometime during the mid-1960s *jamāʿats* working in the U.S. added forays into Canada to their itineraries. A Pakistani Muslim student of the time recalls how one Tablīghī Jamāʿat from Pakistan arrived at the University of Toronto campus in 1968. At that time no mosque existed in the city, and group religious activity consisted of Friday prayer gatherings at the University and special family occasions. The *jamāʿat* stayed for two weeks in Toronto, during which it made personal calls to every Muslim it could find. Appeals were made to attend a religious gathering from where the standard Tablīgh message was advanced, and appeals made for participation in the *jamāʿat*'s further travels. Twelve local Muslims from the Indian Subcontinent, mostly students, joined the Tablīghī Jamāʿat on the next leg of its tour, to London, Ontario. The flavour that Tablīgh activities in Canada have retained ever since is well captured by the sight, portrayed by a participant in this early *jamāʿat*, of a rag-tag collection of fifteen Muslims dressed in Indian Muslim attire publicly calling out the ritual call to prayer, and performing the prayer before bewildered onlookers on a train platform in London, Ontario.

The influx of Indian and Pakistani immigrants into Toronto's Muslim community, which was beginning to take off by the late 1960s, provided the Tablīghī Jamāʿat with a population familiar and receptive to its work. Thereafter, Tablīghī Jamāʿats coming to North America from other parts of the world made Toronto a regular stop in their itineraries. As many as two or three *jamāʿats* would come annually to Toronto and would use the home of a supportive Muslim family as a base.

Development of Local Activities

Locally based Tablīgh activities were beginning to develop since several dedicated workers had either come as immigrants or developed locally. Colonel Amīrud Dīn Khān was a significant figure among the immigrants. He had come as a member of a *jamāʿat* before his eventual immigration to Toronto sometime around 1970. Colonel Amīrud Dīn soon became one of the most active Tablīgh organizers and activists Toronto has seen. As a pious and dedicated worker with some religious learning, he functioned like something of a local *imām* for the Tablīgh-inspired workers. He led efforts to use the recently established Jāmiʿ (Friday) Mosque, Toronto's largest at the time, as a Tablīgh center. He organized five-times-a-day prayers in the mosque, and established a Saturday night *ijtimāʿ* there to focus Tablīgh activity in the city. Later, in 1973, when internal ethnic squabbles led to a faction of the Indian-Pakistani and Arab community obtaining control of the Jāmiʿ Mosque, Colonel Amīrud Dīn came to function as the mosque's *imām*. His position was tenuous, however, because the new administration of the mosque was not necessarily sympathetic to the Tablīgh movement. The administration's loyalties, though not yet hardened, were to the fledgling Muslim Students' Association of the U.S. and Canada (MSA), a group whose modernist leanings were destined to bring it into conflict with the Tablīgh movement. For almost four years Colonel Amīrud Dīn and his followers were tolerated because at the time they were the only group who effectively used the mosque on a regular basis, and for practical purposes Colonel Amīrud Dīn was already functioning as a full-time *imām*.

A) *Jāmiʿ Mosque as a Tablīgh Centre*: While Colonel Amīrud Dīn functioned as the *imām* of Jāmiʿ Mosque the Tablīghī Jamāʿat intensified the use of the mosque. Tablīgh work in Toronto's burgeoning Muslim community became more extensive. Weekly *gasht* activities and Saturday night *ijtimāʿ*s were centered there. Tablīghī jamāʿats coming from abroad and from elsewhere in Canada and the U.S. began to use the Jāmiʿ Mosque as a hostel. Almost weekly some *jamāʿat* would stay overnight there. Large *ijtimāʿ*s of several hundred individuals began to be held at the mosque once or twice a year. It was the visiting *jamāʿats* and the convening of these large *ijtimāʿ*s that led to expression of the once-latent frictions between the mosque administration and the Tablīgh movement. Colonel Amīrud Dīn was ousted and Tablīghī use of the mosque severely curtailed. Use of the mosque as a hostel was virtually eliminated, and only the Saturday night *ijtimāʿ* was allowed to continue.

B) *Madīna Mosque as a Tablīgh Centre*: The loss of Jāmiʿ Mosque as an effective Tablīgh center was offset by the development of a large and stable community in Toronto loyal to the Tablīghī Jamāʿat. This was more the result of immigration patterns than of local Tablīgh initiatives. Immigration to Toronto throughout the 1970s brought large numbers of Gujrātī Muslims, who brought with them their well-known and intense loyalty to the Tablīgh movement. This community provided the basis for establishing new Islamic institutions whose entire design and purpose was oriented toward facilitating Tablīgh activity. In 1974 a large hall was leased in Toronto's East End and converted into a mosque. By the time the lease expired in 1981, enough money had been raised, mainly in the Gujrātī Muslim community, to purchase a large new center which became the Madina Mosque. This mosque has ever since been the real center of Tablīgh activity in Toronto. The Tablīgh leadership attempted to maintain some footing in Jāmiʿ Mosque, and persisted in holding its Saturday *ijtimāʿ*s there until 1987. By the mid-1980s there were open tensions between the pro-Tablīgh community centered at Madina Mosque and the pro-MSA (Muslim Students Association) community at Jāmiʿ Mosque due to ethnic and ideological differences. The Tablīgh community was dominated by Indians and Pakistanis and maintained a more "traditional" outlook on Islamic expression. The MSA community was ethnically more mixed and composed largely of middle-class professionals and academics who were concerned to blend a puritanical version of Islam with the forms of a modern society. This divergence of outlooks led to a heightened sense of competition between the two groups. Inevitably this led in turn to personal conflicts and tensions which forced the cessation of all Tablīgh activities at Jāmiʿ Mosque and the consolidation of these at Madīna Mosque.

The Pattern of Tablīgh Work and Administration

Following the pattern of Tablīgh activities everywhere, their work in Metropolitan Toronto tenaciously adheres to the model established by Mawlānā Ilyās, centered first at Jāmiʿ Mosque then later at Madīna Mosque.

One-day weekly *gasht* rounds are conducted. The problem of finding Muslim homes in a city where they are widely scattered is circumvented by techniques which include finding Muslim names in telephone directories or apartment building listings, establishing contact with Muslims in mosques and Friday prayer gatherings, and basic networking.

Weekly *ijtimāʿ*s or *mashwara* bring together workers and recruits on Saturday nights, where weekend *jamāʿats* are organized to travel to neighbouring towns and cities once a month, and where *jamāʿats* of longer duration, sometimes of several months, are organized for travels to farther destinations. These are often coordinated to allow participation in large national, continental, and international *ijtimāʿ*s around the world. *Jamāʿats* from Canada have been known to travel to destinations in the U.S., the Caribbean, South America, Europe, and frequently to the Indian subcontinent. Everyone travels at his own expense, although some locally arranged financial support is sometimes available. *Jamāʿats* coming into Toronto are received almost on a weekly basis from other centers in Canada and the U.S., and on a less regular basis from international centers. *Jamāʿats* come from Tablīgh centers everywhere, although the greater number tend to come from India and Pakistan.

Organization of large regional and international *ijtimāʿs* and planning involvement in them has emerged as a major activity. In recent years a large Christmas-time *ijtimāʿ* has been convened in the Toronto area on an annual basis. It is held in fairgrounds and arenas and has been attracting several thousand participants. The Toronto Tablīgh community has sent hundreds of participants to international *ijtimāʿ*s in North American locations. The last two, held in the vicinity of Detroit in 1980 and 1985, attracted as many as ten thousand participants, and were far and away the largest gatherings of Muslims in North American history. In all these *ijtimāʿ*s, whatever their size, the pattern of activity is always the same: the day is devoted to congregational prayer, devotions and readings, and frequent lectures on religious subjects confined to the realm of personal religious practice and belief. Political and social subjects are strictly taboo.

Tablīgh Administration in Toronto

As the Toronto Muslim community has expanded so too has Tablīghī Jamāʿat's administration there. A local committee of seven members was established in the early 1970s. An *amīr* was appointed from amongst them, and this individual functioned as such until his death a few years ago. Since then the position of *amīr* has rotated among the expanded committee, which currently has thirteen members. Committee members are loosely accountable to seniors in the Tablīgh centers in India and Pakistan, and often travel there as leaders of *Jamāʿat* groups. They plan and administer local activities. All members of the committee are volunteers; none is paid for their work or expenses.

The enormous growth and dispersal of the Muslim community throughout the Metropolis and surrounding areas has necessitated a further development of local administration of Tablīgh activities. In recent years Metropolitan Toronto has been divided into four administrative zones for which local *ḥalaqa*s (circles) are organized and entrusted to a local *amīr*. The *ḥalaqas* are charged with performing local weekly *gasht* centered at some local Mosque or religious facility, and they meet on a regular basis. All four *ḥalaqas* in the Toronto area participate in the weekly *mashwara* or *ijtimāʿ* held at Madīna Mosque every Saturday night, and they are loosely accountable to the central Tablīgh leaders. These Saturday night gatherings bring together some two hundred core Tablīgh workers and new recruits.

The *amīr* of the Toronto Tablīgh committee is also involved in the North America *shūrā* committee, which coordinates activities across the continent. The travelling of *jamāʿats* within North America and to Tablīgh centers in India and Pakistan facilitates communication with this committee, supplemented by ample use of telephone and mail contacts.

Resistance to Bureaucratic Organization

The Tablīghī Jamāʿat has more or less been able to carry over successfully its characteristic methodology and manner of administration to the context of the Muslim community of Toronto, and indeed of North America. It has not yet made concessions to bureaucratic organizational patterns characteristic of North American social and political structures, as has almost every other major Islamic movement or organization. A clear reflection of this is that the Tablīghī Jamāʿat has no legal presence in North America—no corporate entity, no corporate headquarters, no executive, no treasury, no paid staff, and no newspaper or official newsletter. It is administered by highly dedicated volunteers organized in hierarchical fashion and loyal to the central leadership in India. This has proven effective for coordinating the movement's activities across not only North America but also much of the world.

By remaining true to the simple system of person-to-person contact and the regular travel of groups, the Tablīghī Jamāʿat has developed cadres of devoted volunteers who are able to communicate effectively with one another across the vast spaces of North America. They are able to reach and motivate thousands of Muslims to participate in Tablīgh activities. In terms of numbers and degree of commitment, it is unlikely that any competing Islamic organization in North America can claim equal success.

Institutional Development

The Tablīghī Jamāʿat in Toronto has played a critical role in helping to develop community religious institutions. While these are characteristically supportive of Tablīgh activity, and reflective of its style of Islamic expression, they are not in any official way possessions of the Tablīghī Jamāʿat, for, as noted above, the Tablīghī Jamāʿat maintains no corporate presence in North America.

The establishment of religious institutions loyal to the Tablīghī Jamāʿat in Metropolitan Toronto followed the formation of the Madina Mosque and assured the customary Tablīghī pattern of development. Typically, local community groups sprang up around individuals loyal to or directly involved in Tablīgh activity. These groups came to establish neighbourhood *madrasas* and mosques in facilities rented or borrowed from community centers, schools, apartment building complexes, or commercial units. When these temporary facilities became too small for the local community's needs, fund-raising efforts purchased permanent mosque facilities. Masjid Nūr, founded in 1987 in the northwest side of Toronto, and Masjid Abū Bakr al-Ṣiddīq established in the Toronto suburb of Scarborough in 1992, have both followed this pattern. Two other groups at an earlier stage of development have been established in another corner of Metropolitan Toronto. Within the smaller concentration of Muslims found in smaller towns in southern Ontario, Tablīgh activity has been similarly instrumental in motivating locals to work towards the establishment of local mosques—mosques loyal to the Tablīgh movement have sprung up in at least seven smaller cities within a 200-kilometer radius of Toronto. These include Oshawa, Barrie, Sarnia, Hamilton, Brantford, Cambridge, and Kitchener-Waterloo.

It should also be noted that the Tablīgh institutions referred to above are clearly the most active of all Islamic institutions in the Muslim communities where they are located. Tablīgh activities have not only helped to establish Islamic institutions but have been much more successful than any other group in motivating large numbers of families to actually use them. The three existing mosques loyal to the Tablīgh movement are the only ones in Toronto which have generated communities of devoted persons around them. Consequently, they alone, of the more than ten mosques in the Metropolitan region, are used as something more than weekend drive-in facilities. For example, the Tablīgh-related mosques are the only ones in the city which offer daily after-secular-school *madrasas* for children, and they alone offer regular, well-attended five ritual prayers of the day. The regular use of these facilities for Tablīgh activities uniquely insures an atmosphere of constant Islamic activity.

Development of Boarding Madrasas

Further recent additions to Tablīgh-related institutions have been the formation of three full-time boarding *madrasas*. The first of these was the Al-Rāshid Islamic Institute, established in 1987 at Cornwall, Ontario, a town situated 100 kilometers from Ottawa. The second was Dārul ʿUlūm al-Madaniyya, founded in 1991 at East Aurora, New York, a suburb of Buffalo about 100 kilometers from Toronto. The third and last was the Ajax Islamic Madrasa founded also in 1991 at Ajax, a town just outside of Toronto. The two latter institutions, closer to Toronto, are filled to capacity and are fast expanding.

All three *madrasas* are patterned on those typical of the Indian subcontinent. Their programs are centered on the memorization of the Qurʾān and training in basic Islamic religious subjects. Instructors are from the Indian subcontinent and usually have only a rudimentary knowledge of English; instruction is largely offered in Urdu. Most students come from the Indian-Pakistani Muslim communities of Toronto and Montreal.

The development of all three *madrasas* followed a typical pattern. All resulted from personal effort by individuals from the extended Tablīghī Jamāʿat community. The story of the foundation of the al-Rāshid Islamic Institute will illustrate. It was founded through the efforts of Mawlānā Maẓhar ʿĀlam, its present principal, who came to Canada on the direct instructions of Mawlānā Zakariyyā. Mawlānā Maẓhar ʿĀlam was told to come to Canada and establish a religious institute, which, with enormous personal effort, he did. He arrived in Canada in the mid-1980s not knowing anyone here, and neither English nor French; he had not even made the proper immigration arrangements. Despite being arrested upon arrival, he persisted, working with single-minded determination to raise and borrow funds to establish the Institute, primarily in the Tablīgh-related Muslim communities of Toronto and Montreal.

The Role of the Tablīghī Jamāʿat

The Tablīghī Jamāʿat has spurred religious institutional development in two ways; both by direct intervention in the community through the introduction of motivated individuals from abroad, and by helping to develop motivated individuals from within the local community who then work to establish these facilities. Tablīgh activity has probably also been instrumental in creating and sustaining a community of Muslims who will use the facilities on a daily basis. In addition, it has provided a communication network through which people from various Muslim communities can work together to establish more specialized religious institutions such as the Al-Rāshid Islamic Institute and the other *madrasas*. The Tablīgh-related network of religious institutions in Toronto is clearly more extensive and actively used than any other in the Muslim community there.

The Make-up of the Tablīgh Community

A cursory look at the Tablīgh movement in the Toronto area reveals that its activists and supporters are mainly of Indian descent, coming directly from India or Pakistan or from the various Indian diaspora communities around the world, particularly in the Caribbean, Guyana, South Africa, and Europe. The Tablīgh call is made to all Muslims in the community, but as far as Toronto is concerned, it has been overwhelmingly the community of Indo-Pakistani origin which has responded. Moreover, while Muslims of all educational and class backgrounds are involved in Tablīgh activities, Muslim labourers and merchants make-up the bulk of devotees.

Barriers to Involvement

Most Muslims from non-Indian backgrounds who have participated in Tablīgh activity have done so, it seems, only temporarily. They give several reasons why the work was not for them, even though most express their admiration for the Tablīghī Jamāʿat. One reason cited was the heavy overlay of Indian Muslim cultural practices that characterizes the movement. Reference was made to barriers perceived in the manner of attire, food, and language. That the Friday prayers are said only in Arabic, with only Urdu translation provided before the *khuṭba* (sermon), was frequently mentioned as irritating. Many cited what they perceived to be a narrowness and rigidity in the Tablīgh message. After an initial contact and involvement with the Tablīgh Movement many were not inspired to further engagement.

Similar barriers prevent most acculturated first- and second-generation Muslim youths from participating in Tablīgh activities. The highly motivated Tablīgh devotee involves his children extensively in the movement's various educational offerings, but many peripheral supporters find their acculturated sons uninterested. The movement has been unable to sustain any presence among Muslim students at university and college campuses in Toronto. A few Tablīghī leaders have sensed a threat to the movement's grip on future generations. They have tried to find English-speaking teachers for younger people, and efforts have recently been made to establish recreational opportunities to attract Muslim youth. Such efforts are few and isolated, however, and most Tablīgh leaders appear oblivious to this threat to their future.

Sources of Internal Friction

While the Tablīgh community is mostly composed of people of Indo-Pakistani descent, this does not mean the Tablīgh community is completely uniform. Within the broad ethnic category of "Indian ancestry" are a multitude of smaller ethnic and linguistic groupings. Internal sources of conflict within the Tablīghī Jamāʿat typically stem from either friction between these subdivisions or from competition between individual religious scholars and leaders. Both have affected Tablīghī Jamāʿat in Toronto. The Madīna Mosque, for example, is dominated by the Gujrātī ethnolinguistic subdivision, and while Muslims from other communities are welcome to participate in Mosque activities, positions on the mosque's board of directors are reserved for the Gujrātī-Muslim community. Individual jockeying for position and influence has sometimes complicated relations between religious leaders and teachers of the various existing institutions.

Cohesion of Community and Leadership Roles

While some internal frictions can be discerned, the Tablīgh community nonetheless enjoys a degree of cohesion and commitment unmatched by any other group within the Muslim community. While other Islamic groups often draw larger gatherings for ʿĪd prayers than do the Tablīgh-related institutions, none can rely upon the commitment of their followers as much as the Tablīghī Jamāʿat can. As noted earlier, this is reflected in the network of active institutions that the Tablīghī Jamāʿat has generated, and by the rudiments of a Muslim "ghetto" that it has inspired.

This cohesion and inordinate activity have brought the Tablīghī Jamāʿat influence in the affairs of the Muslim community quite disproportionate to its membership. Tablīgh-related institutions are looked to by a multitude of smaller mosques and religious groups for religious guidance. The Madina Mosque, for example, leads one of the two major factions which have been developed around the issue of sighting of the moon (*hilāl*) for Ramaḍān and ʿĪd. Their *hilāl* committee is perhaps the more influential of the two.

The Response to Challenges

As noted earlier, the Tablīghī Jamāʿat, like other Islamic movements in contexts similar to Toronto, faces two longterm challenges to its survival and success. The Tablīgh Movement's response to each of these will be discussed in turn.

The Challenge of Cohesion

We have identified this as an internal challenge to Muslim community cohesion. Muslim immigrant communities in many Western contexts are enormously diverse, and thus have difficulty in maintaining a cohesiveness which transcends their range of parochialisms. The Muslim community of Metropolitan Toronto is a somewhat exaggerated example of this type of fractious diversity. Islamic movements that claim transethnic relevance need to generate a supporting community which is large and cohesive enough to survive the challenge posed by an assimilationist modern liberal society.

The Tablīghī Jamāʿat would like to resolve the challenge of Muslim community cohesion by establishing a community of Muslims loyal to its unique message, which combines fundamentalist and traditionalist tendencies. However, in Toronto, ethnicity, which has been the movement's greatest strength, has emerged also as its greatest weakness. The Tablīghī Jamāʿat has become perhaps the major Islamic Movement in Toronto's Muslim community by riding the wave of Indo-Pakistani immigration. Being attached to this major ethnic subdivision, they were able to forge a sizable community whose degree of cohesion was unmatched. It was this cohesion which allowed the Tablīghī Jamāʿat to enter into the area with such force. To a large degree, it was this cohesion which allowed them to take a leadership role in the larger Muslim community, and to develop their extensive network of religious institutions.

However, the prominent role played by ethnicity and immigration in the Tablīghī Jamāʿat's development in Toronto has also, it seems, acted as a barrier to the involvement of Muslims from other backgrounds. The movement, while affirming a nonethnic Islamic message, has had difficulty in conveying this message beyond the boundaries established by a broadly defined Indo-Pakistani ethnicity. This is partly because of its own ethnic coating.

Moreover, the Tablīghī Jamāʿat is beginning to exhibit difficulties in accommodating major elements of the post-immigration generation who have become acculturated to Canadian ways. If the Islam presented to these youth is a parochial, Indian Islam, it will cease to be relevant to them once they lose their attachment to Indian ethnicity. Hence, the ethnic element in Tablīghī Jamāʿat's religious message poses a double threat to its survival in Toronto. It has severely reduced the Jamāʿat's relevance for Muslims of other ethnic backgrounds, and shows signs of doing the same for the coming generation of acculturated youth.

The Challenge of Modernity

The second challenge facing Islamic movements in Muslim minority contexts in the West is that of modernity. Modernity at all levels challenges traditional and totalistic conceptions of religion, and insists on the fragmentation of tradition and the secularization of religion. Muslim minority communities living in the West face the external challenge of an overwhelming modern society whose effect is unambiguously corrosive to totalistic religious belief and practice. These Islamic movements face the constant danger of succumbing to these forces and losing their Islamic integrity, or of upholding Islamic norms at the cost of social and political ostracism from mainstream secular society.

Of all major Islamic movements in Toronto, the Tablīghī Jamāʿat alone accepts the prospect of political and social ostracism. The others have to varying degrees been willing to integrate themselves with mainstream society and to accept the modernist consequences of a liberalized and secularized Islam. This is clearly reflected in the willingness of these groups to accept the notions of multiculturalism promoted by the Canadian state. These are firmly imbedded in a liberal framework, and are employed by these groups to redefine the Muslim community and its future role in Canadian society. Virtually every major group in Metropolitan Toronto, save those related to the Tablīghī Jamāʿat, promote multiculturalism, and toward that end involve non-Muslim public figures in their social and religious gatherings. The Tablīghī Jamāʿat has been almost unique in the Muslim community for inspiring in its followers isolationist attitudes which run against the grain of multicultural notions. This is reflected in that it alone, of all the major Islamic groupings in the Toronto area, has been able to inspire the formation of the rudiments of Muslim ghettos. This is problematic given the nature of Toronto's residential patterns and real estate costs.

The Tablīgh community's isolationist tendency is related to the Tablīghī Jamāʿat's "traditional" vision of Islam, which inspires a deep distrust and hostility toward modern society and ways. The Tablīghī Jamāʿat's rejection of modernity was never direct. Mawlānā Ilyās' movement did not arise as a reaction to the corrosive affects of modernity, but more as a reaction to a perceived decay within the Muslim tradition itself. Consequently, since its foundation Tablīghī Jamāʿat's tendency has been to ignore modernity rather than react to it or directly confront it. The primary concern has been for reform of the religious practice of the masses. This led the movement to formulate its message along moralist lines, and did not necessitate an ideological or intellectual rebuttal of the modern threat. Moreover, it also did not require a direct concern for social and political matters which, in accordance with Mawlānā Ilyās' conception of Islam, was de-emphasized. As a result, the Tablīghī Jamāʿat did not articulate an Islamic conception of society and politics. While these two omissions perhaps did not seriously undermine the Tablīghī Jamāʿat's work in the context of the untempered Muslim masses of mid-twentieth century India, they have more serious consequences in the context of modern Canada. The Tablīghī Jamāʿat is intellectually ill-equipped to realize the nature of the threat posed by modernity, let alone articulate an Islamic alternative which is satisfying to minds whose daily activities attune them to secular and liberal conceptions. The Tablīghī Jamāʿat calls upon Muslims living in modern contexts to live their lives in accordance with traditional Islamic teachings, without being able to explain why in the nonmoralist language that the modernized mentality demands.

The challenge of modernity is one that the Tablīghī Jamāʿat handles not by arming its followers intellectually and ideologically, but rather by isolating them from its effects. In the Muslim ghettos of England this strategy might work in retaining the younger generation, but in contexts such as Metropolitan Toronto, where ghettoisation has many barriers, the strategy is unlikely to succeed.

Conclusion

The Tablīghī Jamāʿat has been unusually durable when transplanted beyond its initial domain. Its characteristic message and method have proved relevant to the situation of Muslim communities in many contexts around the world. However, like all movements, the limitations of the initial substantive and formal characteristics of the Tablīghī Jamāʿat may have been exposed during its transportation through time and space. These limitations have perhaps never been so apparent as during its recent expansion into North America.

While the rise of the Tablīghī Jamā'at in North America has been impressive, the situation in Toronto suggests that this success has been more imported than indigenously developed. The movement's phenomenal rise in this city has been closely tied to an equally phenomenal rise in Muslim immigration from Tablīgh strongholds around the world. Limitations inherited from the Tablīghī Jamā'at's foundation in India have retarded efforts to attract a Muslim community-wide following, and retain the next generation of acculturated Muslim youth. The inability of the Tablīgh movement to transcend its Indian ethnic roots has been most obvious, but potentially more damaging in the long run have been the intellectual limitations evident in Mawlānā Ilyās' conceptualization of Islam, and the challenges modernity, in all its dimensions, poses to it.

It is hasty to predict that Tablīghī Jamā'at will become nothing more than an immigrant movement, destined to wither with the passing generations. It can be safely said that the movement will not survive in twenty-first century North America as a movement with the same substantial and formal qualities that Mawlānā Ilyās established to suit the conditions of mid-twentieth century India. North America will increasingly challenge the Tablīghī Jamā'at's characteristic message and methodology. While Tablīgh leaders so far have been able to ignore these challenges they cannot continue to do so for long.

Appendix

(1) *A Movement or a Jamā'at?*

It is important to emphasize that in its conception the Tablīghī Jamā'at was seen as a "movement" or "work" but not as a separate *jamā'at* or faction in the Muslim *Umma.* Mawlānā Muḥammad Yūsuf (for his speech see the appendix to chapter one of this volume) once said:

> We have no party, no formal type of organization, no office, no register and no funds. Our work is to be shared by all Muslims. That's why, according to the times, we have not formed our people into a separate *jamā'at.* We are just working on the pattern of the mosques . . . (Khān 1986, 41)

The idea was that Tablīgh work would flourish in all Muslim communities to reinforce Islam without prejudice to existing *jamā'ats* (in the more proper Islamic sense of 'formal congregations') or mosques. While this may have been the initial conception, it is clear that the idea was unfeasible. Tablīgh work was aimed at fostering a certain approach to Islam, that of

Mawlānā Ilyās, with specific doctrinal and ritual teachings which were not universally accepted in the wider Muslim community. Other *jamāʿats* representing alternate doctrinal viewpoints and ritual norms saw the Tablīgh movement not as a neutrally inspiring Islamic religious practice but as a missionary competitor. Consequently, the Tablīgh movement, which already had some of the trappings of a separate *jamāʿat*, in the form of a distinct hierarchic leadership centered in Bastī Niẓāmuddīn, found it necessary to develop a network of separate and distinct institutions to facilitate Tablīgh work. This work led to the development of virtually all the trappings of a *jamāʿat*, and outsiders naturally came to identify the Tablīgh movement as the Tablīghī Jamāʿat. Tablīgh people, however, continued to see it as a pan-Islamic movement and not as a separate *jamāʿat*. As a result, the Tablīghī Jamāʿat never directly controlled facilities under a corporate name (for a different manifestation see Dassetto, Kepel, and Tozy, this volume), but rather came to develop and control facilities under the name of like-minded individuals and groups. Nevertheless, while the Tablīghī Jamāʿat does not itself possess any institution or facility in the letter of the law, its facilities are distinct and well known to the community as Tablīgh centers. Despite apparently sincere efforts to the contrary, the Tablīgh Movement has indeed emerged as a *jamāʿat*.

(2) *Tablīgh Facilities*

Tablīgh activity created the need for a network of facilities wherever the movement went. Following a typical pattern, the movement came to establish a Tablīgh center (*markaz*) in places owned and operated by local interests. Many of these were existing mosques which were receptive to Tablīgh activity, or newly established facilities specially built for the purpose. These centres invariably established simple facilities to host large travelling groups. Each centre establishes weekly *ijtimāʿ*s, sometimes known as *mashwaras*, to facilitate local Tablīgh activity. The practice of establishing larger regional *ijtimāʿ*s, inaugurated by Mawlānā Ilyās in 1941 in Mēwāt, has since become a regular staple of Tablīgh activity everywhere and has created the need for larger Tablīgh centres in some places. The largest of these was established in Raiwind just outside of Lahore in Pakistan. It can accommodate over a million people under makeshift arrangements, and has done so many times in recent years during large annual Tablīgh *ijtimāʿ*s. The largest Islamic religious facility in the West is undoubtedly the Dewsbury Tablīgh Center in England. It contains the largest mosque in the West, facilities for large *ijtimāʿs*, and a *madrasa* which instructs over 500 boys, gathered from many Western countries, in the memorization of Qurʾān and religious studies (see Faust, this volume).

SELECT BIBLIOGRAPHY

'Abdul Ḥalīm. N.d. *Ḥaḍrat Jī kī Yādgār Taqrīrēn.* New Delhi: Idāra Ishā'at Dīniyāt.

'Abdul Ḥayy, Chaudhrī. "The Freedom Movement in Mēwāt and Dr. K.M. Ashraf." In Kruger (ed.) 1966.

'Abdur Raḥīm. 1968. *Uṣūl-i Da'wat wa Tablīgh.* Delhi: Al-Jam'iyyat Press.

'Abdush Shakūr. 1919. *Tārīkh Mēwāt.* Delhi.

Abū Da'ūd. 1989. *Sunan.* Riyāḍ: Maktab al-Tarbiyyat al-'Arabī li duwal al-khalīj.

Abū Labān, B. 1983. "The Canadian Muslim Community: The Need for a New Survival Strategy." In Waugh and Qureshi (eds.) 1983, 75–90.

Aggarwal, Partap C. 1978. "Rajesthan." In Richard Weeks (ed.) *Muslim People—A World Ethnographic Survey.* Westport (Connecticut): Greenwood. p. 338.

—— 1971. *Caste, Religion and Power: An Indian Case Study.* New Delhi: Shri Ram Centre for Industrial Relations.

Āghā, Mansoor. 1995. "Mawlanā In'āmul Ḥasan." *Muslim and Arab Perspectives* 28 (10):135–141.

Aguer, Béatriz. 1991. "Résurgence de l'Islam en Espagne." *Revue Européenne des Migrations Internationales* 7(3):59–75.

Agwani, M.S. 1986. *Islamic Fundamentalism in India.* Chandigarh: Twenty-First Century India Society.

Aḥmad, 'Abdul Jabbār. 1965. *Sharḥul Uṣūlil Khamsa.* Cairo: Maktaba Wahba.

Aḥmad, Imtiaz. 1979. "Orthodox in Indic Islam: A Comment." *Islam and the Modern Age* 10(3):88–94.

—— 1990. "Mosques, Mobility and Mobilization." *Daily The Statesman.* Delhi. March 25.

Aḥmad, Mumtāz. 1986. "Tablīghī Jamā'at of Pakistan Subcontinent: An Interpretation." Paper presented at the International Seminar on Islamic History, Art and Culture in South Asia. 26–28 March, Islamabad, Pakistan.

—— 1991a. "Islamic Fundamentalism in South Asia: The Jamā'at-Islāmī and the Tablīghī Jamā'at of South Asia." In Martin E. Marty and R. Scott Appleby (eds.), *Fundamentalisms Observed. The Fundamentalism Project* 1:457–530. Chicago: University of Chicago Press.

—— 1991b. "The Politics of War: Islamic Fundamentalisms in Pakistan." In James Piscatori (ed.). *Islamic Fundamentalisms and the Gulf Crisis.* Chicago: University of Chicago Press. Pp. 155–185.

—— 1995. "Tablīghī Jamā'at." In Esposito (ed.) *The Oxford Encyclopedia of the Modern Islamic World* 4:165–169. New York: Oxford University Press.

Aḥmad, Sarfarāz. 1993. "Tablīghī Jamā'at, Ēk Jā'iza." *Ishrāq* 5(11):33–36.

Ahmed, Anis (translator). N.d. *The Teachings of Islam.* English Translation of *Tablīghī Niṣāb.* New Delhi: Idāra Ishā'at Dīniyāt.

Akbarābādī, Mawlānā Sa'īd Aḥmad. 1971. "Islam in India Today." In Lokhandwala (ed.), 1971. 335–339.

'Alī, Hāshim Amīr. 1970. *The Meos of Mēwāt: The Old Neighbors of New Delhi.* New Delhi: Oxford University Press.

'Alī, Mawlawī Murād. 1886. *Jāmi'ul Fatāwā.* Ajmēr.

Alwarī, Muḥammad 'Abdul Ghafūr. 1979. *Tablīghī Jamā'at kā Ṣaḥīḥ Rukh.* Qaṣūr: Faqīr Muḥammad.

'Alwī, Sa'īdur Raḥmān. 1989. "Chār Din Rab kē Ḥuḍūr." Weekly *Nidā* 3(21):27–29.

Amer, M. 1999. "Transnational Religion: A Case of Tablīghī Jamā'at." M.A. Thesis. Faculty of Political Science, University of Amsterdam, Amsterdam, The Netherlands.

al-Āmidī, Sayfud Dīn. 1914. *Al-Iḥkām fī Uṣūlil Aḥkām*. Cairo: Ma'ārif.
Anderson, Benedict. 1991. *Imagined Communities: Reflections on the Origin and Spread of Nationalism*. Second Edition. London & New York: Verso.
Anṣārī, Muḥammad 'Abdul Ḥaq. 1986. *Sufism and Sharī'ah: A Study of Shaykh Aḥmad Sarhandī's Efforts to Reform Sufism*. London: Islamic Foundation.
Anṣārī, Ṣadruddīn 'Āmir. N.d. *Al-Shaykh Muḥammad Ilyās wad da'watul Dīniyya*. New Delhi: Idāra Ishā'at Dīniyat Ḥaḍrat Niẓāmuddīn.
—— 1967. *Six Points of Tabligh*. Delhi: Anjuman Taraqqī Urdu.
Anwar, Zainah. 1987. *Islamic Revivalism in Malaysia—Dakwa among the Students*. Petalang Jaya: Pelanduk Publications.
Arnold, Thomas. 1958 (originally 1908–1926). "Mission (Muḥammadan)." In J. Hastings (ed.). *Encyclopedia of Religion and Ethics* 8:745–749. Edinburgh: Clarke.
—— 1965 (originally 1924). *The Caliphate*. London: Routledge.
—— 1968. *Preaching of Islam, a History of the Propagation of the Muslim Faith*. Lahore: Sh. M. Ashraf. Orig. London, 1893, 1896.
Arqam. 1988. *Muslim News* 2:90.
Aslam, Muḥammad. 1976. "Jamā'atut tablīgh, 'aqīdatuhā wa afkāru mashā'ikhihā." Unpublished thesis. Madina, Saudi Arabia: Jāmi'a Islāmiyya.
Aslam, Shaykh. 1977. *Tablīgh wa Tarbiyyat-e-din kē Pānch Uṣūl*. Bhai Pheru.
'Awda, 'Abdul Qādir. 1959. *al-Tashrī'ul jinā'ī al-Islāmī*. Cairo: Dārul 'Arūba.
'Azmī, S.H. 1989. "An Analysis of Religious Divisions in the Muslim Community of Toronto." *Al-Basirah: Bulletin of Islam and Islamic Social Sciences* 1(1):2–9.
Bade, Klaus. 1994. *Ausländer, Aussiedler, Asyl in der Bundesrepublik Deutschland*. Bonn: Beck.
al-Baghdādī, 'Abdul Qādir. 1928. *Uṣūlud Dīn*. Istānbūl: Maṭba'ul Dawla.
Ballard, Roger. 1994. "Introduction: The Emergence of Desh Pardesh." In Ballard (1994) pp. 1–35.
—— (ed.). 1994. *Desh Pardesh, The South Asian Presence in Britain*. London: Hurst.
al-Bayhaqī, Abū Bakr Aḥmad b. al-Ḥusayn. N.d. *al-I'tiqād 'alā madhāhibis salaf ahlis Sunna wa'l-Jamā'a*. Faysalabad: Ḥadīth Academy.
Bennabi, Malik. 1988. *Islam in History and Society*. Islamabad: Islamic Research Institute.
Bijnawrī, Mawlānā Muftī 'Azīzur Raḥmān. 1958. *Tadhkira Mashā'ikh Deoband*. Bijnawr: Madīna Press.
Bijnawrī, 'Azizur Raḥmān. 1980. *Tadhkira Amīr Tablīgh, Mawlānā Muḥammad Yūsuf Dihlawī*. Bhēra (Sargodha): Dhun Nūrayn Akādemī.
Bijnawri, Muftī 'Azizur Raḥmān. N.d. *Sawāniḥ Haḍrat Jī*. Bijnawr: Idāra Madnī Dārul Tālīf.
Binswanger, Karl. 1990. "Islamischer Fundamentalismus in der Bundesrepublik, Entwicklung-Bestandsaufnahme-Ausblick." In Nirumand (ed.), 1990:38–54.
Blunt, S.W. 1882. *Future of Islam*. Lahore: Sind Sagar (reprint).
Brockelmann, Carl. 1943. *Geschichte der arabischen Litteratur, (GAL)*. Leiden: Brill.
Brown, Seyom. 1974. *New Forces in World Politics*. Washington: Brookings Institution.
Brubaker, Rogers. 1992. *Citizenship and Nationhood in France and Germany*. Cambridge: Cambridge University Press.
Bulandshahrī, Muḥammad 'Āshiq Ilāhī. N.d.a. *Ākhirat kē Fikrmandōn kē Pachās Qiṣṣē*. New Delhi: Idāra Ishā'atul 'ulūm.
—— N.d.b. *Chhe Bātēn*. New Delhi: Idāra Ishā'at Dīniyāt Ḥaḍrat Niẓāmuddīn.
—— N.d.c. *Ikrāmul Muslimīn*. New Delhi: Idāra Ishā'at Dīniyāt Ḥaḍrat Niẓāmuddīn.
—— N.d.d. *Marnē kē Ba'd Kiyā Hōgā*. New Delhi: Idāra Ishā'at-Dīniyāt Ḥaḍrat Niẓāmuddīn.
Bulliet, Richard W. 1979. *Conversion to Islam in the Medieval Period: An Essay in Quantitative History*. Cambridge, MA: Harvard University Press.
Çakır, Ruşen. 1990. *Ayet ve slogan. Türkiye'de islami oluşumlar*. Istanbul: Metis Yayinlari.
Canard, M. 1965. "Da'wa." In C.E. Bosworth (ed.), *The Encyclopedia of Islam*, New Edition 2:168–170. Leiden: Brill.

Carré, O. and Dumont, Paul (eds.) 1986. *Radicalismes Islamiques*. Paris: L'Harmattan.
Chakrawarti, Atulananda. 1934. *Cultural Fellowship in India*. Calcutta: Thacker, Sprink and Co.
Chatterjee, Partha. 1989. "Colonialism, Nationalism and Colonized Women: The Contest in India." *American Ethnologist* 16(4):622–33.
Cilliers, Jacobus Lodewicus. 1983. "Die Tabligh-Beweging en sy Invloed op die Islam in Suid Afrika." Unpublished M. Th. thesis. Department of Missiology, University of the Western Cape, South Africa.
Crooke, William. 1906. *The Castes and Tribes of the North Western Provinces and Oudh*. Calcutta: Office of the Superintendent of the Government Printing Press.
Crozier, M. and Friedberg, E. 1977. *L'acteur et le système*. Paris: Seuil.
Ḍarīf, Muḥammad. 1993. *Al-islāmus siyāsī fī l-maghrib muqāraba wathā'iqiyya*. Casablanca: Al-majallatul maghribiyya li ʿilmil ijtimāʿis siyāsī.
Dassetto, Felice. 1988. "The Tablīgh Organization in Belgium." In Gerholm and Litham (eds.), 1988:59–173.
—— 1994. "L'Islam transplanté: bilan des recherches européennes." *Revue Européenne des Migrations Internationales* 10(2):201–211.
Dassetto, Felice and Bastenier, A. 1984. *L'Islam transplaté: Vie et organisation des minorités musulmanes de Belgique*. Anvers/Bruxelles: EPO/EVO.
—— 1987. *Une manifestation islamique à Bruxelles*. CIACO: Louvain La Neuve.
Denny, Frederick M. 1987. "Daʿwa." In M. Eliade (ed.), *The Encyclopedia of Religion* 4:244–45. New York: MacMillan.
Desroche, H. 1995. "Autour de la sociologie dite des sectes" (book review). *Année Sociologique* 395.
Devji, Faisal Fatehali. 1991. "Gender and the Politics of Space: The Movement for Women's Reform in Muslim India." *South Asia* 14(1):141–154.
Dhaouadi, Z. 1983. "La da'wa: les mots du ciel pour les années de braise." *Peuples Méditerranéens* 25:157.
Diop, Moustapha A. 1994. "Structuration d'un réseau: la Jamāʿat Tablīgh (Société pour la Propagation de la Foi)." *Revue Européenne des Migrations Internationales* 10(1):145–155.
Eickelman, Dale F. 1978. "The Art of Memory: Islamic Education and its Sociological Reproduction." *Comparative Studies in Society and History* 20(4):485–516.
Eickelman, Dale F. and Piscatori, James (eds.). 1990a. *Muslim Travelers: Pilgrimage, Migration, and the Religious Imagination*. London: Routledge.
—— 1990b. "Social Theory in the Study of Muslim Societies." In Eickelman and Piscatori (eds.) 1990:3–25.
Esposito, J.L. (ed.), 1955. *Oxford Encyclopedia of The Modern Islamic World*. New York, Oxford University Press.
Etienne, B. and Tozy, M. 1981. "Le glissement des obligations islamiques vers le phénomène associatif à Casablanca." In C. Souriau (ed.), *Le Maghreb musulman en 1979*. Paris: CNRS. Pp. 261–284.
Etzioni, A. 1971. *Les organisations modernes*. Gembloux: Duculot.
Fabian, Johannes. 1991 [1989]. *Language and Colonial Power: The Appropriation of Swahili in the Former Belgian Congo, 1880–1938*. Berkeley: University of California Press.
Falāḥī, ʿUbaydullāh Fahd. 1987. *Tārīkh Daʿwat wa Jihād: Barr i Ṣaghīr kē Tanāẓur mēn*. Lahore: Maktaba Taʿmīr-e-Insāniyyat.
Farīdī, Iftikhār. 1977. *Tablīghī Kām*. Delhi: Anjuman Taraqqī Urdu.
Fārūqī, Ziyaul Ḥasan. 1971. "The Tablīghī Jamāʿat." In Lockhandwala (ed.), 1971:60–69.
Fārūqī, Muḥammad Riḍwanur Raḥmān. 1976. *Jarāthīmul Wahābiyyah fil Jamāʿat Tablīghiyya: Tablīghī Jamāʿat kī Wahābiyyat awr un kē ʿaqā'id kī Ḥaqīqat kā Ā'inah*. Bareilly: Riḍwī Kutubkhāna.
Fāṭimī, S.Q. 1963. "Two Letters from the Mahārāja to the Khalīfah: A Study in the Early History of Islam in the East." *Islamic Studies* 2:121–140.

Faust, Elke. 1996. "Tablīghī Jamā'at: Auszug auf dem Wege Gottes." Masters thesis. Philosophischen Fakultät der Rheinischen Friedrich-Wilhelms-Universität zu Bonn.

Firishta, Muḥammad b. Qāsim. 1962. *Tārīkh Farishta.* Urdu translation of *Gulshan-i-Ibrāhīmī* by Khāwja 'Abdul Ḥayy. Lahore: Ghulām 'Ali.

Fīrōzpurī, Miyānjī Muḥammad 'Īsā. N.d.c. *Tablīghī Jamā'at kē Liyē Rawāngī kī Hidāyāt.* Delhi: Rabbānī Book Depot.

—— N.d.a. *Tablīghī Taḥrīk Kī Ibtidā' awr Is kē Bunyādī Uṣūl.* Delhi: Rabbānī Book Depot.

—— N.d.b. *Tablīgh kā Maqāmī Kām.* Delhi: Rabbānī Book Depot.

Friedmann, Yohanan. 1990. *Prophesy Continues: Aspects of Ahmadi Religious Thought and its Medieval Background.* Berkeley: University of California Press.

Gaborieau, Marc. 1986a. "What is Tablīghī Jamā'at? Preliminary Thoughts about a New Strategy of Adaptation to Minority Situations." SSRC/CERI workshop on "Muslim minorities," Paris.

—— 1986b. "Le néo-fondamentalisme au Pakistan: Maududi et la Jama'at Islami." In Carré and Dumont (eds.), 1986:33–76.

—— 1987a. "Les lignages savants dans le sous-continent indien, *Lettre d'information* n. 7, Paris, EHESS, Equipe de recherche sur la transmission du savoir dans le monde musulman périphérique 7:44–47.

—— 1987b. "L'islam dans le sous-continent indo-pakistanais." In *Annuaire: Compte rendu des cours et conférences, 1984–1985, 1985–1986.* Paris: EHESS. Pp. 356–357.

—— 1989. "Les oulémas/soufis dans l'Inde moghole: anthropologie historique de religieux musulman." *Annales E.S.C.* 5:1185–1204.

—— 1990. "L'Islam Indo-pakistanais: bilan des activités (1982–1990)." *Lettre d'information* 10:4–17. Paris: EHESS.

—— 1997. "Renouveau de l'islam ou stratégie politique occulte? La Tablighi Jama'at dans le sous-continent Indien et dans le monde." In Catherine Clémentin-Ojha (ed.), *Un renouveau religieux en Asie?* Paris: École Française d'Extrème Orient. Pp. 211–229.

Gaborieau, Marc and Alice Thorner (eds.). 1986c. *Asie du Sud: Traditions et changements.* Paris: CNRS.

Gaborieau, Marc, Grandin, Nicole, Labrousse, Pièrre and Popovic, Alexandre (eds.). 1992 *Dictionnaire Biographique des Savants et Grandes Figures du Monde Musulman Périphérique, du XIXe Siècle a Nos Jours.* Paris: EHESS. Fasc. n. 1.

Gangōhī, Maḥmūd Ḥasan. N.d. *Chashma Āftāb.* Kānpur: Maktaba Niẓām.

Geaves, Ron. 1995. *Muslims in Leeds.* Leeds: Community Religious Project.

Gerholm, Thomas and Lithman, Y.G. (eds.). 1988. *The New Islamic Presence in Western Europe.* London: Mansell.

Ghalūsh, Aḥmad Aḥmad. 1978. *Al-Da'watul Islāmiyyah Uṣūluhā wa wasā'iluhā.* Cairo: Dār al-Kitāb al-Miṣrī.

Ghaytās, Ḥasanī Muḥammad Ibrāhīm. 1985. *Al-Da'watul Islāmiyyah fi 'Ahd Amīril Mu'minīn 'Umar Ibnil Khaṭṭāb.* Beirut: al-Kitāb al-Islāmī.

Al-Ghazālī, Abū Ḥāmid. N.d. *Iḥyā 'Ulūmid Dīn.* Bayrūt: Dārul ma'rifa.

Al-Ghazālī, Muḥammad. 1988. *Al-Ṭarīq min Hunā.* Damascus: Dārul Qalam.

Gīlānī, Manāẓir Aḥsan. 1962. *Al-Dīnul Qayyim.* Karachi: Nafis Academy.

Gilmartin, David. 1991. "Democracy, Nationalism and the Public: A Speculation on Colonial Muslim Politics." *South Asia* 14(1):141–154.

Goffman, E. 1961. *Asylums: Essays on the Social Situation of Mental Patients and Other Inmates.* New York: Anchor Books, Doubleday.

Goldziher, Ignaz. 1952. *Die Richtungen der Islamischen Koranauslegung.* Leiden: Brill.

Government of India. 1910 [1878]. *The Gazeteer of Alwar.*

—— 1911. *Punjab District Gazetteer, Gurgaon District.* Lahore.

Gür, Metin. 1993. *Türkisch-islamische Vereinigungen in der Bundesrepublik Deutschland.* Frankfurt a.M.: Brandes und Apsel.

Ḥālī, Alṭāf Ḥusayn. 1985. *Ḥayāt Jāwīd*. Lahore: ʿIshrat Publishing House.
Hall, John R. 1978. *The Ways Out: Utopian Communal Groups in an Age of Babylon*. London: Routledge and Kegan Paul.
Hamdani, Abbas. 1976. "Evolution of the Organizational Structure of the Fatimi *Daʿwa*. The Yemani and Persian Contribution." *Arabian Studies* 3:85–114.
Ḥaq, M. Anwārul. 1972. *The Faith Movement of Mawlānā Muḥammad Ilyās*. London: George Allen.
Harās, Muḥammad Khalīl. 1952. *Ibn Taymiyya al-Salafī*. Ṭanṭā: Maṭbaʿ Yūsufiyya.
Hardy, Peter. 1972. *The Muslims of British India*. Cambridge U.K.: Cambridge University Press.
Ḥasan, ʿAzīzul. 1985. *Ashrafus Sawāniḥ*. Multān: Tālīfāt Ashrafiyya.
Ḥasanī, ʿAbdul Ḥayy. 1947. *Nuzhatul Khawāṭir*. Hyderabad (Daccan): Jāmiʿa ʿUthmāniya.
Ḥasanī, Sayyid Muḥammad Thānī. 1967. *Sawāniḥ Ḥaḍrat Mawlānā Muḥammad Yūsuf Kāndhalawī*. Lucknow: Maktaba Islām, Queen's Road.
—— 1988. *Tadhkira Ḥaḍrat Mawlānā Muḥammad Yūsuf*. Lucknow: Maktaba al-Furqān.
Hilālī, Taqīud-Dīn. 1979. *Al-sirājul munīr fi tanbīh jamāʿatit Tablīgh ilā akhṭāʾihim*. Casablanca: An-Najāḥ al-Jadīda.
Hitti, P.K. 1951. *History of the Arabs*. London: MacMillan.
Hourani, Albert. 1970. *Arabic Thought in the Liberal Age*. Oxford: Oxford University Press.
Hours, Bernard. 1993. *Islam et développement au Bangladesh*. Paris: L'Harmattan.
Houtsma, M. 1961. "Aḥmadiyya." In H.A.R. Gibb and J.H. Kramers (ed.) *Shorter Encyclopedia of Islam*. Leiden: E.J. Brill.
Hughes, Thomas Patrick. 1964 [1885]. "Daʿwa." In Hughes, *A Dictionary of Islam*. Lahore: Premier Book House.
Ḥusayn, ʿInāyat. 1870. *Ghazā Nāma Masʿūd*. Kānpur: Maṭbaʿ Niẓāmī.
Husin, Mohammad Zain bin. 1984–1985. "Pergerakan Jamaʿah Tablighi di Malaysia: Penekanan Khusus Kepada Metod Penyampaian Daʿwah." Masters thesis. Fakulti Pengajian Islam, Universiti Kebangsaan Malaysia, Bangi.
Hussain, Tanzeem. 1989. "Daʿwat o Tahrik." *Mithāq* 38(10):43–52; (11):51–57; (12):35–45.
Ibn Baṭṭūṭa. 1934. *Tuḥfatun Nuẓẓār fi Gharāʾibil amṣār*. Cairo: Maṭbaʿ Amīriyya.
Ibn Hishām. 1963. *Sīratun Nabī*. Vol. 1. Cairo: Maḥmūd ʿAlī Ṣubayḥ.
Ibn Humām. 1898. *Al-Musāmara*. Cairo: Bulāq.
Ibn Manẓūr. 1988. *Lisānul ʿArab*. Bayrut: Dār Iḥyāit Turāthil ʿArabi.
Ikrām, Shaykh Muḥammad. N.d. *Mawj Kawthar*. Lahore: Ferozesons.
—— 1958. *Rūd Kawthar*. Lahore: Ferozesons.
—— 1992. *Āb Kawthar*. Lahore: Idāra Thaqāfat Islāmiyya.
Ilāhī, ʿĀshiq. 1989. "Six Fundamentals of Islam." In Ḥasan, Ehteshamul and Elahi, Ashique (eds.), *The Teachings of Tabligh*. New Delhi: Idāra Ishāʿat Dīniyāt.
al-Ilūrī, Ādam ʿAbdullah. 1979. *Tārikhud Daʿwa Ila Allāh bayn al-Ams waʾl Yawm*. Cairo: Wahaba.
Ilyās, Mawlānā Muḥammad. 1952. *Makātīb Ḥaḍrat Mawlānā Muḥammad Ilyās*. Edited by Mawlānā Abul Ḥasan ʿAlī Nadwī. Delhi: Anjuman Taraqqī Urdu. Also Delhi: Anjuman Taraqqī Urdu, 1962, 1963 and 1965; and 1976. Karachi: Dārul Ishāʿat.
—— 1960. *Malfūẓāt Ḥaḍrat Mawlānā Muḥammad Ilyās*. Edited by Mawlānā Muḥammad Manẓūr Nuʿmānī. Lucknow: Maktabatul Furqān.
—— 1980. *Irshādāt wa Maktūbāt Bānī Tablīgh Ḥaḍrat Mawlānā Shāh Muḥammad Ilyās Ṣāḥib*. Edited by Iftikhār Farīdī. Delhi: Idāra Ishāʿat Dīniyāt and ʿArshī Publications. Also 1989. Lahore: ʿImrān Academy.
—— 1985 [1944]. *A Call to Muslims: Message to an All-India Conference of Ulama, and the Muslim Political Leaders at Delhi in April 1944*. Lyallpur [Faisalabad]: Malik Brothers Publishers.
—— 1989. *A Call to Muslims*. Translated and edited by Anis Ahmed. Delhi: Idara Ishāʿat Dīniyāt.

Iṣfahānī, Rāghib. 1961. *Al-Mufradāt fī Gharībil Qur'ān*. Cairo: Muṣṭafā al-Bābī.
Islamic Institute. N.d. *Prospectus*. Notinghamshire.
Jain, M.S. 1979 [Original circa 1965]. *The Aligarh Movement, Its Origins and Development, 1858–1906*. Karachi: Karimsons.
Jamālī, Naʿīm. 1987. *Tableegh Jamaʿat in the Light of the Facts and the Truth*. Urdu translation of tract by Allama Arshad al-Qadiri. Durban: World Islamic Mission.
Juynboll, Th. W. 1961. "Daʿwa." In Gibb and Kramers (eds.) *Shorter Encyclopedia of Islam*. Leiden: Brill. P. 71.
Kāndhalawī, Mawlānā Iḥtishāmul Ḥasan. N.d.a. *Ādāb-i Maʿīshat*. New Delhi: Idāra Ishāʿat-e-Islām.
—— N.d.b. *Muslim Degeneration and its Only Remedy*. English translation of *Musalmānōn kī Mawjūda Pastī kā wāḥid ʿIlāj*. Malik Haq Nawaz (trans.) Lahore: Kutub Khāna Faiḍī.
—— 1939. *Musalmānōn kī Mawjūda Pastī Kā Wāḥid ʿIlāj*. In Kāndhalawī 1962.
—— 1957. *Tadhkira Aslāf, Ḥālāt Mashā'ikh Kāndhala*. New Delhi: Idāra Ishāʿat Dīniyāt.
—— 1959. *Payām ʿAmal*. Delhi: Idāra Ishāʿat Dīniyāt.
—— 1962 [1944]. *Tablīgh Kiyā Hay?* Delhi: Idāra Ishāʿat Dīniyāt. The edition includes the following tracts: (1) *Islāmī Ẓindagī*, (2) *Iṣlāh Inqilāb*, (3) *Payām ʿAmal*, (4) *Musalmānōn Kī Mawjuda Pastī Kā Wāḥid ʿIlāj*, (5) *Dīn Khāliṣ*.
Kasōlī, Ẓuhūrul-Ḥasan (ed.). 1950. *Arwāḥ Thalātha*. Sahāranpur: Kutubkhāna Ishāʿatul ʿUlūm.
Kāwish, Fayyāḍ Aḥmad. N.d. *Tablīghī Jamāʿat kā Iʿlān Wahābiyyat*. Karachi: Ḍiyā'ud-din Publications.
Keohane, Robert and Nye, Joseph S. 1977. *Power and Interdependence*. Boston: Little Brown.
Kepel, Gilles. 1987. *Les banlieues de l'Islam*. Paris: Éditions du Seuil.
—— 1994. *The Revenge of God: The Resurgence of Islam, Christianity and Judaism in the Modern World* (*La Revanche de Dieu*). English trans. by Alan Braley. Cambridge, U.K.: Polity Press.
—— 1996. *Allah im Westen. Demokratie und die islamische Herausforderung*. German trans. by Inge Leipold. München: Piper.
—— 1997. *Allah in the West: Islamic Movements in America and Europe*. Cambridge, UK.: Polity Press.
Khālidī, Muṣṭafā. 1964. *Al-Tabshīr wal Istiʿmār fil Bilādil ʿArabiyya, ʿArḍ li Juhūdil Mubasshirīn allatī tarmī ilā ikhḍāʿil Sharq li'l ʿIstiʿmāril Gharbī*. Beirut: Author.
Khān, Shams Tabrīz. 1984. *Tārīkh Nadwatul ʿUlamā*. Vol. 2. Lucknow: Nadwatul ʿUlamā.
Khān, Sir Syed Ahmad. 1858. *Asbāb Baghāwat Hind*. Aligarh: University Publishers.
Khān, Waḥīduddīn. 1985. *Tablīghī Taḥrīk*. New Delhi: Maktabat al-Risāla.
—— 1986. *Tablīgh Movement*. New Delhi: The Islamic Centre.
—— 1988. *Mewāt kā Safar*. New Delhi: Maṭbūʿāt Islāmī Markaz.
Khwāja, Muḥammad Qāsim. 1990. *Tablīghī Jamāʿat apne Niṣāb kē Ā'inē mēn*. Gujrānwāla: Idāra Iḥyā al-Sunnah.
Kifāyatullāh, Mawlānā Muftī. N.d.a. *Kifāyatul Muftī*. Karachi: Sikandar ʿAlī.
Kifāyatullāh, Muftī. N.d. [1875–1952?]. *Taʿlīmul Islam*. Delhi: Idāra Ishāʿat Dīniyāt.
Kopf, David. 1988. *The Brahmo Samaj and the Shaping of the Modern Indian Mind*. New Delhi: Archives Publishers.
Kruger, Horst (ed.). 1996. *Kunwar Muhammad Ashraf, An Indian Scholar and Revolutionary (1903–1962)*. Berlin: Academie Verlag.
Lakhnawī, ʿAbdush Shakūr. 1965. *ʿIlmul Fiqh*. Edited by Muftī Muḥammad Shafīʿ. Karachi: Dārul Ishāʿat.
Landman, Nico. 1992. *Van Mat Tot Minaret. De institutionalisering van de islam in Nederland*. Amsterdam. VU (Free University) Uitgevrij.

Lelyveld, David S. 1978. *Aligarh's First Generation: Muslim Solidarity in British India.* Princeton: Princeton University Press.
Le Roux, C. du P. and Jhazbhay, I. 1992. "The Contemporary Path of Qibla Thought: A Hermeneutical Reflection." *Journal for Islamic Studies* 12:85–100.
Lewis, Philip. 1994a. *Islamic Britain: Religion, Politics and Identity among British Muslims.* London: I.B. Tauris.
—— 1994b. "Being Muslim and British: The Challenge to Bradford Muslims." In Ballard 1994:58–87.
Lokhandwala, S.T. (ed.). 1971. *India and Contemporary Islam: Proceedings of a Seminar.* Simla: Indian Institute of Advanced Studies.
Long, D.E. 1979. *The Ḥajj Today.* Albany: State University of New York Press.
Al-Maghribī, Shaykh ʿAbdul Qādir. 1921. *Al-bayyināt fid dīn wa'l ijtimāʿ wa'l adab wa'l tārīkh.* Part 1. Cairo: Maṭbaʿa Salafiyya.
Magnuson, Douglas Kent. 1987. *Islamic Reform in Contemporary Tunisia: A Comparative Ethnographic Study.* Ph.D. thesis, Brown University. Providence, RI, USA.
—— 1991. "Islamic Reform in Contemporary Tunisia: Unity and Diversity." In Zartman, I. William (ed.), *Tunisia. The Political Economy of Reform.* London: Boulder. Pp. 169–192.
Mahdī, Tābish. 1985. *Tablīghī Jamāʿat: Apnē Bānī kē Malfūẓāt kē Āʾinē mēn.* Deoband: Maktabatul Īmān.
Mahmood, Khurram. 1999. "Tablīghī Jamāʿat in Pakistan: 1947–1997." M. Phil. thesis. National Institute of Pakistan Studies, Quaid Azam University, Islamabad, Pakistan.
Malik, Jamal. 1994. "The Making of a Council: The Nadwat al-ʿUlamāʾ." *Zeitschrift der Deutschen Morgenländischen Gesellschaft* 144(1):60–91.
—— 1997. *Islamische Gelehrtenkultur in Nordindien. Entwicklungs-geschichte und Tendenzen am Beispiel von Lucknow.* Leiden: Brill.
Manṣūrpurī, Qāḍī Muḥammad Sulaymān. 1928. *Tablīgh al-Islām.* Simla: Army Press.
Marty, Martin, and Appleby, R. Scott (eds.). 1991. *Fundamentalism Observed.* Chicago: University of Chicago Press.
—— (eds.) 1993. *Accounting for Fundamentalisms.* Chicago: University of Chicago Press.
Marwah, I.S. 1979. "Tablīgh Movement among the Meos of Mēwāt." In Rao 1979: 79–99.
Massignon, Louis. 1961. "Ṭarīḳa." *Shorter Encyclopedia of Islam.* Leiden: Brill. Pp. 573–578.
—— 1987. "Ṭarīḳa." In M. Th. Houtsma (ed.), In *First Encyclopaedia of Islam 1913–1936.* Leiden: Brill. Pp. 667–672.
Masud, Muhammad Khalid. 1969. "Trends in the Interpretation of Islamic Law in the Nineteenth Century India: A Study of the Fatawa of the Deoband School." Masters Thesis. Institute of Islamic Studies, McGill University, Montreal, Canada.
—— 1990. "Obligation to Migrate: Formulation of the Doctrine of Hijrah in Islamic Law." In Eickelman and Piscatori 1990:29–49.
—— 1992. "Muftī Kifayatullāh". In Gaborieau et al. 1992:14–15.
—— 1993. "The Definition of Bidʿa in the South Asian Fatāwā Literature." *Annales Islamologique* 27:55–75.
—— 1994. "Mawlānā Muḥammad Ihtishamu'l-Ḥasan Kāndhalawī." In Gaborieau (1994).
—— 1995a. "Daʿwa: Modern Usage." In *Oxford Encyclopedia of the Modern Islamic World.* 1:350–353. New York: Oxford University Press.
—— 1995b. "Tablīgh" in Esposito (ed.), *Oxford Encyclopedia of the Modern Islamic World* 4:162–165. New York: Oxford University Press.
—— 1996. *Iqbal's Reconstruction of Ijtihad.* Islamabad: Islamic Research Institute and Iqbal Academy, Lahore.
—— 1996. "The World of Shāh ʿAbdul ʿAzīz." Paper presented at "Seminar on

Mutual Perceptions of Each Other in South Asian Cultures in the Eighteenth Century," Bonn. Germany, 15–18 December.
Mathur, Y.B. 1968. "Tanẓīm and Tabligh Movements in Modern India Before its Partition into Pakistan and India: A Short Historical Description of the Struggle for Survival and Supremacy in India in the Early Twenties between the Religious Ideologies of Islam and Hinduism." *The Islamic Review and Arab Affairs* 56 (11–12):22–24, 40.
—— 1983. *Growth of Muslim Politics in India.* Lahore: Book Traders.
Māwardī, Abul Ḥasan. 1880. *Al-Aḥkāmus Sulṭāniyya.* Cairo. Waṭan.
Mawdūdī, Mawlānā Abul Aʿlā. 1939. "Iḥyā Dīn Kī Jidd-o-Juhd kā Ṣaḥīḥ Ṭarīqa Awr ēk Qābil-Taqlīd Namūna." In M. Nuʿmānī 1980:19–37.
Mawdūdī, Abul Aʿlā. 1940. "Manṣab Tajdīd kī Ḥaqīqat awr Tārīkh Tajdīd mēn Shāh Wali Allāh kā Maqām." in Manzūr Aḥmad Nuʿmānī (ed.) *Al-Furqān*, "Shāh Waliullāh" Nambar, Bareli.
—— 1972 [1939]. *Purdan and the Status of Woman in Islam.* Lahore: Islamic Publications Ltd.
Mayaram, S. 1997. *Resisting Regimes: Myth, Memory and the Shaping of a Muslim Identity.* Delhi: Oxford University Press.
Mazrui, Ali A. 1985. "Religion and Political Culture in Africa." *Journal of the American Academy of Religion* 53(3):817–818.
Merad, A. 1984. *L'Islam contemporain.* Paris: PUF.
Merton, R.K. 1957. *Social Theory and Social Structure.* Glencoe: The Free Press.
Metcalf, Barbara D. 1982. *Islamic Revival in British India: Deoband, 1860–1900.* Princeton: Princeton University Press.
—— 1987. "Islamic Arguments in Contemporary Pakistan." In Roff and Eickelman 1987:132–59.
—— 1993a. "Living Ḥadīth in the Tablīghī Jamāʿat" *Journal of Asian Studies* 52(3):584–608.
—— 1993b. "'Remaking Ourselves': Islamic Self-Fashioning in a Global Movement of Spritual Renewal." In Marty 1993:706–725.
—— 1995. "Deobandis." In Esposito (ed.) *The Oxford Encyclopedia of the Modern Islamic World.* 1:362–363. New York: Oxford University Press.
—— 1996. "New Medinas: The Tablīghī Jamāʿat in America and Europe." In Metcalf 1996:110–127.
—— (ed. and trans.). 1991. *Perfecting Women: Maulānā Ashraf ʿAlī Thānawī's Bihishtī Zewar.* Berkeley: University of California Press.
—— (ed.) 1996. *Making Muslim Space in North America and Europe.* Berkeley: University of California Press.
Mēwātī, Muḥammad Ḥasan Khān. 1963. *Miftāḥut Tablīgh.* Delhi: Kutubkhāna Anjuman Taraqqī Urdu.
Mēwātī, Muḥammad Ḥabibur Raḥmān Khān. 1979. *Tadhkira Ṣūfiya Mēwāt.* Lahore: Maktaba Madaniyya.
Mirzā, Janbāz N.d. [1975?]. *Kārwan Aḥrār.* Lahore: Maktaba Tabṣira.
Mohsin, K.M. 1983. "Trends of Islam in Bangladesh." In Rafiuddin Ahmed (ed.) *Islam in Bangladesh, Society, Culture and Politics.* Dhaka: Bangladesh Itihas Samiti. Pp. 226–249.
Moin, Mumtaz. 1976. *The Aligarh Movement (Origin and Early History).* Karachi: Salman Academy.
Moosa, Ebrahim. 1993. "Discursive Voices of Diaspora Islam in Southern Africa." *Jurnal Antropologi dan Sosiologi* 20(4):27–59.
Muhammad, Shan. 1986. *The Aligarh Movement: Basic Documents 1864–1898.* (Three vols.) Lahore: Islamic Book Centre.
Mujaddidī, Shaykh Abul Ḥasan Zayd Fārūqī. 1992. *Tablīghī Jamāʿat kī Ḥaqīqat.* Lahore: Idāra Maʿārif Nuʿmāniya.

Muslim. 1954. *Ṣaḥīḥ*. Cairo: Dār al-Turāth al-ʿArabī.
Muẓaffar, Chandra. 1987. *Islamic Resurgence in Malaysia*. Petalang Jaya: Fajr Bakti.
Muẓṭar, A.D. 1979. *Shāh Waliullāh: A Saint Scholar of Muslim India*. Islamabad: National Commission on Historical & Cultural Research.
An-Nadwatul ʿĀlamiyya lish Shabābil Islāmī. 1989. "Jamāʿatut Tablīgh." In *al-Mawsūʿatul Muyassara fi'l Adyān wa'l Madhāhibil Muʿāṣira*". Riyādh: An-Nadwatul-ʿĀlamiyya lish Shabābil Islāmī.
Nadwī, ʿAbdul Bārī. 1962. *Tajdīd Dīn Kāmil*. Karachi: Nafīs Academy.
Nadwī, Abul ʿAla. N.d. *Jawāhir Pārē yaʿnī Tablīghi Taqrīrēn*. Hyderabad: Maktaba Islām.
Nadwī, Abul Ḥasan ʿAlī. N.d. *Sawāniḥ Ḥaḍrat Mawlānā Abdul Qādir Rāʾipurī*. Lucknow: Maktabatul Islām.
—— 1943. *Ēk Aham Dīnī Daʿwat*. Lucknow: Maktabatul Islām Al-Furqān. Also 1982, Delhi: Idāra Ishāʿat Dīniyāt.
—— 1973. *Dunyā par Musalmānōn kē ʿUrūjo Zawāl kā Athar*. Lucknow: Majlis Nashriyāt Islām.
—— 1976. *Manṣab Nubuwwat awr us ke Ḥāmilīn*. Karachi: Majlis Nashriyāt Islām.
—— 1977. *Sīrat Sayyid Aḥmad Shahīd*. Lucknow: Majlis Nashriyāt Islām.
—— 1982. *Ḥaḍrat Shaykhul Ḥadīth Mawlānā Muḥammad Zakariyyā*. Lucknow: Majlis Nashriyāt Islām. Also 1983, Karachi: Majlis Nashriyāt Islām.
—— 1983–1990. *Kārawān Zindagī*. Vols. 1–4. Lucknow: Maktaba Islām.
—— 1985. *Ḥaḍrat Mawlānā Muḥammad Ilyās awr un kī Dīnī Daʿwat*. Karachi: Majlis Nashriyāt Islām. Original 1944, Lucknow: Kutub Khāna al-Furqān. Also 1946 and 1979 editions by the same publisher. 1960 and 1964, Lucknow: Tanwīr. 1980, Delhi: Idāra Ishāʿat Dīniyāt.
—— 1988a. *Ḥayāt ʿAbdul Ḥayy*. Pūne: Urdu Marāthī Prakashan.
—— 1988b. *Tārīkh Daʿwat o ʿAzīmat*. Five vols. Lucknow: Majlis Taḥqīqāt wa Nashriyyāt Islam.
Nadwī, Sayyid Sulaymān. 1990. *Sīratun Nabī*. Islamabad: National Book Foundation.
al-Najjār, ʿAbdul Ḥalīm (transl.) 1955. *Madhāhibut Tafsīril Islāmī*. Translation of Goldziher 1952. Baghdad: Maktabatul Khānjī.
Naṣr, S. Hossain. 1991. *Islamic Spirituality: Manifestations*. London: SCM Press.
al-Nawāwī, Imām Abū Zakariya Yaḥyā b. Sharaf Muḥiyud Dīn. N.d. *Les Jardins des vertueux de l'Imam Mohieddine Annawawi*. (Trans. and commentary by Salaheddine Keshrid). Beirut: Dar al-Gharb al-Islami.
—— 1985. *Gardens of the Righteous: Riyadh as-Salihin of Imam Nawawi*. (English trans. by Muḥammad Zafrullā Khān). London: Curzon Press.
—— 1986. *Riyāḍ al-Sāliḥīn min Kalim Sayyid al-Mursalīn* (Edited and annotated by Raḍwān Muḥammad Raḍwān). Bayruth: Dār al-Kitāb al-Miṣrī.
—— 1988. *Riyāḍ aṣ-ṣāliḥīn* (English. Trans. by Abdur Rehmān Shād). 2 vols. Lahore: Kazi Publications.
Nemo, Jacques. 1979. "La communauté Gujrātī a la Réunion: Identité ou identification." In Gaborieau and Thornes 1979, 629–34.
—— 1983. *Musulman de la Réunion*. Saint Denis: Université de la Réunion, Institut de linguistique et d'anthropologie.
Nielsen, Jorgen. 1995. *Muslims in Western Europe*. Edinburgh: Edinburgh University Press. First ed. 1993.
Nirumand, Bahman (ed.) 1990. Im Namen Allahs: Islamische Gruppen und der Fundamentalismus in der Bundesrepublik Deutschland. Köln: Dreisam-Verlag.
Nock, A.D. 1933. *Conversion*. New York: Oxford University Press.
Nuʿmānī, Muḥammad Manẓūr (ed.). N.d. *Daʿwat Tablīgh*. Lahore: Maktaba Zakariyyā.
—— (ed.). 1965. *al-Furqān: Yūsuf Nambar*. Lucknow: Al-Furqān.
—— 1980. *Tablīghī Jamāʿat, Jamāʿat Islāmī awr Brēlwī Ḥaḍrāt*. Lucknow: al-Furqān Book Depot. Also 1989, Lahore: ʿImrān Academy.
Nuʿmānī, Shiblī. 1975. *Sīratun Nabī*. Islamabad: National Book Foundation of Pakistan.

Nye, Joseph S. and Robert Keohane. 1972. *Transnational Relations and World Politics*. Cambridge, Mass: Harvard University Press.

Peacock, James L. 1988. "Religion and Life History: An Exploration in Cultural Psychology." In Edward M. Bruner (ed.), *Text, Play, and Story. The Construction and Reconstruction of Self and Society*. Washington, D.C.: Waveland Press. Pp. 94–116.

Pīrzāda, ʿAbdul Khāliq. 1990. *Al-Shaykh Muḥammad Ilyās Dihlawī: Ḥayātuhū wa Manhajuhū fi al-Daʿwa wa'l Tablīgh*. Qāhira: Maktabatul Ādāb.

Piscatori, James. 1992. "Religious Transnationalism and World Order." Paper read at workshop on "Transnational Daʿwa," 10–13 Oct., Machynlleth, Wales, UK.

Qādirī, Muḥammad Ayyūb. 1971. *Tablīghī Jamāʿat kā Tārīkhī Jā'iza*. Karachi: Maktaba Muʿāwiyya.

Qādirī, Muḥammad Ilyās. 1988. *Fayḍān Sunnat*. Karachi: Maktabatul Madīna.

Qādirī, Arshdul. 1960. *Tablīghī Jamāʿat*. Jamshēdpur.

—— 1967. *Tablīghi Kām*. Delhi: Anjuman Taraqqī Urdu.

—— 1981. *Tablīghī Jamāʿat: Ḥaqā'iq wa Maʿlūmāt Kē Ā'ine Mēn*. (Fifteenth edition). Layallpur: Maẓhar Faiḍ Raḍā.

Qādirī, Muḥammad Ziyaullāh. N.d. *Tablīghī Jamāʿat sē Ikhtilāf Kiyūn*. Sialkot: Qādirī Kutub Khāna.

Qidwā'ī, Āṣif (trans.). 1983. *Life and Mission of Mawlana Mohammad Ilyas*. (English translation of Abul Ḥasan ʿAlī Nadwī's *Ḥadrat Mawlānā Muḥammad Ilyās awr un ki Dīnī Daʿwat,* 1948.) Lucknow: Academy of Islamic Research and Publications.

Qurashi, M.M. 1984. "A Study of Ḥajj as an Index of Islamic Motivation of the Ummah in the Last Two Centuries." *Science and Technology in the Islamic World* 2:59–66.

—— 1985. "A Statistical Analysis of Motivation, Cooperation and Achievement Part V: Some Empirical Data and its Comparison." *Proceedings of the Pakistan Academy of Sciences*. 22:41–54.

—— 1986. "A Study of the Men of the Century in the 14 Centuries of Islam." *Science & Technology in the Islamic World* 4:100–109.

—— 1989. "The Tablīgh Movement, Some Observations." *Islamic Studies* 28:237–248.

—— 1993. "State of Science and Technology, Manpower in the Muslim World from 2nd to 12th Century Hijra." *Islamic Thought and Scientific Creativity* 4(2):29–48.

Qureshi, Naeem. 1999. *Pan Islam in British Indian Politics, 1918–1924*. Leiden: Brill.

Quṭb, Sayyid. 1978. *Milestones*. English trans. of *Maʿālim fit ṭarīq*. Sālimiah (Kuwait): International Islamic Federation of Student Organization.

Rabbānī, Maẓhar Sayyid. 1976. *Tablīghī Jamāʿat Kiyā Hai?* Bareilly: Riḍwī Kutubkhāna.

Raḥīm, A. 1959. *Social History of Muslims in Bengal*. Dacca: Asiatic Society.

Raḥmān, Ṭālibur. 1992. *Tablīghī Jamāʿat kā Islām*. Rawalpindi: Al-maʿhadul ʿālī lidirāsātil Islāmiyyatil ʿaṣriyya.

Rai, Lala Lajpat. 1977. *A History of the Arya Samaj*. (Urdu trans. by Kishwar Sulṭān). Delhi: Taraqqi Urdu Board. First edition London: Longman, 1915.

Ramanujan, A.K. 1990. *Who Needs Folklore?: The Revelance of Oral Traditions to South Asian Studies*. South Asia Occasional Paper Series, No. 1. Honolulu: Center for South Asian Studies, University of Hawaii.

Rambo, R.L. 1987. "Conversion." In Mircea Eliade (ed.), *The Encyclopedia of Religion* 4:73–79. New York: Macmillan.

Rao, M.S.A. (ed.), 1979. *Social Movements in India*. Delhi: Manohar.

Rashid, A. 1985. *The Muslim Canadians: A Profile*. Statistics Canada 1981 Census of Canada.

Rāshid, Nurul Ḥasan. (ed.). 1997. Vols. 2–4. *Aḥwāl-o Āthār*, Kāndhala. Special issue: "Ḥaḍrat Mawlānā Inʿāmul Ḥasan." Vol. 2–4.

Raẓā, Muḥammad S. 1991. *Islam in Britain, Past, Present and the Future*. London and Leicester: Volcano Press.

Rāzī, Fakhrud Dīn. 1938. *al-Tafsīrul Kabīr*. Cairo: Maṭbaʿa Bahiyya.

Riḍwī, Ibnul ʿAlī. 1979. "Tablīghī Jamāʿat kā Pas Manẓar." *Tarjumān Ahl Sunnat* 8:68–73.
Riḍwī, Muḥammad Ḥasan ʿAlī. 1978. "Tablīghī Jamāʿat, Chand Iṣlāḥ Ṭalab Pahlū." *Nawā'i Waqt* (daily) Lahore, 18 May.
Robertson, Roland. 1978. *Meaning and Change*. Oxford: Blackwell.
Roff, William R. and Eickelman, Dale F. (eds.). 1987. *Islam and the Political Economy of Meaning: Comparative Studies of Muslim Discourse*. London and Berkeley: Croomhelm.
Roy, Asim. 1983. *The Islamic Syncretistic Tradition in Bengal*. New Delhi: Sterling Publishers.
Sahāranpūrī, Muḥammad Shāhid. N.d. *Akābir kē khuṭūṭ*. Lahore: Maktaba Zakariyyā.
Sahsawānī, Mawlāwī ʿAbd al-Bāqī. 1924. *Akhbār Qilʿa Rā'i Sēn*. Lucknow: Hindustānī Press.
Saʿīdī, ʿAbdul Mutaʿāl. N.d. *Al-Mujaddidūn fi'l-Islām*. Cairo: Maktaba Namūdhajiyya.
Sakharwī, ʿAbdur-Ra'ūf. 1987. "Tablīgh awr Tablīghī Jamāʿat." *Al-Balāgh* 21:15–22.
al-Ṣāliḥ, al-Subḥī. 1968. *Al-Nuzumul Islāmiyya, nash'atuhā wa taṭawwuruhā*. Bayrut: Dārul ʿIlm li'l-mala'īn.
Sanyal, Usha. 1990. "In the Path of the Prophet: Mawlānā Aḥmad Riẓā Khān Barēlwī and the Ahl-e Sunnat wa Jamāʿat Movement in British India, C. 1870–1921." Ph.D. thesis. Columbia University, New York.
—— 1995. "Barelwis." In Esposito (ed.) *The Oxford Encyclopedia of Modern Islamic World* 1:201–202. New York: Oxford University Press.
Sarsawati, Dayanand. 1915. *Satayarath Parakash*. English Translation *Light of Truth* by Ch. Bharadwaja. Agra: The Arya Pratnidhi Sabha.
Sartre, Jean Paul. 1948. *The Emotions: Outline of a Theory*. New York: Philosophical Library.
Schulze, Reinhard. 1990. "Zum Hintergrund islamischer politischer Bewegungen." In Nirumand 1990. Pp. 9–37.
Seguy, Jean. 1972. "Max Weber et la sociologies historique des religions." *Archive de sociologies des Religions* Vol. 33:71–104.
Shams, Shamsuddin. 1983. *Meos of India, Their Customs and Laws*. Delhi: Deep and Deep.
Shērkotī, M. Anwār Ḥasan. 1985. *Ḥayāt Uthmānī*. Karachi: Dārul ʿUlūm.
Siddīqī, Mājid. 1986, "History and Society in a Popular Rebellion: Mēwāt, 1920–1933." *Comparative Studies in Society and History* 28(3):442–467.
Ṣiddīqī, Manẓūrul Ḥasan. 1964. *Ma'āthirul Ajdād*. Lahore: Maktaba Salafiya.
Sikand, Yoginder Singh. N.d. "The Emergence of the Tablīghī Jamāʿat among the Meos of Mēwāt." Unpublished paper.
—— 1994. "Charisma and Religious Revivalism: The Case of the Tablighi Jamāʿat Movement among Meos of Mēwāt." M. Phil thesis. Jawahar Lal University, Delhi.
—— 1998. "The Origins and Growth of the Tablighi Jamaʿat." *Islam and Christian Muslim Relations* 9(2):171–192.
Snow, David A. and Machalek, Richard. 1984. "The Sociology of Conversion." *Annual Review of Sociology* 10:167–190.
Staples, Clifford L. and Mauss, Armand L. 1987. "Conversion or Commitment? A Reassessment of the Snow and Machalek Approach to the Study of Conversion." *Journal for the Scientific Study of Religion* 26(2):133–147.
Sweeney, Amin. 1987. *A Full Hearing: Orality and Literacy in the Malay World*. Berkeley: University of California Press.
Tarafdar, M.R. 1986. "The Bengali Muslims in the Pre-colonial Period: Problems of Conversion, Class Formation and Cultural Evolution." In Gaborieau and Thornes 1986c. Pp. 93–110.
Tayob, Abdulkader I. 1992. "The Muslim Youth Movement (MYM) of South Africa: Challenging the ʿUlamā' Hegemony." *Journal for Islamic Studies* (Centre for Islamic Studies, Rand Afrikaans University) 12:101–124.
Ṭayyib, Qārī Muḥammad. N.d. *Uṣūl Daʿwat Islām*. Lahore: Idāra Islāmiyyāt.

Temple, R.C. 1962. *Ḥikāyāt Panjāb*. (Urdu translation by Miyān 'Abdur Rashīd). Lahore: Majlis Taraqqī Adab.
Thānawī, Muḥammad A'lā. 1862. *Kashshāf Iṣṭilāḥātil Funūn*. Calcutta: Asiatic Society of Bengal.
Thānawī, Mawlānā Ashraf 'Alī. N.d. *Iṣlāḥī Niṣāb*. Multān: Kutub Khāna Mājidiyya.
—— 1982 [original 1927]. *Ḥayātul Muslimīn*. Lahore: Idāra Islāmiyyāt. Also 1947, Deoband: Dārul Ishā'at.
Tirmidhī, Abū Īsa Muhammad al-. N.d. *Sunan*. Madīna: Muḥammad 'Abdul Muḥsin al-Kutubī.
Tirmidhī, Muftī Sayyid 'Abdush-Shakūr. 1981. *Da'wat o Tablīgh kī Shar'ī Ḥaythiyyat*. Lahore: Idāra Islāmiyyāt. Also 1985.
Tiwāna, Major (Rtd.) Muḥammad Sa'īd. 1992. "Wāpas Ājāo Tumhēn kuch nahīn kahā ja'igā." *Ḍiyāi Ḥaram* 22(10):70–72. Originally published in *Pakistan* (daily), 18 May.
Touraine, A. 1973. *Production de la société*. Paris. Seuil.
Tozy, Mohamed. 1984. *Champ et contre-champ politico-religieux au Maroc*. Ph.D. thesis. Faculté de droit et science politique d'Aix-Marseille 1984 (unpublished microfiche).
—— 1999. *Monarchie et Islam politique au Maroc*. Paris: Press de la Fondation nationale des science politique.
Tozy, M. and Etienne, B. 1986. "La da'wa au Maroc. Prolégomènes théorico-historiques." *Radicalismes islamiques*. In Carré and Dumont 1986. 2:5–32.
Troll, Christian W. 1982. "A Muslim Mission Instruction." *Vidyajyoti, Journal of Theological Reflection* 46(8):391–401.
—— 1985. "Five Letters of Mawlana Ilyas (1885–1944), the Founder of the Tabligh Jama'at." *Islam in India: Studies and Commentaries* 2:138–176. Delhi: Vikas Publishing House.
—— 1994. "Two Conceptions of Da'wa in India: Jamâ'at Islâmî and Tablîghî Jamâ'at." *Archives de Sciences sociales de Religions* 87:115–133.
'Ubaydat, Maḥmūd Salīm. 1989. *Athārul jamā'atil islāmiyatil maidani khilālul qarnil 'ishrīn*. 'Ammān: Maktabatur risālatil ḥadītha.
Vable, D. 1983. *The Arya Samaj, Hindu without Hinduism*. New Delhi: Vikas Publishing.
Van der Veer, Peter. 1992. "Playing or Praying: A Saint's Day in Surat." *Journal of Asian Studies* 51(3):545–565.
—— 1994. *Religious Nationalism, Hindus and Muslims in India*. Berkeley: University of California Press.
—— 1999. "The Moral State: Religion, Nation, and Empire in Victorian Britain and British India". In Van der Veer, Peter and Lehman, Hartmut (eds.) *Nation and Religion, Perspectives on Europe and Asia*. Princeton: Princeton University Press. Pp. 15–43.
Wach, J. 1955. *Sociologie de la religion*. Paris: Payot.
Waheeduzzafar. 1971. *Muslim Socio-Religious Movements*. In Lodkhandwala 1971. Pp. 138–142.
Waugh, Earl H., Abu Laban, Baha, and Qureshi, Ragula B. 1983. *The Muslim Community in North America*. Edmonton: University of Alberta.
Wilson, Bryan. 1963. "Typologie des Sectes dans une perspective dynamique et comparative." *Archives de sociologies des religion* 16:49–63.
—— 1970. *Religious Sects: A Sociological Study*. London: Weidenfeld and Nicolson.
—— 1982. *Religion in Sociological Perspective*. London and New York: Oxford University Press.
——. 1985. "Community." In M. Eliade (ed.), *The Encyclopedia of Religion* 3:566–571.
Yacine, A. 1981. *La revolution à l'heure de l'Islam*. Gignac la Nerthe: Borel et Serand.
Yūsuf, Mawlānā Muḥammad. 1959a. *Amānīl Aḥbār*. Delhi: Maktaba Yaḥyawiyya.
—— 1959b. *Ḥayātus Ṣaḥāba*. [Arabic]. Vol. 1. Delhi: Maktaba Yaḥyawiyya. Vol.

2. 1962. Also 1960, Hyderabad: Dā'iratul Mā'ārif; 1986, Damascus: Dārul Qalam. Reprint by Bayrut: Dārul Ma'rifa.
—— 1960. *Ḥayātus Ṣaḥāba* [Urdu trans.] Three Vols. Delhi: Idāra Ishā'at Dīniyāt. Also printed in 1968 and 1969.
—— 1967. *Muraqqa' Yūsufī*. Karachi: Maktaba Mu'āwiya.
Zakariah, Mawlānā M. (Zakariyya, Mawlana Muḥammad). N.d. *Les enseignements de l'islam* (traduction du Tablīghī Niṣāb par A. Saïd Ingar). St-Pierre (Réunion): Centre Islamique de la Réunion.
—— N.d.a. *Faḍā'il Ḥajj o Ṣadaqāt*. Delhi: Idāra Ishā'at Dīniyāt.
—— N.d.b. *Faḍā'il Tijārat*. Sahāranpur: Kutub Khāna Ishā'at Islām.
—— N.d.c. *Ḥaḍratjī kī Chhē Bātēn awr Ṭarīqi Kār*. New Delhi: Rabbānī Book Depot.
—— N.d.d. *Ḥaḍrat Shaykh awr un kī Āpbītī*. Lahore: Maktaba Zakariyya.
—— N.d.e. *Kutub Faḍā'il par Ishkālāt awr un kē Jawābāt*. Karachi: Maktaba al-Shaykh.
—— 1928–1940. *Tablīghī Niṣāb*. New Delhi: Idāra Ishā'at Dīniyāt. Consists of the following: *Faḍā'il Qur'ān* (1929), *Faḍā'il Ramaḍān* (1930), *Faḍā'il Tablīgh* (1931), *Ḥikāyat Ṣaḥāba* (1938), *Faḍā'il Namāz* and *Faḍā'il Dhikr* (1939). Also published in 1960 and 1966, Lahore: Malik Brothers. 1966 edition includes *Faḍā'il-i Darūd*. 1983, Karachi: Dār al-Ishā'at.
—— 1944. *Faza'il-e-A'maal*. Vol. I. New Delhi: Idāra Ishā'at Dīniyāt.
—— 1960. *Teachings of Islam*. English trans. of *Tablīghī Niṣāb*. New Delhi: Ishā'at-e-Islam. Revised translation 1980, Lahore: Kutubkhāna Faiḍī. Several reprints, 1986, Delhi: Idāra Ishā'at Dīniyāt.
—— 1965. *Faḍā'il Ṣadaqāt*. Delhī: Idāra Ishā'at Dīniyāt.
—— 1969. *Āp Bītī numbar Dō: Yād Ayyām*. Three Volumes. Sahāranpur: Kutubkhāna Yaḥyawiyya.
—— 1972a. *Jamā'at Tablīgh par I'tirāḍāt ke Jawābāt*. New Delhi: Idāra Ishā'at Dīniyāt.
—— 1972b. *Dihlī kī Tablīghī Jamā'at par chand 'Umūmī I'tirāḍāt awr un kē Mufaṣṣal Jawābāt*. Karachi: Maktabat al-Shaykh.
—— 1977. *Faḍā'il Tablīgh*. Delhi: Idāra Ishā'at Dīniyāt.
—— 1987. *Faza'il-e-Aamal* [*Faḍā'il-A'māl*]. Lahore: Kutub Khāna Faiḍī. Reprint 1987, Karachi: Dār al-Ishā'at. Earlier 1980, New Delhi: Idāra Ishā'at-e-Dīniyāt. Also 1990, Lahore: Kutub Khānā Faiḍī. 1990, New Delhi: Iḍāra Ishā'at Dīniyāt in two volumes, vol. 2 titled *Virtues of Charity and Haj*.
Zuḥaylī, Wahba. N.d. *Āthārul Ḥarb fi'l Fiqhil Islāmī*. Damascus: Dārul Fikr.
—— 1986. *Uṣūlul Fiqhil Islāmī*. Damascus: Dārul Fikr.
—— 1989. *Al-Fiqhul Islāmī wa Adillatuhū*. Damascus: Dārul Fikr.

GLOSSARY

In addition to the terms used in this volume, the following glossary includes selected vocabulary which the Tablīghī Jamāʿat use in their discourse.

Ādāb: pl. *adab*, manner.
Ādābul māʿida: table manners.
Ādāb-i-nawm: etiquette of going to sleep.
Ādāb-i-ṭaʿām: table manners.
Aḥādīth: pl. of *ḥadīth*.
Aḥkām: pl. of *ḥukm*, injunctions, divine laws, rules.
Ahli Ḥadīth: followers of *ḥadīth*, a school of thought in South Asia who, like *Salafī*s in the Arab world, does not adhere to any school of law.
Aḥmadī: a follower of Mirzā Ghulām Aḥmad (d. 1908) as a prophet, a renewer of the religion of Islam and the promised Messiah.
Aḥzāb: pl. of *ḥizb*, party, group.
Ākhirat: life hereafter.
Al-Daʿwa: see *daʿwa*.
ʿālim: a scholar, a person learned in Islamic religious sciences.
Aʿmaal: Aʿmāl, actions.
Amīr: leader.
Amīrul Khidma: head of services.
Amr biʾl maʿrūf wa nahī ʿanil munkar: enjoining the right and forbidding the wrong—a basic doctrine of *daʿwa*.
Anjuman: society.
Āpā: sister, a form of address, senior Tablīghī woman.
ʿAqīda: faith.
Aqwām: pl. of *qawm*, peoples, nations.
ʿArsh: throne of God.
Ārya Samāj: a Hindu missionary movement.
ASBL: statutory form of non-profit organizations constituted according to Belgian law.
Ashʿarīs: a school of Muslim theology that denied the role of reason in religious matters, opposed to Muʿtazila.
ʿAṣr: late afternoon prayer.
ʿAwām: ʿAwāmm, people.
ʿAwrat: part of the body that must be covered; woman; weakness.
ʿAyaat: Āyāt, pl. of *āyat*, sign of God; verse of the Qurʾān.
ʿAyn al-yaqīn: faith based on one's observation of facts.
Azaan: Adhān, call for prayer.
Balāgh: message.
Balāgha: rhetoric.
Bārāt: bridegroom's kinsmen and friends; wedding procession (Urdu).
Bāṭin: inner, interior form, meaning.
Bayʿa: oath of spiritual initiation.
Bayān: Tablīghī speech, discourse.
Bazurg: elder—form of address especially in *bayān* (Persian).
Bhāʾī: (Urdu) brother—form of address among the Tablīghīs.
Bidʿa: innovation in religion; heretical practice; any addition in religious matters.

Bīghas: a measure of land equal to 120 square feet.
Birādarī: clan.
Bulūghud daʿwa: communication of *daʿwa*.
Burqaʿ: (Urdu) veil, a type of women's outer garment that covers the body from head to foot.
Chador: (Persian) sheet of cloth; wrapper that women use to cover themselves.
Chaudhrī(s): head of a village; a man of influence in a rural community.
Chhe bātēn: six fundamentals of Tablīgh.
Chilla: forty days; a Ṣūfī practice of reclusion; a forty day Tablīghī tour.
Dāʿī: bearer of *daʿwa*; a Tablīghī.
Dakwa: (Malay) *daʿwa*.
Dars-i Nizāmī: A curriculum for religious studies composed by Mullā Niẓāmuddīn of Farangī Maḥall in the eighteenth century, now used as general term for religious studies.
Dārul ʿUlūm: College for religious sciences.
Daʿwa: invitation to a meal; prayer; invocation; vow; appeal; claim; lawsuit; inviting others to the path of Allāh; conversion; *al-daʿwa al-ʿāmma*: general call; *al-daʿwa al-khāṣṣa*: special call; *daʿwa ilā nuṣrat al-dīn*: call to support religion.
Daʿwat: Urdu version of *daʿwa*.
Dastar khwān: (Urdu) food table.
Dhabīḥa: meat of an animal slaughtered in the proper way as prescribed by Islamic law.
Dhāt: essence of God.
Dhikr: Remembrance—one of the fundamentals of Tablīghī Jamaʿat; incessant repetition of certain words or formulae in praise of God.
Dīn: religion, matters relating to the hereafter; Tablīghī distinction between the worldly (*dunyawī*) and the religious (*dīnī*).
Dīndar: a person possessing *dīn*, a religious person.
Dōstō: a form of address for peers, especially during *bayān*.
Duʿā: supplication.
Dunyā: this world; the physical world; Tablīghī antonym for *dīn* and *Ākhira*.
Faḍā'il: pl. of *faḍīlat*, merits.
Fajr: prayer before sunrise.
Farā'iḍ: pl. of *farīḍa*, obligations.
Farḍ kifāya: communal duty; an act that is formally obligatory for all, but if an adequate number of people perform it that is sufficient.
Fatāwā: pl. of *fatwa*, legal opinion by an expert in Islamic law.
Fawā'id: pl. of *fā'ida*, notes.
Fikr: concern.
Fiqh: Islamic law.
Firaq: pl. of *firqa*, sect.
Fitna: schism; disorder.
Foi et Pratique: faith and practice—the French name for the Tablīghī Jamāʿat.
Futuwwa: manliness, chivalry—a Ṣūfī virtue.
Gasht: evangelical visits; door to door calls.
Ghayr al-yaqīn: faith bestowed by others, based on witness by others.
Ghaybī madad: divine help.
Ghāzī: a participant in a *ghazwa*.
Ghazwa: campaign, *Jihād*, pl. *ghazwāt*.
Ghuluww: exaggeration.
Gusht: another transliteration of *gasht*.
Ḥadd: limit, punishment in Islamic law.
Ḥadīth: a report about a statement, a practice of or the approval of an act by the Prophet Muḥammad.

Ḥaḍrat Jī: Respected. Title for the Amīr of the Tablīghī Jamāʿat.
Ḥāfiẓ: a person who memorizes the entire Qur'ān.
Ḥāji camp: transit camps for intending pilgrims—one of the targets of Tablīghī Jamāʿat.
Ḥajj: pilgrimage to Mecca.
Ḥalāl: lawful; allowed by the Islamic laws; legitimate.
Ḥalaqa: ring; circle.
Ḥaqq al-yaqīn: faith rooted in the direct encounter with truth.
Haraam: ḥarām; unlawful; prohibited by divine laws; illegitimate.
Ḥavēlī: (Urdu) palatial mansion.
Ḥifẓ: memorizing the Qur'ān.
Ḥijāb: veil.
Hijra: departure, emigration; withdrawal, migration.
Hijrī: calendar beginning with the event of Prophet Muḥammad's migration from Mecca to Medina.
Hilāl: new moon.
Ḥisba: censure; censure of morals—an official form of *daʿwa*.
Ḥiṣn Ḥaṣīn: a book of litanies written in the fourteenth century by Muḥammad b. Muḥammad al-Jazarī al-Shāfiʿī.
Ḥizb: a formula of *dhikr*.
Ḥukūma: government.
ʿIbādat: worship; acts of worship.
Iftaar: Ifṭār, to break a fast.
Iḥrām: unsewn pieces of white cloth worn by pilgrims.
Iḥsān: doing one's job only with the intention of earning God's benevolence.
Ijtimāʿ: meeting; *Ijtimāʿāt*: plural of *ijtimāʿ*, major gatherings.
Ikhlāṣ-i-niyyat: sincerity of purpose—one of the fundamentals of Tablīghī Jamāʿat.
Ikrām: respect.
Ikrām-i-Muslim: respect of a Muslim—one of the fundamentals of Tablīghī Jamāʿat.
Iʿlān: announcement.
ʿIlm: knowledge—one of the fundamentals of Tablīghī Jamāʿat.
ʿIlmud dīn: the knowledge of religion.
Imaan: Īmān, faith.
Imām: leader; leader in prayer; ruler.
Īmān: faith; belief.
Indhār: warning—a form of *daʿwa*.
Iqtidār: power, might.
Irshād: guidance—a form of *daʿwa* activity.
ʿIshā: late evening prayer.
Iṣlāḥ: reform.
Ism dhāt: essential name of God, Allah.
Istiḍʿāf: weakness.
Istighfār: seeking God's forgiveness for sins.
Istiḥkām: consolidation of *daʿwa* work.
Iṭāʿat: obedience.
Ittibāʿ: strict emulation of the Prophet.
Jāhiliyya: ignorance or paganism.
Jalābiyya: long gown.
Jamāʿa (h): totality; community; also political party, Tablīghī Jamāʿat.
Jamāʿat: Tablīghī Jamāʿat; *jamāʿat* (non-capitalized): a group of the Tablīghī Jamāʿat.
Jāmiʿ: collective, comprehensive.
Jāmiʿ masjid: central mosque where Friday prayer is held.
Jamʿiyya(t): association; society.
Jawla: round; roaming about; *gasht*.

Jihād: physical struggle; *Jihād bi'l sayf*; war, battle; struggle or confrontation with sword.
Jōr: joining, meeting; joining of two *jamāʿats*.
Junūd: pl. of *jund*, army.
Kabāʾir: major sins.
Kalām: theology, religious science dealing with doctrines of creed.
Kalima: formulae of the profession of faith.
Kalima ṭayyiba: article of faith; one of the fundamentals of Tablīgh: "There is no god but Allah, Muḥammad is his messenger.
Khānqah: hospice.
Khaṭīb: a person who delivers a sermon (*khuṭba*) on Friday or on the occasion of *Īd* prayers.
Khidmat: involving physical service, labour; service.
Khilāfat: an Indian Muslim protest movement for the protection of the Ottoman Caliphate.
Khurūj: outing, *gasht, jawla; Khurūj fi sabīl Allāh*: to go out preaching the word of God, Tablīghī tour.
Khuṣūṣi gasht: special round.
Khuṭba: sermon.
Madāriyya: Madārīs, an order related with Shāh Badīʿ al-Dīn Madār.
Madrasa: school; religious school.
Maghrib: prayer after sunset.
Mahājan: moneylender.
Maḥram: a person with whom marriage is prohibited.
Majlis ugama: (Malay) religious council.
Makātib: pl. of *maktab*.
Maktab: elementary religious school.
Māl: worldly resources.
Māldar: materially wealthy.
Mallam: (Hausa) *al-muʿallim*, scholar of religion.
Maqāmī bāshindē: local populations.
Maqāmī kām: local Tablīgh work.
Marḍiyāt: pl. of *marḍī*, will, wishes.
Markaz: centre, headquarters.
Masāʾil: pl. of *masʾala*, details of the legal or theological doctrines, rules and regulations, problems.
Mashāʾikh: pl. of *shaykh*, spiritual leader.
Meelad: Milād or *Mawlidun nabī*: celebration of the birthday of the Prophet.
Mēwātī: belonging to Mēwāt; an inhabitant of Mēwāt in India.
Miḥnat: effort; work; action.
Miraaj: Miʿrāj: Prophet Muḥammad's ascension to heaven.
Miswak: a twig of a tree used to clean teeth.
Morchid: Murshid, guide; *amīr*, leader.
Muazzin: Muʾadhdhin: one who calls for prayer.
Mubālagha: hyperbole.
Mudhakkir: a person who performs the duty of *tadhkīr*, reminding.
Muftī: The expert on Islamic law who gives a legal opinion.
Muhājir: immigrants.
Muḥalla: neighbourhood—the smallest unit of Tablīghī organization.
Mujāhid: one who is performing Jihād or *mujāhāda* (struggle for a cause).
Munāfiqūn: hypocrites.
Munāẓara: polemics, debates between religious rivals.
Muqriʾ: a reciter or a teacher of the Qurʾān.
Murīd: disciple; Ṣūfī novice.

Muta'addī: contagious.
Mutakallim: speaker, spokesman in a small group (*jamā'at*) of the Tablīghī Jamā'at.
Mu'tazila: a rationalist school of theology in early Islam.
Nafr: going out for *Jihād*, another term used by the Tablīghī Jamā'at for *gasht* or *khurūj*.
Namāz: *ṣalāt*, prayer.
Naqd: cash; prompt, immediate, dispatch of a *jamā'at*.
Naql-o-ḥarkat: movement.
Naqsha: plan; Tablīghī plan.
Nāṣiḥ: the one who performs the duty of *naṣīḥa*, giving advice—a form of *da'wa*.
Nawāfil: pl. of *nafl*, supererogatory prayers.
Nāẓim: organizer, regulator, administrator.
Niyya: intention, motive, objective.
Nufūdh: penetration.
Nuqūsh: signs.
Nūr: light.
Nuṣra: local help, organization of *jamā'at* to meet the incoming *jamā'at*, and going out with them.
Paisa: (Urdu) smallest coin.
Panchāyat: traditional meeting of the elders in a village.
Purdah: veil.
Qādiānīs: *Qādiyānīs* belonging to Qādiyān, a village in Indian Panjab, a popular name for Aḥmadīs.
Qadr: value.
Qārūn: Cora (Korah) in Bible.
Qibla: direction to Ka'ba in Mecca.
Qiyāmul layl: vigil, to stay at night praying or remembering God.
Qiyāmat: resurrection.
Radhiallaho anho: Raḍī Allāhu 'anhu, "May God be pleased with him," salutation for the Companions of the Prophet.
Rahbar: guide.
Rahmatullah Alaih: raḥmat Allāh 'alayh: "May God be merciful to him," salutation for others than the Prophet and his Companions.
Rak'at: one complete act of standing, kneeling and prostrating in *ṣalāt*.
Ramazan: Ramadhan: Ramaḍān: the month of fasting.
Rāsta: path.
Risāla: mission of a prophet.
Riwāyat: report, narration, report of a *ḥadīth*.
Rukh: direction, destination of a *jamā'at*.
Ṣābiriyya: Ṣūfī order associated with Makhdūm Ṣābir of Kalyar (India).
Ṣafwat aṣḥābun nabī: selected companions of the Prophet.
Ṣaghā'ir: minor sins.
Ṣaḥābī: pl. *Ṣaḥāba*, a companion of the Prophet.
Ṣalāt; the five ritual prayers of the day, Islamic way of worshiping Allah; prayer—one of the fundamentals of Tablīghī Jamā'at.
Ṣalātul jamā'a: congregational prayer.
Sallallaho alaihe wasallam: Ṣalla Allāhu 'alayhi wa sallam: "May God's blessings and peace be on him", salutation for Prophet Muhammad.
Shahāda: witness; martyrdom.
Shakl: form.
Sharī'at: Sharī'a, Islamic laws; exoteric juridical practices.
Sheikh: Shaykh, spiritual leader; Ṣūfī mentor.
Sheikh-i ṭarīqat: a master in a Ṣūfī order.
Shūrā: a formal council; council of elders of the Tablīghī Jamā'at.

Ṣifāt: attributes of God.
Sijda: Sajda, the act of prostration.
Siyāsat: politics.
Ṣubḥ: dawn.
Ṣuḥba: company.
Sufra: Dastar khāwn: food table.
Sūrah: Sūra, a chapter in the Qur'ān.
Suraus: (Malay) small mosques without a regular *imām*.
Ta'alluq ma' Allāh: spiritual relationship with Allah.
Ta'awwudh: seeking refuge with Allah against Satan.
Tabdīlī: change in personal and social life.
Tablīgh al-da'wa: communication of call.
Tabshīr: Prophecy; good tidings—a form of *da'wa*; evangelical.
Tadhkīr: reminding—a form of *da'wa*.
Tadrīs: teaching—a form of *da'wa*.
Tafrīgh-i-Waqt: donation of time—one of the fundamentals of Tablīghī Jamā'at.
Tahajjud: after midnight prayer with special *dhikr*.
Taḥakkum: power; control; authority.
Tajdīdud dīn: renewal of religion.
Tajdīdul īmān: renewal of faith.
Tājir: merchant; an informal performer of *da'wa* in early Islamic history.
Tajwīd: correct pronunciation and recitation of the Qur'ān.
Ṭalab: quest.
Taleem: Ta'līm, learning; teaching; a particular activity of the Tablīghī Jamā'at reading prescribed books.
Tālīf/taṣnīf: writing book—a form of *da'wa*.
Taqāḍa: demand; requirements of various places for dispatching jamā'at.
Taqlīd: obedience; adherence to a particular school of Islamic law.
Taraqqiyāt: improvement, promotions, gradual progress.
Ṭarīqa: orthodox Ṣūfī orders.
Tark-i-lā ya'nī: abstention from useless talk—one of the fundamentals of Tablīghī Jamā'at.
Tartībud da'wa: order of priority in *da'wa*.
Tasbīḥ: rosary; formula of dhikr, pl. *Tasbīḥāt*.
Taṣḥīḥ-i-niyyat: emendation of intention—one of the fundamentals of Tablīghī Jamā'at.
Tashkīl: organization, formation of a *jamā'at*.
Tawba: coming back; conversion; change of mind.
Tilāwat: recitation of the Qur'ān.
Torqī: a follower of a Ṣūfī *ṭarīqa* (order).
'Ulamā: plural of *'ālim*.
'Umra: shorter *Ḥajj* (pilgrimage to Mecca).
'Umūmī gasht: a local tour by a *jamā'at* to approach the general public in a locality, distinguished from *khuṣūṣī gasht* in which only specific persons are approached.
Uswa-i Ḥasana: the ideal model, the *sunna* of the Prophet.
Wā'iẓ: a person who delivers *wa'ẓ*.
Walāyāt: territories.
Wa'ẓ: sermon, speech, preaching—a form of *da'wa*.
Waẓā'if: special litanies for *dhikr*.
Wuḍū: Wuzu, ablution for prayer.
Ẓabiha: dhabīḥa.
Ẓāhir: exterior form; apparent; outward.
Ẓakir: Dhākir: one who performs the ritual of *dhikr*.
Ẓamīndār: absentee landlord who monopolizes ownership of land in a village.
Ẓikr: Dhikr.

INDEX